Land and sustainable livelihood in Latin America

Annelies Zoomers (ed.)

Land and sustainable livelihood in Latin America

Royal Tropical Institute - the Netherlands
Vervuert Verlag - Germany

Royal Tropical Institute
KIT Publishers
P.O. Box 95001
1090 HA Amsterdam
The Netherlands
Telephone: 31 (0)20 5688272
Telefax: 31 (0)20 5688286
E-mail: publishers@kit.nl
Website: www.kit.nl

Iberoamericana/Vervuert Verlag
Wielandstrasse 40
60318 Frankfurt/Main
Germany
Telephone: 49 (0)69 599615
Fax: 49 (0)69 5978743
E-mail: info@iberoamericanalibros.com
Website: www.vervuert.com

First published by KIT Publishers and
Iberoamericana/Vervuert Verlag

Editor: Annelies Zoomers
Corrector: Jeremy Rayner

Cover design: Ad van Helmond, Amsterdam,
the Netherlands
Desktop publishing: Nadamo Bos, Driebergen,
the Netherlands
Printing: Giethoorn Ten Brink, Meppel,
the Netherlands

Cover etching: Eric Hermsen, Amsterdam,
the Netherlands

*Land and sustainable livelihood in Latin
America* has been developed by the Royal
Tropical Institute in the Netherlands.
It is co-published with Iberoamericana/Vervuert
Verlag (Frankfurt and Madrid) to increase
dissemination.
KIT Publishers and the authors are responsible
for its content.

ISBN 90 6832 141 2 (KIT Publishers edition)
ISBN 3 89354 128 4 (Iberoamericana/Vervuert
Verlag). This edition is available in Germany and
Spain.
Nugi 651/661

Contributors

Dr. Kisten Appendini, senior researcher and lecturer at the Center for Economic Studies of the *Colegio de México*, Mexico (Kirsten@colmex.mx).

Dr. Anna Bee, lecturer in Human Geography at the University of Leicester, England (aeb12@leicester.ac.uk).

Calogero Carletto, economist with the Poverty and Human Resources Division of the Development Research Group of the World Bank, USA (ccarletto@worldbank.org).

Dr. Geneviève Cortes, Associate Professor at the University of Montpellier and at the Research Group on Latin America (GRAL) of the University of Toulouse, France (genevieve.cortes@univ-montp3.fr).

Dr. Orlando Cortez, senior researcher at the School of Agricultural Economics (ESECA) of the National University of Managua, Nicaragua (eseca@sdnnic.org.ni).

Dr. Benjamin Davis, economist with the UN Food and Agriculture Organization (FAO), Italy (benjamin.davis@fao.org).

Dr. Nancy R. Forster, research fellow at the Institute for Environmental Studies and the Land Tenure Center of the University of Wisconsin, USA (nforster@facstaff.wisc.edu).

Dr. Raúl García Barrios (agricultural economist and biologist), research coordinator at the Regional Center for Multidisciplinary Research of the *Universidad Nacional Autónoma de México*, Mexico (rgarciab@servidor.unam.mx).

José Manuel Gilvonio (anthropologist), lecturer at the *Universidad del Centro* in Huancayo, Peru and research fellow (PhD) at Wageningen University, the Netherlands.

Peter R.W. Gerritsen, lecturer and research fellow at the Manantlán Institute for Ecology and Biodiversity Conservation (IMECBIO) of the University of Guadalajara, Mexico (pgerritsen@cucsur.udg.mx).

Dr. Arthur Morris, Professor at the Department of Geography and Topographic Science, University of Glasgow, Scotland (amorris@geog.gla.ac.uk).

Dr. Monique Nuijten, Royal Dutch Academy research scientist at the Rural Sociology Development Group of Wageningen University, the Netherlands (Monique.nuijten@alg.asnw.wag-ur.nl).

Laura Paulson, research fellow (PhD) in Human Geography at the University of Florida, USA (lpaulson@ufl.edu).

Dr. Susan Paulson, Assistant Professor of Anthropology and Latin American Studies at Miami University of Ohio, USA (paulsosa@muohio.edu).

Norman Piccioni, senior agricultural economist with the Poverty and Human Resources Division of the Development Research Group of the World Bank, USA (npiccioni@worldbank.org).

Dr. Luis Rodríguez, senior lecturer at the School of Agricultural Economics (ESECA) of the National University of Managua, Nicaragua (eseca@sdnnic.org.ni).

Dr. Ruerd Ruben, Associate Professor of Farm Household Economics at the Development Economics Group of Wageningen University, the Netherlands (Ruerd.Ruben@alg.oe.wau.nl).

Ute Schüren (anthropologist), researcher and lecturer at the Latin American Institute of the Free University of Berlin, Germany (u.schueren@t-online.de).

Dr. Beatriz G. de la Tejera Hernández (agricultural economist and sociologist), researcher at the *Centro Regional Occidente* of the Autonomous University of Chapingo, Mexico (btejera1999@yahoo.com).

Dr. Pieter de Vries, lecturer at the Rural Sociology Development Group of Wageningen University, the Netherlands (pieter.devries@alg.asnw.wau.nl).

Dr. Annelies Zoomers, Associate Professor in Human Geography at the Center for Latin American Research and Documentation (CEDLA), the Netherlands (zoomers@cedla.uva.nl).

Table of contents

Livelihood and land-use in a global competitive sphere

Final reflections

List of tables

List of figures

List of maps

Preface

This publication is based on the findings of the workshop Land in Latin America: new context, new claims, new concepts (Amsterdam, 1999). It was organized by the Center for Latin American Research and Documentation (CEDLA) in conjunction with the Rural Development Sociology Group (ROS) of Wageningen University and the Royal Tropical Institute (KIT), and was attended by researchers from Latin America, Europe, and the US. The aim of the workshop was to collect experiences with land policy in Latin America, to make a critical assessment of land tenure reform under neo-liberalism, and to contribute to the debate on how land policy could be used as an instrument for sustainable development.

The results of the workshop and a selection of the papers read at it are published in two volumes. The first—*Current land policy in Latin America: regulating land tenure under neo-liberalism* (KIT Publishers/Vervuert, 2000)—offers a critical reflection on current land policy and shows how, under neo-liberalism, there has been a shift away from the redistributive policies that characterized earlier land reforms in Latin America. Land privatization and individual titles granting full-fledged ownership of land have become the cornerstone of neo-liberal land policies, and attempts are being made to undo the restricted collective and semi-collective forms of ownership originating from previous land reforms. In the volume, attention is paid to the characteristics of neo-liberal land policy (i.e., the process of institutional reform and its underlying assumptions) and the implications for production, social goals (e.g., the rights of women and indigenous people), and sustainable resource management. Furthermore, a number of case studies, from Costa Rica, Mexico, Bolivia, and Honduras, address the complexities of land tenure regulation. They show that actual dynamics in land tenure often elude the attempts at state regulation, as these are recast or circumvented by local populations (Zoomers and van der Haar, 2000).

This second volume—*Land and sustainable livelihood in Latin America*—contains a selection of papers focusing on the role of land in the livelihood strategies of farmers, and analyzes in detail the implications of changing land tenure regimes for land-use (agricultural production, environmental sustainability) and the income generating capacity of farmers (is greater access to land still a way out of poverty?), and the consequences for the non-material aspects of life (e.g., prestige, identity, social relations, etc.). It aims to present a complementary view to the first volume. By focusing on the goals and priorities of rural households, rather than on policy goals, an attempt is made to provide an insider's view of rural life. Irrespective of whether policy makers aim at liberalizing land markets or other goals, farmers respond in their own way to the changing situation. Land is a necessary element of life, even in those cases where it no longer plays a crucial role in terms of income generation. Given the current changes in rural life (farmers are having to cope with multifunctional, and often transnational, spaces, as well as neo-liberal production environments and neo-liberal land policy), it is time to make a conceptual update of the land issue. Being a very important asset of rural life, land needs to be studied in close relation to changes in the portfolios of activities of various groups and the large variety of coping mechanisms. Case studies are taken from Mexico, Nicaragua, Chile, Bolivia, and Peru.

Hopefully, this volume will inspire policy makers to formulate a new land policy, one that does greater justice to the diversity and dynamics of rural life, and make them more aware of the multifunctionality of land and livelihood.

I wish to express my gratitude to a number of organizations whose financial support facilitated the organization of the workshop. In addition to the contributions from CEDLA, ROS, and KIT, I would like to mention the Research School for Resource Studies for Development (CERES), the Department of Social Sciences of Wageningen University, the Mansholt Institute of Wageningen University (WU), the Netherlands Association of Latin American and Caribbean Studies (NALACS), the Royal Netherlands Academy of Arts and Sciences (KNAW), and the Food and Agriculture Organization (FAO), in Rome.

This publication was made possible by support and funding from the Department of Agricultural and Enterprise Development of the Royal Tropical Institute (KIT). Many thanks to Lex Roeleveld of that Department for co-organizing the workshop and making valuable observations and remarks during the preparation of this volume.

Finally, and more personally, my thanks go to Gemma van der Haar (ROS): after the idea for a workshop was born, we decided to develop it as a common effort. We shared a fruitful experience of multidisciplinary collaboration, which resulted in the publication of *Current land policy in Latin America: regulating land tenure under neo-liberalism*, the first of this two-volume series.

Annelies Zoomers
Amsterdam, November 2000

1 Introduction: linking land to livelihood

Annelies Zoomers

Background

Today, people's livelihoods are shifting away from being directly based on natural resources, toward livelihoods based on a range of assets, income sources, and product and labor markets. Rural livelihoods should no longer be analyzed as being directly linked to agriculture and access to land; nor should poverty. It is important to have a wide conception of the resources people need to access in the process of composing a livelihood. "We therefore require a notion of access to resources that helps us not only understand the way in which people deal with poverty in a material sense (by making a living), but also the ways in which their perception of well-being and poverty are related to their livelihood choices and strategies, and the capability that they possess both to add to their quality of life and also to enhance their capabilities to confront the social conditions that produce poverty" (Bebbington, 1999: 2022).

According to Bebbington, livelihood strategies should be considered in terms of access to five types of capital assets, i.e., produced, human, natural, social, and cultural capital.

A person's assets, such as land, are not merely means with which he or she makes a living: they also give meaning to that person's world. Assets are not simply resources that people use in building livelihoods: they are assets that give them the capability to be and to act. Assets should not be understood only as "things" that allow survival, adaptation, and poverty alleviation: "They are also the basis of agents' *power* to act and to reproduce, challenge or change the rules that govern the control, use and transformation of resources" (Giddens, In: Bebbington, 1999: 2022).

This volume analyzes how livelihood systems change and diversify in response to changing agroecological and socioeconomic conditions and opportunities. It focuses on exploring in detail how farmers cope with the ongoing transformation of rural space, concentrating on the link between livelihood and land. What is the effect of differential access to and control of land for livelihood, and how does this affect the development opportunities of individual members of households?

Land is a basis for sustainable livelihood—a necessary element of life—even in those cases where it no longer plays a crucial role in terms of income generation. Its importance needs to be studied in close relation to changes in the portfolios of activities of different groups and the large variety of coping mechanisms. Nowadays, access to resources and institutional spheres is critical in determining the relative viability of livelihoods.

Concepts

Land tenure, livelihood, and sustainability are the central concepts of this publication, and each of these notions is difficult to conceive.

Land tenure normally refers to the system of ownership of land and of title to its use, generally in agriculture. "Landownership is usually relatively straightforward compared with rights to use the land" (Johnston *et al.*, 2000: 425-429). Land tenure may be classified according to its legal basis (i.e., formal, informal, illegal), the relative rights of landowners and land users, the conditions and forms of payment from the latter to the former, if any, and the security of tenants. Many forms of tenure involve very complex combinations of use rights.

Land rights are the institutionalized forms of access to, and control over, land; land rights typically constitute land as property which involves some jural entity (individuals, households, communities, nations, etc.) that has rights and duties over land against other jural entities (property rights). Land rights are, however, always more complex than public versus private: virtually everywhere complex mixtures of group (or communal) and individual (private) control exist. "Rights over land are customarily divided into use rights (grazing, farming, collection, etc.); transfer rights (movement of ownership or possession through inheritance, gift, sale, lending, etc.) and administrative rights (the authority to allocate or withdraw land from use, to tax it, to arbitrate disputes, regulate transfers, etc.). Rights over land do not necessarily imply ownership (i.e., there can be rights of use and rental). Similarly, communal or collective forms of land management (for example in the Andes or in the Mexican *ejido)* may confer substantial 'ownership' security to some individuals; that is to say, there are stable and secure use rights in perpetuity. Fully privatized land rights—fee simple—in which rights to sell are not proscribed by laws that assign ultimate ownership to the state or to the powers of indigenous communities, are far from universal. Rights are often divided among different units of aggregation that claim different 'bundles of rights.' Such bundles may be nested or ranked in 'hierarchies' of estates" (Glucksman, 1965, in Johnston *et al.*, 2000: 425). But a right of access for one purpose (collecting wood) does not always imply automatic access for another (grazing). "Concepts of rights are often rooted in modes of livelihood and their relation to the market. Pastoral communities may have rights to rangelands as a common property system; this does not mean open access, but rather complex systems of regulation which link land and water rights. Forager may have rights of use rather than ownership" (Johnston *et al.*, 2000: 425-429).

The concept of livelihood is also very complex and difficult to define. Whereas the poor farmers in Latin America have long been viewed as passive victims of their surroundings, their active involvement in enforcing and responding to change has gradually gained recognition. For a long time, especially in studies addressing the characteristics and functioning of the *economía campesina*, rural household have been regarded as "a single decision-making unit maximizing its welfare subject to a range of income-earning opportunities and a set of resource constraints" (Ellis, 1997: 12). Although the *economía campesina* is usually regarded from the perspective that households pursue an optimal balance, the absence of such an equilibrium is increasingly proving to be a driving force behind farmers' actions. Families constantly weigh different objectives, opportunities, and limitations as a consequence of external and internal circumstances that change over time.

According to Long: "Livelihood best expresses the idea of individuals and groups striving to make a living, attempting to meet their various consumptions and economic necessities, coping with uncertainties, responding to new opportunities and choosing between different value position" (Appendini, this volume). In this volume, we use the definition currently applied by policy makers (e.g., DFID), which is a slightly modified version of the one originally developed by Robert Chambers and Gordon Conway (Carney, 1998: 2):

"A livelihood comprises the capabilities, assets (including both material and social resources) and activities required for a means of living. A livelihood is sustainable when it can cope with and recover from stresses and shocks and maintain or enhance its capabilities and assets both now and in the future, while not undermining the natural resource base."

Sustainable livelihood refers to the maintenance or enhancement of the productivity of resources on a long-term basis; it only exists when it also provides sustainable livelihood for the next generation.

Livelihood strategies (or the way that households respond to change, handling opportunities and limitations [Zoomers, 1999: 18]) will often result in the reallocation of land, labor, and capital resources. The outcome of livelihood strategies will highly depend on the family's goals and priorities, the availability of resources (land, labor capacity, and capital), the functioning and adaptability of local institutions, and the quality of the external environment, i.e., the agroecological situation, market access, infrastructure, etc.

In order to understand the livelihood strategies of farmers, it is important to acknowledge that what farmers do is not always the result of deliberate and strategic behavior. Changes are not always brought about by systematic or conscious behavior, and many decisions will not imply free choice but adaptation to ever-changing internal and external circumstances. Only a limited number of farmers' actions are to be interpreted as deliberate behavior.

Moreover, it is important to make a distinction between adapting strategies (in the event of an adaptation *ex ante*) and coping behavior (with an *ex post* adaptation). "Adapting (...) is then interpreted as a deliberate household strategy to anticipate failures in individual income streams (e.g., by maintaining a spread of activities), while coping is the involuntary response to disaster or unanticipated failure in major sources of survival" (see Zoomers, 1999: 19). In other words: adapting should be conceived as *ex ante* income management, and coping as *ex post* consumption management in the wake of crisis. "Adapting means making permanent changes to the livelihood mix in the face of changing circumstances, while coping means trying to preserve existing livelihoods in the face of disaster" (Webb *et al.*, 1992; Carter, 1997; in Ellis, 1998). Similar decisions (e.g., diversification of income) may therefore be taken either as a deliberate household strategy or as an involuntary response to crisis.

It is also important that sufficient attention is paid not only to the "appearance" of livelihood strategies at the household level, but also to the "hidden" dimensions at the micro-level. No two households are organized identically or are based on the same operational logic. "An interesting distinction can be made between families within which each member is involved in many different part-time income generating activities, and those for which individual family members are able to engage in full-time specialized occupations" (Unni, 1996; In: Ellis, 1998). There are considerable differences between households with respect to the role of individual family members and the division of labor on the basis of gender relations. It is important to realize that many households do not function as paragons of harmony; there are several grounds for conflicts and divergent interests. What is good for the individual is not necessarily good for the household, and vice versa. In addition, what suits the men does not always please the women in the household, and vice versa. "Gender (...) affects diversification options, in terms of which income earning opportunities are taken up and which are discarded; and also affects diversification patterns, as manifested by unequal male and female participation rates in different categories of non-farm activity" (Ellis, 1998).

Livelihood strategies can only be studied as an element of long-term development. For the short term, it is more realistic to speak about practices (i.e., a set of repeated and related activities conducted by different members of a family over the course of a year). Livelihood strategies concern more extended periods spanning several years; only over time does the course of the farmers' development path become clear. Households with a similar combination of practices (e.g., families which combine market gardening with migration) can progress in very different directions; for example, one family may purchase additional land and concentrate its efforts on commercial production, while another may buy a truck and start a business as a middleman.

Finally, for a true understanding of livelihood strategies, the analysis should go beyond the economic or productive end of life. It was made clear in the above that livelihood is multidimensional: it is built on a combination of produced, human, natural, social, and cultural assets (Bebbington, 1999: 2022). The influence of non-material and extra-household factors on household development opportunities is often greater than initial appearances suggest. "A livelihood encompasses income, both cash and in kind, as well as the social institutions (kin, family, village, etc.), gender relations, and property rights required to support and to sustain a given standard of living. A livelihood also includes access to and the benefits derived from social and public services provided by the state such as education, health services, roads, water supplies and so on. Livelihood is therefore not synonymous with the income situation" (Ellis, 1998). Sufficient consideration needs to be afforded to the various dimensions of livelihood, including the presence of social security mechanisms.

Objective and scope of this publication

This volume contains a selection of papers focusing on the changing role of land in the livelihood strategies of farmers. In the various chapters, an attempt is made to sketch a picture of current transformations of the rural area in various countries in Latin America. Developments at the micro level (households) are connected with processes of institutional change at the meso (village) and macro level (national and international).

The Introduction (this chapter and Chapter 2) focuses on the concept of livelihood and the consequences of this concept for rural development policy. Appendini (Chapter 2) shows that development organizations (FAO, UNDP, DFID, etc.) have for a long time based themselves on economic theories and concepts, but that currently attention is being paid to the holistic concept of sustainable livelihood strategies (i.e., sustainable livelihood approach as a new approach to poverty alleviation). She shows that although livelihood can be seen as a useful analysis concept, as a policy instrument it is not easy to implement. The livelihood approach helps in understanding the realities and needs of rural people at the community and household level in a more flexible way. Once in the field, however, the livelihood approach often faces operational and methodological problems the development agents must be aware of and sensitive to.

The rest of the volume is divided into three parts, each of which reflects important transformations that are currently taking place: international migration (part 1), land privatization (part 2) and the appearance of new market niches (part 3). The following details the contents of the chapters, each of which may be read individually.

Part 1: Livelihood and multifunctional land-use in a transnational space: international migration

In this part, attention is focused on the characteristics of livelihood in traditional communities with communal land management systems in Bolivia, Peru, and Mexico. As a result of the continuing land scarcity and people's increasing ability to move over great distances, in many villages international migration has developed into a structural element of farmers' livelihood (people leave for longer periods to the US, Argentina, etc.). An analysis is made of the consequences of this on access to resources and livelihood, in which attention is primarily paid to processes of institutional change and of adaptation.

In Chapter 3, Susan Paulson concentrates on the characteristics of the traditional land management system in the Bolivian Andes, and demonstrates that "land does not stand alone". She emphasizes the interconnection between the various dimensions of land (ecological, economic, social, etc.), and shows that environmental management systems are characterized by diversity and interdependence, which usually do not fit the reality of development interventions (i.e., agricultural modernization, individual land titling, etc.). Policies based on units of one man and one plot are not compatible with reality: there is a need for an integral approach to environmental degradation and social inequality. Farmers have multiple, often dispersed, land plots and resources which are essentially interrelated. Land has various overlapping and parallel functions, and changes (international migration, etc.) frequently have far-reaching and partly unexpected consequences for the land-livelihood relation at the local level; this has direct consequences for the division of tasks between men and women (land is an engendered space), and for the use of resources (with multidimensional results, both environmentally as well as economically and socially). Land must be seen as a social space.

In Chapter 4, Cortes—taking as her starting point a "holistic" reality (described by Paulson as "a dynamic web of interdependency")—focuses her analysis on the increasing importance of international migration from the Bolivian Andes to Argentina, Israel, and the US, and the consequences of this for access to land and the use of resources. In the livelihood strategies of farmers, land performs various functions simultaneously (nutritive, monetary, social, cultural, and patrimonial), and depending on the specific role, the land is used in a certain manner (individually, collectively, etc.) for certain purposes (consumption, production, status, etc.). International migration and the fact that people generate capital have an important impact on access to land and the practical value of land. International migration is not the harbinger of *decampesinación*, but a dynamic force, one that brings about the redistribution and reorganization of rural space, production methods, and access to resources. In many cases, it is the migrants who buy extra land. Investment in land, thanks to income from migration, sometimes goes beyond a simple economic aim and expresses the wish to maintain the symbolic and cultural function of the land: it is a sign of belonging to the community group—a form of socioeconomic identification—and to Andean society. Like Paulson, Cortes establishes that change processes are selective (they have different consequences for different groups) and that institutional organizations (projects, government, etc.) are insufficiently aware of the complexity of the situation (in this case, land tenure).

It seems that there is a similar situation in Mexico. In Chapter 5, Nuijten emphasizes that—apart from the economic meaning of land (farming incomes)—in many areas the role of land is primarily to maintain continuity in the family (inheritance as a way of keeping families together and of connecting generations); land plays an important role in power relations and in changes in those relations (landowners versus landless), and above all affects social relations; more specifically, having land is very important for the construction of identity (i.e., "transnational" *ejiditarios* who use their land as an instrument for maintaining a peasant identity, in spite of international migration).

In Chapter 6, Appendini, García Barrios and de la Tejera examine how international migration is interwoven with institutional change (transnational institutions). Based on Orstom's definition of property rights (access, withdrawal, management, exclusion, and alienation), they analyze in which ways migration has modified and adjusted institutional practices, such as the way they are inclusive of *comuneros* who are absent from the community. The authors focus on "institutional flexibility" (how despite international migration, old-fashioned institutions persist). Rather than resulting in a breakdown of the communal ability to manage resources and the end of the functioning of local institutions, local institutions show an ability to adapt, allowing migrants to retain access to the local resources (cropland, pastures, forest). Despite international migration, the local community persists: local institutions are adapted to the new situation, allowing the population to live in two worlds. Decision-making and the management of resources are modified, but without destroying the indigenous institutions or excluding the migrants.

Finally, in Chapter 7, de Vries and Gilvonio analyze the situation in Peru and show that community-building and access to land should not be perceived as structural matters. They demonstrate that property (i.e., land) and its regulation are not only connected with material subsistence, but that land is also determinative for the construction of local identity. A community is not a "territorial thing," but a discourse. People must continue to fulfil various requirements in order to retain their rights and access to land. Being a *comunero* is not as easy as so often assumed. It requires commitment, political acumen, and perseverance, especially when facing conflicts over land.

Part 2: Livelihood and land-use change in new a policy context: land privatization

In this part, the focus is on the changes in livelihood and land-use as a consequence of new land policies. As Latin America moves toward full integration into the free market economy, many governments, supported by the World Bank and other international organizations, have determined that the traditional land management structure (e.g., *comunidades Andinos*, *ejidos*, and other examples of collective land) has been a key element in the agricultural sector's lack of competitiveness. Land privatization and individual titles granting full-fledged ownership of land are the cornerstone of current land policies, and a common feature of neo-liberal land policy is thus the undoing of the agrarian reform of previous decades (the parceling out of production cooperatives and other forms of collective land holdings), while creating the conditions to engender a land market. Simultaneously, new forms of land tenure are being introduced, i.e., the establishment of ecological parks or *territorios indígenas* (see Volume 1, this series). Based on various case studies (Peru, Mexico, Nicaragua) the consequences of the new land policy (privatization, enclosing the commons, decollectivization, etc.) are analyzed; in this, the focus is on the consequences for land-use and access to resources (what happens to traditional land management structure, community life and rural welfare).

In Chapter 8, Morris analyzes how far land privatization in Peru has had consequences for "the communal" and the acceptance by farmers of traditional technology. According to Morris, the adherents of protecting communal land are too negative about privatization, and the individualization of land-use does not mean that there is no longer room for collective management. He looks at recent attempts to revive traditional Inca technology (water management) for which—regardless of the land tenure situation—there are good possibilities. Despite land privatization and the one man, one plot policy (see also Paulson), the people still exhibit the "old flexibility" that is so typical of communal living. Differential land-use, which is extensively described by Paulson, is important for flexibility, and—despite privatization—it is likely to stay. Land tenure does not have direct implications for community life.

In Chapter 9, Gerritsen and Foster show how in Mexico in a community surrounded by a biosphere reserve, common land is gradually being enclosed and appropriated by certain groups (especially the *ganaderos*), with the result that the former collective pastures are being fenced off and withdrawn from the use of other villagers. As opposed to what Appendini *et al.* describe, we see here that international migration has led to a situation in which farmers who have earned money in the US invest it in purchasing land and cattle, and are thus putting pressure on the common land (enclosure of the commons). The "rules of the game" are being undermined by the increasing pressure, and a gradual change is taking place in which forest becomes cultivated field and then pasture.

At the village level, an increasing divide is growing between the poor (with multifaceted livelihood strategies, based on differential land-use) and the rich (the *ganaderos* with their specialized land-use). A process of land-use change, coupled with a process of socioeconomic differentiation, is occurring.

The analysis is then focused on Nicaragua, and *inter alia* the link between land, livelihood strategies and rural welfare (the size and composition of income). In Chapter 10, Ruben, Rodríguez and Cortez analyze the implications of the breaking up of the cooperatives; they show how "individuals and households and group characteristics influence the selection of different *pathways of institutional change.*" They analyze changes in membership of cooperatives in relation to changes in land-use and cropping patterns, and analyze the income strategies of individual households. While the parcelation of cooperative property enables some farmers to improve their income situation, it is shown that this is often at the expense of a higher concentration of income derived from arable cropping, giving rise to substantially lower income elasticity for on-farm labor efforts.

Finally, in Chapter 11, Davis, Carletto and Piccioni analyze the structure and distribution of income and assets in rural Nicaragua, and look at the questions: which household assets and characteristics are associated with poverty, and what are the implications for poverty alleviation strategies? They also look at the response capacity of rural producers, focusing on control over land (and other productive assets), transaction costs, market failures and imperfections, and differential access to institutions and public goods. Agricultural income is the most important source of income across different categories of the rural population. Still, across farm households, the structure and sources of income are heterogeneous; sources of income are highly correlated with size of landholding.

Lack of productive assets (land, but also skilled labor) is a key determinant of rural poverty, as are poorly functioning factor markets. Annual perennial and pastureland, and higher levels of education, have a significant, positive impact on household income. Further land transfers to *microfundistas* and *minifundistas* (i.e., the poorest of the population) could lead to a significant increase in income. Greater access to land is still a way out of poverty.

Part 3: Livelihood in a global competitive sphere: between decampesinación, diversification and *specialization*

In this part, the focus is on changes in livelihood and land-use resulting from farmers having to function in global competitive spheres. Worldwide, there has been a fundamental change in the organization of production of goods and services (Dicken, 1992); markets have become integrated and competition has increased (global commodity chains). Production environments are no longer protected; most Latin American economies are now structured according the neo-liberal principle of the market economy. How do farmers adapt to broader, more competitive, economic spheres, and how does this shape their livelihood strategies and agricultural land-use? Based on case studies of Mexico and Chile, it is shown how, in the production areas of new export crops, both positive and negative developments are taking place, which—depending on the local situation—launch the process of *decampesinación* or sustainable development.

In Chapter 12, Laura Paulson illustrates the relationship between agricultural restructuring/land-use change and smallholder participation in the Mexican avocado sector (land-use changes in response to the global restructuring of markets of agricultural production). She shows how farmers have adapted to broader, more competitive, economic spheres, and that private producers and *ejido*/indigenous producers responded differently to agricultural policy shifts from 1970s to the 1990s. It is an example of an area where the local economy has improved and migration to the US is no longer necessary, and where even in-migration is occurring. At the same time, processes of land concentration are taking place, often going hand in hand with increased land fragmentation within *ejidos* and processes of exclusion. The increasing globalization of the avocado sector is creating inequalities among different sets of producers (an elite of avocado producers, and the development of a significant market for wage labor).

In Chapter 13, Schüren describes striking differences in land-use (access to markets, technology, capital, etc.) between Mennonites on the one hand and *comuneros* and landless non-*comuneros* on the other hand in Mexico: whereas the Mennonites concentrate on commercial production (mechanized land/specialized land-use), the majority of the local/indigenous population are involved in food production (differentiated land-use). An increasing number of the latter rent out parts of their land to mechanized farmers who grown cotton on it; as well as receiving rent, they earn money as laborers and cotton pickers; here, too, economic differentiation and land concentration is becoming more pronounced, increasingly excluding the small farmer.

Attention then shifts to Chile, one of the first countries to successfully set off along the neo-liberal road. In Chapter 14, Bee shows that there are disparities between capitalistic and peasant farming (table grapes); a heterogeneous rural population experiences the expansion of nontraditional exports in different ways. The expansion of export production does not necessarily herald the destruction or marginalization of more traditional forms of agricultural production; even the small-scale farmers survive. In some villages, the population has sold their land to the table grape producers and now work as laborers, whereas in others they have continued the "old farming" and/or switched to growing tomatoes, simultaneously profiting from the local work possibilities. Changing land tenure patterns have had repercussions on both labor and community organization.

Part 4: Final reflections

Finally, Chapter 15—on the basis of the earlier chapters— makes clear that man-land relationships need a conceptual update. The role of land in the livelihood strategies of farmers cannot be described in general or static terms. The relationships cannot be understood unless sufficient attention is paid to the diversity and dynamics of livelihood strategies (objectives and priorities being closely linked to the family development cycle), the multidimensionality of land, and the institutional setting. Even though there is an important link between access to land and livelihood strategies, giving access to land will often not be sufficient to alleviate poverty or solve the problems of rural development.

References

Bebbington, A., "Capitals and capabilities: a framework for analyzing peasant viability, rural livelihoods and poverty". *World Development,* Vol. 27, no. 12 (1999), pp. 2021-44.

Carney, D. (ed.), *Sustainable rural livelihoods. What contribution can we make?* Department for International Development. Overseas Development Institute, London, 1998.

Dicken, P, *Global shift: the internationalization of economic activity.* New York, 1992.

Ellis, F., "Household strategies and rural livelihood diversification". *The Journal of Development Studies,* Vol. 35, no. 1 (1998), pp. 1-38.

Johnston, R.J., D. Gregory, G. Pratt and M. Watts, *The dictionary of human geography.* 4th edition. Oxford, 2000.

Zoomers, A., *Linking livelihood strategies to development.* KIT, Amsterdam, 1999.

Zoomers, A. and G. van der Haar (eds.), *Current land policy in Latin America: regulating land tenure under neo-liberalism.* KIT/Vervuert, Amsterdam, 2000.

2 Land and livelihood: what do we know, and what are the issues?

Kirsten Appendini[1]

Introduction

The title "Land and livelihood" suggests that rural populations are still tied to land as a basis for their livelihoods. This is the general premise of rural policy, whether it focuses on agricultural activities and/or poverty alleviation. However, the viability of agriculture (certainly for smallholding farmers or peasants, for whom food production is often the main agricultural activity) is under serious stress due to the liberalization of economies and global competition.

There is hence an underlying tension between the aims of improving the livelihood of peasants and the viability of farming, particularly of basic food crops that constitute the bulk of small farmers production. This has not been ignored by policy makers, and in the new economic model[2], poverty alleviation policies have become entrenched in the policy agenda in order to mitigate the negative effects of structural adjustment policies and economic reforms.

This has led to a focus on broader issues than agriculture within rural policy design and implementation. For example, the fact that the importance of agriculture as a means of rural livelihood tends to be diminishing, as rural households engage in multiple economic activities in order to achieve their subsistence, is not new, but it has gained a new dimension in the policy agenda. Off-farm and non-farm employment is now part of the development solution for rural areas. At the same time, land reform, access to productive resources, and sustainable agriculture/forestry are argued for as means to improve the income of rural populations, and particularly of poor peasants (de Janvry *et al.*, 1999).

Is there then still considered to be space for the smallholder, the family farm, the peasant? And who is this economic and social actor? The "efficient" peasant in an export "niche"? The "poor" peasant household engaged in complex, multi-activity income strategies for survival? The post-modern "peasant" moving about in the space of transnational communities? In the development discourse, they are referred to dichotomically as "winners and losers," or "potential competitive peasants or poverty assisted peasants," having "opportunities and costs" and being subject to differential policies.

But the livelihoods of rural population throughout Latin America are evolving in much more complex ways than can be accounted for by simple dichotomies. Understanding and taking account of these complexities is the challenge for those of us concerned with rural issues. As researchers, we are deeply involved in finding out more about how rural people adjust, cope, create, and re-create their livelihoods under the impact of macroeconomic and policy change. As policy advisors/designers, we are concerned with finding better ways to support and strengthen the potential of people's strategies that are aimed at improving their livelihood.

In these endeavors, some consensus has been reached around certain themes, new (or perhaps not so new) issues have been brought up, our theoretical and methodological frameworks are being revised, and policy design is facing new challenges framed by "deregulation," "decentralization," "democratization," seeking solutions that in the "new" development discourse stresses "participation," "empowerment," and "gender sensitiveness."

This chapter concerns some of the current issues mentioned above and discussed in several articles included in this book: the meaning of and approach to livelihood as seen from different perspectives; the strategies undertaken by rural households for maintaining or enhancing their livelihoods and incomes—such as income diversification; the importance of land for livelihood strategies; the implication of different land tenure regimes for land-use and investment behavior; and the social and cultural dimensions of land in rural life. An attempt will be made to answer the questions: what do we know, what are the issues, and what are the policies?

Livelihood

Livelihood and sustainable livelihood concepts have become entrenched in the development discourse. Several international agencies and donors have adopted the concept as an approach to poverty alleviation. This is part of the constant search for more effective methods to support people and communities in ways that are more meaningful to their daily lives and needs, as opposed to ready-made, interventionist instruments. This is a response to former approaches—and policies—to poverty alleviation, such as those based on income and consumption criteria, the basic needs perspective, or the basic capability perspective. According to DFID (Department of International Development), the sustainable livelihood approach provides a holistic means of understanding and analyzing poverty, bringing together former experiences, but also relating other analytical concepts and focuses, such as the households, gender, governance, and farming systems. A sustainable livelihood framework is considered an analytical device for improved understanding of livelihoods and poverty, and can support poverty eradication by "making enhancement of poor people's livelihoods a central goal of development efforts" (Farrington et al., 1999: 1). Hence, the approach is wrapped in a discourse of participation and empowerment. It can also be understood in the trend of decentralization, and providing space for the "local" in the emerging "globalizing" world.

Defining the concept of livelihood is complex, because it is an all-encompassing topic, and when incorporated as an approach in policy design and implementation, the concept needs to be operationalized in ways in which development agencies and practitioners can use the approach. This requires a methodological framework, and a working concept that may be translated into quantitative and qualitative variables.[3] This is not the place to discuss this debate, although some issues relevant to the topics discussed in this book will be highlighted. First, the definition of the concept will be looked at, then some examples will be given of how the main agencies that have proposed this approach in a policy framework have incorporated it, and then the discussion will be linked to land and livelihood.

Long (1997) defines "livelihood" in its broader concept: "Livelihood best expresses the idea of individuals and groups striving to make a living, attempting to meet their various consumption and economic necessities, coping with uncertainties, responding to new opportunities, and choosing between different value positions...". This should be understood in a broad and dynamic perspective identifying the relevant social units and fields of activity, and not only the analysis of economic life. Or, as Wallman says:

> "Livelihood is never just a matter of finding or making shelter, transacting money getting food to put on the family table or to exchange on the market place. It is equally a matter of ownership and circulation of information, the management of skills and relationships and the affirmation of personal significance....and group identity. The tasks of meeting obligations, of security, identity and status, and organizing time are crucial to livelihood as bread and shelter" (Wallman, 1984).

Policy-oriented literature has incorporated the concept of livelihood in a more narrow way, since—as mentioned above—it is necessary to operationalize the concept as a tool for development programs and policies for addressing poverty alleviation.

In this perspective, the concept of livelihood implies the idea of "strategy," since people manage an array of resources or assets (natural capital, social capital, human capital, physical capital, financial capital) within a dynamic context in which assets and decision-making interact:

> "A livelihood system is a dynamic realm that integrates both the opportunities and assets available to a group of people for achieving their goals and aspirations as well as interactions with and exposure to a range of beneficial or harmful ecological, social, economic and political perturbations that may help or hinder groups' capacities to make a living" (Hoon, Singh and Wanmali, 1997: 5).

> "A livelihood is sustainable when it can cope with and recover from stresses and shocks and maintain or enhance its capabilities and assets both now and in the future, while not undermining the natural resource base" (Carney, 1998: 4).

According to UNDP—one of the first international agencies to propose this approach to poverty alleviation—the attractiveness of sustainable livelihood "lies in its applicability to different contexts, situations of uncertainty and in its capacity as a consultative and participatory process for the cross-fertilization of ideas and strategies between various stakeholders" (Hoon et al., 1997: 4).

The sustainable livelihood program of UNDP has focused on coping and adaptive strategies "pursued by individuals and communities as a response to external shocks and stresses such as drought, civil strife and policy failures" (Hoon et al., 1997: 5). There is a holistic approach to understanding livelihoods at the community and the individual level, as well as the context of livelihoods such as the macro, micro, and sectoral policies that affect people's livelihoods. UNDP has proposed a methodology to translate a holistic approach into a conceptual "model"[4] in order that people's strategies for survival, or coping with stress and shocks, can be acted upon in a program or policy context. At the operational level, it is the knowledge and/or technology component which is underlined and becomes the aim of specific program or project interventions.[5]

FAO has also incorporated the concept of livelihood systems into some of the agency's units, as a diagnostic tool for project formulation, for example by the Investment Center Division and recently in a large-scale fishery project in western Africa.

DFID has defined a methodological framework for analyzing sustainable livelihoods, which focuses on identifying five types of capital assets which people can build and draw upon: human, natural, financial, social, and physical assets. The policy is to support people in their own efforts and strategies by focusing "on the impact of different policy and institutional arrangements on people's livelihoods and seeking to influence these arrangements in order to promote the agenda of the poor" (Farrington et al., 1999: 2). The experience required to implement this approach has been related to project and/or program design, as well as project or program review and impact assessment.[6]

In sum, while such multidisciplinary and holistic efforts as the sustainable livelihood approach are now among the forefront issues in the discussion on poverty alleviation, there is still a wide range of issues to be discussed, such as solving methodological questions[7], how to link the participatory process beyond the community (and specifically to the macro policy context), and how to mainstream the concept within development policy as opposed to ready-made, interventionist approaches.[8]

Livelihood strategies of rural households: income and the importance of land

This section reviews some of the topics concerning livelihoods that are discussed in this volume, namely those related to land. First, the more economic aspects of livelihood strategies are dealt with, that is, how households generate their income, and the importance of agriculture, and hence land, in the income strategies of rural households. When looking at income strategies, the conceptual approach is on well-trodden ground: mainstream economics. There is a vast tradition of the study of household economics and empirical assessment of rural household's income strategies.[9]

Empirical studies show that rural households involve themselves in a range of activities in order to reproduce/re-create their livelihoods. Income diversification, in off-farm and non-farm activities, is an income strategy adopted by most rural households. This evidence has underlined that agriculture is but one of several activities of rural families, often being partially sustained by non-farm activities (Ellis, 1998; de Janvry et al., 1997; Reardon et al., 1998).

The issue of the complexity of rural households in their endeavor to survive is not a recent issue, but the debate has changed. In Latin America, the multiple-activity of households was recognized from a political economy perspective and was the core of the *campesinista* debate of the 1970s, when the importance of wage-work (both rural and non-rural) was arduously discussed among *campesinistas* and *proletaristas* (Appendini, 1992). *Campesinistas* assessed that semi-proletarization was the means by which poor rural households survived and resisted the process of proletarization, by reproducing both farming activities and the labor force for non-farming activities.[10] Today, no-one would sustain the "functionality" of peasant households as suppliers of cheap food and cheap labor: the former has been surpassed by the uncompetitiveness of peasant as basic food producers, and the latter has become redundant (or has it, considering the transnational migration flows?). The question has changed: the multi-activity of rural households is a strategy for the livelihoods of rural families in a context of limited opportunities in both the labor and product market, a context which has become harsher within economic liberalization, in which basic food crops are being priced at international levels, and labor markets are being deregulated within national economies.

But coming back to the present, hard data provided by economists have now brought the issue of the multi-activity of rural households to the consideration of policy design for poverty alleviation purposes; whereas formerly, rural policies were mainly focused on production, they now incorporate employment and non-farm activities (Melmed-Sanjak *et al.*, 1998: 16; Stamoulis, 1996).

Assessing the importance of income diversification by rural households associated with the resource base (water, farm implements, credit, etc.), and the characteristics of the family (labor force, lifecycle, ethnicity, etc.) helps to identify trends of households strategies on the basis of which we can construct "typologies" (subsistence, medium, and better-off peasants).

For Latin America, some overall trends seem to have emerged: households with little land have become integrated into labor markets as wage workers, and agriculture is now a small component of income, being mainly for self-consumption; medium peasants are less reliant on off-farm income; and better-off households are diversified, but in a variety of activities ranging from wage-work to self-employment and investment in a small business.[11]

This kind of evidence has provided guides for policy interventions based on the implications that the ability to classify and categorize households also enabled the identification of different needs of households and their members in improving livelihoods/incomes, leading to differentiated policies. For example, in Mexico this led to the categorization of farmers into three groups: efficient, potential, and non-viable producers. The first two became subject to differential credit policies, whereas the third came under a poverty alleviation program *(Pronasol/Solidaridad)*. Hence, in both the livelihood strategy approach and the income strategy analysis, farming is one of many activities pursued and land one of the many assets of the rural household.

One interesting focus for the above type of study is the analysis of the role of land and whether it is the basic asset of rural household. One question is how important land is for food production, cash crops, etc. for specific contexts and household types, and how households decide on resource allocation between farm and non-farm activities. It is also important to extend this to an intra-household perspective: the decision-making on resource allocation according to sex, age, and status within the family[12]. Another question is the importance of land in a broader perspective, for example, as an entitlement that is related to claims and access to other resources which may be economic, social, or cultural; or the different meanings of land in a household and community context.

As for the first question, an issue to be explored more is the dynamics between income sources and the importance of land. With more income diversification, is land and natural resources less important for livelihoods? Studies on household income strategies mainly underline the importance of agricultural production by socioeconomic groups, but do not explicitly look at the above questions. A review of economic literature exploring the relationship between off-farm income and patterns of ownership (tenure) shows that there is little evidence of links between off-farm income and farm investment, including the purchase of land. Empirical evidence is scattered and does not prove that off-farm income is a source of investment in land; where this type of analysis is available, evidence is context specific (Melmed-Sanjak *et al.*, 1998).

In conclusion, the income strategies of rural households, and the role of agriculture and off-farm activities, have been well documented in many countries, thus providing information that policy advisors have incorporated into recommendations for supporting people's access to assets (such as land and credit) and employment, and for designing rural development programs. Of the complex array of livelihood strategies, it is perhaps this subset that relies on a most concrete set of tools, since they are based on mainstream economics. However, setting this understanding within a multidisciplinary approach—that is, understanding people's decision-making in a wider context, such as the cultural and historical processes— remains a challenge for researchers and policy makers interested in constructing a holistic approach to development. The following reflections on current land policy may illustrate how a narrow economic approach is limited in understanding the complex process of access to land and tenure security.

Access to resource and security of tenure

Though giving lip-service to the importance of land as a means of access to broader entitlements, policy advice has mainly focused on issues of land that relate to individual households, and the importance of land as an economic asset. Under the "new economic model," security of tenure became the main concern of land reform policies rather than land distribution, as it was in former agrarian reform policies (Herrera *et al.*, 1997). During the wave of privatization, security of tenure (meaning formal titles to land) was considered the main condition for incentivizing investment (and obtaining credit) in order to increase productivity and achieve agricultural growth, and hence to improve income and the general welfare of rural households.

However, the literature is increasingly questioning the basic assumption concerning the impact of land titling on agricultural performance and the welfare of peasant households. First, the beneficial outcomes of private property rights has been critically confronted by the debate on common property and resource management (Ostrom, 1998; Baland *et al.*, 1996). There is now a significant amount of literature which concludes that common property may be efficient in managing resources in specific contexts (Quan, 1998; see also Volume 1, this series).

Second, the World Bank has reviewed its position on the matter: instead of viewing formal land title as a precondition for "modern development," empirical studies analyzed by the Bank have provided controversial evidence on these basic assumptions: for example, credit markets are often non-existent for peasant farmer communities (Deininger *et al.*, 1998); benefits of titling when land is used as a collateral may pose the threat of land loss because of foreclosure to small farmers to the benefit of the better-off; land markets may not develop, and land titling may not have any impact on peasants: "Where private property as a tenure form is not dominant, however, land titling has little consequence or utility because land holders acquire tenure security through other mechanisms (e.g., membership in a group or family). This explains why titling programs in some areas either have little impact, unintended effects, or quickly become outdated" (Melhed-Sanjak *et al.*, 1998: 3-5).[13]

Third, agriculture in general has lost profitability in the open market context; this applies particularly to food crops, which are the main peasant staples. Incentives for credit and investment are associated with profitability, but small farmers are not competitive (or need to restructure their cropping patterns, as in the case of the successful Guatemalan peasants turning to high value horticulture, which is not replicable in general).

Concerning the two first points, in many peasant communities where family fields are individually cropped, possession or ownership of plots is defined and recognized by the community, whether the tenure system is private or communal, and whether or not plots have legal titles. In fact, studies undertaken by FAO have found that even in the absence of titled land, land transactions continue to take place. Security of tenure in informal land market transactions is based on the local character of the markets. Land transactions take place among people of the same community or between family members; in the absence of land titles, land rights are assured by community tradition and kinship networks.[14]

However the simplified relationship of titling and positive impact in the agricultural production, income, and welfare of rural households, is still an accepted association at the core of many current land tenure policies in Latin America; particularly titling programs still focus mainly on privatization and the individualization of landholdings. Although research has shown that the poorer households are often excluded from the beneficial impacts of titling, this fact seems of little concern to the advocates of land titling. International funding agencies continue to emphasize land titling as one of the main subjects when dealing with assistance to countries on land tenure issues. National titling projects in Central American countries, Ecuador, and Mexico, among others, are part of the on-going funding initiatives of these institutions today.

Hence, there is indeed a challenge as to how the empirical knowledge accumulated on the complexities of land tenure systems and the impact of reforms can be incorporated into policy issues.[15]

For example, a study was performed in Ecuador to assess the impact of land titling on agricultural production and the general welfare of rural families. This study, which was carried out in the Andean Highlands, found that the main issue concerning land was not titling, but access to land. In indigenous communities with communal property, individual plots were assigned to families and recognized as private possessions with no need for formal titling. Communities had obtained land at different periods. The oldest communities under agrarian reform in the 1960s, and the most recent had made collective purchases of land with the support of NGOs and regional peasant organizations. The performance of agriculture and the income of households varied from one community to the other. Those households that had had the support of NGO programs in the form of credit (both to buy land and for agricultural and livestock production) and organizing skills, were better off than communities without such support (the case of households with a titling program without other support). Titling was related to a time dimension; that is, individual titling was advanced in the older communities, while in the newly formed the process was just beginning. The Ecuadorian experience showed that access to land and organization, rather than the holding of individual titles, were the key factors for agricultural performance. Peasant organizations and NGOs supported the Andean peasants in gaining access to land mainly through collective purchase. Titling was not an issue, and security was attained through the recognized rights as members of a peasant association or organization (DyA, 1999).

FAO is involved in various activities concerning land tenure security and attending to a number of related issues. For example, in Brazil, the government is designing settlements for agrarian reform recipients with FAO cooperation, in which special efforts are being made to go beyond mere land distribution and to ensure that the beneficiaries develop sustainable family farm enterprises, so that they will not end up selling their land to speculators. This FAO approach of combining land tenure reform with sustainable farm development, is also being applied in the Philippines, where it serves as a basis of rural infrastructure loans by the World Bank and the Asian Development Bank.

FAO has also been engaged in the analysis of "traditional" ownership rights and in encouraging local participation in resource management. For example, in Niger in supporting customary land tenure for resource management; similar activities have been supported in the Philippines (Herrera *et al.*, 1997); and through the FAO Forests, Trees and People Program (FTPP) in Latin America, particularly in Peru and Bolivia. However, securing property rights in a collective form—although undertaken through the FAO Agrarian Reform projects during the 1970s and 1980s—has not been attended to under the privatization trends of today, and is a challenge to be included in a relevant way in the agricultural and land policy agenda for Latin America.[16]

Livelihood, land, and the institutional environment

The previous section concerned the formal institutional aspects of land tenure, which is the aim of policies. But the relationship between formal institutional frameworks and the performance of agriculture and management of land resources is much more complex and dynamic than the hypothetical questions that led to the study in Ecuador referred to above.

A land tenure system is constructed by an institutional setting that goes from the macro level, with the formal institutions that determine the legal frame of land tenure in a country, to the local institutions that may have particular specificities, and is mediated by the organizing practices of people around institutional settings, which may (or may not) lead to new institutional arrangements (Nuijten, 1998). For example, at the local level, the indigenous communities of Oaxaca are under communal land tenure regimes, and are constituted as moral legal entities that are recognized as communities that have their own internal rules, such as established by "custom and norms" which are recognized by constitutional and state laws. But in the forest communities, institutional practices have changed due to out-migration leading to processes that have changed the property rights institutions at the local level (Appendini *et al.*, this volume).

The impact and response to legal reforms still need to be researched and better understood in their particularities in the regional and local contexts: how do people access land, water, and other natural resources? How does the institutional setting determine and interact with groups or individuals who appropriate, reinterpret, adapt, and modify the norms and rules at the community and household levels?

Evidence of these processes is being constructed both theoretically and empirically. Literature dealing with access to and management of resources is vast and multidisciplinary; sociological and anthropological approaches provide insight into the complexity of institutional processes. Examples of case studies providing empirical evidence of the way people and communities construct institutional practices in complex ways attending to economic, social, historical, and cultural processes are included in this volume: Paulson provides a fine-tuned analysis of the gender organization of access to land and the division of labor, by analyzing the production and reproduction practices of the households as embedded in the cultural "meanings" of the social and economic as well as environmental practices. The impact of modernization policies implemented to improve agricultural production in a village did not take into account the organizational practices related to the role of women in resource management, and hence negatively affected the livelihood of women and quality of life for the family.

Cortes (this volume) shows how international migration from villages in the Andean valleys of Bolivia has resulted in multiple arrangements to access land among migrants and non-migrants. Migration has also changed the meaning of land according to the type of household (importance and market orientation of agriculture), and has reinforced its symbolic and social value even when losing importance as an economic asset. Appendini *et al.* (this volume) analyze the flexibility of institutional practices relating to common resources (including land) due to migration.

The role and meanings of land stand out in various chapters also presented in this volume. Nuijten shows how land has different roles: within the family according to who possess land and how power relations within the family are played out; the relations between landowners and the landless in the political struggles of the village; and the meaning of land in constructing a "peasant" identity in a trans-nationalized community. De Vries and Gilvonio discuss an example of how a specific strategy to obtain land is constructed intertwined with the playing out of identities in a political negotiating process. Córdova (Volume 1, this series) looks at how women in a village in Veracruz have appropriated and used their formal rights to inherit and control land, and used this to change the power relations within their household.

But it is again economics, in this case institutional economics, that provides a theoretical/methodological frame which is having an impact on the policy debate in order to analyze the interaction of households and/or agents with the institutional framework related to access to land and natural resources. Referred to here is the literature on property rights (Ostrom, 1998; Baland *et al.*, 1996). For example, the chapter by Gerritsen *et al.* (this volume) looks at a common tenure system in Cuzalapa (Sierra de Manantlán, Mexico), and underline the complexities of the institutional practices of peasants creating unequal access and use of land—particularly grazing lands—due to power structures within the community. They argue that in the case of protected areas that have been established, "clearly defined 'rules of the game' and effective measures for sanctioning violators should be negotiated between local people and managers of protected areas."

The normative and regulative structure defining institutions make institutional economics a powerful tool for policy design.[17] As neo-classical economics and structural adjustment policies recommended getting "prices right," institutional economics recommends getting "institutions right."

For example, on property rights, if we look at the eight principles for constructing long-enduring, common-pool resource institutions as proposed by Ostrom (1998), there is a series of possibilities for policy interventions. By analyzing how people access resources through a bundle of rights (access, withdrawal, management, exclusion, and alienation), we may understand the institutional arrangements set by formal institutions at the macro and local levels, and the actions or practices that individuals undertake in order to observe those rights in the context of normative behavioral codes, determined by the cultural values which legitimize the institutional arrangements and their constraints from below.

In the case of the forest community of Oaxaca, these could be: promoting and recognizing the social rights and legitimacy of local institutions; providing information about resources; providing space and methods for conflict resolutions; provide mechanisms for monitoring and sanctioning; and providing information and capacity-building for designing the structures of community enterprises. The challenge of assigning attributes and designing interventions is indeed vast (Garcia *et al.*, 1999: 4).

Hence, there is an instrumental logic in the approach: institutions can be regulated but, as Engberg-Pedersen says, their legitimacy is more due to their status of rule-setting than to the agents' normative relationship to institutions (Engberg-Pedersen, 1997).

The economic paradigm's assumptions that people are always pursuing self-interest, that people are opportunistic agents, making cost-benefit judgements in relation to objective institutions, and that preferences are universal and not context-specific, is contested. It is unlikely that individuals are constantly evaluating institutions, that they are rational maximizers across all cultures and beliefs (Engberg-Pedersen, 1997).[18] People are not neutral agents: they act and make decisions according to a context, embedded in the norms, codes, and practices of the culture (traditions) and history of their community and society.

So, the challenge for policy designers and implementers goes beyond the normative, and should be more complex because the basic assumptions underpinning the property rights approach is not so evident when we move onto the findings of other research disciplines as the case studies mentioned show: land and resource management intertwines economic factors with social, cultural, ethnic, and gender dimensions which are not subject to, or escape, formal institutional frameworks. The real challenge if policy programs and projects are to be relevant, is to disentangle the dynamic relationships between the institutional setting at the community level and the web of normative behavioral codes embedded in economic, sociocultural practices at the local level, in order to understand how households access resources, how resources are managed at the household and community levels, how different actors are involved or excluded, and how class, ethnicity, and gender cuts across these practices. And finally, how policy can best support and strengthen the groups that are disadvantaged, excluded, or otherwise encounter barriers to productive resources, for example, by supporting or constructing appropriate institutional frameworks.

Conclusion

Research and many case studies—examples of which are included in this volume—point to the complexities of social and institutional processes in relation to the context in which they evolve embedded in the history and culture of the communities. Asking simple questions—such as is there space for the family farm or the peasant, and how can policies promote "winners" (efficiency) or assist "losers"?—is a false approach to complex processes that are the realities of rural livelihoods today. In recent years, we have learned much about these livelihoods and their specificities rooted in local contexts. We have also developed much more sophisticated tools for gathering data and analyzing it.

The theoretical debate on land reform, property rights, and other institutions has provided a paradigmatic framework for policy design. However, once we depart from the more formal (quantitative analysis) and normative approaches (institutional economics) and enter the socioeconomic and cultural context of specific local situations, we confront the challenging task of coming to grips with understanding the dynamic web of relationships and translating this into the design of policies, both from above, such as macro policies, and from below, i.e., policy interventions at the community level.

The livelihood approach discussed in the first section may be suggestive for policy makers and development agents in understanding the realities and needs of rural people at the community and household levels in a more flexible approach. This certainly applies to the discourse on whether "participation and empowerment" is more promising than "interventionist policies" at the community level. Yet, these approaches once in the field often face implementation and methodological problems that the development agents must be sensitive to and aware of. There are no ready-made, clear-cut solutions to the problems of rural development or poverty alleviation.[19]

Also, the livelihood approach implicitly works within the given macro framework, and does not question the macro policy environment under structural adjustment and economic reforms that have often negatively affected the agricultural activities of the peasantry and national labor markets. The link between micro/meso and macro policy is disarticulated and depoliticized, a discussion which goes beyond the scope of this chapter, but has to be kept in mind if the "sustainable livelihoods" approach is to be more than assistance programs and be oriented toward rural development.

What have we learned? By identifying the differential impacts and responses, we should be able to design "better" or more "appropriate" policies. The complexity and context specificity also underlines the need for policies to be participatory and community based. But participation must not stop at the community or meso level. Hence, the lessons from research are that we are confronting a question of not just what the appropriate policies are for different communities, social groups, and types of rural constituencies, but how we should go about doing the business of policy-making.

Notes

[1] This chapter has benefited considerably from discussions with Adriana Herrera (FAO/SDAR Land Tenure Service), who provided inputs for and critical comments about various versions of this paper, for which I am indebted. I am also grateful to Pieter de Vries for his valuable comments. Needless to say, the final result is my sole responsibility; the views presented in this paper are my own and do not necessarily reflect the position of FAO.

[2] Scott (1996) refers to the new economic model as that which is being implemented under neo-liberal policies. The main features are: a redefinition of the role of the state, giving priority to macroeconomic stability, trade and financial liberalization, and commitment to poverty reduction.

[3] For a recent discussion, see the results of the Sustainable Livelihoods Web and email conference "Operationalising participative ways of applying sustainable livelihoods" Coordinated by FAO and DFID, February-March, 2000.

[4] See e.g., Hoon, Singh and Wanmali, 1997, who refer to several models of livelihood evolution.

[5] See e.g., country case studies of South Africa and Kenya and policy issues in Zimbabwe and Burkina Faso.

[6] In the cases of Pakistan and Zambia for program design; the economic and livelihood impacts of wildlife enterprises in Kenya, community-based natural resource management in Namibia. (Farrington *et al.*, 1999: 3).

[7] UNDP has worked on "indicators for sustainable development," see Hoon *et al.*, 1997.

[8] See efforts in that direction as mentioned in footnote 2.

[9] There is no clear articulation in the livelihood approach or the economic approach. In a pragmatic way, income strategies are included in livelihood strategies and the methodology used may be quite eclectic. For example, a participatory rural appraisal may capture income data in a community diagnosis, or an income survey may be carried out (see Appendini and Nuijten, 1999). The methodological and conceptual issues concerning multidisciplinarity approaches is beyond the reach of this paper. See Garcia *et al.*, 1999.

[10] The term "reproduction" used in the literature was associated with the reproduction of the labor force and thus associated with the tasks of women (though the gender perspective was actually not present in the literature (de Janvry, 1981)). For a critique of the conceptual distinction of "production" and "reproduction," see the chapter by S. Paulson in this volume.

[11] This U-shaped association with level of income and income diversification is mostly observed in Latin America and Asia. According to Reardon, the presence of labor markets associated with dynamic agriculture and urbanization, as well as unequal access to land is associated with off-farm incomes. On the other hand, "households with high asset holdings are able to diversify into more capital intensive activities, self-financing this diversification or else using their assets as collateral to obtain credit." Data from various data sources gathered by Reardon *et al.* indicate that non-farm income sources for rural households account for 40% of total household incomes in Africa, 32% in Asia, and 40% in Latin America (Reardon, 1998: 10). See also the chapter by Davis, Carletto and Piccioni in this volume, which is a good example of this type of research.

[12] In an article by Melmed-Sanjak *et al.* (1998), the authors refer to several studies that focus on land, land security, and access to income. See also Carter, 1999; Carter *et al.*, 1993; Carter and Weibe, 1990; de Janvry *et al.*, 1997.

[13] For a review of issues related to land markets, property rights, economic performance, and examples of impact on peasants in Latin America, see Carter, 1999.

[14] See volume I of this publication series, also Carter, 1999.

[15] Also how this knowledge is constructed and the methodological issues of field research.

[16] The World Bank has also reviewed the issue: "...communal resource ownership provides a public good or allows to take advantage of synergies that would be difficult to provide under fully individualized cultivation: such as risk reduction, economies of scale to break seasonal labor shortage or investment in community infrastructure; in low density population areas when pay-offs from land related investment are limited, disincentives associated with communal tenure is low, or when the cost of delimiting and enforcing boundaries to individual plots are high" (Deininger *et al.*, 1998).

[17] See Gordillo, 1999.

[18] For a discussion from a sustentativist perspective on the limits of neo-institutionalist perspective and co-operative institutions for understanding livelihood strategies/income strategies and the institutional setting at the community level, see Garcia *et al.*, 1999.

[19] For a discussion on methodological perspectives in a flexible framework for analyzing community/households and the institutional setting, see Appendini *et al.*, 1999.

References

Appendini, K., "La modernización en el campo y el futuro del campesinado: iniciamos el debate de los 'noventa'". *Estudios Sociológicos,* Vol. X, no. 29 (1993). May-August, Mexico, El Colegio de México.

Appendini, K., M. Nuijten, "The institutional environment and household income strategies: a methodological framework". Draft for discussion. SDAR, Rome, FAO, 1999.

Baland, J.M. and J.P. Platteau, "Halting degradation of natural resources. Is there a role for rural communities?" Rome, FAO, 1996.

Carney, D., "Implementing the sustainable rural livelihoods approach". In: D. Carney (ed.), *Sustainable rural livelihoods. What contribution can we make?* Department of International Development, Nottingham, Russell Press Ltd, 1998.

Carter, M., "Old questions and new realities: land in post-liberal economies". In: A. Zoomers and G. van der Haar (eds.), *Current land policy in Latin America: regulating land tenure under neo-liberalism.* KIT/Vervuert, Amsterdam, 2000.

Carter, M. and D. Mesbah, "Can land market reform mitigate the exclusionary aspects of rapid agro-export growth?" *World Development,* Vol. 21, no. 7 (1993).

Carter, M. and K. Weibe, "Access to capital and its impact on agrarian structure and productivity in Kenya". *American Journal of Agricultural Economics,* December 1990.

Córdova, R., "Gender roles, inheritance patterns, and female acess to land in an *ejidal* community in Veracuz, Mexico". In: A. Zoomers and G. van der Haar (eds.), *Current land policy in Latin America: regulating land tenure under neo-liberalism.* KIT/Vervuert, Amsterdam, 2000.

De Janvry, A., *The agrarian question and reformism in Latin America.* Baltimore, John Hopkins University Press, 1981.

De Janvry, A., G. Gordillo and E. Sadoulet, "Mexico's second agrarian reform". Household and Community Responses, USCD, La Jolla, 1997.

De Janvry, A., and E. Sadoulet, "Access to land for the rural poor: how to keep it open and effective for poverty reduction". Paper presented at the Latin American and Carribean Economic Association, New York, 1999.

Deininger, K. and H. Binswanger, "The evolution of the bank's land policy". Document photocopy, April 17, 1998.

DyA, "Estudio de impacto de la regularización predial en Ecuador: el caso de la provincia de Cotopaxi". Informe Preliminar Roma, FAO, enero, 1999.

Ellis, F., "Household strategies and rural livelihood diversification". *Journal of Development Studies,* Vol. XXXV, no. 1 (1998). Frank Cass Publishers.

Engberg-Pedersen, E., "Institutionel teori I 1990erne" *Den Nye Verden,* Vol. XXX, no. 3 (1997). Copenhagen, Centre for Development Research.

Farrington, J. D. Carney, C. Asshley and C. Turton, "Sustainable livelihoods in practice: early applications of concepts in rural areas". *ODI, Natural resource perspectives,* Vol. 42, June (1999). UK, DFID.

FAO, "Rome declaration on world food security and world food summit plan of action". World Food Summit, Rome, November, 1996.

García Barrios, R, B. de la Tejera *et al.* "Estrategias de ingreso en los hogares rurales para alivio de la pobreza e interacciones con las instituciones locales". Caso México, Draft report. CRIM/UNAM/FAO, 1999.

Gordillo, G. "Dismantled states and fragmented societies: a plea for reconstructing institutions". Paper presented at the workshop Land in Latin America: new context, new claims, new concepts. CEDLA/CERES/WAU, Amsterdam, May 26-27, 1999.

Herrera, A., J. Riddell and P. Toseli, "Recent FAO experiences in land reform and land tenure". *FAO Land Reform.* Rome, FAO, 1997.

Hoon, P., N. Singh and S.S. Wanmali, "Sustainable livelihoods: concepts, principles and approaches to indicator development". A draft discussion paper, presented at the workshop Sustainable livelihoods indicators, social development and poverty eradication division, UNDP, New York, August 1997.

Kearney, M., *Reconceptualizing the peasantry. Anthropology in global perspective.* Oxford, Westview Press, 1996.

Long, N., "Agency and constraint, perceptions and practices. A theoretical position". In: H. de Haan, and N. Long (eds.), *Images and realities of rural life.* The Netherlands, van Gorkum, Assen, 1997.

Melmed-Sanjak, J. and S. Lastarria-Cornhiel, "Land access, off-farm income and capital access in relation to the reduction of rural poverty". *FAO Land Reform*, 1998/1, FAO, Rome, 1999.

Nuijten, M., "In the name of the land. Organization, transnationalism, and the culture of the state in a Mexican *ejido*". PhD thesis. University of Wageningen, 1998.

Ostrom, E., "Efficiency, sustainability and access under alternative property-rights regimes". Paper presented at the UNU/WIDER project on Land reform revisited: access to land, rural poverty and public action, Santiago, April, 1998.

Quan, J., "Land tenure and sustainable rural livelihoods". In: D. Carney (ed.), *Sustainable rural livelihoods. What contribution can we make?* Department of International Development, Nottingham, Russell Press Ltd, 1998.

Reardon, T., K. Stamoulis, M.E. Cruz, A. Balisacan and J. Berdegué, "Rural non-farm income in developing countries, importance and policy implications". Special chapter in State of Food and Agriculture, FAO, Rome, 1998.

Scott, Ch., "El nuevo modelo económico en América Latina y la pobreza rural". In: A.P. de Teresa and C. Cortés Ruiz, *La nueva relación campo-ciudad y la pobreza rural.* Serie on La sociedad rural mexicana frente al nuevo milenio, INAH/UAM/UNAM/PyV, Mexico, 1996.

Singh, N. and P. Kalala (eds.), "Adaptive strategies and sustainable livelihoods: community studies". Kenya; Adaptive strategies and sustainable livelihoods: community studies. South Africa; Adaptive strategies and sustainable livelihoods: policy studies. Burkina Faso; Adaptive strategies and sustainable livelihoods: policy studies. Zimbabwe. International Institute for Sustainable Development Canada, IISD.

Stamoulis, K., "Perspectives on off-farm income, access to assets and rural development". Rome, FAO, 1996 (manuscript).

Wallman, S., *Eight London households.* London, Routledge, 1984.

Zoomers, A. and G. van der Haar (eds.), *Current land policy in Latin America: regulating land tenure under neo-liberalism.* KIT/Vervuert, Amsterdam, 2000.

Part 1

**Livelihood and multifunctional land-use
in a transnational space: international migration**

3 No land stands alone: social and environmental interdependency in a Bolivian watershed

Susan Paulson

Introduction

The Andean region is characterized by extraordinary geographic and ecological diversity, and by a great complexity of cultural practices and patterns. During millennia, symbolically marked social groups have controlled different spaces, resources, and activities; developed different botanical, zoological, and technical knowledge; and maintained different rights and responsibilities over land and other resources. We have long understood that the organization of these social differences is, in itself, a sophisticated technology for environmental management (Balan and Dandler, 1986; Harris, 1985; Lehmann, 1982; Mayer, 1974 and 1985; Murra, 1956 and 1985), but little attention has been paid to the gender dimensions of this organization.

This chapter contributes to a better understanding of the dynamics of mixed farm management in a changing historical context. The study discussed here is part of an effort to better understand relationships between two disturbing phenomena manifest in many parts of Latin America: environmental degradation and social inequity (Paulson, 1998). Both phenomena have been consistently linked to loss of soil fertility, impoverishment, deforestation, erosion, migration, poor health and nutrition, breakdown of families and communities, and other symptomatic problems, but we know little about the causal relations *between* environmental degradation and social inequity.

One barrier to this understanding is that in Latin America, environmental issues have been studied and responded to largely within the natural and applied sciences (agronomy, biology, and forestry), while issues of social inequity have been addressed by social scientists and social movements, such as those embracing Marxism, feminism, and indiginism.[1] In our universities, natural and social sciences have separate buildings, budgets, administrators, curricula, epistemological bases, and methods. In our governments, ministries of natural resources, forestry and agriculture have little to do with ministries of health, welfare, education and human development. This polarization of knowledge and action limits our capacity to develop a more comprehensive vision of tenure rights, rules, and responsibilities, which are always and inseparably social and environmental. This chapter, based on studies carried out during the past decade on changing land management practices in several watersheds in central Bolivia, aims to contribute to a more integral approach.

The social and geographic context

(Re)productive strategies[2] predominant in central Bolivia encompass multiple types of diversity including dissimilar geographic and ecological spaces; numerous species and varieties of plants and animals; multiple economic systems; and a wide gamut of knowledge, techniques, and organizational strategies. Multiple types of tenure, together with the rights, rules, and practices associated with them, are overlapped and interrelated in essential ways.

If we start with the classic liberal assumption that each actor manages his resources based on rational, self-interested equations of cost-benefit, it is difficult to imagine how one farmer might handle so many components, let alone allocate *his* resources "economically" between them. Perhaps we need to look beyond that one man.

In different historical periods and different parts of the Andes, ayllus, ethnic groups, larger polities that we call empires or kingdoms, and myriad local cultural forms have variously orchestrated these diverse elements. In *all* these cases, social differentiation and interdependence—expressed in terms of ethnic, gender, generational, and spatial terms—seem to have been key factors.

Today in the Departments of Mizque and Campero, we observe that communities in the upper watershed differ markedly from those in the central valleys in terms of spatial organization, ethnic identity, and resource management practices. Upper watershed communities like Raqaypampa and Mizquepampa are largely monolingual and dress in striking ethnic costumes; they manage important areas of land and other resources through peasant syndicates, which, since the agrarian reform, have controlled communal grazing lands and allocated lands to newly formed families. In contrast, the bilingual people in Mizque and Aiquile valleys are more assimilated into national culture, use more modern clothing, household supplies, farming inputs and technologies, and have divided their entire valleys into private property, with the exception of roads, irrigation canals, schools, and syndicate headquarters. These explicitly differentiated groups maintain multiple interdependencies played out in ritual and symbolic expressions, as well as in the exchange of seed, labor, products, medical and ritual knowledge, and other elements (CIDRE, 1987; Mercado, de la Fuente and Rojas, 1990; Paulson, 1992).

These and other communities are crosscut by *socioeconomic differentiation*, which in many areas is increasing as certain families consolidate land and/or key resources such as trucks, stores, and tractors, while others suffer diminished and degraded resources (Blanes, 1984; Dandler, 1987; Lagos, 1988 and 1994; see also Morris, this volume).[3] Amongst other impacts, this differentiation interferes with the capacity for concerted decision and action by community organizations, specifically in reference to communal tenure arrangements and rules for grazing, fallowing, water, and fuelwood usage. Ostrom's (1990) scheme for identifying nested levels of governance institutions can be useful here. We observe that under a constitutional-choice regime where private tenure is foregrounded, some community groups are failing to maintain consensus on traditional collective-choice rules for managing resources and resolving conflict, in some cases leading to situations where more powerful families and individuals began to stretch or circumvent the operational rules for daily practice. Another crosscutting dimension of resource management is that of gender, which we will explore in the following sections.

Gender organization of land, labor and knowledge

In the past decade, methodologies for the study of gender and resource management have been widely disseminated, inspiring much new research, as well as ongoing revisions and approaches. These proposals include research tools such as daily hour sheets and annual calendars to catalogue men's and women's work, matrices charting access, control and use of resources by sex, and maps locating men's and women's spaces and resources (Balarezu, 1994; Care, 1994; Rao *et al.*, 1991).[4]

In 1993-94 I worked with an interdisciplinary team to apply these tools in research carried out in the higher region of the Department of Carrasco, a steep mountainous area with an average altitude of 2,800 meters and an annual rainfall of 60 cm that has suffered increasingly severe erosion over the past two decades. Our efforts to implement this approach with local communities led to numerous confusions and disagreements, which are well worth considering.

To begin with, virtually all of the published methods assume that gender identities are construed as two discrete and polarized categories: men vs. women. Yet when Carrasco residents were asked to describe women's resources and responsibilities, they asked "What woman? A young woman *(sipas)*? Or a mature woman with family *(warmi, madre)*?" suggesting that the essentially *biological* category "women" does not coincide with the multiple gender identities and resource management roles within the community.[5]

We also applied research tools designed to characterize relationships between individuals and their resources. In this case, we found that given tenure categories did not necessarily resonate with the locals, who asked "What do you mean, do I *own* or *use* these sheep? My duty is to make sure that the herd is healthy and reproduces." Finally, when we asked whether certain tasks were carried out by men or by women, many community members balked, insisting that "everyone is involved with everything."

We will focus here on the last issue: the division of labor. It is likely true that "everyone is involved with everything" in this region, but *not in an undifferentiated way*. Further research contributed to a more subtle understanding of the gender organization of labor as a series of nested complementarities: each task or responsibility is considered feminine or masculine on one level, but also encompasses differentiation and collaboration. Moreover, we found that variables of age, socioeconomic status, and others intersect with gender in labor arrangements, and that historical changes give rise to contradictions between the symbolic or prescriptive organization of labor and its practical implementation. For the purposes of this example, we will focus mainly on two basic categories of this complex social system: adult women and men who are joint heads of household.

Figure 1 helps us visualize gender organization in Carrasco valleys. In the communities studied, agriculture is considered a male domain, and is in practice the most important focus of most men's labor, while women are more closely associated (both practically and symbolically) with silviculture (management of fuelwood, forage, fruits) and with the care of livestock (medium sized herds of sheep and goats, a few cows). At the same time, each of these sectors encompasses multiple levels of participation and differentiation: "Everyone is involved in everything."

Taking as an example the agricultural sector, we see that men take greater responsibility for principal crops (mainly potatoes and wheat), which are cultivated in the larger, flatter fields, whereas women have greater responsibility for and participation in secondary crops (broad beans, peas, *quinua, millmi, poroto, tarhui, squash*, and others,) which are planted in scattered patches of land, on hillsides, garden plots, and intercropped with wheat or corn. A larger portion of the principal crops are destined for sale, whereas secondary crops go mostly toward exchange and family consumption, which women administer according to social and culinary customs.

Within principal crops, there is also differentiation between men, who focus more on commercial production with improved seeds, and women, who focus more on

Figure 1   Gender organization of labor and resources surrounding wheat production

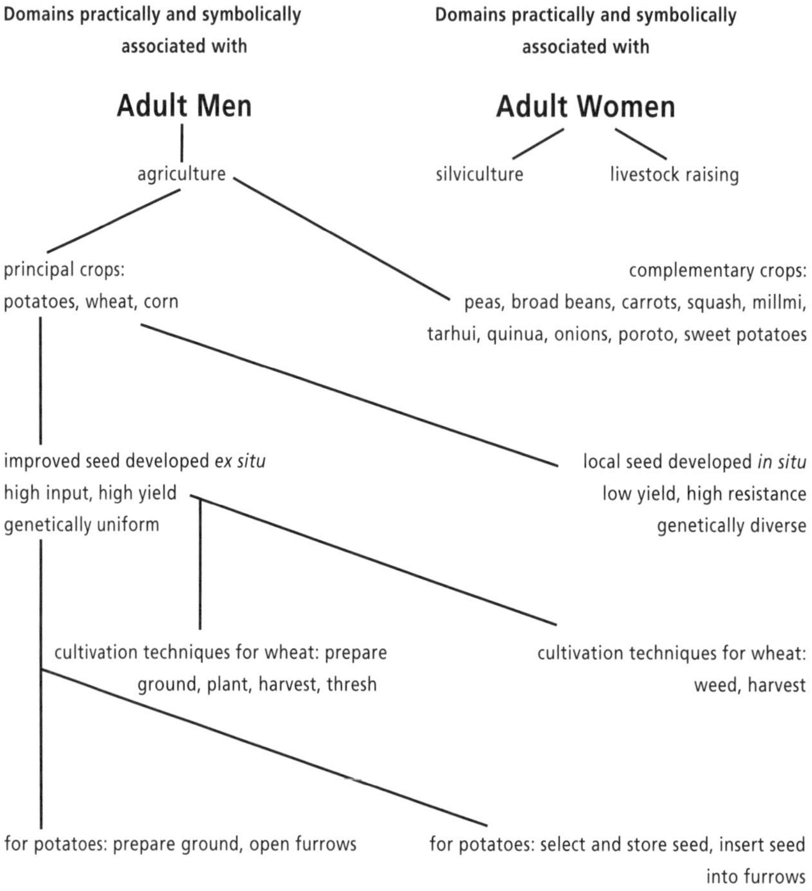

Domains practically and symbolically
associated with

Domains practically and symbolically
associated with

Adult Men

Adult Women

agriculture

silviculture   livestock raising

principal crops:
potatoes, wheat, corn

complementary crops:
peas, broad beans, carrots, squash, millmi,
tarhui, quinua, onions, poroto, sweet potatoes

improved seed developed *ex situ*
high input, high yield
genetically uniform

local seed developed *in situ*
low yield, high resistance
genetically diverse

cultivation techniques for wheat: prepare
ground, plant, harvest, thresh

cultivation techniques for wheat:
weed, harvest

for potatoes: prepare ground, open furrows

for potatoes: select and store seed, insert seed
into furrows

diverse local varieties for family consumption and exchange. Improved seeds give higher yields, but depend heavily on modern training, technology, and inputs, often obtained by men from agricultural extension institutions. Most families also cultivate as many as a dozen local varieties of potatoes and wheat, which are variously resistant to droughts, floods, frost, and plagues. Seed for these varieties is obtained through exchange, or is selected and stored at home, usually by women, in practices of *in situ* germplasm management oriented toward assuring family nutrition within changing ecological and socioeconomic contexts.

   Even within each crop and each field, gendered actors apply different knowledge, skills, and strategies. Family members work together in the field, but there is also specialization. In wheat, for example, men tend to prepare the earth and sow the seed, while women and children do much of the weeding. In potatoes, men plow with oxen, while women sow the seed and manage the seed selection and storage. In sum, different activities, spaces, and spheres of knowledge are nominally feminine or masculine, while at the same time there is differentiated collaboration at every level. This social organization is not only practical, but also always meaningful. Women's selection, storage, and planting of potato seed, for example, is symbolically charged through identification with *Pachamama*, the female force behind soil fertility, who is said to "nourish the potatoes at her breast."

Multiple interdependence

We could go on for pages enumerating each task within each sector, but that would provide us with a mere catalogue of men's and women's activities. To develop a *gender analysis* we need to explore the multiple relations *between* the different activities, relations that are practical, economic, psychological, symbolic, ritual, cosmological, erotic, as well as ecological, which is our focus here.

To start with, the interdependence between agriculture and livestock is widely recognized as a basic land management strategy, in which one of the many important interdependencies is the use of manure from livestock to regenerate the fertility of agricultural soils. Indeed, farm research and extension in Bolivia is explicitly based in the integral concept of *ciencias agropecuarias* (agrohusbandry sciences), and local symbols and discourse emphasize men's ability to cultivate food, and women's contribution to regenerating the conditions for food production through manure.

In contrast to the agrohusbandry binomial, pitifully little attention has been given to the role of silviculture in integrated land management. Yet local men and women show us that the landscape is not constituted exclusively of agricultural parcels and pasturelands, but also of networks of paths and canals lined with grasses, shrubs, and trees, corridors of trees and bushes, fallow fields and irregular, rocky or inclined slopes covered with greenery, and forested ravines in distant, steeper parts of the watershed.

They explain that these areas serve as physical barriers to wind and water erosion; biological barriers to crop-specific pests and diseases; nesting places for birds and animals; shade for humans, animals, and crops; and that they produce forage, fuelwood, green fertilizer, fruits, roots, medicinal and culinary herbs, and other products. Why then, has the role of silviculture been so neglected in land management research and extension projects? One reason is that these uses do not provide immediate market value, and thus are not considered "productive" or "economical." Another reason is that in many regions, like this one, it is women and children (and not men) who invest large amounts of time and energy in silviculture, especially in relation to pasturing and fuelwood collection.

Gender organization shapes the social and physical topography in countless other ways. In many families, when a man plants a parcel of wheat (whose slender stalks and thin roots make it vulnerable to erosion) his wife and/or daughters plant around it a living fence of *tarhui*, *millmi*, or other robust native plants that protect against erosion and repel pests.

Men and women also affect the landscape through their different practices of germplasm management. Men often obtain improved seed, generated *ex situ*, through agricultural extension institutions, while *in situ* selection and inter-community exchange are carried out by men and women who manage different species and varieties of seed, and who also select for different characteristics within varieties (Watson and Almanza, 1994). It is also crucial to consider women's and men's impacts on semi-domesticated and wild grasses, shrubs and, trees whose growth they encourage, discourage, or otherwise affect through collection and pasturing practices.

If we look at the landscape in nutritional terms, we see large fields of principal crops (primarily men's responsibility) which provide carbohydrates, calories, and energy, and many smaller swatches of diverse crops (largely women's responsibility) which provide proteins, vitamins, and minerals. Culinary practices and preferences reflect and influence the spatial organization of the landscape and the annual climatic cycle: bread from a certain wheat baked for *Todos Santos*, fresh corn soup at Christmas time, and *T'impu* at carnival, have powerful symbolic value. At the same time, gender-specific knowledge and techniques in relation to seed selection, food production, menu planning, and meal preparation play a significant role in environmental change and sustainability (see Weismantel, 1988). If these communities organized their production so as to enjoy beef barbecues every day, the watershed would quickly turn into desert. On the other hand, if they ate nothing but barley broth, the people would become weak and children's development would be retarded.

In sum, gender is a basic principle in the organization of diverse sectors, spaces, species, knowledge, and responsibilities; it saturates the landscape. Now, in addition to exploring the multiple relations between gendered elements of a system, we also need to explore the dynamic evolution of these through time and space, and their role within larger contexts.[6] With Zoomers, I agree that we must move beyond explaining static situations, and focus on *lack of equilibrium, dynamic change*, as a point of departure for rural studies (Zoomers, 1998: 14). In the next section we will explore ways in which certain changes in gendered resource management are interrelated with social and environmental changes in the region.

Agricultural modernization

In the introduction to her study of Tiraque, which is not far from the Carrasco valleys discussed here, María Lagos describes the historical processes that set the scene for agricultural modernization in the region:

> "When vallunos *seized* hacienda *lands after the revolution of 1952, claiming that they had rights over these lands because they worked them and because the lands had belonged to their ancestors 'since time immemorial,' they were at the vanguard of rural mobilization in Bolivia and were one of the major forces pressuring the revolutionary government to pass, in 1953, one of the most radical agrarian reforms in Latin America... It did not take long, however, for them to rediscover that direct access to land made them vulnerable to new forms of exploitation and domination (1994: 2)."*

The decisions and actions of the farmers and institutions studied here are situated within a national and international push toward modernizing land tenure and rural production that has indeed contributed to both more rights and new kinds of oppression.[7] Starting with the 1953 Agrarian Reform, the Bolivian government promoted a series of programs (SNRA, *Desarrollo de Comunidades*, IBTA, CIAT, PDAR, PDAC, etc.) directed toward intensifying small farm production, increasing offer to national markets, and substituting food imports. These programs have been largely based on the triumvirate of land privatization, expansion of area cultivated, and increased yields per unit of land (Urioste, 1987: 11).

Farmers' participation in these processes has contributed to what Morris (this volume) describes as a widespread "modernization of thought" amongst the farming peoples of the *Sierra*. One outcome of that process, observed by Morris in Peruvian highlands, is the fact that the latest government measures to privatize farmland are actively supported by the majority of farmers.

During the past four decades, Bolivian state and non-governmental institutions, as well as research scientists, have identified (and indeed created) individual farmers as the basic actors, decision makers and units of analysis in the process of agricultural modernization. Given the well-documented complex social geography and organizational systems described above for Carrasco, and described by Morris for Peru,[8] how can we explain policies based on units of one man and one plot of land?

According to critic Naila Kabeer, "Liberal neo-classical economics has always played a central role in the evolution of development studies and in the formulation of development policy" (1994: 13). And the basic atom of liberal theory is, of course, the self-serving individual, a type of universal economic man whose essentially human ability for rational economic decision-making underlies all cultural forms. In cases like the Andes, where rational man was deeply buried beneath other lifeways, modernization theorists argued that the establishment of socioeconomic institutions that value and reward rational individualism would allow him to flourish and break through even the darkest superstition. And what institution is better at promoting competitive economic behavior than *private property?*

If we want to motivate individuals to maximize their own production, so the argument goes (and thereby contribute to expanding production on larger political economic levels), we must guarantee them rights to the results of their individual efforts. So Bolivian agencies set up programs to implement the "one man, one private land" policy through agricultural reform (SNRA) and extension (IBTA) as well as through colonization (DIRECO). At the same time, little or no effort was invested in studying, supporting, or improving communal systems for managing grazing lands, wooded ravines, fallow cycles, and other practices that interact and overlap with individual management of agricultural plots.

Agents of rural development encouraged and facilitated individual titling, partly so that each farmer might use his title as collateral on loans for improvements and equipment that would increase production on his plot of land. International agencies and NGOs collaborated by transferring to individual farmers a series of modern techniques and inputs designed to increase productivity and net production of commercial crops, in a widespread process that has been criticized for its environmental as well as social impacts in different parts of Latin America.

Timothy Finan summarizes numerous anthropological assessments of agricultural modernization processes that focus on, amongst others, the appropriateness of high-yielding grain varieties that might subperform traditional varieties in poor climatic years; the reduction in crop diversity on subsistence farms; negative and lasting environmental impacts; and the disregard of local indigenous knowledge in the development of technological options (Finan, 1997: 82). And in the preface of his 1994 book, Douglas Murray writes:

"Since World War II, the Green Revolution has boosted agricultural production in Latin America and other parts of the Third World, with money, technical assistance and other forms of aid from US development agencies. But the Green Revolution came at a high price—massive pesticide

dependence that has caused serious socioeconomic and public health problems and widespread environmental damage."

Studies of numerous Latin American contexts show that privatization, modernization, and capitalization of agriculture has coincided with exacerbated social inequalities (see León de Leal and Deere, 1980). Warren and Bourque sum up notable gender dimensions of this impact, as identified by Boserup (1970), Etienne and Leacock (1980), Rogers (1980) and others studying agricultural modernization in the Third World. "As a result of the differential access of each gender to novel technologies—to plows, high-yield seed varieties, fertilizers, training to grow commercial crops, mechanized equipment, or motor-driven transportation—women's powers in community affairs were eroded" (Warren and Bourque, 1991: 281).

Despite these criticisms, national agencies and international development interventions in Bolivia continue to promote classic agricultural modernization for the land-holding man, giving us an opportunity to ask a different kind of research question: what, if anything, do the oft-noted social impacts have to do with the widely observed environmental impacts of this process?

A classic example

Since this historical process is much too broad and complex to analyze here, we will start by looking at a relatively typical agricultural modernization project in the Department of Carrasco. Throughout the 1980s, and until its program was changed significantly in the mid-1990s, an internationally funded NGO implemented a relatively typical agricultural improvement project whose purported principal objective was "to improve the quality of life of local families."

The project's major activities included: technical training and institutional support to farmer syndicates and wheat producer associations (whose members were virtually all male), provision of certified wheat seed and chemical inputs (to those men who had sufficient land and were willing and able to take the risk), and sale of tractors and threshing machines on credit (to a few men who could obtain land titles to use for collateral).

Technically, the project was a tremendous success, and squarely fulfilled its operational goals of increasing the area of land cultivated, increasing yield per hectare, increasing net tons of produce, and increasing money income of participants. But how is any of this related to quality of life of local families? If we believe that quality of life has anything to do with family health and well-being, food and energy security, beauty of the landscape, sustainability of resource base, social relationships or community solidarity, we must look well beyond the project indicators to consider the people, spaces, and resources that were excluded from the project framework.

If we return to our earlier characterization of labor organization, it is clear that this project, like many others carried out in the region, was directed exclusively at selected productive sectors, spaces, and social groups. Agricultural production was strengthened, but not silviculture or livestock management; commercial production was improved, but not production for family consumption or exchange; monoculture of improved varieties was expanded, but not the cultivation of diverse local species and varieties. Individual production on private plots was supported, while cooperative management of other watershed resources was ignored. Men's activities and efforts were strengthened, and not women's.[9] Production was expanded at the cost of reproduction, posing significant threats to sustainability.

In terms of the spatial organization of the watershed, this project (and, more importantly, the regional historical process of which it is but a minor part) motivated and facilitated expansion of the agricultural frontier, impelling farmers to open larger fields on increasingly steep slopes, which displaced and degraded the communal spaces that women and poorer families had been using in their silvicultural and livestock management. Consequent overgrazing and intensified fuelwood collection in reduced green areas contributed to deforestation and erosion, leading numerous observers to conclude that women and land-poor peasants are the main perpetrators of ecological destruction in the region, and that their "irrational" management of silviculture and pasturage slopes is the primary cause of the severe erosion and flooding that is destroying agriculture plots. The following excerpt from an Environment Profile of Bolivia demonstrates the point:

> "The land users have not developed any awareness about the problems of soil erosion. Overgrazing and trampling by livestock, together with the removal of shrub cover for fuel in the Altiplano and the Mesothermic Valleys, are the most important causes of soil erosion" (International Institute for Development and Environment and United States Agency for International Development, 1986, cited in Zimmerer, 1993b).

As green areas are degraded and eroded, women are forced to take their herds longer distances to find forage, which takes a toll on the health and vitality of both women and livestock. Increasingly, families are forced to sell livestock or arrange for it to be pastured in other communities. Reduced access to manure, milk, and meat limits women's capacity to reproduce the fertility of the soil through organic fertilizer and to reproduce family labor through nourishing food. At the same time, reallocation of land, labor, and water to commercial fields reduces the quantity and variety of complementary crops, contributing to increasing dependence on purchased foodstuffs.

Even within principal crops, diversity is reduced. Since wheat that suffers wind-induced cross-pollination cannot be certified, farmers must curtail their traditional cultivation of up to a dozen varieties of wheat that are resistant to different climatic risks, display different nutritional, cooking, and storage characteristics, and have cultural significance as key ingredients in traditional meals prepared throughout the annual cycle.

Finally, while the tractors and threshing machines provided by the program easily reduce men's labor, especially in preparing the soil for planting, women's and children's tasks—notably weeding—are increased by the greater area and density of wheat and by stringent certification standards.

As women lose access to key resources, and as the resources they do control become degraded, they are less able to provide balanced food to family and livestock, and fail to assure the health and fertility of soils, animals, and people. Both men and women suffer the consequences. One man complained, "The cost of buying fertilizers and food for the family is constantly increasing, and we men have to earn more and more money to buy these things that everyone used to make at home." Local women testify: "My husband hits me because I don't cook well, like they're used to." "My mother-in-law criticizes me because I don't make my herd multiply like she did." "My child got sick because I was off herding on a distant mountainside."

Production vs. reproduction

These practical changes in environmental management are accompanied by new ideas and values; one of the most important of which is the conceptual distinction between "production" and "reproduction" in which the first is construed as a highly valued technical and economic system, and the second as a social issue of peripheral importance.

Since 1953 the UN National Accounting System has globalized formulas to measure "economic production" in GNP (later GDP) figures, and Bolivia's political economic apparatus is explicitly geared to maximize economic production, thus defined. In much of rural Bolivia, however, production and reproduction remain spatially and temporally inseparable. Women produce livestock by fostering the reproduction of the herds, which produce manure to reproduce the fertility of fields in which men produce food to reproduce the strength of their families, and, of course, to produce children, who reproduce the community. All of these activities are carried out in ways that pass on social customs and organization, together with productive knowledge, technology, and tradition, thus reproducing culture, society, and landscapes across generations.

Because development programs, together with the liberal economic theory that propels them, rest on the separation of economic production from the rest of life, they indeed must create this distinction in the process. In the region studied, men "producers" have for decades received public esteem and technical and financial support in "production training" and "producers' associations," while women have been associated with "reproduction," a category conspicuously absent from agricultural improvement and environmental management efforts, and egregiously confused with the western urban concept of housewife.

It is surprising to see how many researchers and practitioners accept the historically and culturally specific distinction of production vs. reproduction as a universally valid analytic framework. Thus what is a specifically industrial capitalist division of life into spatially and institutionally segregated spheres is applied in attempts to understand non-industrial societies and production systems. Even leading authors who critique development from a gender perspective acritically reproduce these categories in their zeal to characterize the lives of women all over the world in terms of the "triple role" of production, reproduction, and community organization (Moffat *et al.*, 1991; Moser, 1989 and 1993; Overholt *et al.*, 1984).[10]

Rural development programs, explicitly grounded in the production vs. reproduction framework, have prioritized agricultural production and allocated little technical, financial or symbolic support to assure the health, nourishment, and regeneration of family forces, nor to regenerate the fertility of the soils, slopes, and livestock.

Responses from the "Women and Development" camp have largely ignored the importance of these "reproductive" activities for environmental and social sustainability, and focused on the diminishing social power of women who are associated with the marginalized domain of reproduction. The way to remedy this inferior position, according to USAID WID policy, was through projects to support women's participation and opportunity in *productive*, income-earning capacities.[11]

Indeed, programs throughout Latin America have reacted to perceived asymmetrical development by trying to "empower" women through productive projects and technical training. While these projects may move some women out of low-status "reproduction," they appear to do little to arrest the accelerating *crisis of reproduction*, and may indeed further erode relations between production and reproduction, the most basic crux of social and environmental sustainability.

A gender effort?

Back to our case study: the institutional trajectory sketched above took an interesting turn in the early 1990s when the principal financing agency evaluated the project using indicators disaggregated by sex to discover that virtually all participants and direct beneficiaries were men, and that men accrued disproportionate social value as the only "producers" recognized and supported by the project.

Consequent demand for gender focus evoked a sadly typical response: "Incorporate women into productive activities." The program began to distribute improved seed and chemical input packets to women, formed an association of women wheat producers, and provided technical and productive training to female members. Warren and Bourque describe the theory behind this kind of effort.

> To the extent that feminists and development critics defined access as the crucial issue, the logical solution was to equalize it. Poor women needed the ability to use tools and machines, as well as literacy and education. The message was explicitly protechnology: women had lost ground because of restricted access. The solution to inequities was to open the restricted channels of education and training (1991: 28).

This resolutely liberal response exemplifies a widespread reformist approach aimed at ensuring, in the words of the UN Decade of the Woman, "the integration of women into development." In our Carrasco case, women in wealthier families in which both husband and wife were able to obtain and implement improved seed packages, did enjoy some benefits. These women valued the opportunity to participate in a formal organization and converse with extension workers. The sale of certified seed provided income that allowed them to buy more foodstuffs and farm inputs, and to hire women from outside the family to carry out traditional female labor. Thus these better-off women were liberated from increasingly burdensome "female" chores, and could dedicate themselves to other activities through which they obtained greater status and income.

It should not come as a surprise, however, to find that these changes exacerbated the ruinous environmental impacts discussed above, in addition to exaggerating socioeconomic inequalities between families, and more specifically, between women. The adjustments reveal little concern for environmental sustainability, nor do they make any kind of structural challenge to the social inequities intrinsic to the modes of development into which women were to be "incorporated."

In contrast to the narrow response exemplified here with its focus on private production, Gerritsen and Forster (this volume) suggest that to begin resolving the entangled social and environmental problems in a Mexican region they studied, it is absolutely necessary to better understand the existing tenure systems, in particular how the competing regimes interface, and how rules and regulations are applied and bent in practice. It is most likely that a very complex and messy picture will emerge. Actor-oriented empirical analysis could help untangle this and shed light on the human dynamics of tenure in Cuzalapa.

Gender, space, and socioeconomic differentiation

A more comprehensive reading of tenure and management in the Carrasco case reveals that the improved conditions enjoyed by the new "women producers" are intrinsically tied to increasingly inequitable distribution of land and related natural, financial, and technical resources on the community level. The access of certain families to a double quota of seed, credit, and technical support allows those families to exploit a greater share of community resources reaching far beyond their private plots. Many poorer families had earned a livelihood by gathering and selling fuelwood, pasturing other people's livestock, and other activities that depend on watershed resources *beyond and outside of* private agricultural plots. Thus, the expansion and intensification of the latter, at severe costs to the former, affects land-poor families in a disproportionate way, often pushing them to further degrade the surrounding resources. Members of these families are forced to sell their labor; many men migrate elsewhere, and women become servants to their "producer" neighbors.

Spatial and socioeconomic differences shape key dynamics within all watersheds, where diverse inhabitants are dependent on the hydrological system that they share and influence in different ways. A heated controversy arose in another part of this region when a development agency helped more wealthy and assimilated commercial farmers to expand an irrigation system and line the canals with cement. In this case, the long-established right of valley farmers to capture water from far beyond their private property was not disputed, but the poorer middle watershed communities argued that the generations-old irrigation system had allowed for abundant seepage, promoting lush greenery along canals and around storage areas, which was necessary to their livelihood. They argued that the cement-lined system would cause their own wells and springs to dry up and the ground cover to die, accelerating erosion on their already degraded land.

In Bolivia, recent innovative approaches to rural planning and development ostensibly address the conflict of interests between spatially and culturally differentiated groups. During its 1993-97 administration, the MNR/MRTKL coalition government passed an unprecedented number of legal reforms, including the *Ley de Participación Popular*, which sought to redistribute a certain degree of political power and decision-making to local communities. The law provides for the transfer of 20% of state revenues directly to municipalities and *Organizaciones Territoriales de Base* (OTBs), each of which chooses its own leaders, according to "*usos y costumbres*" and elects representatives for the Vigilance Committee, whose function is to supervise the use of municipal funds by elected officials.

Participatory planning procedures establish mechanisms for differentiated groups to be represented in local decision-making processes, and attempt to transform the long-standing situation in which centralized national elites planned the development of a vast and varied populace, while elites in provincial towns controlled and exploited the rural hinterlands. According to official documents, "The meeting of the institutional and social actors in the municipality is causing a new relational dynamic. Contradiction is being substituted by consensus between these actors in which objectives for development are determined jointly" (Mercado,1995: 46, cited in Lagos, forthcoming).[12]

Theoretically, the new organizational units integrate the idea of geographical and ecological territory with the idea of sociopolitical territory, and incorporate a temporal dimension through multi-year management plans. Is it possible that these units promote the kind of concerted supra-farm management strategies, rules, and tenure systems that appear to have been atrophying under recent models of rural development? Morris (this volume) expresses confidence that interfamily and community collaboration, interdependence, and flexibility can be retained, even as land units are broken up and privatized in highland Peru.

In order for the Carrasco families studied to manage their communities/territories in ways that allow sustained access to different resources, and to promote equilibrium and collaboration in the multiple enterprises needed to reproduce their territories, they will need a very different kind of support than they have been receiving from conventional agricultural modernization projects and state agencies. Gerritsen and Forster (this volume) argue that managers of protected areas should incorporate conflict management and negotiation of tenure understandings into the overall conservation strategy to help address the political aspects of conflicts over land access and natural resource use. And I argue that this strategy is useful well beyond protected areas in all kinds of land management context.

The advances and shortcomings of Bolivia's *Participación Popular* experiment in terms of balancing the different spatial, socioeconomic, and gender interests within each territory will make important future studies. And, significantly, we have yet to see if and how local participation can liberate rural people from extra-local forces of domination and exploitation.

Ultimately, all of the relations of difference and interaction that we glimpse within the rural watershed are intrinsically connected to and influenced by relations that extend far beyond it. Rural agricultural products are transferred to urban centers in exchange for sums of money grossly insufficient to regenerate the natural and social resources that enable such production. In similar relations, farmers migrate to sell their labor at wages barely sufficient to reproduce a worker's daily strength, let alone fuel the reproduction and socialization of new working classes. In a study of Cochabamba, Bolivia, Cortes (this volume: 66-67) observed three types of impacts of farmers' temporal migrations to sell labor off their farms. The first one, "a regressive recoiling toward self-sufficient agriculture," seems to be a last-dash effort to withdraw from exploitative extra-community relations which have contributed to situations in which these families find themselves in extreme poverty and economic vulnerability, to such an extent that some are forced to sell their land. In Bolivia, this continuous drain of human and ecological energy has contributed to degradation of the hinterlands and a rural exodus manifest in the rampant growth of cities like Montero, Quillacollo, and El Alto (now over a half million people), many of whose inhabitants are refugees from failed farms.

The degradation, erosion, and deforestation observed here are widely recognized in Andean valleys, and many authors have suggested some kind of connection between these "environmental problems" and separate "social problems" of inequality and disintegration of rural families and communities. With this study I hope to contribute to a better understanding of the internal dynamics that link these processes together.

Webs of interdependency and inequity

Liberal policies and programs that reduce land tenure and productive improvement to the individual unit of "one man, one private plot of land," facilitate asymmetrical historical processes that contribute to a continuous bleeding of energy that has both social and spatial-geographic dimensions.

In rural watersheds, the forage, wildlife, moisture, and soil on slopes and pasturelands, together with women's silviculture and herding management efforts, assure the fertility of agricultural plots. With the expansion of commercial agriculture and with increasing male migration, however, these silvicultural areas are shortchanged: more energy is extracted from them than is invested in them, and they began to degrade (Collins, 1998; Zimmerer, 1993a).[13] In regional and urban markets, commercial agricultural products, together with migrant labor of rural men, are sold at prices too low to maintain and regenerate the social and environmental resources necessary to continue producing them. On the national level, outrageously cheap food supplies and labor allow for production and export of manufactured products as well as natural resources at prices too low to maintain the system.

On each of these levels, the net energy flow is away from women, sheep, and mountainsides, toward urban centers, and ultimately, to international poles of wealth. Numerous analysts have brought attention to the fact those rural hinterlands and indigenous women suffer the most immediate symptoms of degradation in this process. But, unfortunately, many of these criticisms tend to reduce the complexity of the situation and polarize the problem. In the introduction to the book called *Ecofeminism*, for example, Maria Mies and Vandana Shiva argue that both nature and women have been colonized and exploited for the short-term profit motives of affluent societies and classes.[14] They write:

"Capitalist patriarchy or 'modern' civilization is based on a cosmology and anthropology that structurally dichotomizes reality, and hierarchically opposes the two parts to each other: the one always considered superior, always thriving, and progressing at the expense of the other. Thus, nature is subordinated to man; woman to man..." (Mies and Shiva, 1993: 5).

If, in this dualistic analysis, women and nature are the "losers" of lopsided development, is it fair to say that men in rural Bolivia are "winners?" That they are thriving and progressing at the cost of their wives, daughters and natural resources? A Carrasco farmer could receive training, credit, inputs, technical support, and more; he could redirect family and community resources to his own project and profit; he could sell more produce for more money. But he himself is exploited by the egregiously low market value of his produce and labor within a system of multiple inequalities. Moreover, the very process of which he is "protagonist" makes him vulnerable to degraded environment, increased dependency on volatile markets, lack of nutritional security, weakening of community solidarity, increased family and marital tensions, and other conflicts.

In the long run, unbalanced social and environmental change is not good for anyone. When historical processes favor one sector at the cost of others, it is not a simple problem of injustice to the marginalized people and resources, which can be resolved by incorporating these into the winner's team: the problem is that the development model itself is inherently asymmetrical. Nor is it an issue of exclusion or inclusion of different kinds of individuals: virtually everybody in the world *is already involved* in asymmetrical relations of development, not as rational individuals, but as members of complex networks of inequitable interdependencies which are shaped by class, gender, space, ethnicity, and the international economic order. Finally, these relations are never separate from, but are inherently embedded in and indeed constructed from the material resources and environmental contexts through which people move and which they continually shape and recreate.

Conclusion

Numerous studies in Andean regions describe how socially differentiated persons— together with the land and other resources that they manage—are bound together in relationships variously expressed in terms of ethnic, gender, or generational complementarity and conflict; of class and racial exploitation; and of market exchange and competition (Alberti and Mayer, 1974; Collins, 1988; Dandler, 1987; de la Cadena, 1997; Izko, 1992; Lagos, 1994; Molina, 1987; Orlove, 1974). But our historical and theoretical understanding of the relations between social difference and environmental processes needs to advance significantly in order for us to understand the effects that current liberal market policies are having on different groups of Andeans and on the environments with which they interact.

This paper explores multiple interactions between cultural organization and meaning, specifically in terms of gender, and land-use, biodiversity, biomass, organization of the landscape and other environmental factors within a context of changing legal and political-economic forces. The dynamic relations of mutual causal impact illuminated here contribute to a more integral understanding of the processes that shape the social and physical landscape. Following are a few of the key ideas developed in the analysis:

- No land stands alone. Multiple far-reaching land plots and resources are essentially interrelated. Private property must be understood in the context of more complex and integrated systems of tenure, access, and use.
- No man stands alone, and neither does the famous Andean man-woman unit *(qhari-warmi* or *chacha-warmi)*. All actors are interconnected in webs of exchange with neighbors, relatives, commercial intermediaries, employers, urban markets, and others.
- Neither social, nor environmental conditions evolve alone. Resources such as soil, water, green coverage, and others can not be divorced from the human labor, knowledge, and social organization with which they have evolved.

From this point of view, the people with whom we work tell us an environmental history, a history of the land they came of age in, a land which is engraved upon their bodies. Every body tells of the fruits that have fueled its growth; of the spaces it has frequented and the activities it has carried out; of the illnesses and humiliations it has suffered; of the symbols and values it has internalized as it moves through the land. And since different groups of people do not walk in the same places, do not have access to the same spaces, do not carry out the same labors, they do not carry the same environmental history in their bodies.

The landscapes that we study also tell a social history: a history of the visions, values, appetites, ambitions, and technologies of the people who have transformed the land through generations; a history of the collaborations, conflicts, and exploitations between differentiated groups and their resources. It shows their strengths and their triumphs, as well as their weaknesses and excesses, amongst them, social inequity.

Notes

[1] Warren and Bourque marvel at the way production issues are defined as purely technical problems. "That much of the international development community and many social scientists are able to identify technological concerns as primarily technical and to 'factor out' or "'bracket' cultural context, political economy, and history is something we need to treat in our research and writing" (Warren and Bourque, 1991: 279). Conversely, much work on gender and the environment "factors out" the details of ecological change and reduces environmental management to a social characteristic: having access to different resources influences men's and women's relative social power. Both of these approaches—the technical and the social—promote detailed analyses of environmental management that conveniently disregard larger historical and political economic forces and contexts.

[2] While an institutional divorce between production and reproduction is central to modern industrial economies, I believe that this division should be a topic of investigation, and not a conceptual framework used to interpret all forms of economic organization. Because it is difficult to identify a practical or symbolic separation between production and reproduction in the life strategies studied in central Bolivia, I use the hybrid term "(re)productive" to refer to the integral livelihood process.

[3] Lagos writes of the Tiraque region, "The struggle of peasants to gain direct access to land and to maintain a certain degree of control over the labor process has enabled them to produce use values outside the influence of the market. But, in order to preserve this delicate autonomy, paradoxically, they have increased participation in well-developed markets for their labor, cash crops, chemical fertilizer, and transport for their cash crops, even for the 'traditional' manure that many now obtain outside their farms. In producing, buying and selling, peasants are constrained by the practices of a new dominant class of merchants, transporters, and usurers, who have arisen from within rural villages and towns" (1994: 4).

[4] These "gender and environment" approaches are explicitly based in the widely used gender and development frameworks published by Overholt et al. (1984) and Moffat et al. (1991).

[5] Andean anthropologists have long identified multiple gender categories linked to sexual status (Harris, 1980; Isbell, 1997; Arnold and Yapita, 1996), and in her recent article, Los Diez Generos de Amarete Bolivia, Ina Rösing (1997) describes how ten named gender identities are defined by and in turn influence each individual's access to agricultural plots, political voice, and other resources.

[6] Concerning a similar study carried out in Africa, Louise Lamphere observes that "accepted concepts like 'the sexual division of labor' or 'female farming systems' seem too simple and naïve when actually applied to the change in Beti women's and men's agricultural activities during the colonial and contemporary period in Southern Cameroon. Such categories are not only stagnant but mask

complex relationships between men and women and between local cropping techniques and larger systems of markets and capital as they affect the agricultural strategies of men and women" (1991: iii).

[7] Douglas Murray sums up, "Agriculture was particularly important to the new [post WWII] development scheme, insofar as it was the means to increase food production and raise nutritional levels, thus providing relief from disease and hunger. Agricultural development also offered, according to development planners, a relatively quick means of generating the capital necessary to drive Third World industrialization (Kaimowitz, 1992)" (1994: 3).

[8] Morris (this volume) writes, "Traditional communities, as is clearly visible on the *altiplano*, chose to locate villages at the break of slope between plain and hills, with access to lands in both zones. The *pampas* or plains land is used for occasional crops of bitter potatoes, *quinua* or *cañihua*, and for grazing, the slope land is used for other crops, such as beans, barley, and sweet potatoes. These communities often also had access to marsh lands around the lake with the possibility of using water resources (reeds, fish), the whole making a rounded resources system. Just as the traditional community provided flexibility and varied human resources, so the physical environment provided flexibility of resources to reduce the risk of droughts, frosts, and floods, all major problems in the *altiplano*. Individual farmers could not hope for this flexibility, and cannot locate their farms so as to combine resources" (this volume).

[9] Based on Latin American experiences, one might gather that the exclusive emphasis on men's agricultural production is not a gender bias, but a simple fact of rural development. Cases from Africa, however, reveal that where women farm and men herd, rural development has focused on cattle. In a chapter titled "The men in the field" Barbara Rogers reports on a series of interviews with development planners, citing the following testimony of a FAO country representative in Africa: "I've just been filling in a questionnaire from headquarters about women. But you know there's hardly anything to say, because we don't have the sort of projects that would involve them. We have nothing against them, in fact we'd like to have more for them, but you see all our projects here are concerned with cattle, and it just so happens that women have very few cattle. Of course, we get criticized because cattle are owned by the richer people." Rogers asked "Is it perhaps more than just coincidence that all the money is going into cattle and almost nothing for crops, when cattle are men's responsibility and crops are women's?" The representative answered, "I never really saw it like that. But I suppose there is a connection" (Rogers, 1980: 54-55).

[10] The idea of the "triple role" of Third World women has been widely promoted by Caroline Moser, who uses the concept to encourage a broader understanding of women's activities. Whereas development planners had stereotyped women as "housewives," responsible only for "reproductive" activities, she urges a consideration of women's productive and community roles as well. While this triple role framework is an effective planning tool for Western development planners who think in terms of their own industrial capitalist categories, it has little empirical resonance in the lives of most Third World women.

[11] Naila Kabeer observes: "The WID neglect of the interconnections between production and reproduction in women's lives is echoed, for instance, in USAID policy, which in 1979 officially defined WID projects as those which increased women's participation, opportunity and income-earning capacities. Explicitly excluded from the WID definitions are those projects in which women are recipients of goods (such as contraception or health projects) or of food and services for themselves or their children (Staudt, 1985: 52). Women were being redefined as the agents of development rather than the recipients, but their agency was premised on a very truncated understanding of their lives" (1994: 30).

[12] In their discussion of the Zapatistas demands for indigenous autonomy, Stephan and Collier identify similar proposals: "In contrast to the *autonomy* of the mythical 'economic' man who freely chooses among choices afforded by the global capitalist market, what the proposals for indigenous autonomy

in Mexico are really calling for is participatory democracy in which local and regional populations make their own decisions about a) how economic development proceeds, b) what should be done with government resources allocated to them, and c) how their communities should be run through specifically indigenous political representation at the regional and national levels" (Stephen and Collier, 1997: 12).

[13] Zimmerer's case study, in an area near the region discussed in this paper, "demonstrates that soil erosion in the Bolivian Andes worsened during recent decades (1953-91) due to changes in production as peasants shifted labor from conservation techniques to nonfarm employment" (1993a: 16659).

[14] "The relationship between colonized and colonizer is based not on any measure of partnership but rather on the latter's coercion and violence in its dealings with the former. This relationship is in fact the secret of unlimited growth in the centers of accumulation. If externalization of all the costs of industrial production were not possible, if they had to be borne by the industrialized countries themselves, that is if they were internalized, an immediate end to unlimited growth would be inevitable" (Mies, 1993: 50).

References

Alberti, G. and E. Mayer (eds.), "Reciprocidad e intercambio en los Andes peruanos". Lima, Instituto de Estudios Peruanos, 1974.

Arnold, D. and J. de Dios Yapita, "Los caminos de género en Qaqachaka: saberes femeninos y discursos textuales alternativos en los Andes". In: S. Rivera Cusicanqui (ed.), *Ser mujer indígena, chola o birlocha en la Bolivia postcolonial de los años 90*. La Paz, Ministerio de Desarrollo Humano, 1996.

Balan, J. and J. Dandler, "Marriage process and household formation: the impact of migration in a peasant society". Report submitted to the Population Council. Cochabamba, CERES, 1986.

Balarezu, S., "Guía metodológica para incorporar la dimensión de género en proyectos forestales participativos". Quito, FAO/FTPP y FAO/DFPA, 1994.

Blanes, J., F. Calderon, J. Dandler *et al.*, "Agricultura, pauperización, proletariazación y diferenciación campesina". La Paz, CERES, 1984.

CARE Perú, "Género y desarrollo, guía del facilitador". Lima, OCISA, 1994.

CIDRE (Centro de Investigación y Documentación Regional), "Monografia sobre la Provincia Esteban Arze". Serie de Estudios Regionales. Cochabamba, CIDRE, 1985.

CIDRE, "Monografía de la Provincia Mizque". Serie de Estudios Regionales. Cochabamba, CIDRE, 1987.

CIPCA, CERES, Ayllu Sartañani, DSU, Stockholm University CDS and University of Hull, "Popular participation: democratizing the state in rural Bolivia". Report to SIDA, commissioned through Development Studies Unit, Department of Social Anthropology, Stockholm University, 1997.

Collins, J.L., *Unseasonal migrations: the effects of rural labor scarcity in Peru*. Princeton, Princeton University Press, 1988.

Dandler, J., "Diversificación, procesos de trabajo y movilidad espacial en los Valles y Serranías de Cochabamba". In: O. Harris, B. Larson and E. Tandeter (eds.), *La participación indígena en los mercados surandinos*. La Paz, CERES, 1987.

De Leal, L., M. and C.D. Deere, *Mujer y capitalismo agrario: estudio de cuatro regiones Columbianas*. Bogotá, Asociación Colombiana para el Estudio de la Población, 1980.

De la Cadena, M., "Matrimonio y etnicidad en comunidades andinas". In: D. Arnold (ed.), *Más allá del silencio: las fronteras de género en los Andes*. La Paz, CIASE/ILCA, 1997.

Finan, T., "Changing roles of agriculture in global development policy. Is anthropology (out)standing in its field?" *Culture and Agriculture*, Vol. 19, no. 3 (1997), pp. 79-84.

Harris, O., "The power of signs: gender, culture and the wild in the Bolivian Andes". In: C.P. MacCormack and M. Strathern (eds.), *Nature, culture and gender*. London, Cambridge University Press, 1980.

Harris, O., "Ecological duality and the role of the center: Northern Potosí". In: S. Masuda, I. Shimade and C. Morris (eds.), *Andean ecology and civilization*. Tokyo, University of Tokyo Press, 1985.

Isbell, B.J., "De inmaduro a duro: lo simbólico femenino y los esquemas andinos de género". In: D. Arnold (ed.), "Más allá del silencio: las fronteras de género en los Andes". La Paz, CIASE/ILCA, 1997.

Izko, X., "La doble frontera: ecología, política y ritual en el altiplano central". La Paz, HISBOL/CERES, 1992.

Kabeer, N., *Reversed realities: gender hierarchies in development thought*. London and New York, Verso, 1994.

Lagos, M.L., "Pathways to autonomy, roads to power: peasant-elite relations in Cochabamba (Bolivia), 1900-1985". PhD dissertation. Department of Anthropology, Columbia Universit, 1988.

Lagos, M.L., *Autonomy and power: the dynamics of class and culture in rural Bolivia*. Philadelphia, University of Pennsylvania Press, 1994.

Lagos, M.L., "Bolivia la nueva: constructing new citizens". *Journal of Latin American Anthropology*, forthcoming.

Lamphere, L. "Forward". In: M. di Leonardo (ed.), *Gender at the crossroads of knowledge*. Berkeley and Los Angeles, University of California Press, 1991.

Lehmann, D. (ed.), *Eology and exchange in the Andes*. Cambridge, Cambridge University Press, 1982.

Mayer, E., "Las reglas del juego en la reciprocidad Andina". In: G. Alberti and E. Mayer (eds.), *Reciprocidad y intercambio en los Andes Peruanos*. Lima, Instituto de Estudios Peruanos, 1974.

Mayer, E., "Production zones". In: S. Masuda, I. Shimade and C. Morris (eds.), *Andean ecology and civilization*. Tokyo, University of Tokyo Press, 1985.

Mercado, D., J. de la Fuente and L.H. Rojas, *Produccion y vida rural en las provincias Mizque y Campero*. Cochabamba, Centro de Formacion e Investigacion Interdisciplinaria, Universidad Mayor de San Simón, 1990.

Mercado, M., "El municipio y la planificación participativa". *Participar* (Organo de la Secretaría de Participación Popular), Año 2, no. 7-8 (1995). La Paz.

Mies, M., "The myth of catching-up development". In: M. Mies and V. Shiva, *Ecofeminism*. London, Zed Books, 1993.

Mies, M. and V. Shiva, *Ecofeminism*. London, Zed Books, 1993.

Moffat, L., Y. Geadah and R. Stuart, *Two halves make a whole*. Ottawa, Canadian Council for International Cooperation, 1991.

Molino Rivero, R., "La tradicionalidad como medio de articulación al mercado: una comunidad pastoril en Oruro". In: O. Harris, B. Larson, E. Tandeter (eds.), *La participación indígena en los mercados surandinos*. La Paz, CERES, 1987.

Moser, C. and C.A. Levy, "Theory and methodology of gender planning: meetings women's practical and strategic needs". DPU Gender Planning Unit, 1986.

Moser, C., "Gender planning in the Third World: meeting practical and strategic needs". *World Development*, Vol. 17, no. 11 (1989).

Moser, C., *Gender planning and development. Theory, practice and training*. London, Routledge, 1993.

Murra, J., "The economic organization of the Inca state". PhD dissertation. Department of Anthropology, University of Chicago, 1956.

Murra, J., "El archipielago vertical revisited". In: S. Masuda, I. Shimade and C. Morris (eds.), *Andean ecology and civilization*. Tokyo, University of Tokyo Press, 1985.

Murray, D.L., *Cultivating crisis: the human cost of pesticides in Latin America*. Austin, University of Texas Press, 1994.

Ostrom, E., *Governing the commons: the evolution of institutions for collective actions*. New York, Cambridge Press, 1990.

Orlove, B.S., "Reciprocidad, desigualdad y dominación". In: G. Alberti and E. Mayer (eds.), *Reciprocided e intercambio en los Andes Peruanos*. Lima, Instituto de Estudios Peruanos, 1974.

Overholt, C., M. Anderson, K. Cloud and J. Austin, *Gender roles in development*. West Hartford, Kumarian Press, 1984.

Painter, M., "Agricultural policy, food production and multinational corporations in Peru". *Latin American Research Review*, Vol. 18 (1983), pp. 201-18.

Paulson, S., "Gender and ethnicity in motion: identity and integration in Andean households". PhD dissertation. University of Chicago, 1992.

Paulson, S., *Desigualdad social y degradación ambiental en America Latina*. Quito, Abya Yala, 1998.

Rao, A., M.B. Anderson and C.A. Overholt (eds.), *Gender analysis in development planning*. West Hartford, Kumarian Press, 1991.

Rogers, B. *The domestication of women: discrimination in developing societies*. London and New York, Tavistock Publications, 1980.

Rösing, I., "Los diez géneros de Amarete, Bolivia". In: D. Arnold (ed.), *Más allá del silencio: las fronteras de género en los Andes*. La Paz, CIASE/ILCA, 1997.

Stephen, L. and G.A. Collier, "Reconfiguring ethnicity, identity and citizenship in the wake of the *Zapatista* rebellion". *Journal of Latin American Anthropology*, Vol. 3, no. 1 (1997), pp. 2-13.

Urioste, M., *Segunda reforma agraria: campesinos, tierra y educación popular*. La Paz, CEDLA, 1997.

Watson, G. and J. Almanza, *Manejo in situ de cultivares de papa: caracterización, producción difusión y el rol de género en Cochabamba*. Cochabamba, PROIMPA, 1994.

Weismantel, M.J., *Food, gender, and poverty in the Ecuadorian Andes*. Philadelphia, University of Pennsylvania Press, 1994.

Zambrana, J. and S. Wade, "Análisis participativo de género como medio de cambio social". In: S. Paulson and M. Crespo (eds.), *Teorías y prácticas de género: una conversación dialéctica*. Cochabamba, Embajada Real de los Paises Bajos. Unidad Departamental de Asuntos de Género (UDAG), Cochabamba. 1995-1996 Diagnóstico complementario de género en la provincia de Tiraque. Subsecretaría de Asuntos de Género. Cochabamba, 1994.

Zimmerer, K.S., "Soil erosion and labor shortages in the Andes with special reference to Bolivia, 1953-91: implications for 'conservations-with-development'". *World Development*, Vol. 21, no. 10 (1993a), pp. 1659-75.

Zimmerer, K.S., "Soil erosion and social (dis)courses in Cochabamba Bolivia: perceiving the nature of environmental degradation", *Economic Geography*, Vol. 69/3 (1993b), pp. 312-27.

Zoomers, A., "Estrategias campesinas: algunas consideraciones teóricas y conceptuales". In A. Zoomers (ed.), *Estrategias campesinas en el surandino de Bolivia: intervenciones y desarrollo rural en el norte de Chuquisaca y Potosí*. KIT/CEDLA/PLURAL, Amsterdam/Bolivia, 1998.

4 Rooted migrants: land and rural development in the Valle Alto of Cochabamba, Bolivia

Geneviève Cortes

Introduction

In relaunching the debate around the agrarian question in Latin America—a theme much explored in the 1960s and 1970s by researchers in the social sciences—the new economic and social realities of the Latin American rural world are taken into account.

One of the new realities for Latin America at the end of the twentieth century is the crisis affecting peasant models of production, which are very significant in Bolivia. The destabilization of traditional peasant economies[1], which play an essential role in providing food for the entire country (Franqueville *et al.*, 1992) is the result of a complex economic, social, and political process.

The agrarian and agricultural history of Bolivia is marked by various key events. The national revolution of 1952 and the agrarian reform which followed (1953) set in motion a crucial stage of social and economic liberalization of the peasant sector, which allowed individual ownership of land. The redistribution of the land after the dismantling of the system of *haciendas* and *colonato*[2] accelerated the integration of the peasants into a national society while, at the same time, there were parallel movements toward urbanization, the development of new commercial networks, and greater spatial mobility of the population.

The governments of this period, preoccupied by the need to achieve self-sufficiency in food supplies, supported the traditional peasant sector by launching credit and technical assistance programs. But, at the same time, there emerged new dynamics for the development of the Amazon regions through agricultural colonization, particularly in the sub-tropical region of Santa Cruz. The conquest of these virgin lands had three objectives: to even out spatial inequalities, to attain self-sufficiency in particular crops (rice, sugar), and to boost the development of agricultural exports and agribusiness.

The economic crisis of the 1980s, which hit most Latin American countries (inflation, debt, underemployment), caused a significant rupture in the socioeconomic development of the entire country and, consequently, in the progress of the agricultural sector. To respond to the crisis and conform to the model imposed by international bodies, the government adopted new development strategies based on the liberalization of the economy and the retreat of the state. These strategies led to the reinforcement of the politics of aid for the agribusiness sector of the *Oriente* (higher credits, overtures to foreign investors, the introduction of new industrial crops and, more recently, the liberalization of the land market), policies which have not improved the socioeconomic marginalization of peasant populations in the Andes. Besides structural factors such as climatic conditions (drought, frost) and the small size of family holdings, the Andes population is today confronted with a lack of credit and technical assistance, inadequate road transport infrastructure, as well as the constraining conditions of commercialization and a deterioration in the agroecological environment. According to various sources, the Andes region has experienced new levels of impoverishment during the past two decades[3] (PNUD, 1996; Franqueville, 1997).

This has led to the development of strategies of survival, or of resistance to impoverishment. Historically, diversification has always been a characteristic of the Andean peasant economy, as a way of spreading risk by having several sources of revenue with which to face climatic and economic conditions (Morlon, 1996; Zoomers, 1998). But, with the persistent crisis, this reality has assumed a new magnitude. The diversification and "informal" tertiarization of the peasant economies (small-scale commerce, craft activities, wage labor) is becoming more general, in particular in the rural areas around the principal urban centers (La Paz, Sucre, Cochabamba). This process is accompanied by an increase in temporary migration not only to different regions of the country (zones of colonization, urban centers), but also abroad (Argentina and the US).

This article sets itself very precisely in the context of these international migrations that affect the Bolivian rural world. The hypothesis is that the growing spatial mobility of the population, along with the diversification of activities, drastically changes the relationship of this peasant society with the land, both as means of agricultural production and as object of socialization or symbolic representation.

Starting from observations and surveys carried out in two villages of the Andean valleys of Cochabamba (Arbieto and Santa Rosa, in the Valle Alto), rural migration is approached from the angle of the peasants' strategies[4]. After the study region has been described, an attempt will be made to evaluate the consequences of mobility and diversification on family economies, focusing attention on the reciprocal relationships between agrarian structures and migration. An analysis will then be made of the transformation of the system of agricultural production in these villages, examining the economic, social, and cultural functions of the land.

The agroecological and agrarian context of Cochabamba

The region of Cochabamba—which is situated in the central zone of the country, halfway between La Paz and Santa Cruz—has a long tradition of agriculture, characterized by a very diversified production. This region has always played a key role in feeding the country, even during the period of the Inca Empire. Its ecological diversity constitutes a major reason for its exploitation and development. In the areas above 3,000 meters in altitude *(puma)* dominates a family agriculture specializing in traditional Andean crops (potatoes, *oca, quinoa*[5]) and the raising of sheep and llamas. The valleys *(intermedio, bajo, y alto)*, where the study area is situated, benefit from agroecological conditions which are more favorable for the development of a diversified and intensive agriculture (production of corn, potatoes, vegetables, fruit, and cattle raising). As they are prone to recurrent drought, the various systems of production are largely determined by the possibilities of irrigation.

The peasants of the valleys of Cochabamba have inherited a long tradition of struggle for the land, which is linked to the sociohistoric formation of the whole region (Larson, 1992). As a veritable granary of *Alto Peru* during the Spanish colonization, *haciendas* were more developed here than anywhere else in the country. But, at the same time, they were contested at a very early date, and already by the 19th century there began a fragmentation of colonial landed property. The sale of land allowed the emancipation of a whole sector of small independent landowners (the *piqueros*), who played an important role in the final phase of the expulsion of the *hacendados* and the agrarian reform of 1953.

The emergence of a peasant sector is one of the reasons for the heavy fragmentation of the land and the small size of holdings that characterizes this region. The political orientations of the 1960s have only reinforced the traditional agrarian duality of the country: excessive subdivision on the high plateaus and mountainous regions, concentration and large agricultural holdings in the lower regions of the *Oriente*. The valleys of Cochabamba constitute an exemplary case of this microdivision of the land. At a regional level, 80% of farmers have between 0.1 and 5 hectares (Caro *et al.*, 1992). If one considers only the valley sector, 63% of the rural families have less than two hectares and 40% less than one hectare.

Diversification and international migrations in the Valle Alto of Cochabamba

In Bolivia, and more generally in Andean societies, pluri-activity is structural to the peasant economy (Figueroa, 1981; Gonzales de Olarte, 1984; Zoomers, 1998). But this phenomenon is particularly visible in the valleys of Cochabamba (Dandler *et al.*, 1982; Laserna, 1982). A study by Caro *et al. (op. cit)* found that only 40% of the heads of holdings had agriculture as a principal activity.

In the Valle Alto, the diversification of activities is very much tied up with another reality: temporary migration abroad. The migration of Bolivians to Argentina is an old phenomenon, very well known today[6]. On the other hand, migration to the US is much more recent, but has become prevalent since the early 1980s. The Argentinean economic crisis, which reduced the prospects of entry into the labor market in Buenos Aires, has contributed to the emergence not only of the US as a new destination, but also of Israel and Japan (in Santa Rosa and Arbieto, migration involved 54% of the population in 1992; of these people, 75% were living outside Bolivia: 58% in Argentina, 39% in the US, and 3% in Japan and Israel).[7]

Migration in the lifecycle of the peasant

In the Valle Alto of Cochabamba, international migration has taken on a structural character within the peasant economies. Transmitted from father to son according to well-established rules of behavior, this migration can only be understood within the lifecycle of the individual and the family. The first departure abroad, which is made as early as the age of sixteen and has Argentina as the principal destination, constitutes a period of apprenticeship which determines the future itinerary of the young migrant. Migration to Argentina, which may be regarded as temporary (alternating sojourns in the village and in Buenos Aires), lasts generally for several years until the migrant can establish a family holding. The savings made from migration (around 100 dollars a month in 1992) are thus destined for the upkeep of family members who have stayed in the village, the construction of a house, and the purchase of land.

After several years of migratory experience in Argentina, the migrant can envisage a departure to the US, a more profitable destination in terms of income (monthly savings in 1992 were 400 dollars). Nevertheless, the cost of the fare (around 3,000 dollars) obliges the migrant to borrow money from close family, members of the neighboring communities, or professional creditors, who can be found at Cochabamba. As the interest rates are generally very high (up to 3% per month), the migrant exposes himself to the risks of debt that are sometimes irreversible.

This international migration, which rarely turns into a definitive move abroad, has very important financial impacts in the departure zones. The families that stay in the village continually receive money from the migrant parent. Economic surveys show that 85% of the revenues of these families come from non-agricultural activities or loans. Migration alone contributes up to 40% of the revenues (in some families, the proportion exceeds 60%). The importance of income from migration causes a new socioeconomic differentiation in the peasant communities. Families with low revenues (between 260 and 790 dollars annually) are those which remain sedentary and struggle to combine agricultural and non-agricultural activities. Families with a member in the US, Israel, or Japan have the highest levels of revenue (between 1,580 and 3,000 dollars a year). At an intermediate level are the families of migrants to Argentina (between 800 and 1,500 dollars). However, some families suffer a high level of debt (sometimes more than 2,000 dollars) which is tied to an abortive departure to the US.

The least poor are those that migrate

According to a well-known theoretical model, demographic pressure on the land is considered the principal factor behind the migration of rural populations. The propensity to migrate is therefore proportional to the size of the family holding. For Bolivia, there are no exhaustive and reliable figures that would permit this relationship to be shown, but many local studies confirm it (Blanes, Flores, 1983; Vargas, 1998; Mercado *et al.*, 1990)[8]. However, in the study zone, where international migration is predominant, the relation between agrarian structures and migration behavior obeys a contrary model: a correlation between the size of the family holding and the overall time of migration of the heads of the families shows that it is the peasants with the most land who migrate the most.

This paradoxical relationship is the result of a double process. Firstly, only families with agricultural revenues, that is, those who have access to a relatively large area of land (at least two hectares), can support the period of debt entailed by a first departure abroad. The women who stay in the village must be able to live on their own resources while the money earned from the migration is used to pay off the debt. After this period (which varies from six months to a year), the family can use the savings from migration to meet other expenses. Secondly, migration allows the families to amass or raise their land capital by buying more land from the community. This type of investment, however, does not occur until after several years of migration.

Thus, a double relationship between agrarian structures and migration can be observed:
- The lack of land obliges the peasant to look for alternatives to subsistence but, at the same time, this limits the possibility of international migration.
- The greater the size of the holding, the lower the risk and the greater the possibility of long-distance migration.

In the villages of the Valle Alto, the fact of migration introduces new uses of the land, based upon traditional practices of the Andean world. Insofar as migration does not entail an abandonment of the family holding, the principal challenge to the peasants is to maintain agricultural activity. For this, a system of land transfers is played out amongst the migrants and non-migrants, which takes many different forms. The *compaña* system, the most frequently used, consists of entrusting a plot of land to a member of the village who undertakes to cultivate it. The harvests are shared between the owner and the *compañero*. Certain families prefer the *al partir* system that consists of a trade between two families to cultivate their plots. The *anticrético*, which is much less widespread, is a system which allows the landowner to confer the usufruct of a plot on a non-migrant in exchange for a sum of money, which he must repay at the end of the contract (around 1,500 dollars per hectare).

Amongst the families of migrants, the cultivation of land holdings falls almost entirely on the women. To even out the lack of manpower caused by the departure of the heads of families and children, the women resort very often to these practices. It is generally close family, non-migrants who benefit from the usufruct of the land. In the same way, in order not to lose their community rights (rights of irrigation, etc.), the migrants entrust their portion of collective work *(faenas)* to non-migrants (help at meetings, upkeep of paths or irrigation canals). For the poor peasants who are unable to migrate, these practices allow them to compensate for their feeble land resources, while the migrant peasants are able to maintain agricultural activity on their land and thus preserve their community rights.

International migration also engenders an informal system for selling land. According to surveys, investment in land funded by savings from migration is quasi-systematic. In certain families, more than 50% of land capital has been built up in this manner. The purchase of land, which is a general tendency in all of the Valle Alto (Dandler *et al.*, 1982; Blanes, 1983; Deheza, 1991), is directly related to the system of transmission of patrimonial property. According to custom, land is inherited only on the death of parents, but rather than wait, the families of migrants seek to create their own patrimony from a very young age.

Thus, migration constitutes an essential strategy for gaining access to property. The selling of land involves a new process of agrarian concentration that curbs the fragmentation of the land and reduces the dispersion of plots (it is a priority of migrants to buy land close to their own holdings). The peasants who sell their land are of two types. They may be sedentary families with meager land resources who renounce farming and take up non-agricultural activities (small-scale commerce, transport), while staying in the village. These families are direct participants in the passage of agricultural society to a diversified and tertiarized rural society. But the majority of those who sell their land are peasant farmers who have failed in their attempt to migrate and find themselves in a situation of irreversible debt. This is a process of veritable agrarian "decapitalization", which accentuates the socioeconomic inequalities within the village.

The land market, which is very dynamic in this region, is paradoxical: land is very expensive in the Valle Alto. However, it continues to be bought, even if we are talking about small quantities, sometimes less than half a hectare (Dandler *et al.*, 1982: 50). The value of land is even higher because availability is limited. The good agroecological conditions of the Valle Alto (despite the risks of drought), favorable topographical conditions for agricultural modernization, and the proximity of the urban market, explain why land is in such demand. In 1992, the price of a hectare varied between 6,000 and 9,000 dollars, which represents more than five years of wage labor in the US[9]. How, therefore, can one explain these strategies of land investment when agricultural production offers so few possibilities for accumulation, particularly in comparison with international migration?

Toward new systems of agricultural production

At first sight, the dynamic nature of land dealings contradicts the conditions of the local agrarian market and the monetary possibilities of agricultural production and, in fact, hides a profound transformation of agricultural production systems. In terms of income, agriculture is a secondary activity of family economies (15% of annual income on average). However, this does not signify that the region is undergoing a process of "de-agriculturalization" of the rural areas. It is rather that migration introduces a structural change into the modes of production and the development of the land, involving relatively complex mechanisms. The monetarization of family economies which is tied to the importance of migratory revenues may provoke one of three processes: either a regression to subsistence agriculture, the maintenance of a semi-commercial type of agriculture, or an evolution toward an entrepreneurial type of family agriculture.

A regression toward a family subsistence agriculture

The first group of families practice an exclusively subsistence form of agriculture. Production is generally limited to traditional crops, like potatoes or corn, and is primarily intended for family consumption. Several types of family follow this pattern: first of all, sedentary peasants who have little land and receive a non-agricultural income (crafts, commerce, transport). In this group, one also finds families which migrate to Argentina. One can distinguish (a) the young migrants who begin a migratory itinerary of long duration and who have very little land and, (b), the migrants who have a long migratory experience, but have not succeeded in saving enough to be able to build up their land holdings.

There are some heads of families who are too much in debt and are unable to break the process of migration, while the women struggle to maintain an "agriculture of survival" on the family holding, where the logic of subsistence is *de rigueur*. These families often find themselves in an extremely fragile economic situation and a process of impoverishment that often obliges them to sell a part of their land capital, including plots they were able to buy only a few years before.

The maintenance of semi-commercial family agriculture

The families of the second group practice a type of agriculture that is aimed at both consumption and commercialization. This is the case, in particular, of the families of migrants to Argentina, who manage to maintain a satisfactory level of income, thanks to the complementary nature of agricultural activity (between 10 and 30% of annual revenues) and the migration of one member of the family (father or son).

This system of production favors traditional crops (potatoes, maize, wheat) while always aiming to produce a surplus for sale. These households, who generally do not have a lot of land (less than two hectares), are very prominent in the informal system of land transfers. Thanks to the usufruct of plots of land that the "richer" migrants concede to them as *companía* or *al partir*, they are able to maintain a certain level of agricultural production, while migration permits them both to cover current expenses and to finance the costs of production (to buy seed, to rent a tractor). Some families have supplementary revenues from raising cattle and selling cheese in nearby urban markets. For these families, migration does not upset the traditional patterns of agricultural production, but without migration, the reproduction of the family holding system would be compromised.

An evolution toward an entrepreneurial type of family agriculture

The third group of families is very interesting from the point of view of the impact of international migration on the rural and agricultural development of the region. Revenues from migration and, in particular, those earned in the US, bring about profound transformations in the systems of production. The amount that migrants invest in agriculture over the course of their lifecycle can be considerable (Table 1).

Table 1   Example of agricultural investment

Year	Type of investment	Amount (US$)	
1971	Acquisition of land (600 m²)		Not known
1979-1981	Acquisition of land (10,800 m²)		6,000
1984	Acquisition of land (5,300 m²)		3,000
1988	Acquisition of a tractor with the help of credit	Cost:	21,000
		Loan:	16,000
		Own capital:	5,000
1988	Planting of peach trees, acquisition of an irrigation pump, costruction of wells		3,000
1991	Planting of peach trees		2,000
1992	Reimbursement of debt (for the tractor)		7,000
Total investment			26,000

Source: Reconstitution of migratory itinerary of Orlando S., 50 years old, 21 years of migration to Argentina and the US, Arbieto.

As well as buying land, these families have also become innovative by introducing new types of crops destined for the regional market (fruits, flowers, vegetables) while reducing their traditional crops (corn, potatoes). Such diversification of produce is accompanied by a multiplication of individual wells for irrigation and by agricultural mechanization. From all the evidence, the number of families who are able to buy a tractor is very small. They are, in all cases, obliged to borrow, generally from technical and financial assistance associations. From another point of view, the mechanization of the systems of production would seem paradoxical, given the large degree of fragmentation of the land. In reality, the farmers who have a tractor amortize the investment by renting it out to other members of the community (20 bolivianos per hour).

These dynamics of the transition of agriculture imply a monetarization of the normal modes of production. The restructuring of the systems of production is accompanied by a new definition of work relationships within the village. While the heads of families are away, the intensification of the work of women and children does not allow them to take on all the tasks of the farm, tasks that have become more important and more technical. Some women have recourse to the traditional *ayni* (reciprocal exchange of services between two families), but in an asymmetrical form (such as the use of a tractor for one hour in exchange for labor). For the most part, these women must hire temporary wage laborers from amongst the non-migrants of the village. The recourse to wage labor, agricultural mechanization, the growing use of chemicals, the use of higher quality seed, are the factors which contribute to the monetarization of agriculture.

Thus emerges a system of production which is moving progressively further away from "peasant logic" as strictly defined by the theories of Chayanov (1966). The process of migration participates directly in the transition of agriculture toward an entrepreneurial family type with profit from investments as the chief objective. The most remarkable aspect of these mutations is the key role that the wives of migrants will henceforth play in the running of land holdings. The feminization of agriculture, a direct consequence of international migration, is one social and cultural change of great importance in this Andean valley region of Bolivia.

The different functions of the land

The restructuring of agriculture in the Valle Alto of Cochabamba modifies the function of the land within the modes of existence of the peasant families. One can distinguish five functions of the land, both material and non-material. The criteria are the following: the role of the land, the type of usage and the peasant's unit of sociospatial frame of reference (Figure 1).

Figure 1   Functions of the land

		Role of the land	Usage of the land	Sociospatial frame of reference
Material function		biological/nutritive	production/consumption	individual/family
		economic/monetary	production/commercialization	regional/national society
Non-material function		social	status	national society/community
		symbolic/cultural	world-view	Andean *quechua* group
		patrimonial	transmission	family

The first function of the land in the material domain, which is evident within the context of traditional peasant economies, is the function of nourishment. Land is perceived and used above all as a means of production and consumption. It is an instrument of individual and family reproduction, the unit of reference of the first group. This function maintains itself differently in each of the three types of agricultural economy. For the families of the third group, the nutritive function of the land disappears, while it is reinforced in the first group.

Another possible function of the land in the material domain is the commercial and monetary function. In this category, the relationship of the peasant to the land changes. The land is no longer perceived only as a means of subsistence, but also as a source of profit. This functionality of the land places the peasant within a type of production that is monetarized and dependent on the market. The monetary function of the land is dominant and limited almost exclusively to families who have set in motion new agricultural dynamics, using the income from migration.

The social function of the land is defined by the role it plays in the identification of the individual with the community group and society as a whole. This function is very important for the second and third groups of families, particularly for those peasants who have used the proceeds from immigration to invest in land, because how otherwise can one explain the fact that certain families who buy land do not put it into cultivation? The first reason is that the women do not always have the time or the means to do so. But one also has to take into account the fact that the land does not have only an economic role. The possession of land, even in very small amounts, assures the landowner of a certain recognition and social prestige within the community of which he is a member (Deheza, 1991). Moreover, the colonial past of the region, which gave birth to a strong tradition of struggle for the land, has forged a collective conscience and a territorial attachment amongst the *Quechua* peasants. To be a landowner is equally a manner of affirming a specifically "peasant" identity as a means of differentiating oneself from the rest of the national society and, particularly, urban society.

In the specific context of Andean society one cannot ignore the symbolic and cultural function of the land. The man/earth relationship in the Andean world-view is very rich (Albó, 1987; Albó et al., 1990). The work of the land takes place within a mode of symbolic representation, which gives birth to ritual practices of a mystical character, within which the divinity *Pachamama* (mother earth) plays a central role. Besides the traditional *ch'alla*[10,] the traditional agricultural calendar is marked by a multitude of ceremonies (burial of foodstuffs in homage to *Pachamama*, reading of the coca leaf). In the villages of the Valle Alto, the intensity of the symbolic and cultural relationships of man and the earth varies widely from one group to another. Amongst the families who exclusively practice subsistence agriculture, this function of the land is very present. In contrast, the families of the third group maintain very little symbolic relationship with the land. This is not necessarily a sign of weakening cultural identity. It could be related to a simple lack of time, or to the fact that they often concede the work of the land to hired labor. Thus, it seems that the higher the monetary function of the land, the more the symbolic function diminishes.

Finally, the patrimonial function of the land is the only one that does not show any differentiation between the three groups of families. Peasant discourse makes continual reference to the problem of the transmission of land and the prospects of inheritance. The sale of land nearly always corresponds with cases of extreme necessity, and represents a traumatic social and cultural experience for those who are forced to sell:

"I have worked for years so that my children could have a future. And during those years, I had to leave my wife and my children in the village so that I could go and work in Argentina. We couldn't have survived any other way. Now, I am too much in debt and I have to sell my land. Without land, who am I?" (Domingo, Arbieto).

Conclusion

The magnitude of temporary migration in Bolivia, and particularly in the region of Cochabamba, brings us back to the crucial question of what is happening to Andean peasant societies. According to certain theoretical interpretations, migration and the accompanying diversification of activities are considered as indications of the destructuring and proletarization of the peasant sector (Goodman, Redclift, 1982). However, processes observed in the Valle Alto of Cochabamba show no clear relationship between temporary migration and impoverishment of the peasantry.

According to other interpretations (Stavenhagen, 1970; Figueroa, 1981; Morlon, 1996), migration constitutes a strategy of survival and even enrichment for the peasant society. It is true that in the Valle Alto, where land fragmentation is extreme, international migration prevents a final exodus of the population and thus assures the maintenance of rural society, and even engenders the dynamics of development and agricultural modernization, with the emergence of new systems of production. These structural changes are accompanied by a displacement of the functionality of the land, which serves simultaneously as a means of production, a source of income, an object of socialization, and a symbol of cultural identification. Investment in land, thanks to income from migration, sometimes goes beyond a simple economic aim, and expresses the permanence of the symbolic and cultural function of the land as a sign of belonging to the community group, of socio-ethnic identification and of the territorial attachment of Andean society (Cortes, 1999).

Thus, the peasants of the inter-Andean valleys of Cochabamba show a great capacity for "self-organization" in a situation of crisis. Facing a lack of means of production, the families develop their own strategies outside all institutional frameworks except those of the community. The strong social cohesion of these communities allows recourse to a network of traditional exchange and trade that the peasants reappropriate in order to gain access to the process of international migration (exchange of information, loan systems). However, migration is selective. In marginalizing a part of the population, particularly the poorest peasants who have few land resources, it helps to accentuate the inequalities within the peasant societies. In other words, international migration remains a "privilege" of the least poor and fails to solve the fundamental problem of the unequal distribution of land.

Finally, particular attention should be paid to the huge complexity of the agrarian situation and the types of land ownership in this region of Bolivia. The modes of access to the land are very diversified. The informal and not very visible character of the system of land transfers, intimately bound up with migration, is integral to the ongoing debate on the INRA law of 1992-96, which claims to be compiling an agrarian register of the country[11]. The complexity of the tenure of the land in the Valle Alto of Cochabamba, which is also found in other parts of the country (Zoomers, 1998), often goes unrecognized by institutional organizations. This reality should be urgently and explicitly integrated into the programs of rural and agricultural development, particularly in the context of the debate around agrarian questions animating national and international political spheres.

Notes

[1] By "traditional peasant economy" is meant economies based on the modes of production, of work and of consumption essentially articulated around the family and community group.

[2] In exchange for the usufruct of a small plot, the *colonatos* must work a certain number of days on the owner's land.

[3] The country saw a diminution in its gross national product of 1.5% between 1980 and 1992. It is estimated that 86% of the rural population live in conditions of poverty.

[4] In the two villages we carried out surveys at the community level (census of migrants, social organization of work, types of exchanges), at the family level (follow-up of land holdings, revenues, expenses and food consumption) and at the individual level (determination of migratory itineraries).

[5] *Oca*: Andean tuber. *Quinoa*: Andean grasses.

[6] In the villages of the Valle Alto, international migration is a veritable local "specialization". The racial mix and urbanized nature of the rural populations (the bilingual *Quechua*-Spanish) are factors which favor the diffusion of international migration. But in the 1980s, when the price of coca leaves was at its highest, a number of peasants stopped migrating to Argentina in order to dedicate themselves to the illegal cultivation of coca and its preparation. In 1992, migrants to Chapare (a coca production zone) were in a small minority.

[7] Until the 1960s, Bolivians went to work as agriculture wage laborers in the frontier zones of Salta, Jujuy and Mendoza, where there was a growing export agriculture (sugar, tobacco, fruit). Nowadays, Buenos Aires is much more attractive. The migrants integrate themselves into construction, the textile industry, domestic services, and suburban horticultural agriculture (Benencia, Karasik, 1992).

[8] J. Blanes and G. Flores calculate, for example, that 64% of the immigrants in Chapare own less than one hectare in their communities of origin. According to the study carried out by D. Mercado in the Mizque and Campero region, 70% of the migrants to Chapare are landless.

[9] In the same year, one hectare in Chapare (illegal zone of coca production) was worth between 150 and 500 dollars, depending on the location of the land.

[10] The *ch'alla* is a homage paid to the *Pachamama*, and consists of spilling several drops of liquid on the ground.

[11] See the article by M. Urioste and D. Pacheco (In: Zoomers and van der Haar, 2000: 259-270).

References

Albó, J., "Culturas y cosmovisión andina". *Shupihui*, enero, no. 41 (1987), 9-28. Centro de Estudios Teologicos de la Amazonia, Lima.

Albó, J. K. Liberman, A. Godinez and F. Pifarre, *Para comprender las culturas rurales en Bolivia*. MEC/CIPCA/UNICEF, La Paz, 1990.

Barrón, J. and I. Goudsmit, "Hacerse la vida: migración definitiva". In: A. Zoomers (ed.), *Estrategias campesinas en el surandino de Bolivia. Intervenciones y desarrollo rural en el Norte de Chuquisaca y Potosí*. KIT/CEDLA/CID, La Paz, 1998.

Benencia, R. and G. Karasik, *Immigración limítrofe: los Bolivianos en Buenos Aires*. Buenos Aires, CELA, 1996.

Blanes, J., "Bolivia: consecuencias de los movimientos migratorios en el ambito rural". Congreso Latinoamericano de Poblacion y de Desarrollo, Mexico, 8-10 de noviembre, 1983.

Blanes, J. and G. Flores, "Campesino migrante y colonizador. Reproducción de la economía familiar en el chapare tropical". CERES, Serie Estudios Regionales, no. 3, 1983, La Paz.

Caro, D., J. Riordan and M. Cables, "Encuesta de hogares rurales de Cochabamba: resultados preliminares". USAID/Bolivia, OWD, AID, 1992.

Chayanov, A.V., "The theory of peasant economy". In: D. Thorner, B. Kerblay and R.E.F. Smith (eds.), The American Economic Association, Illinois, 1966.

Cortes, G., "L'émigration rurale dans les vallées inter-andines de Bolivie". *Revue Européenne des Migrations Internationales*, Vol. 11, no. 2 (1995), pp. 113-28.

Cortes, G., "Mobilités paysannes et identités territoriales dans les Andes boliviennes". In: J. Bonnemaison *et al.* (eds.), *Les territoires de l'identité*. Coll. Géographie et Culture, Ed. L'Harmattan, 1999.

Dandler, J., B. Anderson, R. León, C. Sage and J. Torrico, "Economía campesina en los valles y serranias de Cochabamba: procesos de diversificacíon y trabajo". CERES, Cochabamba, 1982.

Deheza, G.D., "Estudio socio-económico del area del proyecto Laka Laka". Informe del CIDRE, Mayo, Cochabamba, 1991.

Figueroa, A., "Economía campesina de la sierra del Perú". Pontificia Universidad Católica del Perú, Lima, 1981.

Franqueville, A., "D'un pillage à l'autre, la Bolivie". Institut Français de Recherche Scientifique pour le Développement en Coopération, Paris, 1997.

Franqueville, A., R. Léon, C. La Vega and M. Aguerre, "El consumo alimentario en Bolivia". IDRC, CERES, Orstom, Cochabamba, 1992.

Gonzales de Olarte, E., "Economía de la comunidad campesina". Instituto de Estudios Peruanos, Lima, Perú, 1984.

Goodman, D. and M. Redclift, *From peasant to proletarian: capitalist development and agrarian transition*. New York, 1982.

Guerrero, E., "Ahorro y crédito en San Juan. Estudio de caso". In: A. Zoomers (ed.), *Estrategias campesinas en el surandino de Bolivia. Intervenciones y desarrollo rural en el Norte de Chuquisaca y Potosí*. KIT/CEDLA/CID, La Paz, 1998.

Larson, B., "Colonialismo y transformación agraria en Bolivia. Cochabamba, 1500-1900". La Paz, Ed. CERES/HISBOL, 1992.

Laserna, R., "Constitución y desarrollo regional de Cochabamba". Cochabamba, Ed. CERES, 1982.

Mercado, B.D., J.J. de La Fuente and V.L. Rojas, "Producción y vida rural en las provincias Mizque y Campero (Bolivia)". CEFOIN/IESE, Cochabamba, 1990.

Morlon, P. (ed.), "Comprender la agricultura campesina en los Andes Centrales". Perú, Bolivia. Institut Français d'Etudes Andines, Centro de Estudios Regionales Andinos. Bartolome de Las Casas, Cuzco, Perú, 1996.

Pizarro, R.A., "Los terratenientes de Cochabamba". Cochabamba, CERES/FACES, 1992.

PNUD, "Rapport mondial sur le développement humain". Paris, 1996.

Stavenhagen, R., *Agrarian problems and peasant movements in Latin America*. New York, 1970.

Vargas, S., "La migracíon temporal en la dinámica de la unidad doméstica campesina". In: A. Zoomers (ed.), *Estrategias campesinas en el surandino de Bolivia. Intervenciones y desarrollo rural en el Norte de Chuquisaca y Potosí*. KIT/CEDLA/CID, La Paz, 1998.

Zoomers, A., "Titulando tierras en los Andes bolivianos: las implicaciones de la ley INRA en Chuquisaca y Potosí". In: A. Zoomers (ed.), *Estrategias campesinas en el surandino de Bolivia. Intervenciones y desarrollo rural en el Norte de Chuquisaca y Potosí*. KIT/CEDLA/CID, La Paz, 1998.

5 What's in the land? The multiple meanings of land in a transnationalized Mexican village

Monique Nuijten

Introduction: the multiple meanings of land

This article focuses on the role of land in the forging of social relationships in La Canoa, a village in western Mexico.[1] It shows that the possession of land may have many different roles. Much of the literature has too easily taken for granted the importance of land as an economic means of production. Because of this economic bias, the importance of land for the non-economic domains of life, have often been overlooked. These other roles become especially clear when we study the history of local politics and the transnationalized context in which many households in rural Mexico operate today. In this article, the role of land in three specific fields will be discussed.

First, it is shown how land possession influences relations between different generations in the family, and can unite or disrupt entire families. Subsequently, it is analyzed how land possession influences the relations between landowners and landless villagers, and how this is related to local politics. Finally, it is discussed how land can be important for maintaining a "peasant style of life," especially in a transnationalized community where migration to the US has become prevalent. The article starts with the presentation of an image of life in La Canoa, a village that in 1938 received land to form its own *ejido*.

The village and the construction of a situated community

La Canoa is a small village in the Autlán—El Grullo valley in Jalisco, a predominantly agrarian region. Nine kilometres along the paved road from Autlán to El Grullo, is the exit to La Canoa. A further six kilometres along a dirt road leads to the village. In the rainy season, this road can be in a terrible state. On the way to the village, the dirt road runs alongside the irrigation canals that irrigate part of the *ejido* lands of La Canoa. The dominant crop in this irrigated zone is sugarcane. At a certain point, the road crosses the main canal, leaves the irrigated zone behind, and enters the dry area. Here, the predominant crop is maize, which is cultivated in the rainy season (May to November). During the rest of the year, there are only the leftovers of the maize and cattle grazing. Some fifteen minutes after turning off the main road, the dirt road enters the village and becomes the broad, main street. At this entrance, there is a small chapel, a shop where men can be found drinking and talking, and a wooden bullring. The main street leads to a small central *plaza*, where the *ejido* house is situated, as is a small park with benches. This area is called *el pueblo abajo* (the village below), and is considered to be the rich part of the village because most of the bigger landowners and politically influential families live here. There are certain parts in the *pueblo abajo* where several houses together belong to certain families, such as the Romeros, the Garcías, the Cosíos, the Fábregas, and the Lagos. This is the oldest part of the village. From the *plaza*, two sandy roads continue to the part of the village that is called *el pueblo arriba* (the village higher up). *El pueblo arriba* used to be the poorer part of the village. One of the sandy roads leads to the neighboring villages. On this road there is a big Catholic church, a new building that has never been completely finished. Today, the difference between *el pueblo abajo* and *el pueblo arriba* is less pronounced than in former days. According to villagers, the reason is that many families in the latter have migrated to the US, and so they are no longer poorer than the families in *el pueblo abajo*.

La Canoa has 196 households (approximately 800 inhabitants) and is very much a rural village.[2] From any house, it is possible to walk directly to the fields, the *cerro* (mountainous terrain), and the river. There are a large number of cattle, and in the street there are often herds of cows, on their way to the field or back again to the stalls. Many men ride horses, but this is considered to be more a sign of wealth and leisure than of work. Today, most plowing on the arable land is done by machines. The houses used to have large *corrales*. In these corrales people have their fruit trees, plants, chickens, goats, a pig, and so on. People do not grow their own vegetables, but buy them in the shops in the village. Some fruits and vegetables are freely collected in the commons of the *ejido*.

There are several small shops and one public telephone (in Lupe Medina's store) in the village. At certain hours of the day, people queue up to make their calls. There is little privacy when speaking on the telephone, and thus it is a good place to learn the details of the latest village dramas: as the phone line is often bad, people tend to shout and everybody in the shop can follow the conversation and hear the latest news. This one telephone in the village is very important for the relations of migrants in the US. Around the many small shops in the village, men may gather, buy their liquor, and talk about the latest developments. There are also several bars in the village; rooms with a few tables and chairs. The village has a large school complex for kindergarten, primary school, and secondary school (the lessons are taught via television), a small clinic, and a football field.

Village life is very rich in various kinds of social gatherings. Religion plays an important role in the life of the people. Most villagers belong to the Catholic Church. The many Catholic celebrations during which relations of *compadrazgo* (ritual kinship) are established form the motive for big parties. Any event may be the reason to hold a big party, if the family has money to spend. According to the importance of the event and the wealth of the family, chicken, goat, or pork may be served. Other festive meals are *pozole* and *tamales*.[3] Sometimes a pig is slaughtered, and the participants in the party spend the whole day eating the various parts of the animal. During these festivities, a lot of alcohol is consumed. The favorite drinks are beer and *tequila*, or brandy mixed with soft drinks. Besides these private parties, to which only people from a close circle of friends and relatives are invited, there are numerous public festivities in the village and region.

At the beginning of November, La Canoa celebrates its saint, the Virgin of Guadalupe. Although this saint's official day is December 12th, according to the villagers they have always celebrated it in November, as otherwise their festivities would coincide with the national celebration of the Virgin and then nobody would visit their village. During the twelve days of festivities in honor of the Virgin, they have many activities. A fair is brought to the village, dances are organized in the evenings, and bull riding takes place during the day. The last and most important day of the 12-day celebration is November 12th. On that day, several priests come to the village, the *mariachi* from Autlán plays during the mass, the first communion of several children is celebrated, and then the festivities end with a display of fireworks. The villagers contribute the money for the fireworks, but the wealthy families pay most of it. For the organization of the many activities, a special group is formed which also takes care of collecting money from the villagers. Normally, this group is composed of young people of the village.

Another important event takes place at the end of each year. During the last days of the year and the first days of the new year, bull riding and *rodeos* take place in the village. This is a common form of diversion in rural villages, in which young men try to stay as long as possible on the back of a bull. Besides the achievements of the men on the bull, the men on horseback can show off their ability to lasso the legs or the head of the bull when the bull needs to be caught and taken from the ring. This spectacle takes place in the bullring in the village and is very popular among the villagers. The villagers share the costs of organizing these festivities. The organizers of the bull riding sell tickets to people who want to watch the spectacle, and also sell beer and food. The idea is that if there is any money left over after paying the costs, it is used for village projects. This is why the organizing committee is called the *Junta de mejoras* (committee of improvements), but as one woman remarked: "The only point is that they do not do the *mejoras* anymore. The money stays with the organizers."

There is always a lot of gossiping and talking going on around these events in the village. It is often said that the organizers keep the profits in their own pockets, or that they drink all the beer that is left over. So every year it is said that this time, there will be no bull riding as the people will no longer cooperate. But in the end, it is always organized. Many people say that the bullring discredits the village, and that it is the worst to be found in the surroundings. It is true that it is in a terrible state and many women do not go to the bull riding in La Canoa because one has to make an awkward climb to get onto the boards that serve as seats surrounding the bullring. In 1992, one of the boards broke and a group of people dropped to the ground.

The most important of these village feasts are those of the regional towns of el Grullo and Autlán. The carnival of Autlán is especially well known, and many people come from the US to be part of these festivities. Besides the bull riding, real *corridas* are then organized with famous Mexican *toreros*. During the days of the carnival in Autlán, all offices in the town are closed. These festivities have an important function in the consolidation of friendship bonds, *compadrazgo* relations, and also in the striking of business deals.

As regards the villagers' perceptions of their own village, they never talk with pride about the state of it: they talk in negative terms about the condition of the roads, the *plaza*, and the general filthy state of the village. The villagers always compare La Canoa with other villages, which are much better organized, have a nice *plaza* with flowers and trees, and have paved instead of earth roads. However, what people greatly appreciate about life in La Canoa is the freedom, quietness, and healthy way of life. This is especially valued in comparison with the unhealthy, stressful life in Autlán, the big Mexican cities (Guadalajara and Mexico City), and especially the US. They also appreciate the "natural richness" of the village, in terms of the fruit and vegetables that are out there in the commons, just waiting to be collected.

There have been a large number of serious conflicts within and between families in the village. For example, several murders have influenced relations in the village for decades. There is much resentment about inheritance problems, and there have been several conflicts over land. Some of these conflicts are old, and others are very recent. Many are painful for the people involved, and are not easily talked about.[4] As kinship and ritual kinship are so highly valued, people try to avoid commenting upon conflicts with their next of kin or *compadres*. Hence, the majority of people in the village are connected to each other by long-standing relations of real and fictive kinship, they share histories of violent conflicts, and in their daily life they have to get on with each other.

Much has been written about the internal division, distrust, and conflictive nature of Mexican villages (see the debate between Redfield, 1930, and Lewis, 1951). It has often been argued that *mestizo* villages in particular are riddled with internal conflicts, gossip, and distrust. This is in contrast to Indian communities, which are said to be much more egalitarian and cohesive. The explanation for this difference is often sought in the fact that *ejidos* are "not only of more recent formation but also tend to group together people from a large number of *ranchos*, such that internal ties of kinship tend to be thinner than in the Indian communities and *ejidos*" (Lomnitz, 1992: 178). These theories about the lack of cohesion in *mestizo* villages in comparison to the Indian communities may be criticized for several reasons. First of all, as Ouweneel (1990) points out, the romantic image of the egalitarian Indian community is losing its footing, and being challenged by several authors who show the internal differentiation and unequal distribution of resources in Indian villages. Secondly, a mythical and romanticized view of community underlies these theories. Namely, the view that communities with a long and stable existence are not characterized by division, conflicts, and gossip. However, there is no practical evidence to support this position. Furthermore, the idea that kinship relations reduce conflicts is arbitrary. Barth shows in his study of a Balinese village that "closeness and loyalty also entail control, interference, and disapproval" and are accompanied by gossip and slander (Barth, 1993: 127). Thus, the assumption that kinship is a factor which prevents conflicts and divisions is a doubtful one. La Canoa is a good example of the contrary.

Yet, conflicts and tensions do not mean that there is a lack of "community." All feelings which refer to belonging to certain networks of groups of friends and enemies are part of the construction of situated communities (Appadurai, 1997). The construction of situated communities also implies the marking of distinctions between different social categories and processes of "exclusion and constructions of otherness" (Gupta and Ferguson, 1997: 13). Furthermore, the construction of community is always related to forms of dominance (Sabean, 1984). In the same way as the history of numerous conflicts, the many village festivities strengthen "feelings of belonging." Hence, in La Canoa, the community as an imagined and lived entity to which a large proportion of the feelings and intimate social worlds are related, plays a very important role. This imagined and lived community also remains important in the lives of many migrants who spend most of their time across the border.

Land and the relation between generations

In 1938, the village La Canoa received an endowment grant to enable it to establish its own *ejido* as part of the Mexican land reform. Although the use of *ejido* land was restricted by many rules, the Mexican agrarian law allowed the "individual" possession of *ejido* plots by the *ejidatarios*, and also allowed the *ejidatarios* to choose their own heir. The agrarian law only made the restriction that the *ejido* plot could not be divided and that the agrarian right had to be left to one heir.[5] Since the 1930s, inheritance practices have developed in which several elements play a role. The agrarian law and the bureaucratic rules and procedures obviously influenced the inheritance practices that have developed over the years. However, the inheritance practices can only be really understood by taking into account the strong moral value placed on reciprocal care relations between parents and children, and the fact that land is considered to be individual property and family patrimony at the same time. Inheritance of land is strongly embedded within dense webs of relations within the family.

The custom in the village is that a child who marries, leaves the parental house to establish his or her own household. It is not common for a married couple to stay in the parental house. It is not difficult for the newly weds to find a house to rent or borrow, as many houses in the village are empty. Many marriages in La Canoa take place within the village itself. Even with the migration to the US, many men return to the village to marry their girlfriend and then take her back to the States. If possible, the family of the man helps the young couple to get started and provides a house. Traditionally, the economic support follows the paternal line, and parents will especially support the household of their sons. Property is mostly inherited by one of the sons. However, there are no fixed inheritance rules, and the son or daughter who looks after his or her aged parents until their death develops certain rights to the property, even if that person is a woman.

Parents and children support each other considerably, although no fixed rules can be given and much depends on the position of the specific families and children. Unmarried children contribute to the household economy of their parents. The girls work in the house and the boys work on the land, and if they have jobs, the earnings go to their parents.[6] However, this general rule is applied with great flexibility, and it appeared that in many households it was not so strictly followed. When the children get married, the obligation to contribute to the parents' household diminishes. From this point on, the contribution is more voluntary and is normally more irregular. However, although these mutual support arrangements diminish, if necessary parents and children continue helping each other in different kind of ways.

When the parents grow old, the care relation is reversed and the children become responsible for their parents. They may provide the necessary money, but will also look after them if they cannot live on their own anymore. Many old people prefer to stay on their own, and are visited and looked after by their children and grandchildren in the village. When the parent cannot live on his or her own anymore, he or she chooses to live with one of the children. The child who remains in the parental house longest, usually looks after their parents. So, "whether single or married, young or old, offspring are entitled to affection and help from their parents and are obliged to reciprocate, especially in their parents' old age" (de la Peña, 1984: 211). As many children now live in the US, they often try to convince their parents to come and live with them.

With the growing group of landless in the village, the difference between generations has become more pronounced. For example, only 15% of households with young children possess an *ejido* plot, as opposed to 48% of older households without young children.[7] Many landless people are the sons of *ejidatarios* for whom land was no longer available. That *ejido* land remains in the hands of the older generation is also illustrated by the age composition of the *ejidatarios*: in 1993, 84% of the *ejidatarios* were 51 or older.

The fact that land remains in the hands of the older people means not only that the young families are in a much more difficult economic position, but also that the older generation maintains significant control over the distribution of resources. Parents normally help their children when they need economic support, and this means that they retain a certain amount of control over them. Economic support by *ejidatario* fathers may be accompanied by considerable interference in the life of the children. Another important and delicate issue which plays a significant role in the relation between parents and children, is the inheritance of the *ejido* land.

Ejido land tenure is seen as a form of private property, but also as family patrimony within patriarchally organized families. There is a strong feeling that the "owner" of the land has certain moral obligations to take good care of the land and make sure that it will be there for his or her children. Land and the inheritance of land are used to maintain continuity in the family. Mutual obligations of care between parents and children influence the choice of the heir, and ensure that there is no fixed person in the family with a "natural right" to inherit the land. This makes the inheritance of land a long-lasting process, in which any new development may lead to a change of the heir. Obviously, this gives rise to much tension and many conflicts. As Sabean points out: "Property can focus attention and create expectations, provide opportunities to exhibit skill and character, and establish connections and cooperation or points of resentment and disruption" (Sabean, 1990: 33).[8]

The notion that the land is family patrimony and should be used to maintain and support the various members of the family, means that if it is left to one son, he is often made to promise that he will look after the other brothers and sisters once the parents have passed away. For the same reason, the land is also often passed from the husband to the wife, who can continue looking after the land for the benefit of the whole family. F. and K. von Benda Beckmann talk in this respect of "the social continuity function of inherited property" which "instills a sense of responsibility to guard and maintain the property" (F. and K. von Benda Beckmann, 1998: 18). Inheritance by a wife may be seen as the postponement of the transfer to the next generation (see also Córdova Plaza. In: Volume 1, this series). Often it is not yet clear who will be the most appropriate heir to the land in the future, and then the land can better remain with the longest living partner. At the transfer to the next generation, the land normally returns to a man, as parents prefer a son to inherit the land. Only when there are no sons left in the family, or in special cases, is the land passed to a daughter or a granddaughter. There are, for example, several cases of *ejidatarios* who left the village with the whole family except a daughter. In these cases, the father passed the land to the daughter.

An important element that influences inheritance decisions is that of care and obligation. A son who has looked after his parents until their death will have created certain rights to their land. This sometimes leads to awkward situations between brothers and sisters, who do not want each other to look after their parents too much and thus create rights to the land. In their turn, parents also consider another element of care in their decisions: they often prefer to leave the land to children who really need it, and preferably to those who still live in the village. For example, they may decide to leave the land to the only son who has no job. Alternatively, a son who migrated to the US and declares that he does not intend to come back, may be replaced as heir by a son in the village. All this implies that the choice of heir is not an easy one. It also explains why officially registered heirs are often changed. For example, most of the people who were listed as the heirs of the *ejidatarios* in the register of the RAN (National Agrarian Registry) in 1942, in the end did not inherit the land. The *ejidatario* can change the designated heir whenever he or she wants to.

The fact that so many factors influence inheritance decisions, and that no fixed inheritance pattern exists, is reflected in the inheritances between 1942 and 1993. Although many people tend to give a common rule for inheritance such as: "The custom here is that the youngest son inherits the land," research reveals a great variety of types of inheritance. Between 1942 and 1993, twelve different types of inheritance were found, and 81% of all inheritances were not from father to youngest son (Nuijten, 1998).

Inheritance of land is a sensitive subject, one not often openly discussed within the family. Although there may be a lot of speculation and gossip, it is considered to be a decision of the *ejidatario* himself or herself, and not open to discussion between siblings and their parents. Although inheritance decisions may cause tension, expectations, friction, disappointments, and joy among would-be heirs, we find the same feelings among testators. Many *ejidatarios* have great difficulties in deciding on the heir to their property, and women *ejidatarias* in particular talked to me about their problem in choosing an heir. When I asked people about inheritance customs in La Canoa, many said that the custom was that the youngest son inherits the land, unless he could be described by the phrase *no sirve*. Then another son inherits. "*No sirve*" generally means that the man in question does not work and spends his money on women and alcohol; in other words, he is considered irresponsible. People are afraid that he will sell the land, and thus they choose another heir. The case of Juana Sánchez illustrates this.

Juana Sánchez

Juana is a woman of 73. She inherited five hectares of rainfed land from her husband. She has six sons and three daughters. Four of her sons live in the village. The youngest son, Heriberto, is still living with her in the house; the others are married and have their own house. The most obvious solution would be to leave the land to Heriberto, but he is a drunkard and Juana is afraid that he might sell the land. She has three other sons in the village to whom she could leave the land instead. However, besides the fact that this would cause a conflict with Heriberto, she is faced with another difficult decision: to which of the three brothers—Jaime, Angel, and José—would she leave it? All three have an interest in the land. At the moment, the brothers in the village work their mother's land together with a brother in Autlán. They divide the produce and give a part of it to their mother.

Angel is the son who has been the most successful: he is a teacher and school inspector. His wife is a teacher as well, and they are doing very well. However, Angel also uses his position to support his relatives. For example, he organized a job as a cleaner in a school nearby for Jaime, who had been unemployed for quite some time. He also tried to help Jaime's wife to get a job as a teacher in La Canoa. Angel is also the son who most supports their mother. So, besides being successful, Angel is considered to be the typical good, responsible son and brother. Therefore, Juana put Angel down as the heir to her land. Her wish is that the land will be for Heriberto and that he will till the land, but that Angel will see to it that he does not sell it. As the land will formally be Angel's property, Heriberto will not be able to sell it. However, not everybody is sure that Angel will keep the promises he has made to his mother, namely that Heriberto has the right to till the land. Some of these doubts were expressed in the following conversation between Jaime (Juana's son) and Javier Romero.

Jaime: "My father always wanted Angel to inherit the land, although he's the one who needs it least. I'd like to inherit the land myself, as I need it more than Angel, who's a school inspector and has a wife who works as a teacher as well. We all agreed that Heriberto is the one who has most rights to the land, as he lived with my mother, works the land, and does not have another job. But he's an irresponsible drunkard, and we agreed not to let him inherit the land. Angel is the heir and I'm sure he'll help his brothers."

Javier: "That remains to be seen.... The one who has more, always wants more..."

Juana's case was often mentioned by the people in La Canoa as an example of the difficult situation an *ejidatario* can be in when he or she has to designate the heir to the land. Although most people understand Juana's decision to put Angel down as the heir instead of Heriberto, they are not convinced that it will produce a good outcome. Although there is an informal agreement between Angel and his mother, legally the land will be Angel's when she passes away. These informal agreements do not have any legal value, and in the past there have been many problems with this kind of agreement. In several cases, whole families split up over conflicts concerning the inheritance of land. Furthermore, it means that in the next generation, the land will stay with Angel's children. If Heriberto marries and has children of his own, there is no way the land will ever go to his children. Most *ejidatarios* expect that when Juana dies, serious problems will emerge in this family about the inheritance.

The different principles that guide inheritance practices offer flexibility, but also cause difficulties and tension for *ejidatarios* as well as their children. It is a dream of many *ejidatarios* that their children will work the land together, or at least will all benefit from its produce once they pass away. However, they realize at the same time that this is not a realistic option. Although a son who inherits the land may promise that he will give part of the revenue of the land to his brothers and sisters, one never knows what will happen in the future. People are quick to mention cases in which this type of arrangement did not work out.

In conclusion, in the inheritance practices, ideas concerning the land as family patrimony and mutual care and obligation between parents and children all come together. These notions which guide the inheritance decision can lead to many different outcomes in the ultimate choice of a heir. Family relations are complex and can change over time. In an increasingly transnational context, sometimes contradictory considerations are taken into account in the choice of a heir (trying to get children back to the village through inheritance or, on the contrary, favoring children in the village). The inheritance of an *ejido* plot can be used to stimulate children to return to the village. However, if they make clear that they will not return to the village and will sell the land if necessary, a new heir has to be chosen. However, too, this is not without its problems. Thus, inheritance can be a source of tremendous tension within families, and can strongly influence the relation between different family members. In this way, *ejido* land ownership "marks periods of transition between generations, demarcates areas of competence, and creates bonds of dependence" within the family (Sabean, 1990: 33).

The *ejido* and the creation of different categories of villagers

The possession of *ejido* land has influenced the relation between people in the village, and this has gradually led to the creation of different categories of villagers. In administrative terms, a separation exists between the village La Canoa and the *ejido* La Canoa: the *ejido* is an agrarian institution, which falls under the responsibility of the Ministry of Agrarian Reform, while the village is an administrative unit, under the municipality of Autlán. The *ejido* La Canoa received approximately 400 hectares of arable land—which was divided into individual plots—and 1,800 hectares of common lands, which remained in common use. In the beginning, almost every household received an individual plot of land, but over the years the population in the village grew and today the majority of households in the village are landless. More precisely, 138 of the 196 households in the village now do not have access to an *ejido* plot. On the basis of a similar situation in an *ejido* in Michoacán, Gledhill concluded that "the problem of the countryside is not the problem of the *ejidatarios*, who constitute a relatively privileged minority, but the problems of the landless who remain in the countryside, or move between countryside, city and the US" (Gledhill, 1991: 9).

Since the 1960s, half of the arable land of La Canoa is watered by an irrigation system constructed by the Mexican government. Almost half of the arable land in the Autlán—el Grullo valley is irrigated, and production and economic activities in the region have greatly increased. In the 1960s, a sugarcane refinery was built in the valley and sugarcane is now the dominant crop on the irrigated lands. Since irrigation was introduced, agriculture in the region has acquired a boom-bust character (see van der Zaag, 1992). Changes in agriculture are directly felt in household economies. When agriculture in the region is in crisis, the whole village La Canoa is in crisis, and when agriculture is booming, the entire local economy is booming. During periods of crises, there is a tendency for people to leave the village. However, people from other poorer regions of Mexico often come to look for work. Many of the landless households get their income by working as day laborers in the fields of the landowners. Others manage to get jobs in the sugarcane refinery or in the service sector in Autlán. Women also perform many different activities. Many, for example, prepare meals for sale on Sundays, wash for other people, sew or embroider. Only the women of the poorest families work on the land, for example, during the tomato harvest. Women working in agriculture is seen as a sign of poverty. Migration, especially to the US, is another important source of income.

What struck me from the beginning in La Canoa, was that in the reflections of the local people—*ejidatarios* as well as landless people—land was considered to be one of life's central assets. In these local reflections, land was the only source of wealth, and the lack of land was used to explain the poverty of those without land. Estela Lagos, for example, who comes from a landless family, but is now married to one of the few young *ejidatarios*, said to me: "My mother always says: the people with land are millionaires." However, Estela and her husband were having difficult times, and were certainly not living as millionaires. In contrast, Estela's mother was doing quite well without land. Landless people often reacted with amazement or irritation when I asked if there were any differences between *ejidatarios* and other villagers. It was as though I was asking something very obvious and was blind to what was going on. Cristina, the woman of a poor landless family in the village said to me: "There is a lot of difference between *ejidatarios* and non-*ejidatarios*. *Ejidatarios* have land, they have more money than we have." Cristina still speaks with great indignation about her parents-in-law who had *ejido* land but sold it at the beginning of the 1960s and left for Guadalajara. Cristina (angrily): "And they left their two sons in the village without any land!" Other authors have also described this strong value attached to the possession of land in rural Mexico. Luis González, a well-known Mexican historian, writes that "many consider the rancheros' obsession with possessing land that produces very little and is the source of a thousand quarrels and pains, a foolishness. However, in the rural environment, almost the only way to stand out, to be taken seriously, to become a respectable and respected person, is to be the owner of arable and pastoral lands" (González, 1988: 56, own translation). Although González description refers to rancheros who are private landowners and are not organized in *ejidos*, his characterization of the value attached to land, and even to poor land, also applies to La Canoa.

At first, this glorification of land seems understandable in a region characterized by agriculture and animal husbandry. At a first glance, we could even say that in La Canoa the poor landless households provide the labor for the wealthy landowners. But although many people in the village would agree with this conclusion, the situation is much more complex. Among the *ejidatarios*, there are some big entrepreneurs but also many smallholders who cannot possible live off the land. Without going into a complicated economic discussion of how much land a family would need in order to be able to live off it, a rough indication can be gained from the figures the villagers gave me. Many people told me that in order to maintain a family, one needed at least four hectares of irrigated land or eight hectares of rainfed land. Based on these figures, the majority of *ejidatarios* in La Canoa do not possess enough land to live on. Thus, land is not the only, or the most important, source of income for the *ejidatario* households.

With the exception of some of the bigger entrepreneurs with irrigated land, most households with an *ejido* plot have several sources of income besides the land. Several *ejidatarios* work as day laborers on the land of others, or combine their small plot with other activities, such as running a shop or small business. Many *ejidatarios* also receive money from migration. As Gledhill points out, "the possibility of sustaining a rural household by means of seasonal migration, often supplemented by income remittances by children working elsewhere, was what permitted the eventual resurrection of *ejidal* farming... Migration is therefore a facet of a dialectical process of decomposition and recomposition which has marked the history of the peasantry as a social category" (Gledhill, 1991: 154).

Hence, among the *ejidatarios* there are many people who possess only a very small plot of rainfed land, and who cannot possibly live off it. While it is true that the richest families in the village are *ejidatarios*, it is also true that these days many landless families are richer than their *ejidatario* neighbors. This can primarily be explained by migration to the US, which has reduced the importance of the land as the main factor in socioeconomic differentiation.

Thus, in order to understand the value attached to land, we have to look at the many different meanings attached to the possession of an *ejido* plot. First of all, the possession of an *ejido* plot is related to the agrarian struggle at the beginning of the twentieth century. Several people lost their lives in the fight against the *hacendados* during the period in which *ejidos* were established. The *ejidatarios* like to refer to this period as a dangerous time, during which their fathers and grandfathers heroically fought for the establishment of the *ejido* La Canoa. Hence, the people who possess land today claim that they are directly related to this heroic past, while at the same time they argue that the landless villagers have no relation whatsoever with the agrarian struggle.

Yet, there are other reasons for which the possession of an *ejido* plot is important. When I talked to Aurora García, an *ejidataria* in La Canoa, about the many conflicts over land in the village, she commented: "All this fighting over land, while it doesn't produce very much. But for the people it is important to have land, even if it doesn't produce very much. It's the idea of having something; the security that the land provides." Besides security, the land is also important for the production of maize for home consumption. The production of one's own maize has a strong cultural significance, and is important even for those who have enough income to buy maize. Maize and beans are the central ingredients of meals in the village. Today, beans are mostly bought in the shops, but people try to be at least partly self-supporting in their annual maize consumption. Maize is used to make tortillas, and for festivities it is used to prepare tamales.[9] Households that do not possess land often cultivate some maize in their corral. Hence, land also has a more symbolic value as the provider of the main ingredient of the rural diet.

It will be obvious that the possession of an *ejido* plot provides a certain status. There is a clear social distinction between *ejidatarios* and landless families in the village. Although in middle-class circles of private landowners, or in the cities, people tend to talk in a denigrating way about these smallholder *ejidatarios*, in the village their image is quite different: the *ejidatarios* are the independent and proud people. The richer *ejidatarios* are very aware of their position and feel superior to landless laborers. For example, Lorenzo Romero explained that the sons of *ejidatarios* do not work in the fields: "They pay very little for the work on the land, and the laborers on the land are generally poor people from other regions. They are paid 15 thousand (US\$ 5), whether it is man, woman, or child. In contrast, the *ejidatarios* receive 25 thousand (US\$ 8) a day, and they only work when they want to." However, this quote is more an illustration of Lorenzo's feelings of superiority than a practical rule concerning day laborers. During economic crises, the sons of *ejidatarios*, including Lorenzo's, also have to work as day laborers and for the same salary as others.

Besides the elements mentioned above, which give the possession of an *ejido* plot all kinds of values besides economic ones, being an *ejidatario* also means that one can participate in government programs for the *ejido* sector, such as credit programs, subsidy programs, and so on. Landless families are excluded from most of these programs. Thus, membership of the *ejido* provides access to many different resources. Some *ejidatarios* are also capable of appropriating resources which are meant for the whole village, including the landless families. As a woman of a landless family said after expressing herself very negatively about *ejidatarios*: "The government only helps the people who already have things; government support is directly taken by other people, the poor don't get anything. The government only helps the farmers." This comment illustrates the view of landless people that not only are the *ejidatarios* better off, but they also monopolize other resources and support that may come from outside. As we will see in the next section, several *ejidatarios* did indeed control projects which were meant for the entire village. But there are other fields where the differences between *ejidatarios* and landless villagers come to the fore, for example, the common lands.

Most of the land the *ejido* La Canoa received was common land (i.e., approximately 1,800 hectares, as opposed to 400 hectares of arable land). Unlike the arable land, the agrarian law did not allow the division of the commons into individual plots. All members of the *ejido* had the right to an individual plot of arable land and to the use of the commons. The mountainous commons of La Canoa have always been used for different activities and provide many resources. According to the season, they may be used for collecting fruits *(pitayas, tunas)* and vegetables *(nopales, guamuchiles)*, hunting, gathering firewood, agroforestry, and for herding of cattle. Although officially the commons belonged to the *ejidatarios*, nobody complained if other families collected fruits and vegetables, or hunted on this extensive land. Many landless families were even allowed by the *ejidatarios* to take a part of the commons for a *coamil* (an extensive form of maize cultivation). For the landless families, a *coamil* can make a difference to the household economy: it makes it possible for them to produce their own maize and have some animals, which they feed with the waste from the crop. Many landless families cherish their *coamil*. This also has to be seen in the light of the fact that many landless men are the sons of *ejidatarios*, who did not inherit their father's plot. Hence, the *coamil* is their only remaining link with the land. It is a poor substitute, for they possess the land only as a loan from the *ejido* and are excluded from the *ejido* community. In this way, they are second-rate peasants. Still it makes it possible for them to continue the "peasant way of life", which is very important for most villagers. Although the commons the *ejido* La Canoa received in 1938 were extensive, over the years almost all of the common land has been brought into use. Fifty-seven percent of households in La Canoa do not have access to individual plots or a *coamil*; 13% have access only to a *coamil*.

Although the users of the commons—*ejidatarios* as well as landless families— realize that officially they cannot claim individual rights to specific plots, people who have been working the same *coamil* for many years feel that they have developed certain property rights. As we saw, over the years the pressure on the commons has increased. Now that land in the commons is becoming scarce, many *ejidatarios* have started to openly question the possession of *coamiles* by non-*ejidatarios*. In their turn, the landless people recognize that the *ejido* only lent them the land and remains the "real owner." Yet, they are very angry with what they call the selfish and egoistic attitude of the *ejidatarios*, who are better off and yet are claiming lands that landless families have been working peacefully for many years. However, the non-*ejidatarios* are very careful about expressing these feelings in public, as they realize their position is one of dependence, and that the *ejidatarios* have the legal right to decide. Some groups claim to have more rights to the commons than others, and in this way they use a language of differing rights (see also Volume 1, this series). The *ejidatarios* use a language which is based on the agrarian law, which states that the commons belong to the *ejido* and not to the village. The non-*ejidatarios* use a language of moral rights, and of the principles of social justice propagated during the Mexican revolution, to claim rights to their *coamil*. Hence, around the problems with the commons, different categories in the village are distinguished and different groups organize. These social categories have different interests, and sets of different rights are claimed.[10] In the following section, the distinction between *ejidatarios* and landless families when it comes to the organization of local projects and village politics is discussed.

The role of the *ejido* in the organization of local projects

As explained above, there is an administrative separation between village and *ejido*: the latter falls under the responsibility of the Ministry of Agrarian Reform, while the former falls under the municipality of Autlán. The official administrative term for the village La Canoa is *delegación*. The administrative head of the *delegación* is the *delegado*. He is responsible for village affairs and has two local assistants, who operate as armed police officers at public events and other occasions that may require their intervention. However, the villagers use a different terminology. They talk in terms of the *pueblo* and the *comunidad*. The *delegado* belongs to the *pueblo* (village) and the *comisariado* (*ejido* commissioner) to the *comunidad* (*ejido*). Unlike the *ejido* commissioner who does not receive a salary, the *delegado* receives a small remuneration for this work.

The most important activities of the *delegado* are the organization of local projects, and the coordination of government programs for the village. According to the villagers, another important responsibility (although not an official one) is the organization of the village festivities in November and December. The position of *delegado* is not seen by the villagers as one with much influence, but more one that gives opportunities to line one's own pocket through the administration of government projects. The management of resources and the organization of these projects, always provides room for negotiation and some enrichment.

The *delegado* in La Canoa has always been appointed by the municipality of Autlán. Only on one occasion did the municipality allow the *delegado* be elected by the villagers (the *delegado* of 1986-1988). These appointments are made through PRI (Partido Revolucionario Institucional) party networks. The most influential *ejidatarios* in La Canoa have always had political connections in Autlán, and they decide who will be appointed *delegado* of the village. During the period this research was being carried out, several of the Romero men (Lorenzo, José, Gustavo) were among those who decided on the who would be appointed the village *delegado*: one of their nephews was the police inspector in Autlán, and he made sure that their candidate would be appointed. The interesting thing here is that *ejidatarios* appoint the *delegado*, although the *delegado* represents the whole village and not only the *ejido*. Hence, not only is the practice of appointing the *delegado* the privilege of a small group, it is also a form of control of the village by the *ejido*. This becomes especially clear if we look at the people who have been *delegados* in the village. All the *delegados* since 1946 are listed in the village archive: from 1946 to 1983, all sixteen *delegados* were *ejidatarios*.[11] Only since 1983 have non-*ejidatarios* also been appointed. After four non-*ejidatarios* (one of whom held the post for only a year), in 1992 an *ejidatario* was again appointed. This clearly shows the dominance of the *ejido* in political matters at the local level. The two important public functions at the local level (*ejido* commissioner and *delegado*) were filled by *ejidatarios* even when the majority of the villagers were landless.

However, it is not only by appointing *delegados* that these dominant *ejidatarios* influence village affairs: their political networks in Autlán also make it possible for them to influence village projects, because government projects for the villages are administered by the offices of the municipality in Autlán. For that reason, the contacts villagers have with the PRI networks in the municipality are crucial for gaining access to municipal resources and different kinds of projects. In La Canoa, some influential *ejidatarios* have always maintained these contacts. In this way, these *ejidatarios* brought many government projects to the village. For example, Ricardo García managed to get electricity brought to the village through his contacts with General García Barragán when Ricardo was *ejido* commissioner (1970-1973). The next *ejido* commissioner, Rubén García (1973-1976), also had important political allies in Autlán, and arranged for houses to be built in the village as part of a special government program for poor families. In addition, he got a piped water system built with a subsidy from the government. Lorenzo Romero, in his turn, also maintained good relations with several influential figures in Autlán. In 1980, the mayor of Autlán asked Lorenzo to become *delegado* of La Canoa (1980-1983) and through his good contacts with the mayor, Lorenzo managed to get a nursery and a small clinic built in the village, and arranged for an extra water well to be dug.

Although one might say that the villagers should be pleased to have these well-connected *ejidatarios*, all these projects are surrounded by gossip, scandals, and criticism. The people who organized these projects are criticized for giving houses to friends rather than poor families, for not listening to the needs and wishes of the villagers but deciding on their own what the village needs, and keeping part of the money to line their own pockets. A well-known characteristic of Mexican government projects in rural areas, is that participation by the village itself is demanded in the form of labor or money. This gives rise to yet more negotiations between officials and local organizers. This leads to a situation in La Canoa where many villagers stress that these local leaders have always enriched themselves from these projects, while these men and their children feel frustrated that the villagers have never appreciated the effort they put into developing the village.

However, the *ejido* was also important for village projects for other reasons: the *ejido* provided the necessary land and money. Many of these projects needed a plot of land for the construction of buildings, and required the financial participation of the village. As the *ejido* owned all the land, it was the *ejido* which had to decide on the gift of a plot of land. By renting out the pasture of the commons, the *ejido* also had the possibility of generating money for some of the projects. The *ejidatarios* are very conscious of the fact that the *ejido* provides many services to the landless families: even the football field and the bullring are situated on *ejido* land. Whenever problems arise in the village, the *ejidatarios* are eager to stress that landless families have access to the school (built with *ejido* money and on *ejido* land) and to many other privileges, thanks to the benevolence of the *ejidatarios*.

In this context, one could even argue that the *ejido* meetings have a strong symbolic function. Although no important decisions are taken at these meetings, they make painfully clear who the "insiders" and who the "outsiders" are. These meetings are held in the *ejido* house in the center of the village, and only members of the *ejido* are allowed to attend. They are held with the doors and windows open, and thus can easily be followed by people outside the building. However, although other villagers sometimes hang around the building, they never enter during an *ejido* meeting. On the other hand, the meetings for the village, which are organized by the *delegado*, can be held at different places, sometimes in the open in the center of the village or in the school, and sometimes in the *ejido* house, when it is made explicit to the people that the meeting is meant for the entire village. Thus, the meetings function symbolically to discriminate between the *ejidatarios* and the landless.

Other authors have also written about the phenomenon of the *ejido* dominating the village in local government. Jones points out that although not legally recognized as such, in many municipalities it is the *ejido* which has traditionally functioned as the local government. This means that non-*ejidatarios* depend on *ejidatarios* for access to services which have often been acquired through direct negotiation between the *comisariado* and the appropriate federal agency. Furthermore, the management of these services is often conducted by the *ejido*. This autonomy of the *ejido* often means that both the municipality and the non-*ejidatarios* are excluded from the decision-making process, even when the latter are in the majority (Jones, 1996: 195).

Zendejas and Mummert (1993) describe a case involving a village in Michoacán, in which non-*ejidatarios* participate in the *ejido* structure and in this way constitute broader arenas of local organization, in which landless villagers and *ejidatarios* together participate and struggle to press for roads, piped water, and so on. This situation is different from La Canoa, as some landless villagers improved their position by "using" the *ejido* structure, while in La Canoa landless villagers were kept at a distance by dominant *ejidatarios* who used the *ejido* as a political platform. However, these different cases have in common that the *ejido* structure was central for obtaining village projects via political networks. In this way, the *ejido* has been a central element in the construction of a situated community, and the ownership of *ejido* land was important for its political implications.

However, things are changing—so too, perhaps, is the privileged situation of *ejidatarios* changing. An important factor in this, is that the economic differences between *ejidatarios* and landless people are diminishing and that landless people are less dependent on the *ejidatarios*. In general, the link with the US makes people much less dependent on income from the land and government resources. Although *ejidatarios* are still appointing the *delegado* of La Canoa, since 1983 they have also appointed landless villagers. Furthermore, the influential *ejidatarios* of former times are losing influence in power games in the regional arena.

Hence, the ideology around *ejido* land in the village can best be analyzed in relation to the development of force fields in which villagers and family members with *ejido* land dominate the landless, not so much in material, but more in political and ideological ways. This also explains the bitterness and frustration in the way landless people talk about their poverty and explain this in terms of a lack of land. Landless families feel frustrated not only about not having land, but also because of their second-rate position in the village. The *ejido* means not only access to land, but also political control. The landless families not only had to work as laborers on the land of the *ejidatarios*, but for a long time were also politically dependent on the most powerful of them. It is in this way that the significance of *ejido* land came to be power and wealth: not because all the *ejidatarios* are powerful and wealthy, but because some are wealthy and also manage to control village politics.

Migration, land, and the peasant way of life

In this context, it is interesting to study what happens to the role of land in an increasingly transnationalized context. One might assume that land has become less important in villages where migration to the US has become prevalent. It was already mentioned that migration and the remittances from migrants have reduced the socioeconomic differences between families in La Canoa, and has made land a less important factor in this socioeconomic differentiation. However, the research also showed that land possession can acquire new meanings in a transnationalized context. In these transnationalized settings, in which many people struggle to build livelihoods out of activities at different sides of the US-Mexican border, the possession of *ejido* land can become a central element in the maintenance of a "Mexican peasant identity."

The village La Canoa has always been characterized by the considerable mobility of people. This started before the establishment of the *ejido* and continued afterwards. Migration to the US is not a new phenomenon: the state of Jalisco is characterized by long-standing and extensive migration to the US. Many men from La Canoa went to work in agriculture in the US in the 1940s and 1950s. This was augmented by the *bracero* program (1940-1963), which was introduced by the US in order to get Mexican laborers for the American harvest. In this way, peasant farming in Mexico was combined with wage labor in the US. However, since the 1970s, a new form of migration has developed in which not only the men go to the US, but complete families leave the village. This change in the form of migration in western Mexico has also been documented by other researchers (see Massey *et al.*, 1987).

There is no single pattern of migration, and people often do not know beforehand whether they will ever come back to stay in the village. Migration often starts when one or two sons of the family join relatives in the US. If work goes well, other children may follow and in the end the parents as well. Alternatively, the head of the family may decide to go to the States and leave his wife and children in the village. Sons, and even the whole family, may later follow him. There can, of course, be various reasons behind migration, apart from simple economic ones: it is an escape possibility for people with various types of problem in the village. Drug dealers, people with large debts, and those who have murdered someone in La Canoa, for example, have also left for the US.

An indication of the importance of migration to the US is the fact that, of all people born and registered in La Canoa between 1946 and 1986 and who were still alive in 1993, 23% lived in the village and 31% in the US.[12] Another indication of the extent of migration is the fact that, today, 66 of the 262 houses in the village are empty. Many *ejidatarios* have also left the village. Today, many *ejidatarios* even have their permanent residence outside the village. Of the 97 officially recognized *ejidatarios* of La Canoa, in 1993, 37 lived outside the village.[13] *Ejidatarios* with small plots of rainfed land, as well as those with large irrigated plots, have left the village. Some regularly return to till the land, others rent the land out or leave it to a son or another relative. Most of the *ejidatarios* who live outside the village, still show great interest in their land and would not think of selling it.

Although the migration to *El Norte* has a large impact on the local economy, it is difficult to be precise about the resources coming from the US. The main reason is that remittances fluctuate greatly. Some men in the US are retired, and receive a monthly pension, but such a regular income from the US is rare. Most households have children in the US. However, some children send money while others do not. Furthermore, migrant husbands may regularly send money, and then suddenly stop sending. There may be many reasons for this fluctuation in the flow of money from *El Norte*. Naturally, one obvious reason is the type of work the migrants can find in the US.

When we study how transnationalism works out in the daily lives of members of the family, we find that strong support networks can exist between households in La Canoa and the households of their children in the US. As Long points out, "in many situations confederations of households and wide-ranging interpersonal networks embracing a wide variety of activities and cross-cutting so-called 'rural' and 'urban' contexts, as well as national frontiers, constitute the social fabric upon which livelihoods and commodity flows are woven" (Long, 1997: 11). Rouse (1989) talks about a transnational migrant circuit to refer to the circulation of people, money, and services involved in migration. However, in my view, Rouse too heavily stresses the formation of a "single community spanning a variety of sites on both sides of the border" (Rouse, 1989: 3). It is better to talk about a variety of migrant circuits and transnational settings, instead of speaking in terms of a single community. While some children may maintain their links with the village, others do not cherish these connections and are more involved in the formation of new communities which have little relation to their "home village."

Despite the money arriving from the US, in the village the "peasant" or "*ejidatario* way of life" remains important for a large part of the population. As Kearney describes for the town in Oaxaca, where he did research, the seemingly "traditional" community and corresponding "peasant culture and mentality" were in fact maintained by remittances from migrants. Hence, transnational patterns of production and consumption are supporting an apparently traditional society (Kearney, 1996: 16-17). One of my experiences with one of the oldest *ejidatarios* in La Canoa (Pedro Bautista), fits in well with Kearney's analysis. Pedro Bautista belonged to the small group of the first *ejidatarios* who were still alive. I knew that he was a migrant who traveled between Chicago and La Canoa, but in the village he fitted the image of a real "Mexican *campesino*." He took great interest in *ejido* affairs, and liked to talk about the history of the *ejido* and the difficult times in the past. One day, after we had had a typical "peasant" conversation, he said that he had to return to Chicago as there were problems with his apartments. At first I thought that he must mean the apartments he was looking after as a cleaner or concierge, but then it became clear that he was the owner of an apartment complex in Chicago. This "typical" *campesino* who took so much interest in tilling his *ejido* plot and living in the village, is an entrepreneur in Chicago. This shows that land possession and the relation to identity processes is a complex one in the lives of transnational migrants. Studies of migration have been primarily framed within issues of the development and underdevelopment of rural communities, but we should also pay attention to the other aspects of migration. We have already seen that *ejido* land, or a even a *coamil* in the commons, may be very important in maintaining a peasant identity. Land may also fulfil this role for migrants who earn the largest part of their income in the US. Migration has changed the role and importance of land in the economic and political domains, but it also seems to have made the link between land and the "peasant style of life" more pronounced.

A phenomenon that clearly shows the importance of identity issues around transnational migration and land issues is the return of migrants to the village. Many villagers do not "make it" in the US, and return to La Canoa to see if they can make a living there. Several men from La Canoa who returned from the US, did not manage to make it within the regular disciplinary system. Several are engaged in illegal activities, while others are unable to keep a job. The cases of these men show that although for migrants who "failed" in the US, their "home village" may be their last resort, it is often not the place they would prefer to be. The return of migrant children means that during certain periods, adult children come to depend again on their parents' income and set of sociopolitical relations. In this way, *ejido* land as a source of income, and the *ejido* as the provider of important political networks, remain central factors in the lives of *ejidatarios* and their children. Yet, accepting support from the family also means that the sons have to comply with patriarchal authority again. The profound interdependence within the family, and the strong emphasis on respect and authority in the father-son relationship, easily lead to forms of control which are experienced as stifling (see also Barth, 1993: 130; den Ouden, 1995).

In addition to the difficulty of accepting parental authority again, for some migrants it is also difficult to adapt to the village lifestyle again. As Kearney points out, migrants who are denied naturalization in the US, and also cannot make a living in their homeland, "construct a new identity out of a bricolage of their transnational existence" (Kearney, 1998: 129). These transnational identities can take forms which do not easily fit into rural Mexican village life. A central problem for the men is that they have not been successful in transforming themselves into wage laborers in the US, but are not peasants either. Although the "peasant style of life" is much more relaxed than that of a laborer in the US, a specific discipline also reigns in the village. Rouse (1989) discusses in detail the differences in lifestyles between the rural Mexican village and the US. In the former, there is no sharp distinction between working hours and leisure time, nor between the work place and one's private home. A peasant family in La Canoa defines "fulfillment primarily in terms of the capacity to create and maintain independent, family-run operations, ideally based on land" (Rouse, 1992: 34). Notions such as hard work and honor are central in the village, as are socializing activities that might seem like aspects of leisure in the US, such as hosting and attending parties, and partying with friends (Rouse, 1989: 133). Non-adaptation to village norms by returned migrants can be a serious problem. The return of several less successful migrants to La Canoa made this very clear. In the peasant lifestyle, a man does not stay in bed the whole day relaxing, drinking, and smoking marihuana. This behavior is not appreciated and certainly does not help a man develop the sociopolitical networks which are indispensable in a rural Mexican setting. This difference in lifestyle has also proved to be problematic for sons who have to be prepared to become future *ejidatarios*. Migrant sons sometimes have a long way to go before being the worthy heir to an *ejido* plot.

However, we must be careful not to give the impression that *ejido* land and the peasant identity is highly idealized by all villagers. There are many people, especially among the younger migrants, who do not show much interest in *ejido* land. Yet, this makes it all the more important to recognize that *ejido* land signifies different things to different people, and that land can fulfil many roles besides being an economic means of production.

Conclusion: the multiple significiations of land

In this article, the role of land within different fields of social relations was discussed, based on research carried out in a transnationalized village in western Mexico. Although much of the literature on the *ejido* has focused on the productive aspects of *ejido* land, the possession of such land has functions other than the merely economic. As F. and K. von Benda Beckmann argue, it would be silly "to deny that the production aspect of property in many historic and contemporary situations plays a considerable role in social and economic life," but we also have to recognize the many other roles of property (1998: 15). Property may have functions for social security, for the continuing of social groups, for political positions, or for a socially acceptable fair or equitable distribution of wealth (ibid.: 2). We noted many elements that constitute the value of *ejido* land in La Canoa: the fact that the possession of land is related to the agrarian struggle and establishment of the *ejido*; that it is the provider of maize, the central ingredient of the rural diet; that the *ejido* has been central for local politics, and that it gives one the identity of being an independent peasant. Even migrants who have done well in *El Norte* may still cherish their plot and peasant identity. Hence, when we talk about *ejido* land, we do not refer to one type of resource, but to many different resources according to the situation and people involved. Land possession is an important factor in the shaping of relations in different sociopolitical fields.

More specifically, the role of land in three contexts was discussed. Firstly, in the field of the family in which inheritance of land strongly influences the relation between generations and among siblings. Inheritance practices are strongly embedded within the ideology of the family, as land possession is part of family patrimony within patriarchally organized families. Mutual obligations of care between parents and children influence the choice of the heir, and ensure that there is no fixed person in the family with a "natural right" to inherit the land. This makes the inheritance of land a long-lasting process in which expectations and commitments may be created, as well as resentment and conflicts. Secondly, the role of land was discussed within the context of local politics. It was shown that the *ejido* structure is central to obtaining village projects through political party networks, and that this has aggravated the differences in the village between *ejidatarios* and landless villagers. Besides these village projects which are determined by the *ejidatarios*, the landless families also depend on the *ejido* for their *coamiles* in the commons. These processes explain the frustration of the landless families and the ideology which surrounds *ejido* land, even in a time when land is no longer the most important means of production. In this way, the possession of *ejido* land has been central to the construction of a situated community in which processes of domination went hand in hand with the creation of different categories of villagers. Finally, it was shown how land also plays a role in the field of transnational processes, where land possession may become important for a certain group of migrants who want to maintain a peasant identity as part of their transnational existence.

Notes

[1] The research was carried out during several periods of fieldwork from 1991 to 1994, and was made possible by a grant from the Dutch Organisation for the Advancement of Tropical Research (WOTRO) and by financial support from the Department of Sociology of Rural Development, University Wageningen.

[2] According to the government census of 1990, La Canoa has 837 inhabitants. My own research suggests that this is an overestimate, and that many sons and daughters who live in the US, or elsewhere in Mexico, had been included in the census. In 1993, I counted 690 inhabitants (or approximately 803, including unmarried migrant children).

[3] *Pozole* is a special Mexican dish consisting of a soup of cooked maize with pork. *Tamales* are made of maize dough cooked in maize leaves, and often contain meat or sugar and fruit.

[4] See Nuijten "Memories of the land: local struggles and fragmented histories". In: H. Hermans, D. Papousek and C. Raffi-Beroud (eds.), *México en movimiento: concierto mexicano 1910-1940; repercusión e interpretaciones*. Centro de Estudios Mexicanos, Groningen (1997).

[5] The agrarian law stated that the *ejidatarios* could designate the heir to the agrarian right from amongst their partner and children; if there were no children or partner, the right could be designated to a person who was economically dependent on the *ejidatario*. Article 83 states that if the *ejidatario* has never designated the heir to his/her agrarian right, the right will be given to one of the persons described in Article 81, according to which the agrarian right is considered to be vacant if inheritance in the foregoing way is impossible. In that case, the *ejido* assembly can assign (following certain guidelines) the right to somebody else.

[6] When sons work on the land of their fathers, various arrangements may be used. If it is a poor family, or when there is a general crisis in the village, the boys are not paid for their labor. However, if the family is doing well, the boys may be paid the same money as the other day laborers.

[7] In order to show the distribution of land over households with different care tasks, I distinguished four types of household in La Canoa. 1 = young households with young children, 2 = household with young children and older children who have started working, 3 = household without smaller children, only older children of whom some have left the house, 4 = old couples without children to take care of, and old bachelors.

[8] See also Den Ouden, 1995, for a discussion of the role of inheritance in family enterprises among the Adja in Bénin, where there were no rules of succession and fathers had the difficult task of picking out the sons who were best able to take over from them.

[9] Formerly, the women spent much of their time every day preparing tortillas by hand. Today, many families buy their *tortillas* in the *tortillería* in the village; twice a day, one can see people, especially young children, queuing up at the *tortillería*. Even so, home-made *tortillas* are specially valued, and in some houses only *tortillas* prepared by the women of the house are consumed.

[10] When we look at the agrarian law, we see that in contrast to the parceled land, the individual right to a *coamil* is not legally protected. According to the old agrarian law (pre-1992), the commons cannot be divided into individual plots and nobody can claim individual rights to parts of the commons. The right to the use of the commons is the collective right of all *ejidatarios*. *Ejidatarios* and non-*ejidatarios* are very aware of this rule. However, in the same way as with the parceled land, it is not clear what the role of these rules will be in future conflicts. Although nobody has been removed from the commons so far, as with the arable land, these official rules may play a role in the future. We saw that in the case of the parceled land, the prohibition on selling or renting *ejido* land, influenced the way in which these transactions were organized, but did not prevent the large-scale selling and renting of *ejido* plots.

[11] Several *delegados* stayed on for less than three years.

[12] Before 1946, births in La Canoa were registered in Autlán. Since the end of the 1980s, a growing number of women from La Canoa go to the clinic in Autlán to give birth, and registration again takes place in Autlán. Therefore, I take the period between 1946 and 1986 when births were registered in La Canoa.

[13] In the case of *ejidatarios* who passed away or who sold their plots, the residence of the new owner of the land is used.

References

Appadurai, A., *Modernity at large; cultural dimensions of globalisation*. Minneapolis, University of Minnesota Press, 1997.

Barth, F., *Balinese worlds*. Chicago, University of Chicago Press, 1993.

Benda Beckmann von, F. and K., "A functional analysis of property rights, with special reference to Indonesia", forthcoming.

Córdova Plaza, R., "Gender roles, inheritance patterns, and female access to land in an *ejidal* community in Veracruz, México". In: A. Zoomers and G. van der Haar (eds.), *Current land policy in Latin America: regulating land tenure under neo-liberalism*. KIT/Vervuert, Amsterdam, 2000.

De la Peña, G., "Ideology and practice in Southern Jalisco: peasants, *rancheros*, and urban entrepreneurs". In: R. Smith (ed.), *Kinship ideology and practice in Latin America*. Chapel Hill, University of North Carolina Press, 1984.

Den Ouden, J., "The management of labour in Bénin". *Africa*, Vol. 65, no. 1 (1995), pp. 1-35.

Gledhill, J., *Casi nada; a study of agrarian reform in the homeland of Cardenismo*. Austin, University of Texas Press, 1991.

González, L., "Lugares comunes acerca de lo rural". In: J. Zepeda (ed.), *Las sociedades rurales hoy*. Zamora, el Colegio de Michoacán y CONACYT, 1988.

Gupta, A. and J. Ferguson (eds.), *Anthropological locations; boundaries and grounds of a field science*. Berkeley, Los Angeles, London, University of California Press, 1997.

Jones, G., "Dismantling the *ejido*". In: R. Aitken, N. Craske, G. Jones, and D. Stansfield (eds.), *Dismantling the Mexican state?* London, MacMillan Press, 1996.

Kearney, M., *Reconceptualising the peasantry; anthropology in global perspective*. Boulder, Oxford, Westview Press, 1996.

Lomnitz-Adler, C., *Exits from the labyrinth; culture and ideology in the Mexican national space*. Berkeley, Los Angeles, and Oxford, University of California Press, 1992.

Long, N., "Agency and constraint, perceptions and practices". In: H. de Haan and N. Long (eds.), *Images and realities of rural life*. Assen, van Gorcum, 1997.

Nuijten, M., "Memories of the land: local struggles and fragmented histories". In: H. Hermans, D. Papousek and C. Raffi-Beroud (eds.), *México en movimiento: concierto mexicano 1910-1940; repercusión e interpretaciones*. Centro de Estudios Mexicanos, Groningen, 1997.

Nuijten, M., "In the name of the land: organization, transnationalism, and the culture of the state in a Mexican *ejido*". PhD thesis. Wageningen University, 1998.

Ouweneel, A., "Altepeme and pueblos de Indios: some comparative theoretical perspectives on the analysis of the colonial Indian communities". In: A. Ouweneel and S. Miller (eds.), *Fifteen essays on land tenure, corporate organisations, ideology and village politics*. Amsterdam, CEDLA Latin America Studies, 1990.

Rouse, R., "Mexican migration to the US: family relations in the development of a transnational migrant circuit". PhD dissertation. Department of Anthropology, Stanford University, Stanford, California, 1989.

Rouse, R., "Making sense of settlement: class transformation among Mexican migrants in the US". In: N. Glick, L. Basch and C. Blanc-Szanton (eds.), *Towards a transnational perspective on migration: race, class, ethnicity, and nationalism reconsidered*. New York, New York Academy of Sciences, 1992.

Sabean, D., *Power in the blood: popular culture and village discourse in early modern Germany*. Cambridge, Cambridge University Press, 1984.

Sabean, D., *Property, production, and family in Neckerhausen, 1700-1870*. Cambridge, Cambridge University Press, 1990.

Van der Zaag, P., "Chicanery at the canal: changing practice in irrigation management in Western Mexico". Amsterdam, CEDLA, 1992.

Zendejas, S. and G. Mummert, "Impacts of *ejido* reform in a regional setting of western Michoacán". Unpublished research project prospectus. Zamora, El Colegio de Michoacán, 1993.

6 Institutional flexibility in a transnational community: managing collective natural resources in Mexico[1]

Kirsten Appendini, Raúl García Barrios, and Beatriz G. de la Tejera Hernández

Introduction

The *Zapotec* communities of the Sierra Júarez, Oaxaca, have complex institutional structures rooted in the history of the indigenous populations of rural Mexico and the specificity of ethnic groups.[2] Constituted as *comunidades agrarias* with a collective property regime, under Article 27 of the Mexican Constitution, the *comunidad* is based on the agrarian rights that are recognized for indigenous people in order that they may live in a specific territory and undertake the social, political, cultural, religious, linguistic, and productive practices according to their traditions.[3]

In Oaxaca, communities are entitled to a number of community rights, which are recognized and protected by the government, such as: the freedom to determine and protect the social and political organization, as well as the system of governance with its internal norms, jurisdiction over its territories, access to natural resources, decisions related to training and education, elaboration of development plans, promotion of religious and artistic forms of expression, protection of the cultural common assets, and in general, of all the elements which form the identity of the community and its population.[4]

In this chapter, we discuss how the institutional arrangements governing access to natural resources (cropland, pastures, and forest) and the management of these resources, constitute dynamic processes, which are changing according to the every-day practices of the people in a community of the Sierra Júarez in the highlands of Oaxaca. In particular, we want to see how migration is interwoven with institutional change, and bring up some issues of discussion on what we call institutional flexibility. This refers to two dimensions: a time dimension, i.e., how institutions change over time (in this case, their adaptability to change related to migration), and a spatial dimension, which focuses on the concept of territory and its transformation as a result of the changes in the social space generated by migration. By this, we hope to provide new insights into institutional change and the relations members of the community (*comuneros*) have established with their territorial space and its resources.

The above also leads to the questioning of some approaches in development literature on property rights and resource management that see institutional change as the result of exogenous forces, such as state intervention, market penetration, demographic change, etc., often underlining the disruptive forces of external impacts on resources and their management. In the case of migration, we propose that in the case studied, migration is related to institutional change that has not been disruptive, nor has the organizational capacity of the community been eroded, though the process has not been without tension. Hence, we also briefly refer to issues of cooperation/conflict in collective action concerning resource management. In sum, the argument constructed on institutional change and migration has two main ideas: i) The relations communities establish with other agents are endogenized by the local institutional transformations, and ii) the local institutional context is dynamic and continuously changing.

We chose to approach this study of how institutional arrangements concerning natural resources are being modified within a social space permeated by migration, by performing an analysis of property rights; hence, how the rules of rights and obligations related to the access and management of natural resources are changing in a transnational context, meaning that institutional practices integrate a social space that is defined beyond the communities' physical territory, as we will explain later.

The first section of this chapter is a brief introduction to the community of San Pablo, its social and political organization, and its economy. Next, we look at the property rights and how they have evolved in the community. In the final section, we reflect on the more conceptual issues presented above relating institutional flexibility and its territorial dimension; in this context, we bring up the issue of institutional change and how tension leading to conflict or cooperation has emerged and been dealt with in the community of San Pablo.

The community of San Pablo

San Pablo is a small, indigenous community with fewer than 500 inhabitants, located in the Sierra Norte or Sierra Júarez of the State of Oaxaca in southwestern Mexico.[5] Its legal status is that of *comunidad*, meaning that it is based on collective property and subject to internal rules established by the community itself according to use and customs, which are enforced by the village and community authorities via the various entities of community governance. The political structure of San Pablo (and of indigenous communities in general) is as follows:
- *La Asamblea de Comuneros* (the Community Assembly) and the *Asamblea Municipal* (Municipal Assembly). The highest ranking body is the *Comisariado de Bienes Comunales*, which is in charge of matters related to community property (agricultural lands, pastures, and forest). The *Asamblea Municipal* is in charge of matters of governance, and of maintaining the community infrastructure as well as public order.
- *Cargos* (civil and religious responsibilities). These are the responsibilities of the population to perform certain religious tasks (from the age of 8-9 years), as well as municipal civic duties or *cargos* when reaching legal age.[6] The *cargos* are mandatory, are practiced for a determined period of time, and are alternated among the citizens of the community.
- *El tequio* (compulsory collective work). The performance of collective work, such as the construction and maintenance of public infrastructure, e.g., roads, community buildings, water and drainage systems. The *tequio* is obligatory.
- *El Consejo de Ancianos* (Council of Elders). Composed of men 60 years or older who have performed all the *cargos*.[7]

The economy of San Pablo is based on activities carried out both locally and outside the community, such as agriculture, livestock, forestry, trade, and migration. Land for agriculture is assigned to households in an individual manner by the community assembly. The plots for cropping are defined by the peasants as property *(de propiedad)* or private. The possession of this kind of land is individual according to use and custom, and the plot is inherited. On the household plot, the family grows maize and associated crops like beans *(frijoles)* and *squash* for self-consumption. Cattle raising is an important activity carried out on common pastureland and/or on individual pasture plots. The individual plots are former cropland which has been left fallow and is now used for grazing. These plots *(potreros)* are fenced and considered private.

The forest covers 41.5% (1990) of the area of the community, and is used in a collective manner; the wood is processed in a lumberyard, which is collectively owned by the community.

During the summer-fall of 1998, when part of the field research was carried out, 56% of the population was living outside of the community, and a third of the houses in the village were empty due to migration. This resulted in a shortage of economically active adults, which in turn resulted in the abandonment of former *milpas* (plots cultivated with maize) located on the slopes of the mountains, and the conversion of some of these plots into private pasture plots *(potreros)*.

Migration has also meant that remittances are an important part of household incomes; of the households surveyed in 1998-99, 85% obtained income from migrant remittances.

Migration is not a new phenomena in the community, at least not in Oaxaca. Male migration began in the 1940s and continued in the 1950s. Migratory flows went to the US under the *Programa Bracero;* this was a temporary form of migration. Another migratory flow was that of the women who traveled to Mexico City to work as domestic servants. Since then, the remittance has become a basic component of the income of most households.

In the mid-1960s, migration abroad re-emerged after a downturn at the start of the decade[8], and women also started to migrate to *El Norte*. In this period, temporary male migration to Mexico City in order to join the army began. The construction of new migrant networks to other parts of the country began as well, together with those already being formed with the US.

In the 1980s, labor migration continued; to this was added a new flow of migration for educational purposes to the cities of Oaxaca and Mexico. Labor migration increased in the 1990s, now with strong, established migratory networks, and began to include the migration of all members of the family. Up to now, two kinds of migration can thus be observed: one for the purpose of education with a national destination, the other for the purpose of work with a destination abroad, mainly California.

Migration has thus permeated the economic and social fabric of the community. This has direct and decisive consequences on the decisions peasants make regarding the allocation and management of their physical, human, and social resources, as well as on the institutional practices of governance and the rules and regulation of property rights in the community. Hence, these rules are continuously changing over time; however, the spatial dimension of decision-making is also changing, since absence from the community does not mean exclusion from participation in the institutions of governance and resource management. Due to the fact that migrants are members of the community, and therefore are citizens, they are not exempt from performing the *cargos* that have been conferred on them. This situation has resulted in important changes in the way these obligations are fulfilled. Migration merges with the dynamics of the institutional arrangements in such a way that they go beyond the geographical limits of the community in order to include a national (migration to the cities of Oaxaca and Mexico) and international dimension (migration to California, primarily). It is in this context that we may say that the institutional changes and reconstructions are part of a transnational institutionality.

In order to study the ways in which institutional arrangements have been affected by migration, we may look at the practices concerning property rights, by focusing on the institutional practices by which the inhabitants of San Pablo have access to natural resources, and how these are managed under a land tenure system which, formally, is of collective or communal property.

Property rights and institutional practices in San Pablo

Property rights are defined as a bundle of rights established by individuals in relation to an asset. Ostrom (1998: 5) defines the following five rights:
- Access: the right to enter a defined physical area and enjoy nonsubstractive benefits.
- Withdrawal: the right to obtain resource units or products of a resource system.
- Management: the right to regulate internal use patterns and transform the resource by making improvements.
- Exclusion: the right to determine who will have an access right and how that right may be transferred.
- Alienation: the rights to sell or lease management and exclusion rights.

We will now use the case of San Pablo to examine how this group of rights and the corresponding obligations and sanctions are expressed within the institutional practices related to natural resources, and how these practices have been.

In San Pablo, not all the inhabitants have the right to community resources. This right is defined by being a *comunero* (commoner) or *ciudadano* (citizen). All persons who were born in the community are members of the community, but only men have the right to be a *comunero* or *ciudadano*. This right is acquired when a man reaches legal age (18). The rights and obligations remain in force until *comuneros* reach the age of sixty. Thus a large group is excluded: the women.

Migrants are counted as members of the community because they were born in the community and do not lose their rights due to their absence, as long as they fulfil their obligations. However, there is some flexibility concerning the definition of the rights of migrants. For example, informants gave imprecise information about whether there is a limit to the time a migrant may continue to be a *comunero* when permanently absent. Some informants said that the rule is five years; others simply stated that it is for a limited period of time. But is was clear that despite the fact that *comuneros* frequently are migrants, the right of access to land is not lost. Another example of changing institutional practices is that when migration for education became important in the 1980s, it became a practice that male students were not *comuneros* until they had finished their studies and/or had stated their interest in gaining access to the rights and acquiring the obligations of a *comunero*.

We will now look at how the right of access to resources (cropland, pastures, water, and forest) has been made flexible to accommodate migrants. Cropland is assigned in individual plots, recognized by use and customs by the community. The plot is considered *de facto* as private property and, as we have said, is inherited. Historically, the private usufruct of agricultural plots has been customary. Pastures include common pastureland with collective access as well as the individual grazing plots *(potreros)*, which are considered private. Collective pastures have always existed with private usufruct (private ownership of livestock). As migration increased in the 1980s and there was less pressure on land, agricultural plots were abandoned, particularly on the slopes and in the ravines. These plots were then fenced off by the owners and used to graze cattle; this type of semi-extensive livestock production needs little labor input. Hence, the community recognized the existence of private grazing lands, rather than incorporate fallow lands into common grounds.

The right of subtraction of resources refers mainly to the forest. The forest is a collective resource. The right of subtraction comprehends the extraction of timber wood for self-consumption, lumber to build a house, and the collection of firewood, mushrooms, etc. These rights have always existed, and migrants retain it when they return to the community.

Commercial exploitation of the forest began in the 1950s by a parastatal enterprise, which had the right to exploit the forest through a concession from the Federal government. In the mid-1980s, after a long struggle, the community regained the right to exploit the forest and established a community-managed lumberyard. It is administered by the *Comisariado de Bienes Comunales*, comprising the president, secretary, treasurer, and a *Consejo de Vigilancia* (monitoring council). Each of these positions corresponds to a *cargo*.

At present, not all *comuneros* are interested in working in the forest in order to extract lumber; in fact, during the field work, only sixteen *comuneros* working in pairs were in the forest. For those who do want to participate, the right to exploit the forest is rotated, and turns are decided by lottery. In this way, migrants, even though they have not been excluded formally from the right of subtraction of resources, do not actually practice this right. Even so, they participate in the benefits of the forest, because a great part of the earnings of the forest enterprise have been used for public services enjoyed by all members of the community, as well as for festivities that are for the common enjoyment, and many migrants return for these occasions. The enterprise also hires workers who do not belong to the community.

The right of management of resources is assigned through the *cargo* system. Due to the rotating nature of the *cargos*, often responsibilities are given to persons who migrate or live outside the community. This has resulted in practices that make the performance of obligations more flexible, such as changing the length of the *cargo* or allowing for substitution. For instance, since the 1980s, it has been a common practice, in the case of less important *cargos* or to perform the *tequio*, the person assigned with a *cargo* is allowed to name another person of the community as a substitute to perform the tasks assigned, and it is usual for this person to be paid by the assignee, since the substitute does not have the obligation to perform the *cargo* or *tequio*. The "absent" person to whom the *cargo* was assigned, may intervene in matters related to the duties pertaining to the *cargo* through his substitute, and will practice this right according to the importance of the matter.

In these cases, the community may also call directly on different persons to perform the tasks involved. In this way, women have been hired for certain tasks, giving them a job and a salary. Hence, at the same time that they are excluded as citizens, women have occupied roles destined for *cargos*, obviously without acquiring any rights as *comuneras* or changing their status as members of the community. In the case of the more important *cargos* (such as *Comisariado de Bienes Comunales)*, it is probable that the migrant will return to the community to perform his obligations.

The right of exclusion is established by the rules imposed by the *comuneros* and by precedent cases of sanction which have led to exclusion. In the latter case, if a person does not perform the *cargo* within the established time limit, sanctions may include public exhibition and punishment. A recent example was a case in which a butcher was not granted permission to slaughter cattle in the community, because he had not performed a *cargo* assigned to him. A case of partial exclusion occurred when a group of cattle ranchers were excluded from access to an area of common pasturelands, while another group was not excluded. Hence, common grazing lands were actually divided into two areas, and access to one or the other depended on the rancher group to which one belonged.

The right of alienation refers to the right to take part in the management of resources and/or to transfer that right. As we have mentioned, in the case of individual plots, practices relating to the right of alienation are in fact carried out as though the plots were private property. Hence, land is inherited and can be transferred within the community. There are cases in which plots have been sold to persons who are not members of the community, e.g., indigenous people from other communities who have come to work at the forest enterprise. The community recognizes the alienation of the plots in practice, and the transfer of plots is often due to the migration of *comuneros*.

In conclusion, the construction of property rights, and the manner in which the rights and obligations are practiced, is interwoven with the rights and obligations of the *comuneros* within a context of migration. The examples above show that alternative solutions have been implemented in relation to property rights as well as the *cargo* system; these solutions are aimed at attaining a certain continuity and avoiding ruptures in the institutions which govern the economic life of the community. The main institutional practices influenced by migration are thus:
- Not to lose rights of access, subtraction and management of resources, even if migration occurs.
- Flexibility in the right of alienation and management in order to include immigrants and for migrants to retain this right.
- To hire a person to perform the tasks of a *cargo* with a salary.
- To change the period of time assigned to a *cargo*, for example from full time (during a year and a half) to a rotating system for shorter periods.
- To hire a person to perform a *tequio* on behalf of the person assigned the *tequio*.

Some reflections on the dynamics of institutional practices in San Pablo

We have argued that the institutional practices concerning property rights in San Pablo are embedded in the economic and social processes intertwined with migration. Migration has modified and adjusted institutional practices in such a way that they are inclusive of *comuneros* who are absent from the community. Hence, the institutions related to access and management of resources acquire different dimensions to those generally considered by the acknowledged literature on the management of resources to be under collective or common property regimes.

In the following, we make some reflections on the case of San Pablo concerning the flexibility of institutions and institutional practices, and underline issues we think are important to consider when analyzing the dynamics concerning property rights institutions. These issues concern the concept of territoriality and the changing practices around property rights.

The literature on property rights and the management of collective resources implicitly considers the idea of geographical territoriality, because resources are limited to a physical territory and it is within these boundaries that institutional practices are defined and carried out (Ostrom, 1998; Baland and Platteau, 1996). However, in the case of San Pablo (and in general, the indigenous community of Oaxaca) the concept of territory has changed historically: it has evolved and hence changed the spatial dimension to which resources and property rights refer. We can distinguish three periods in which the territory has been conceived:

- The pre-reform period (before 1864), when human populations were circumscribed by spaces without boundaries or with diffuse limits, defined by the established relations with visible or invisible non-human beings[9] with whom they shared the space and its resources. The appropriation of resources was performed through a balance of different practices concerning these beings, including rituals. Resources were clearly defined and located, but the territory was not; the conquest of other villages implied the direct control of the goods produced by men, but only indirectly and mediated by natural and cosmic forces, with the occupied territories.
- The period of the liberal reform (1864 until the Mexican Revolution); during this period, under the protection of liberal laws, individuals reclaimed private property on areas of immediate usage, such as agricultural plots, grazing lands, and forests near populated areas. Private property deeds were granted to the indigenous people. However, the boundaries with other communities and the property of lands without direct usufruct (forests) continued being diffuse.
- The post-revolutionary period; starting from the 1950s, private property was formally annulled and communal property was established according to Article 27 of the Constitution. However, private rights to the land were still recognized by the community, including possibilities to inherit and alienate land. When the parastatal concessionary companies arrived in the region and started to exploit the forest resources commercially in the 1950s, the demand to define the boundaries of a common territory became imminent. It was not until then that specific authorities *(Comisariado de Bienes Comunales)* were established in order to administer and control a specific territory now identified by its physical limits.

With migration, a social space has been constructed beyond that of territoriality, as migrants to Mexico City and California constructed social relations that intertwined the society of origin and that of their destiny. This process evolved particularly from the 1980s onwards, when the community regained control of the forest resource. In other words, a modified institutional dimension concerning property rights has been constructed or transformed, integrating a social space beyond the limits of the physical territory of the community. Hence, it is a social space in which the institutional dimension acquires transnational dimensions.[10]

In sum, over time, physical space takes different forms when the social space is transformed by the relations that communities establish within themselves, as well as with external agents in accordance with their economic, political, ethical, and religious relations.

In the case of San Pablo, we have shown that the flexibilization of property rights has a spatial dimension, and that it is also historical: it is connected with the relations with external agents as well as the correlation of forces within internal power groups. During the history of the community, several property regimes have existed which have been considered legitimate and have retained a normative importance, such as: the ancient communal property, private property and the modern communal property. Property rights have proved to be quite flexible in responding to the changing conditions of the more general institutions (for example, government structures), to the growing importance of the public forest enterprises in the economic public life, and to the changes in the income strategies (including migration) of the peasant families. We must not forget that these changes are due mainly to the presence of migratory flows, and that they are also related to the diminishing importance of agricultural activities to monetary income, as well as to less demographic pressure on resource.

Up to now, we have presented the process of change as a flow of continuity, but the history of the community shows tension as property regimes are modified and institutional practices change. These tensions are played out in a force field internal and external to the community, and giving way to different dynamic balances as well as to changes in the institutional arrangements. Though we will not go further into the history of the community,[11] we do want to pose some questions that may lead to further reflection on institutional change: when does institutional change reflect flexibility and adaptability, and when does it generate or become a product of social tension or social erosion?

We propose that there is flexibility when the institutional order is transformed together with changes in the superior normative order which gives legitimacy and stability to the above-mentioned institutional order. For this to occur, it is necessary to have living and open traditions.[12] When institutions are transformed and contradict the superior model order and create conflicts, we find institutional erosion and loss of legitimacy.

In the case of San Pedro, both situations were identified. The changes to which we have referred to until now, are of the first kind: the institution of citizenship, which implies rights and obligations, has been adapted to the requirements of the migrants who live in other places. They retain their property rights, political participation, and access to the community benefits as long as they fulfil certain obligations, which have been made flexible in order to permit their adequate performance. These are the cases we have mentioned: absence from community assemblies can be compensated for with small donations to the community, labor for the *tequio* can also be compensated for, etc.

We call institutional changes that create tension and have appeared at various times in the history of San Pablo, compulsive. For instance, several years ago in San Pablo, "private" land was expropriated in order to build a public service (an ecological and tourism project), thanks to the pressures of one of the power groups. Despite the fact that it was possible to obtain the approval in a general assembly, the project has not reached a legitimate consensus. This expropriation was performed within a context of an inner struggle among several groups, and was a part of the damage that one of the groups, at present in power, could inflict on the other group. This caused the emigration of an important number of families, as well as an erosion of the institutions created by migrants in Los Angeles, since the *Asociación de Migrantes* (Immigrants Association) became divided, and two associations were formed, reflecting the rivalry caused in the community.

To determine institutional erosion can be difficult. The creation of the communal property regime of the forest was initially prompted because of pressures from external agents (the revolutionary government, private investors, etc.) and could have conflicted with the former normative property regimes. However, internal cohesion of the community led to the control of the forest resources and the end of the concession to the parastatal enterprise.

Concluding thoughts

As a final reflection, we contest some general ideas on integration and the impact of external forces, and argue that, in the case of indigenous communities such as San Pablo, migration has not been disruptive, but rather has transformed the social and institutional space of the community. This means that the community has constantly re-created its organizational capacity in dynamic ways.

Conventional development literature based on a modernization theory, considers the economic and social change of communities to be the result of external impacts that often have disruptive effects on the livelihoods of the communities. These are often characterized as "autochthonous" or "traditional" in a static focus.

From a conceptual or normative focus, the models of collective resource management have also been elaborated around the idea of traditional societies, understood as "societies….. that are relatively closed to external influences, in particular, to those forces which bring in their wake the market mechanisms, significant and more or less continuous technological change, new sets of values and aspirations centered on consumption and individual development, as well as a centralized state system bent on organizing and regulating economic and social life over a unified national space…." (Baland and Platteau, 1996: 235). Hence, there is the idea of a bounded physical territory and a closed economic and social system. External impacts are seen as disruptive forces on resources and their management, notwithstanding that Baland and Platteau (*idem*) state cases in which the interrelations are complex and go in several directions, and that they recognize that the situation of the majority of rural societies are not isolated and have been exposed to external influences since the colonial period.

Concerning the impact of market integration, Baland and Platteau consider that, as a group or population has other opportunities to obtain income, the individuals will loosen their ties to the local context (by, for example, migrating), this will affect the capacity to undertake collective actions for collective resource management at the community level. Hence, these resources will be affected, and there will be less interaction and collaboration concerning the management of these resources. Also, "Western" influences (e.g., education, culture, etc.) may weaken the traditional patterns of authority and networks of loyalty, which again will have an impact on resource management, since the economy will depend less on these resources.[13] (*Idem*: 281-2).

In the case of the indigenous communities of Oaxaca— and particularly the case we have studied, San Pablo—presents a very different situation. For more than two centuries, San Pablo has been integrated into the national economic life of Mexico: in the nineteenth century, the population traveled all over the country as traders and transporters with mule caravans. A large proportion of the population used to transport regional goods (coffee, eggs, clothes, brown sugar, etc.) from the lowlands of the Gulf of Mexico to the City of Oaxaca. Also, families sent their sons to work as *mocitos* (domestic servants) to the upper-class houses of the City of Oaxaca; young boys would work for food and board in order to be able to study and thus receive a basic education.[14] Thus, a particular kind of migration existed for the purpose of education, and this integrated communities into the national culture and provided them with human capital. These forms of integration took place despite the very difficult physical access to the community, which is located in the deepest part of the ravines and foothills of the Sierra de Juarez.

Forestry and livestock activities have also been integrated into the regional and national markets, and for more than forty years now, the population has been strongly integrated into national and international labor markets. Even though migration has resulted in less pressure on collective resources, it has not meant a withdrawal from either the land or the forest, nor a reduced capacity to organize the management of the community and its resources. The struggle for the appropriation and management of the forest, against external forest companies (in the early 1980s), and the establishment of a community enterprise and its management were performed during periods of intense migration and renewed migratory flows.

What resulted was more than a rupture or withdrawal, as we have shown in former sections, but the transformation of institutional practices in regard to the access and management of resources adopting different mechanisms but always withholding the rights of migrants.

As a final remark, we want to briefly comment on the polemic relation between migration and cooperation, concerning whether the organizational capacity and hence collective action of the community has been eroded by migration, as argued by Baland and Platteau (1996).

In San Pablo, migration has had an impact on the organizational capacity in several ways: even though migration generated higher cooperation costs, it did not generate disruption in the management of resources. There were several reasons for this: on one hand, in the case of the forest, management methods were not dependent on cooperation. That is, the extraction and transformation techniques of resources did not depend on cooperative forms. It is enough to work in pairs, and the extraction of wood for domestic use is carried out individually.

On the other hand, for the non-migrants—i.e., for those who stayed in the community and took part in the process of the struggle for the appropriation of the forest resources—cooperation costs may have been high, but the expectation of higher benefits surpassed the increase of costs, when the organization process fell on a smaller number of individuals.

Thus, and in certain circumstances, when resources do not compensate, or when the characteristics of the resources and their management techniques depend on collective exploitation and management, the disruptive effects of migration can be valid, as Baland and Platteau have stated. But concerning resources whose management does not require collective exploitation, or exploitation by large groups, and/or when the expected benefits of the resource compensate for or exceed the increase of costs, then migration may not have the above-mentioned impacts. What is more, the impacts may be different depending on the activity, even within the same community. In the case of San Pablo, organization for the management of the forest activity was not weakened, although it was in the case of agriculture.

The above-mentioned processes are complex, and even if the migration-cooperation dilemma has been resolved in some cases, this has not been attained without tensions. Both the new forms of cooperation as well as the tensions are dynamic processes that can generate balances and ruptures. At certain times, the tensions could not be resolved in a favorable manner. This was the case already mentioned of the ecological and tourism project, which is a case of an inner conflict that generated a rupture in the organization of the community, when two groups of leaders confronted each other in a conflict concerning the management of the forest enterprise.

In short, in order to understand the changes that migration has created, one needs an approach which analyzes every resource and the practices generated around them, and which can provide a vision of the complexity of the processes (Nuijten, 1998). In San Pablo, the decision-making and the management of resources, etc., have been modified, but without a rupture of the indigenous institutions and without the exclusion of the migrants. Migrants retain their rights and obligations, and the institutional practices have been transformed in such a way as to accommodate the migratory processes. But there have also been processes of institutional erosion that have had repercussions on the migratory processes and on their cooperative forms, as we have observed.

But, why is it that migrants have been able to retain their rights and obligations, and have not withdrawn from the community? Some thoughts on this complex question are related to the idea that the community must be considered within its transnational context. It is a community in which migrants and non-migrants cannot be distinguished, in which some people stay and others leave (and only send remittances to the families who stayed). Migrants are part of all the families of the community: to be a migrant or a non-migrant is not a definitive condition; people are migrants and non-migrants alternatively. Hence, the interest in retaining rights, and in recognizing obligations.

There are practices where the institutional rules and regulations have been made flexible, yet they continue to support both counterparts: the rights and the obligations. In this way, the change of rules seems "fair" to the non-migrants. This may be a way of obtaining general acceptance, not only because any person may become a migrant tomorrow, but also because today, rights and obligations are compensated for.

The notion of space also acquires another dimension when local, national, and international dimensions are fused, creating a *sui generis* institutional social space. In the case of San Pablo, the space in which the natural resources are located is geographically limited, while the practices concerning property rights—such as the obligations and sanctions—have an extra-territorial dimension; the same applies to government structures as well as to the inner structures of the community, which in different ways are related to the whole institutional fabric of a community. As Besserer (1998) puts it, there is a creation of a institutional social space in which a continuous flow of people, goods, information, and decision-making exists, and this constructs one social space based on a community with multiple territorial bases, given the transnational dimensions of the community.

Notes

[1] This work is based on a larger field study carried out by CRIM/UNAM and CRUCO/UACH, in collaboration with the Rural Development Division, FAO, as part of the Program on Rural Household Income Strategies for Poverty Alleviation and the Interaction with the Local Institutional Environment. See also García Barrios *et al.*, 1999. The opinions in this paper are those of the authors and do not necessarily reflect those of FAO.

[2] Oaxaca is characterized by its multiple ethnic population. For the study, communities located in the Sierra de Juárez in which forest areas and the *zapotec* ethnia predominate were chosen. In this paper, we refer to one of the communities studied.

[3] The regime of *comunidad* (communities with collective property) is one of the forms of property regimes known as social property (which includes *ejidos* and *comunidades*). The Mexican Constitution recognizes two forms of land property: small private property and social property.

[4] Some of these rights are stated in the Constitution, which also specifies which reglementary laws will establish the measures, norms, and procedures which guarantee the protection and respect of such social rights.

[5] The name of the community has been changed.

[6] The positions are: *topil*, chief of police (peace officer), mayor *(alcalde)*, secretary of the municipality, *regidor, síndico*, municipal president, etc.

[7] Today the *Consejo* is not very important in San Pablo. Some years ago there was a *Consejo de Caracterizados*, an advisory body of citizens with the best reputation, generally elder men.

[8] The *Programa Bracero* ended in 1964.

[9] People have known and used the forest around their communities, but did not define its limits, and there were no boundaries between the forest of one community and the other. In order to use its resources, people requested the permission of supernatural beings, since they did not consider themselves owners of the forest, but rather were permitted to use it by the divinities they believed in.

[10] The concept of transnational community has been formulated by researchers working on migration from an anthropological perspective (Besserer, 1998; Kearney, 1996; Portes, 1995). By a transnational community we understand "the process by which migrants create and maintain social relations founded on the multiple basis that interrelate the society of origin with that of destiny. We emphasize that many migrants nowadays construct social fields that cut across geographical, cultural and political boundaries... A basic element... is the multiplicity of involvements that migrants support both in their communities as well as in their place of destination" (Basch, Glick, Schiller and Blanz-Szanton, 1994, quoted by Portes, 1995: 6).

[11] See García *et al.*, 1999.

[12] By living and open traditions we mean that the visions of people which have been constructed historically by the evolutionary and rational process of human social life, are open to interests and views that are alien to their own views. These external views may be internalized and legitimized, and incorporated into the rational and emotional structures of the people of the community.

[13] However, the authors also recognize that, awareness of the importance of resources and their adequate management and conservation may be promoted and migrant remittances may contribute to a positive approach *(idem)*.

[14] This was the case of Benito Juarez, the famous Oaxacan liberal reformer who became president of Mexico. For a broader view of the social and economic background of the community, see García *et al.*, 1999.

References

Baland, J.M. and J.P. Platteau, "Halting degradation of natural resources: is there a role for rural communities?" FAO, Rome, 1996.

Besserer, F., "A space of view: transnational spaces and perspectives". Paper presented at the international conference: Transnationalism: an exchange of theoretical perspectives from Latin America, Africanists and Asian anthropology. ICCCR International Conference, University Manchester, UK, May 1998.

García Barrios, R. *et al.*, "Estrategias de ingreso en los hogares rurales para alivio de la pobreza e interacciones con las instituciones locales: caso México". Draft report, CRIM/UNAM/FAO, 1999.

Kearney, M., *Reconceptualizing the peasantry. Anthropology in global perspective*. Oxford, Westview Press, 1996.

Nuijten, M., "Memories of the land: local struggles and fragmented histories". In: H. Hermans, D. Papousek and C. Raffi-Beroud (eds.), *México en movimiento: concierto mexicano 1910-1940; repercusión e interpretaciones*. Centro de Estudios Mexicanos, Groningen, 1997.

Nuijten, M., "In the name of the land: organization, transnationalism, and the culture of the state in a Mexican *ejido*". PhD thesis. Wageningen University, 1998.

Ostrom, E., "Efficiency, sustainability and access under alternative property-rights regimes". Paper prepared for the UNU/WIDER Land reform project conference, Santiago, Chile, April 1998.

Portes, A., "Transnational communities: their emergence and significance in the contemporary world system". Working paper series, # 16, Department of Sociology, John Hopkins University, Baltimore, 1995.

7 Debating property: property relations and the cultural construction of community in Usibamba, Central Andes of Peru

Pieter de Vries and José Manuel Gilvonio

> *"Property not only provides a central focus of negotiations between spouses, but it also marks periods of transition between generations, demarcates areas of competence, and creates bonds of dependence. We must not think of property simply as a set of rules or hard structures, an account, that exhausts analysis. Property can focus attention and create expectations, provide opportunities to exhibit skill and character, and establish connections and cooperation or points of resentment and disruption. The fact that many small dramas repeat stereotypical performances attests to the power of the syntax established by property dynamics. But, like any language, its structure provides endless opportunity for innovation and creativity, its direction was never predetermined and any acquaintance with the variety of rural social forms demonstrates the endless creativity of the active appropriation of circumstance" (Sabean, 1990: 33, 34).*

Introduction

In this paper, it is argued that property and its regulation pertain not only to material subsistence, but may be central to the construction of local identities and the establishment of territorially defined community regimes. The focus is on recent developments and events in the *comunidad* of Usibamba, which is located in the Central Andes of Peru, in order to show that notions and images of community are instrumental in the establishment of such regimes. In doing so, special attention is paid to practices of inclusion/exclusion and forms of social categorization. It is also argued that a variety of actors are involved in the construction of such notions and images; among these actors are intellectuals, administrators, and—last but not least—the *comuneros* themselves. On a conceptual level, the contention is that, rather than adopting a culturalist notion of community, one should inquire into the strategies social actors develop in order to gain access to communal property, and thus acquire the status of *comunero*. This requires an analysis of the livelihood strategies and social careers of situated actors. In developing the argument, the focus is on several critical events, followed by the presentation of a case study of a *comunero* who is struggling to assert his rights to property in order to pursue a political career.

The frustration of not being a *comunero*

Whenever Vicente—a non-*comunero* resident of the *comunidad* (and village) of Usibamba in the Central Highlands of Peru—starts drinking, he begins to complain about the *comuneros*. He accuses them not only of being egoists and reluctant to share, but also—and even worse—of despising and denigrating the non-*comuneros*. As he puts it:

"As a non-comunero, you're worth only half; people don't take you seriously. When you participate in faenas [communal work parties], they only let you do half the work of a comunero. If you fail to show up, the fine is half that of a comunero. In this way, they let you know that you're worth less than a comunero. You then feel like half a man [medio hombre]. Half the duties, half the punishments [medio trabajo, medio castigo]. It's the same treatment that's given to a comunera. As a non-comunero, you're treated like a medio hombre, also comuneras are medio hombres."

In order to contextualize this statement, it is important to explain what a *comunidad* is. In short, it is a form of social organization characterized by corporate control of land and other communal resources, the existence of rules and obligations enforced by communal decision-making bodies and, related to this, forms of reciprocal and communal labor *(faenas)* for the construction and maintenance of roads, irrigation canals, buildings, etc. Membership of the *comunidad* is open to sons and daughters of *comuneros* and to others holding affinal ties to them, provided the *comunidad* agrees. In addition, prospective *comuneros* are required to participate in *faenas* and local organizations, including communal decision-making organizations and service-oriented organizations, such as school, sanitation, and irrigation committees. By taking part in such organizations, *comuneros* build up a record of service to the *comunidad*, by which they become entitled to larger amounts of land during their lifecycle. *Comuneros* can lose their record in case of misbehavior or absence.

Vicente is a proud man, who on the one hand, claims to be lucky and independent. As a skilled master builder with many contacts in the highlands and the jungle lowlands, he has never lacked work. He does not need communal land or cattle to subsist, nor does he think his children would like to become herdsmen on the pastures of Usibamba. He likes to recount that in terms of economic success, as a non-*comunero* he has been more successful than most *comuneros*, and insists that he does not need the *comunidad* in order to live well. However, Vicente has applied several times for land in order to become a *comunero*, always without success. There is no doubt that Vicente is a good villager, although he can become quite nasty when drunk. He has participated in various committees and is known as a good neighbor. Especially his construction skills are much appreciated.

On the other hand, however, Vicente feels frustrated. He feels excluded from the communal decision-making process, while being expected to contribute to all sorts of community activities. By virtue of having lived for so many years in Usibamba, he shares a number of interests, commitments, and duties with *comuneros* who do have access to communal resources. To begin with, the *comunidad* has allotted him an urban plot. He has participated in the school committee and various commissions established to improve living conditions in Usibamba, such as the sanitation, street cleaning, and electrification committees, all of which come under the umbrella of the principal decision-making body of the *comunidad*, the *Asamblea Comunal* (Communal Assembly).

Vicente mostly resents the fact that he is not considered a full member of the *comunidad*, even though he has complied with the new rules introduced by the *comuneros* over the last ten years, as a way of strengthening unity in the face of the terrorists of the Shining Path and the vexations of the military. For Vicente, being a non-*comunero* means being excluded from a series of discussions about the future of the locality, which are conducted at the meetings of the Communal Assembly. At the same time, he has to bear all the consequences of a newly installed disciplinary regime instituted by the same body that, in his view, discriminates against him. These complaints are voiced not only by Vicente, but also by other "local outsiders," such as sons-in-law who have married a *comunero* daughter but are denied access to property in Usibamba.

It can be said, then, that being a non-*comunero* signifies for Vicente much more than the lack of access to communal property: it means not being taken seriously as a man or as a local resident of Usibamba—in other words—having to accept the dominance of the *comuneros* in the various organizations that have been set up to deal with issues that are important to the whole village. And, interestingly, his complaints also reveal that the ideology and language of community is a gendered one, as he suffers most from the equivalencies established by male *comuneros* between male non-*comuneros* and female *comuneras*. Here is a case, then, of someone who wants to become a *comunero* in order not to be excluded from local politics and decision-making, while being independent of *comunidad* resources for his subsistence. Interestingly, Vicente does not make a neat distinction between the village and its interests and the *comunidad* as a property-holding institution.

In order to explain the importance for *Usibambinos* (inhabitants of Usibamba) of being a *comunero*, it is necessary to take a look at the relationship between the *comunidad* and the state as mediated by, on the one hand, the administrative territorial system of which the *comunidad* forms part, and on the other hand, its relationship with the *Sociedad Agrícola de Interés Social* (SAIS, Tupac Amaru State enterprise), a huge pastoral state enterprise formed on a *hacienda* owned by the Cerro de Pasco Mining Company after the land reform of the 1970s (see also Morris, this volume). In addition, the recent history of Usibamba—in particular the role it played in the struggle between the military and the Shining Path guerrilla organization—needs to be examined, as do current attempts by the state to introduce a neo-liberal land privatization scheme.

Usibamba: negotiating the future of the *comunidad*

Usibamba is a highland community (3,700-4,000 m) located in the Mantaro Region of Central Peru. It was recognized as an indigenous community (*comunidad indígena*) in 1939. In 1972, it became a *comunidad campesina* during the land reform implemented by the military regime of President Velasco Alvarado, the principal change being that land under the model of the *comunidad campesina* had to be worked collectively. The village consists of 504 inhabitants, of whom 80 are non-*comuneros*. It is noteworthy that the number of non-*comuneros* has increased steadily during the last decades.

Members of the *comunidad campesina* are the *comuneros activos* (active *comuneros*) and *comuneros pasivos* (or *exonerados*), the latter being retired *comuneros* who are exempted from carrying out a series of communal tasks (such as *faenas*), by means of which the construction and maintenance of roads, irrigation canals, and other rural works is effected. The *comuneros pasivos* retain rights to smaller plots than the *comuneros activos*. The land they return to the *comunidad* is allotted to younger *comuneros*, in principle sons or daughters of *comuneros*, who in this way acquire the status of *comunero activo*, thus becoming active members of the *comunidad*. In addition, there is a third category of villagers in the locality who are not registered as *comuneros*: these are called *no comuneros* or, quite paradoxically, *comuneros no agrícolas* (Vicente is one of them). Their status is ambiguous, as they are not allowed to be part of the decision-making bodies of the *comunidad*. Membership of the *comunidad* is thus predicated on access to *comunidad* land. Of the 424 *comuneros*, 237 are active *comuneros* and 192 passive *comuneros*.

The *comunidad* is governed by the *Asamblea Comunal*, which elects a Communal Directive Board *(Junta Directiva Comunal)*. The latter legislates about access to natural resources, administers justice, and elects from among its members a political representative to send to the provincial government. Administratively, the village of Usibamba is a subdistrict of the District of San José de Quero. It is divided into eight *barrios* (neighborhoods). Each *barrio* has its own Directive Board, which in turn sends a representative to the Directive Board of the *comunidad*. We see thus a close entanglement between the village, as an administrative element of the territorial local government system, and the *Comunidad* of Usibamba, which falls under the law of *Comunidades Campesinas* established by the 1970 land reform. Usibambinos, however, do not make a distinction between the village and the *comunidad*. This explains why the Communal Assembly and the Directive Board function as the main forums representing the interests of both *comuneros* and non-*comunero* villagers vis-à-vis state representatives and other outsiders.

During the last decade, important changes have taken place regarding authority relations within the *comunidad*. A new generation of young *comuneros* has taken over positions on the Directive Board. In the past, only older, experienced *comuneros* were elected to the Board, after having assumed a series of functions, or *cargos*, in various committees (those representing the various neighborhoods of Usibamba, the school committee, etc.). It should be noted that there is a difference between major *cargos*, which are attached to the Directive Board of the *Comunidad* (the positions of treasurer, secretary, and president, and the representatives of the neighborhoods), and lower *cargos*, which involve dealing with village issues by being a member of the school, sanitation, or road construction committee.

Nowadays, however, it is possible for younger *comuneros* to be appointed to the Directive Board without having had to assume a series of lower *cargos*. This severance of the relation between seniority and authority within the *comunidad*, is related to the important role the younger men have played in defending the community against the violence of the Shining Path and the army. This is a common phenomenon throughout the region. These younger generations of *comunidad* leaders agree on the importance of strict rules that ensure a strong commitment to the authority of the *comunidad*. Communal Assemblies and meetings of the Directive Board are regulated by very strict rules regarding who is and who is not allowed to speak, and interventions are highly formal. This internal discipline is the result of experiences with revolutionary labor unions in the mines, where generations of Usibambinos have worked in the past. In addition, high fines—in the local language, *castigos* (punishments)—are imposed on those who do not participate in work parties or do not attend Assembly meetings. Also, *comuneros* engaged in temporary migration have to pay high taxes to compensate for their non-participation in *comunidad faenas* and meetings.

The administrators of the SAIS Tupac Amaru State enterprise, which was created during the land reform, mediate the relationship with the state. The new agrarian structure was designed as follows. On the one hand, *comunidades indígenas* were restructured into *comunidades campesinas*, in which both agricultural land and pastures were held collectively. On the other hand, the large pastoral *haciendas* were converted into state enterprises, the *Sociedades Agrícolas de Interés Social*. Officially, the *comunidades* surrounding the SAIS Tupac Amaru were the owners of the enterprise. The purpose of this restructuring was to eliminate the exploitative relationship between *comunidades* and *haciendas* (in which the former had to provide the latter with labor services), while retaining the potential economies of scale of the *hacienda* landholding. *Comunidades*, according to this scheme, would receive technological and administrative support from the SAIS, while providing labor to create, and benefiting from, the profit made by the SAIS. An important role in this strategy was to be played by the *empresas comunales* (communal enterprises), which are in charge of agricultural and pastoral processing activities.

This modernization model of peasant agriculture under the direction of the SAIS proved to be a failure for reasons that, for lack of space, cannot be discussed here. Moreover, the SAIS associational model has always been regarded with suspicion by the *comunidades*, due to the tendency of the SAIS administrators to reproduce the same authoritarian paternalistic patterns of relations that existed with the *haciendas* in the past. The increased interference of the SAIS in communal affairs has been perceived by Usibambinos as a loss of local autonomy. Furthermore, the situation has been complicated by the violence between the Shining Path and the Peruvian state. Currently, *comuneros* resent the authoritarian attitude of SAIS administrators.

Usibamba, in effect, has been in a remarkably difficult political position during the violent years of war between the Shining Path guerrillas and the Peruvian military. The SAIS Tupac Amaru was one of the four SAISs created after the land reform in the 1970s. Two were destroyed at the end of the 1980s by the Shining Path, who expected to win the support of the *comunidades* by forcing the distribution of SAIS lands among them. The SAIS Tupac Amaru was one of the two that survived. Relations between the villages and the SAIS have been no less difficult than they were with the *hacendados* in the past. The SAIS has been accused by *comuneros* of exploiting their labor and of denying them resources that should belong to them. This mutual distrust has been aptly exploited by the Shining Path, which during the years of violence set out to destroy all the SAISs in the Central Andes with a view to gaining the support and compliance of the *comunidades*. Usibambinos resent the fact that the SAIS directives have never acknowledged the role played by Usibamba in resisting the Shining Path guerrillas, and hence the dissolution of the SAISs.

Usibamba responded to the violence of the Shining Path and the military in a way that was different from that of other villages in the region: whereas the latter migrated *en masse* to the lowlands, Usibamaba decided to discourage such migration by taking away the property rights of those who fled. The Shining Path *guerrilleros* made several incursions into Usibamba. In 1988-89, they staged an attack on the SAIS, during which the sheep-wool processing plant and the store were burnt, and the administrator was killed. Shortly after, accusations were leveled by

SAIS functionaries against *comuneros* of Usibamba of having supported the Shining Path *guerrilleros*. The army then decided to take repressive action against the *comunidad*. Several Usibambinos disappeared after being forced at gunpoint to accompany unidentified members of the secret intelligence service. The army and the SAIS denounced Usibamba as a stronghold of the Shining Path, and this created much anxiety. As one *comunero* told us:

> *"The fact is, we functioned as a barrier against the incursion of the Shining Path into the SAIS, and if it hadn't been for us they would've succeeded in destroying the SAIS, like they did elsewhere. The subversives tried to involve us and put us on their side, but we didn't agree to play their game. On the other hand, the army, incited by the SAIS, started treating us as subversives. Two* comuneros *were detained by the army and never returned. Yet, we showed that we were resisting the subversives, by staying here and forming our own* ronda campesina."*

These events have had strong repercussions on the relationship between the state and the *comunidad* of Usibamba. This is evinced by the latter's reaction to state efforts to introduce a neo-liberal land privatization program in the countryside.

Current developments in property relations

Usibambinos have experienced various types of land tenure over the last 40 years. In 1958, when it was still a *Comunidad Indígena*, lands were parceled out and divided among the individual *comuneros*. In 1972, during the revolutionary regime of Velasco Alvarado, a restructuring took place entailing the collectivization of land tenure under the model of p*ropiedad comunal* and/or *asociativa de la tierra*. As a consequence of the failure of this program, it was decided, in 1989 and later in 1993, to divide the arable land into individual plots. However, arable land cannot be inherited, and when a *comunero* dies, the *Asamblea Comunal* redistributes his/her plots. Recently, the urban plots were privatized.

Currently, there are three forms of communal property: arable plots (irrigated or rainfed) allotted by the *comunidad* to *comuneros* for individual usufruct; communal pastures; and individual urban plots owned by *comunero* and non-*comunero* villagers. The extension of land for cultivation purposes has grown over the years, thanks to the installation of several irrigation canals. In addition, on several occasions in the past, the SAIS has made grants of land to the *comunidad*. A new communal property law—*Proyecto Especial de Titulacion de Tierras y Catastro Rural* (Special Titling and Rural Land Registry Project)—has just come into force. The aim is to achieve the privatization of *comunidad* land by facilitating the issuance of private land titles. However, the law has caused much debate within such communities as Usibamba about the future role of the *comunidad*. Officials of the Ministry of Agriculture, the implementing agency of this law, are trying to entice *comuneros* to privatize the land by offering them the possibility to obtain credit, with land as collateral, and to dispose of the land in the way they want to.

Thus, lately, Usibamba has received from the SAIS 1,117 hectares of land, of which about half is suitable for agriculture. Each villager, whether *comunero* or non-*comunero*, has received one arable plot of one hectare, while the pastures have been granted to the *comunidad*. This runs counter to past practice when all land (pastoral and arable) was granted to the *comunidad*. In a parallel fashion, the Ministry has offered Usibambinos new credits for seeds, fertilizers, and machinery for the lands granted by the SAIS. The reaction of the *comuneros* has been one of suspicion. They fear that this offer is part of a wider program intended to weaken the *comunidad* of Usibamba.

After the twin offers by the SAIS and the Ministry of Agriculture, a Communal Assembly was organized in which the following reactions from *comuneros* were heard: "Why're they helping if they've been claiming all the time that there've been subversives here?" And, as a retired *comunero* put it: "This must involve revenge on the part of the SAIS. Their real intentions have to be revealed. No one gives something for nothing. Not even God does that."

It should be underlined that the distrust expressed by the *comuneros* is not mere resistance to a development program and the modernizing attempts of the SAIS, but is based on the real confusion created by the modalities in which the new lands are going to be distributed, i.e., as *de facto* private property and for the benefit of all villagers, including non-*comuneros*. Does this signify the start of a process of privatizing all *comunidad* lands? The *comunidad* is divided on this issue. However, this is not the only division within the *comunidad*: there is a divide between *comuneros* and non-*comuneros*, and one between the older and the younger *comuneros*. To begin with, the older *comuneros* resent the ease with which the younger *comunero* leaders have been able to take up important positions in the *comunidad* without having had to develop a long record of participation in committees and activities, as in the past. While the young leaders of the Directive Board staunchly defend the collective property of arable and pastoral land, the retired *comuneros* are in favor of individual property rights for at least the arable lands. The point is that the younger leaders consider that, in principle, all descendants of *comuneros* should have access to land provided they fulfil the required obligations of the *comunidad*, i.e., to participate in *faenas*, or to pay a fine and taxes if they are absent. Decisions regarding access to property should, in their view, be taken by the *comunidad* (i.e., the Directive Board) and endorsed by the Assembly. The older retired *comuneros* would like a property regime in which the usufructuaries could choose an heir, thus enhancing the authority of the older generations. The younger *comunero* leaders, in turn, are against the inheritance of property, as it would weaken the solidarity between *comuneros* and thus make the *comunidad* more vulnerable in its relation with the state. In their view, access to property through the *comunidad* is important in order to uphold the regulatory and representative functions of the *comunidad* vis-à-vis the state, while ensuring access to *comunidad* resources to all sons and daughters of *comuneros* who really need it. From this view, state attempts to grant private titles to *comuneros* are seen as an outright assault on the *comunidad* (see also Morris, this volume).

It can be seen here that notions of locality and communal belongingness are closely linked to membership of the *comunidad*, and hence to community property rights. On the basis of this, it is possible to ask a series of questions regarding the *comunidad*'s role in relations/negotiations with the state, with regard to access to land, and its centrality vis-à-vis the different sections of the population. As Sabean puts it, "property is not a relationship between people and things but one between people about things" (Sabean, 1990: 18). Thus, a distance should be maintained from legalistic notions of property or "property regimes", and the various meanings property may acquire for different categories of social actors at different points in their lifecycle should be focused on. It also means inquiring further into the role of notions and practices of community in regulating access to property, in other words, in making effective and legitimating a defined property regime.

Conceptualizing community in the Andes

Usibambinos use the term community in two ways:
- Inside the locality, the use of the discourse of community serves to differentiate specific social categories according to their rights of access to certain types of communal resources. Thus, there is a distinction between *comuneros* and non-*comunero* residents with access to urban property, and a distinction between active and passive *comuneros*
- Outside Usibamba, however, Usibambinos present themselves as inhabitants of Usibamba, hence blurring the distinction between the village and the community.

These local conceptualizations of community are rather different from those manufactured by administrators and intellectuals. Notions of community are negotiated and imagined differently in different contexts. The same applies to the strategic use to which they are put. The following is an examination of how intellectuals and state administrators have conceived of notions of community and communal property.

In an article written in 1980, Yambert sets out to unpack the concept of community and to establish the intimate connection between the conceptualization of community by state authorities and wider projects of nation-state formation. As he argues, "images or conceptions of rural society are not simply reflections of existing arrangements but also play an active role in social change when they guide the behavior of concrete groups of people" (1980: 55). He is interested in "the mutual influences that policy and theory, on the one hand, and social organization, on the other hand, have exerted on each other" (ibid.).

In seeing community as a form of social organization (visualized as one pole of the "community-*hacienda*" model) he discerns a number of constituent characteristics, such as "the existence of a recurring configuration of sociocultural features including Indian ethnicity, corporate control of land and irrigation systems, and strong internal organization that is reinforced by the participation of adult males in hierarchical civil-religious posts and sponsorship of public fiestas" (Yambert, 1980: 56). He also cites other characteristics, such as reciprocal (or even communal) labor on major projects (preparing fields for planting, harvesting crops, building houses), and inwardly directed social relationships based largely on ties of actual or ritual kinship.

What distinguishes him from other fellow Andeanists is that he pays attention to the role of the *comunidad* model in the creation of administrative structures geared to the incorporation of formerly isolated regions and social groups in Peru. Thus, according to the discourse of the state, *comuneros* are assumed to share common diagnostic social and cultural traits and, in consequence, become entitled to a legally specified set of administered privileges and resources. In current jargon, one would talk about the social and administrative construction of the *comunidad*.

Yambert also notes with much perspicacity that these understandings of what is meant by "community" do not exhaust the numerous meanings and implications of the term. For, "[j]ust as the material and ideological commitments of governments to rural communities have varied, so also may it reasonably be hypothesized that the essence of the concept of community has been considerably transformed as it was carried by different social groups in diverse sociohistorical circumstances (1980: 75)." In his analysis, Yambert privileges the state which he sees as playing a key role in the mediation of "the dialectic between thought and reality" (1980: 76) as a central element in attempts by nation-states in the Andean region to expand the size of their participating sectors by incorporating formerly marginal groups into national politics.

Yambert had good reasons to focus on the manipulation of the concept of community by intellectuals, state administrators, and a variety of social groups for political and economic aims when writing at a time when the reformist regime of Velasco Alvarado was engaged in one of the most radical land reform programs of Latin America. Here, however, rather than inquiring into the construction of images of community within wider debates on national integration and state penetration, the focus is on understanding the role of such notions and images in the livelihoods of situated actors; that is, how people interpret and manipulate notions of community, and of communal property, so as to support particular aspirations and commitments (see, on the concept of livelihoods, Long, 1997). Notions and images of community should, therefore, be seen as part of local debates concerning the character and future of the locality; debates in which different kinds of livelihood projects are put forward. The task at hand, then, is to inquire into the multiple ways people use discourses of community, the ways in which meaning is attached to the concept, and the possibility it offers to express aspirations, convey contradictions, and visualize/conceive of various levels and dimensions of social conflict. One way of inquiring into these issues is to examine the social process by which sons and daughters of *comuneros* gain membership of the *comunidad*.

The social process of becoming a *comunero*

In Usibamba, villagers do not become *comuneros* merely by ascription, as is so often assumed in much of the literature. It is not a social identity you are born with. Nor is this social identity the product of unconscious structural relations, as assumed by students of Andean cosmologies. Being a *comunero* is the outcome of a long process of achievement, in which constant proof of ability has to be provided. It implies acquiring skills, establishing strong social connections, participating in a series of committees, commissions, etc., passing through a number of positions, and providing continuous evidence of willingness to participate in communal labor and forms of reciprocal mutual support. Being a *comunero* means choosing a specific set of commitments. And the truth is that many, and now increasingly so, choose not to become a *comunero*.

This is the case of many young men who have been to the American Midwest to work as herdsmen on cattle ranches. This form of transnational migration was introduced by the Cerro de Pasco Company, the former owner of the SAIS holdings. Usibambinos, like other villagers in the Mantaro Valley, have had a long experience with seasonal and temporary migration to the mines. They have also provided labor services to highland *haciendas* where they worked as herdsmen. When labor for sheep ranching in the American Midwest became scarce, the Cerro de Pasco Company was glad enough to use its connections to recruit the necessary field labor.

The upshot has been that Usibambinos have been intensively engaged with this kind of migration for a couple of decades.

Transnational migration has become increasingly important in the livelihoods of a large proportion of families in Usibamba. Recruitment takes place through local networks, in which a good standing of the individual and his family is pivotal. Thus, every family strives to have one son in the US in order to improve its livelihood possibilities. Migration to the US, however, is anything but pleasant for young Usibambinos. The work is hard, but what they dislike most is the loneliness in the American prairies. The benefits, on the other hand, are substantial as the subsistence needs of the migrants are provided for. They might return with savings of US$ 10,000-15,000. A large number of return migrants have invested their savings in a small bus or minibus, many of which circulate throughout the whole region of Altos Cunas (to which Usibamba belongs). Besides investing in transport, migrants invest in commerce or in restaurants, often in lowland villages.

Comuneros who migrate have to pay a yearly sum to the *comunidad* in order to compensate for their absence from work parties and other communal activities. Lately, there have been a number of cases of *comuneros* who have stopped paying their dues to the *comunidad*, and thus have decided to stop being a *comunero* when they return to Usibamba, which means withdrawing from pastoral and agricultural activities on common property land. Also many sons of *comuneros* who decide to migrate to the US reflect extensively about the advantages and disadvantages of becoming a *comunero*. The advantages of having access to communal property do not always outweigh the attendant duties and obligations, especially when other options, such as running a transport or other small-scale business, are available. Arguably, this was already the case in the past when transnational migration was not an option. As is shown by the case of Vicente, Usibambinos in the past have engaged in migration to the jungle and urban areas, as well as in non-agricultural activities in the lowlands, while maintaining residence in Usibamba.

Becoming a *comunero* is the result of hard work and proven skills, rather than being a birthright. Membership of the *comunidad* is predicated on participation in *faenas* and the assumption of a series of *cargos*. Becoming a *comunero* also implies subjection to the authority of the elders. Becoming a *comunero* thus implies entering into a close relationship of dependency with the father, as it is he who has to negotiate with the authorities and see the right moment to propose his son, which is when another *comunero* dies or is dispossessed of his plots. Fathers are always testing the *comunero* vocation of their sons, hence imposing a strict discipline, which for many is difficult to bear. And, as argued, through the regime of the *comunidad* different social categories are created, such as *comuneros no-agrícolas*, and passive and active *comuneros*.

Yet, the *comuneros* of Usibamba have been quite successful in presenting an image of their *comunidad* as united, cohesive, and well organized—so successful, in fact, that many anthropologists consider Usibamba to be a very traditional *comunidad*. One reason why Usibamba is viewed as traditional is its endogamous pattern of marriage choice. Besides deciding to stay and confront both the Shining Path and the military, the *comuneros* of Usibamba decided that sons-in-law would no longer be eligible for *comunidad* land. This decision was based on the limited amount of land available for *comuneros* in the face of increasing demographic pressure. It also led to the strengthening of ties within the *comunidad*.

However, rather than being an index of traditional mechanisms ensuring communal solidarity, these choices were the result of active debate among Usibambinos about how to tackle current problems. It is interesting to note that under conditions and circumstances which according to many scholars are conducive to the disintegration of the *comunidad*, Usibambinos have been able to establish a strategy for survival, by establishing a very strict disciplinary regime which, in fact, has little to do with received academic views about the *comunidad* in the Andes.

The following is a case study of a *comunero* for whom land and membership of the community is important, not so much in order to construct a livelihood as a farmer but in order to pursue a political career. It shows the role that communal forms of regulating access to property play in the construction, and deployment, of a set of notions and practices that constitute a community disciplinary regime.

The case of Pedro Huanuco

Pedro is the only son of a daughter of a *comunero* and a former teacher at the local school of Usibamba. His mother became a *comunera* as an unmarried mother. Having been born out of wedlock was a cause of anxiety for Pedro, as he felt it as a hindrance in his efforts to become a full member of the *comunidad*. Pedro was a talented student. He attended the primary and secondary school in Usibamba, and was one of the few to complete the latter. While young, he started to travel regularly to Lima to visit his father's relatives and help an uncle who had a chicken farm. In Lima, he followed short courses in accountancy and English. At the moment, he is registered at the Technical Institute, where he is studying agronomy. Here the notion of "record" is at work, i.e., the idea that status should be achieved through study and hard work.

Though Pedro has always traveled to Lima to work with his uncle for three months at a time, he has never really considered settling there. Being a son of a *comunera* gives him the right to apply for *comunero* status. In contrast to other young men, Pedro never doubted that he wanted to become a *comunero*. He was registered as a *comunero* in 1994 (at the age of 24), the year that he married. He started out with half a hectare, and had two hectares when the social drama occurred which disqualified him from the *comunidad*.

A social drama

As a young man, Pedro had a love affair with a girl from the neighboring village, but she ended up marrying a *comunero* from her village. Soon after the marriage, her husband left for Wyoming to work as a shepherd. Pedro then met his current wife, Julia, whom he married in 1995. Julia comes from a typical *comunero* family. She is one of the youngest daughters and, being her father's favorite, maintains close relations with him. About half a year later, they realized that she cannot bear a child. They went to the doctor and discovered that she is infertile. For Pedro, having a child was extremely important, as a fatherless *comunero* is considered only half a man. Pedro is more sensitive than Julia to this situation, due to his former condition of medio hombre as the son of a foreigner and unmarried *comunera*. In fact, by having no or few children, few rights can be claimed to communal lands. So they decided to adopt a child, after pressure from Pedro and despite the doubts of Julia.

They first adopted a son, and then a daughter. In highland pastoral areas in the Mantaro region, it is common for an orphan to be adopted by relatives, but rather uncommon for a young couple to adopt a "strange" child (however, it is more common for older people to do so). The fact that Pedro adopted two orphans with the idea of treating them as his natural offspring is viewed as rather strange in Usibamba and not really understood by his wife. The situation led to conflicts between them. Pedro explained the problem as follows:

> "To begin with, like all men, I've always wanted to have a child, but my wife has never been able to give me one, because she's sterile. Given the situation, I twice decided to adopt a child. The first was a boy of seven, but my wife treated him badly, and he sought another family to live with. Then I brought a girl of nine, and my wife treated her badly too, and so she left. As a result, we started to quarrel."

At that time, Pedro was starting his political career in Usibamba. In November 1995, he was elected President of the *Comunidad* of Usibamba, after having been a *comunero* for only four years. As commented, this is an example of a new phenomenon in highland communities, generated by the violence of the last decade: young *comuneros* with little *cargo* experience are elected for major *cargos*, including that of president of the *comunidad*, despite opposition from the elder *comuneros*. Pedro, as a representative of the younger *comuneros*, proposed in 1996 the elaboration of a new statute *(estatuto)*, which would establish three types of major crime/misdemeanor which would lead to disqualification as a *comunero*: acting against communal property, poisoning the rivers, and acts against good habits/mores. The two first were intended to defend the community against the influences of outsiders (such as the Shining Path), the third as a response to the increased incidence of adultery in the community resulting from the migration of shepherds to the US.

One day, he met his former girlfriend in the market of Chaquicocha, and seeing that her husband in Wyoming was not taking care of her, he offered to help her financially. As he put it: "I got connected with this woman because her husband had left her, because he was an irresponsible man who didn't support her. So I decided to help her, and we started again with our love affair, and she became pregnant."

When this love affair, and thus his infidelity, became known, his wife with the help of her family denounced him before the communal authorities and the *Juez de Paz* (Peace Judge). The latter arranged his disqualification as a *comunero* with the Directive Board of the *comunidad*. As Pedro emphasized, this is uncommon, as disqualification demands should be put to the judgement of the whole Assembly, the latter deciding the due course of the process. It is the Assembly which decides whether the misdemeanor merits whole or partial disqualification. In this case, however, the Assembly was obviated and the Judge took the issue into his own hands, deciding that the couple should live apart for three months. Pedro was ordered to leave his house, but he challenged the decision and was permitted to live in a room in the house. The Directive Board decided to take away one and a half hectares, leaving him with just one. What is very important for Pedro, however, is that he was not entirely stripped of his record.

So, Pedro lost one and a half hectares of land, and his house was given to his wife (with the exception of the one room), yet he retained his record and one hectare. His wife and her family then sought to obtain property rights over the house, and she applied for the status of *comunera*.

> *"After my disqualification, my wife immediately tried to become a comunera. Probably in order to get my house and my communal plots, but that could not proceed. I was disqualified at the demand of my father-in-law and my wife. Especially my father-in-law, who had a lot of influence over her. They did this even though they knew that my only source of income was the pastures. I was disqualified from May 20, 1997 until February 20, 1998. I'd been a comunero since 1992 and had obtained two and a half hectares. Sometime later, I was able to regain half a hectare. In total, I kept one and a half hectares of irrigated land. But it was important for me to keep my record, otherwise I would have lost all my property."*

Having been sanctioned by the judge and the Directive Board, and having lost his house and most of his land and being scorned for being an adulterer, he decided to move to Lima, where he worked with his uncle on the chicken farm. After a period of reflection, he decided to continue his struggle in Usibamba. An important reason for returning was that his son was due to be born. Another reason was that the three months of separation ordered by the judge had passed. As Pedro reported:

> *"I remember that I returned for Santiago [the fiesta patronal of Usibamba, on July 25], after three months, and in July and August I was already helping with the construction of the houses of the neighbors, and in September I was working on the inauguration of the canal of Pacha."*

So, how should his decision to return to Usibamba be understood? Pedro is not an unsuccessful migrant: it cannot be said that he had to return for lack of possibilities to integrate himself in Lima. He emphasizes that he went to Lima to reflect on his dire circumstance and develop a strategy for dealing with the problems in Usibamba. He returned for the *Huajiti* (the building of houses), during which he reconstructed and reinforced his social network. The *Huajiti* is a reaffirmation of the status and social position of someone in the locality, and the fact that Pedro was invited is telling, given his disqualification and dispossession.

At a wider level, he sought to be invited to the inauguration of the canal of Pachas, a public event in which social relations are reaffirmed, recognized, and endorsed. This, again, was a stratagem for regaining acceptance by his fellow Usibambinos. In Usibamba, Pedro fought against the attempts of his wife and in-laws to extend the period of separation. He asked the judge to be an intermediary in his attempts to reconcile himself with his wife and her family, and sought contact with his father-in-law, thus setting in motion a process of dispute resolution in which the judge changed role from prosecutor to reconciler. This strategy proved to be a consistent and intelligent one. After regaining a position in the intimate world of Usibamba, reasserting his social and political capital, and thus showing his interest in and ability to again become a "good *comunero*," he set out to restore his marriage and resolve his differences with his father-in-law. These attempts to reinforce his status as a *comunero* foiled the attempts by his wife and in-laws to dispossess him and gain access to his plots. As he put it:

> *"The decision to disqualify me was a contingent one, without any moral basis. I recognize that I did wrong becoming an adulterer and that I deserved to be punished, but this was not the real*

reason for being dispossessed. The issue is that given the lack of land, no one objects to the dispossession of a comunero as everyone is hoping for a new redistribution. For that reason my case was not discussed during the assembly. Thus there is a saying that when there is a struggle for land, people do not respect family relations or friendships."

His relation with his in-laws was also complex, and it changed when they realized that their attempts to dispossess him had been unsuccessful and that their claims for reparation were losing ground. His wife's father then put aside his revengeful intentions and turned into an intermediary. Thus he decided to talk with his daughter, telling her that "it's up to you to decide whether you're going to remake your marriage or aim for a total separation."

At the same time, a process of negotiation ensued, and Pedro sought a *rapprochement* with his wife. However, this was not easy, as she refused to have any contact with him. Pedro attempted to talk to her every day and waited for her outside the house, but she did not give in to his requests. Only after a couple of months was he able to talk to her, force her to accept his excuses, and convince her of his good intentions. As he recounted:

"Though she didn't want to, I insisted, but she shunned me, and I begged and almost cried for her to come back. At first she didn't bother, she didn't even listen, but I went on insisting. When possible I tried to approach her to talk. Once I saw her and I begged her to listen to me for only five minutes in order to tell her of my sufferings. I told her that if after five minutes she didn't understand me, I'd leave her in peace. She agreed to listen and we went to my room, and I started telling her all what I had lived through, and I didn't talk for five minutes but for hours, for all the time she wanted to listen to me."

Julia's father, seeing Pedro's ability to reaffirm and reassert his position in the village, realized that his daughter's chances of becoming a *comunera* had diminished, and so he decided to adopt a more conciliatory position. Yet, certain arrangements had to be reached, such as what to do about Pedro's son. Upon the birth of his son, Pedro had "collected" him and taken him to his mother to care for. Pedro had legally recognized his son and visited him regularly, expressing his hope that he will become a professional as he would have liked to be himself.

After having resolved his domestic problems, and thus dispelling the grounds for being sanctioned for immoral behavior, Pedro set out to seek his reincorporation into the *comunidad*. He strengthened his relations with the young leaders of the *comunidad*, and played an important role in the campaign of the current president of the *comunidad*. He also became active in all kinds of political activities and festivities at the municipal level. Soon after his friend was elected president, he solicited his reincorporation by asking the Directive Board to reconsider his position. The Board decided to reinstate Pedro as a *comunero* and informed the Assembly.

Pedro then resumed his political career. In his effort to prove himself a good *comunero*, his role in negotiations with the SAIS and his contribution to the debate about the privatization were of major importance. Furthermore, he sought to develop alliances with leaders of the various communities and *anexos* that compose the district of San José de Quero. In 1998, his tenacity was rewarded when he was elected mayor of the municipality.

Discussion and conclusions

This case study shows that being a *comunero* is not as easy as so often assumed. It requires commitment, political acumen, and perseverance, especially when facing conflicts over land. Constructing a local identity as a *comunero* requires securing access to land and developing a record of service to the *comunidad*. Pedro chose to invest in such a local identity, as a good *comunero* and a man of honor, despite his marital problems. In the end, he was able to achieve his aim of having a son, while resolving the dispute with his wife and in-laws. For Pedro, being a *comunero* is not merely an issue of securing a material livelihood, nor is it merely an issue of holding to cultural notions of community. For him, it is a condition for being able to pursue a political career. In Usibamba, several livelihood projects can be distinguished. Some *comuneros* combine small-scale enterprise/commerce with pastoral activities, while others engage in migration. For Pedro, being a political leader is central to constructing such a livelihood project.

This case study shows the importance of avoiding restricted definitions of community and property, not merely in terms of access to natural resources or in terms of cultural notions of Andean society, but in terms of engagement in local struggles and debates. As Sabean put it:

> *"What is common in community is not shared values or common understanding so much as the fact that members of a community are engaged in the same argument, the same raisonnement, the same rede, the same discourse, in which alternative strategies, misunderstandings, conflicting goals and values are threshed out. In so far as individuals in a community may all be caught up in different webs of connection to the outside, no one is bounded in his relations by the community, and boundedness is not helpful in describing what community is. What makes community is the discourse" (Sabean, 1984: 29-30).*

Property, likewise, should be conceptualized not merely in terms of rules of access, but as a signifier of social change, modes of categorization, and practices of inclusion/exclusion. Property can also become a means of resisting the interference of powerful outsiders.

Concluding, this article focused on Usibambinos' struggles to defend themselves against the violence of the Shining Path and the Peruvian state, by instituting a locally defined disciplinary community regime. The strengthening of communally mediated mechanisms for regulating access to property was central to the establishment of such a regime. It was also argued that such a regime is effected by the enforcement of strict rules regarding the duties and rights of a *comunero*. A community regime entails the categorization of locals as outsiders and insiders, hence underwriting practices of inclusion/exclusion which are heavily resented by "local outsiders" (Nuijten, 1998). At the same time, being a *comunero* is not an ascribed status—many choose not to become one—and depends on actors' abilities to display skills, commitment, and character. A critical event in the history of the *comunidad* was presented in order to show that the defense of community required resisting attempts by the state to break local solidarity by introducing a logic of privatization in the redistribution of former *hacienda* land to the *comunidad*. A case study of a *comunero* politician was presented in order to show that access to property is not merely an issue securing material subsistence. In the case of Pedro, access to property underlines his commitment to a defined livelihood project and is central to his political aspirations. Discourses of community and debates over property should thus be seen as part of local people's engagement in struggles for constructing livelihoods.

At the same time, it is important to stress the futility of attempts to define a concept of community in terms of a territorially bounded corporate group with clear rules of membership, functions, and organizational structure. Rather, one should look at "discourses of community" in order to analyze the precise practices through which a defined disciplinary regime is negotiated, and local identities are constructed. Notions, images, and discourses of community vary across social categories. In addition, such notions and images are constructed in radically different ways by state authorities and local people. Finally, it is important to realize that these notions, discourses, and images do not represent some objective reality, but denote a realm of experience, struggle, and identity construction.

References

Long, N., "Agency and constraint, perceptions and practices. A theoretical position". In: H. de Haan and N. Long (eds.), *Images and realities of rural life*. Assen, Van Gorkum, 1997.

Nuijten, M., "In the name of the land: organisation, transnationalism, and the culture of the state in a Mexican *ejido*". PhD thesis. Wageningen University, 1998.

Sabean, D., *Power in the blood; popular culture and village discourse in early modern Germany*. Cambridge, Cambridge University Press, 1984.

Sabean, D., *Property, production, and family in Neckerhausen, 1700-1870*. Cambridge, Cambridge University Press, 1990.

Yambert, K.A., "Thought and reality: dialectics of the Andean community". In: B. Orlove and G. Custred (eds.), *Land and power in Latin America: agrarian economies and social processes in the Andes*. New York, Holmes and Meier, 1980.

Part 2

Livelihood and land-use

in a context of land privatization

8 Land reform and technology in Puno, Peru

Arthur Morris[1]

Peru—following a 25-year experiment in the area of socialized agriculture along the lines of the Yugoslav model of large community organizations—has moved on to the capitalist and neo-liberal model of individual farmers, with individual private holdings. Various evaluations have been made of the previous reforms, and it is now possible to make initial reviews of the current regime and its relation to agricultural progress.

The critical surveys made of previous Latin American agrarian reforms, such as those by Thiesenhusen (1989) and Dorner (1992), focus preeminently on the turbulent processes of reform, the incomplete nature of reforms in most countries of the region, and the production results. The present chapter, however, focuses on the old problem of tension between the forces of modernization and those of tradition. Reform in the 1960s, in Peru, was oriented toward the retention of the Andean tradition of community, while seeking economies of scale and the elimination of *latifundistas*. Today, the economic power of individual farmers is paramount, and community is regarded as a secondary concern for the government.

A case will be made in this paper that the new structures are capable of success, that they are actively supported by the majority of farmers, and that they do not necessarily mean the destruction of communities. To make this case, the positive and negative critiques will be reviewed at a general level, followed by an examination of the 30-year history of Peruvian agrarian reform, with a case study of an area in Puno Department, north of the city of Puno by Lake Titicaca.

Peruvian reforms

To go back first to the pre-reform period, in the years 1890 to 1920 (Orlove, 1980), Puno became a region of massive sheep ranches whose main function was the production of wool for export markets and for those of Peru itself. This expansion of *haciendas* took place far later than in most of Latin America, or even most of Peru, where it had been typical of the colonial period (Matos Mar, 1976), but the Puno expansion was like those elsewhere in the country, being an expansion made partly through the violent taking of land from Indian communities. At the beginning of the twenty-first century, this land theft is still strong in the memories of families and groups in this region of the southern *Sierra*, whose grandparents lost land to the great estates. In the second half of the 1900s, when the possibility of reform emerged, this area proved to be one of the most actively resistant to landowners linked with efforts to force change.

In the 1960s, the Belaunde government made a first response to unrest in rural regions of the *Sierra*, especially in the La Convencion valley north of Cuzco (Fioravanti, 1976), by declaring (Law 15,037 of 1964) a total of 38 *haciendas* in Puno subject to reform. This limited, timid effort at reform was followed, under the military government of Velasco which assumed power in 1968, by a massive and fairly complete reform (Decree Law 17,716) affecting 1,451 properties in the department, and over two million hectares of farmland.

This reform placed half the Puno reform area, some one million hectares, into SAIS *(Sociedades Agrícolas de Interés Social)*, i.e., giant land units which agglutinated both the *haciendas* and the ring of dependent Indian communities around them, to form an economic unit which, in theory, would be self-sufficient for labor and operate as an integrated whole. Other large units, effectively forms of producer cooperatives—the CAPs and EPS—made up nearly two million hectares divided over 42 huge pseudo-cooperative land holdings. It is now generally accepted that for Puno, as for most of Peru (Caballero and Alvarez, 1980), a major fault of this reform and the resulting land holdings was the failure to recognize most of the *comunidades campesinas*, which numbered 486 in 1969, and the over 500 *parcialidades* which were peasant groupings on the *hacienda*, giving land to only 76 of them, and an area of only 58,500 hectares. The reform failed to make any recognition of the major losses from the 1890-1920 period, losses that were still resented and led to active claims and to irredentist attitudes in the *campesino* mind.

As a result, there were renewed land invasions, starting in December 1985 and rumbling along over a two-year period. Under the government of Alan Garcia, in February 1986 a new special presidential decree ordered the "Restructuring" of the great SAIS as well as of the other corporate land holdings in Puno. Continued unrest up to June 1987 ensured a radical restructuring process. A total of 1.01 million hectares were "restructured" (effectively, handed back to the communities) at this time, still leaving 729,000 hectares in the great holdings.

Following the restructuring, many of the communities which were beneficiaries began working the land as individual holdings. This *de facto* situation was recognized by subsequent legislation, in Laws 24,656 and 24,657 of 1987, and Presidential Decrees (PD) 008-91, 004-92, and then supported actively with the Ley de Tierras of 1995, No. 26505, and the PD 011-97, which finally spelled out the mechanisms for forming individual lots from communal land. The neo-liberal model had finally been applied to Peruvian farmland.

Critiques

Negative critique

There are various kinds of critique which can be applied to this 1990s process of final reform, or in some views, counter-reform. We may begin by rehearsing the negative criticisms. In Peru itself, it is held that the privatization of land has been more applicable to the *Costa* and not to the *Sierra*. Lands of the *Costa* are already in use for commercial, market-oriented agriculture, and have not, in recent times, been organized in a community fashion, so that private holding is most appropriate. In the *Sierra*, division into parcels may break up communities, as individual farmers adopt different production strategies and rely less on their neighbors. Because a market economy has not been fully established in the *Sierra*, a few farmers with money are able to expand rapidly at the expense of others, and an inequitable farm holding system, and social structure, will be reinstated in the region (Mayer and Cadena, 1989).

In other countries, such as Mexico, there is evidence that increasing private control of land leads to polarization between rich landowners and poor people who are landless or have very little land (Gerritsen and Forster, this volume). Counter-reform measures are only partially responsible for this change, and other factors include the greater support being given at national level for livestock and declining support for maize farmers; however, the liberalization movement away from the *ejido* has been a major factor.

At the social level, the breakup of community life is criticized, since many farm families are unable to survive and have to leave their lands and migrate to the city. This leaves mostly the old and the infirm to look after the land and to keep the community together. The retention of communities may also be linked to the retention of traditional culture, which is lost as the community itself loses its coherence (Kervyn, 1992)

At an economic level, the economies of scale and flexibility of the large group are lost, so that major tasks—such as harvesting, land and water engineering works, and transport services—cannot readily be undertaken. Access to markets and credit is lost, because of the lower levels of information, lower creditworthiness, and lesser availability of means of transport, for the individual as compared to the large group.[2]

Finally, at a physical, resource level, the criticism is that the large, differentiated resource pool of the community is lost, and the individual family is exposed to greater risk of total failure and loss of crops and products. Traditional communities, as is clearly visible on the *altiplano*, chose to locate villages at the break of slope between plain and hills, with access to lands in both zones. The *pampas* or plains land is used for occasional crops of bitter potatoes, *quinua* or *cañihua*, and for grazing, the slope land is used for other crops, such as beans, barley, and sweet potatoes. These communities often also had access to marsh lands around the lake with the possibility of using water resources (reeds, fish), the whole making a rounded resource system. Just as the traditional community provided flexibility and varied human resources, so the physical environment provided flexibility of resources to reduce the risk of droughts, frosts, and floods, all major problems in the *altiplano*. Individual farmers could not hope for this flexibility, and cannot locate their farms so as to combine resources.

In addition, individual holding is said to be responsible for overcultivation of the land and for initiating soil erosion, since the communal restraint through rotations and rest years is lost (Orlove, Godoy and Morlon, 1992). This may be true at least in an early stage, before farmers begin to abandon the land as insufficient for their support. Elsewhere in this volume (Gerritsen and Forster) there is commentary on the threat to conservation of a biosphere reserve through the appropriation of land by private livestock farmers in Mexico (see also Volume 1, this series).

Positive critique

Countering the negative points made above, a general, positive point is that, regardless of governmental policy, there has been what may be termed a "modernization of thought" amongst the farming peoples of the *Sierra*. In all probability, the 1969 land reform was already too late to capture the community idea in Peru, and thus it was doomed to failure. At the time of the reform, it is probable that much of the land was actually transferred to individuals rather than to groups, especially in the case of the *Grupos Campesinos* who received 15% of the reform land, in standardized areas (i.e., making allowances for the different capabilities of good and bad lands) (Caballero and Alvarez, 1980, p. 27). But certainly by the 1980s, individual land holding was accepted as desirable. Today, most *campesinos* do support the splitting of lands into private lots, whether because they are keen to work the land more fully and successfully than they could in community, or because they wish to leave the community and sell out. The primary evidence for acceptance is the fact that there have been no riots against the process of *parcelación*, in any area of Peru. Thus, quite apart from technical, environmental, or economic arguments, the attitude of people is in favor of the process now underway.

Countering the specific negative criticisms above, in order, the matter of *Costa* farming being more capitalistic, versus *Sierra* farming being subsistence and community oriented, is a factual commentary. On the other hand, the trend is inevitably toward the formation of a capital-based economic system, as indicated in the previous paragraph, and this is affecting the *Sierra* as well as the coastal region. The new legislation does not counter this trend. In regard to the matter of breakup of community, and migration to cities, this is not a process confined to Peru, and has been widespread in the less developed countries. It is not finished as a process even in France and Spain. Current land reform in Peru may have accelerated the process in that country, but can hardly be accused of causing it. Mayer and Cadena (1989) make a useful distinction between land tenure in the strict legal sense, and a broad social understanding of tenure—where rights to land-use, for specific types of product, are common and separate from legal ownership of the land—in the Central Andes. Communal land ownership has sometimes been misunderstood by legislators, who have created tenure forms giving all rights to the community, when in fact individual families have always been involved in a dialectic with communities in seeking to maintain a balance between the interests of both.

Another negative criticism above concerned the loss of flexibility and diversity in peasant economies. To some extent, this argument is valid, but every farmer, and every economic producer everywhere, must choose between specialization—with its attendant risks, but also its possibilities of great success—and diversification, which ensures survival but not economic success. For modern producers the world over, these specialization risks are countered by capital accumulation and investment with which to overcome difficult years or difficult markets. In other words, flexibility and diversity are not absolute values, but must be compared to other values.

It may also be posited that some flexibility can be retained amongst farmers in a Latin American rural society, despite the breakup of the communal land units. Purpose-made groupings are possible, of groups of families or producers, to buy inputs, to market goods, to get credit from banks, to manage tractors and other machinery. In traditional society, the community or village is all-important, and acts as an integument enclosing the economy. In modern society, however, the economy is independent, and forms its own groupings as needed.

In one way, the counter-reform and transition to private holdings is actually needed to help flexibility for some producers, who combine off-farm work with their land to have different sources of income. This is the case noted, for example by Ruben, Rodríguez, and Cortez (this volume) in Central America. In Bolivia, pluri-activity including farming alongside other work has a long tradition which is still being maintained (Cortes, this volume).

There are two areas of comment in regard to the physical environment and changing tenure. First, flexibility is possible even for small individual farms, at the physical level, because family and friendship networks can provide access to different ecological niches when needed, and exchange systems between families in different environments can also replace the self-sufficiency of the old community territory with its varied environments. Another feature, which comes as a result of the use of Napoleonic inheritance legislation and the continuous subdivision of lands between inheritors, is the ownership by one family of many different plots of land, some of them located in different areas with their own special aptitudes. This subdivision is usually presented as a problem, and in extreme cases it obviously is (Morlon, 1992), but it also has the advantage of dispersal of risk.

A second point is in regard to environmental deterioration. There is no clear indication to date that individual farming has created any more soil erosion or other kinds of deterioration, than communal farming to date, in the countries of the Central Andes. Small pockets of pressure have been seen where too many new farmers have been given too small an area of land, but there is no overall pattern (Preston, 1997; Zimmerer, 1993)

Peru and the Department of Puno

As mentioned above, *parcelación* has been generally well received by farmers in Peru. The public register offices have not recorded most of the transitions to individual farming, as inscription of individual parcels, but this is because of the costs and difficulties of finding lawyers, notaries, land surveyors, and other specialists involved in the correct definition and description of the parcels. All Peru stands out in the degree to which it had supported the nativist, traditional idea of community, from the 1930s *Apristas* onward, and in this respect Peru is, or has been, more community-oriented than Ecuador or Bolivia, its Central Andean comparators to the north and south.

The situation is, however, always complex, as in each department the pre-reform circumstances were different and the function of a standard reform procedure has varied. The focus of this chapter is Puno Department, where the dominant pre-reform figure was the great *hacienda* exporting wool through Arequipa. Puno and the *altiplano* around Lake Titicaca stand at 3,800 to 4,000 meters above sea level, which means a unique farming environment, including large diurnal temperature range and night-time frosts, as well as droughts and floods associated with *El Niño* events. Despite the risks imposed by nature, these lands are capable of intensive arable agriculture if properly managed. From colonial times onward, however, an extensive ranching economy was imposed by the Spanish, and retained thereafter by the Peruvian Republic. Significantly, it is possible to regenerate intensive agriculture here, using prehistoric techniques such as the raised fields or *waru waru*, *q'ochas*, terraces, and traditional crops (Morris, 1999). *Waru waru*—raised fields—are of particular interest, because their function was completely lost in Inca and colonial times, and has been rediscovered only since the 1980s. These were low ridges a meter high and 30-50 meters long, formed by piling up the topsoil of the flat plateau using manual labor, and using the ridge tops, some three meters wide, for cultivation. Between them were ditches. In pre-Inca times, these raised fields served to improve the micro-climate and protect against frost, and to help soil structure and drainage. In modern reintroductions, the technology has been shown to give greatly increased crop yields, under favorable conditions (Berastain, 1992). Under Spanish colonial control, the raised fields were totally abandoned and their uses forgotten, so that a false impression of sterility and marginality of the high plateau land is now given. However, full reintroduction of the ancient technology would require integration of regions and activities, or some way of handling the high risks in this unique environment, posed by night-time frosts, droughts, and occasional floods. It would also require a stable property regime with security of tenure and incentives to work the land. To date, these conditions have not been present.

In this department, contrary to what might be expected given the strength of traditional communities, there has been a wholesale transition to individual holdings of land. Investigation at the Public Register offices in Juliaca and Puno,[3] revealed that in January 1999 only about ten communities had had their division into individual units recognized and inscribed. However, fieldwork and assurances from competent authorities,[4] lead to the conclusion that throughout Puno Department the farmland has been converted to individual working, though the older, pre-1969 established communities retain their communal land while working other portions as individual units. Within the department, the results of reform over the past ten years have been uneven, and it is necessary to use examples in order to establish the net effect.

Buenavista

A first, more detailed, level is that of the major economic unit of land under the previous regime, the SAIS. In the 1969 Agrarian Reform, the great *hacienda* El Moro, like the 40-odd others of Puno Department, was given the status of SAIS (*Sociedad Agrícola de Interés Social*). The *hacienda* had grown up with the wool trade in the early twentieth century, to reach a size of 47,000 hectares, and it was a typical *latifundio* with a salaried staff at the center, plus extra labor from the ring of surrounding communities, which also retained a little land of their own, and other plots or cattle in usufruct from the *hacienda*.

The 1969 solution was to combine all these units into a giant communal operation, the SAIS Buenavista. Traditional communities were swallowed up in this structure. But the memory of land loss earlier in the century meant that small farmers from the communities were not happy with being absorbed into yet another great estate, and there was unrest. In 1985-87, the government achieved a restructuring of the land which broke up the SAIS, and land was distributed to over 30 communities in the area, an urgent measure because of the land invasions and riots which were taking place. The main aspects of the distribution in geographical terms are indicated in the map, which shows a status that has officially continued to the present. We may make some general comments at this level, based on the map itself (Map 1).

First, the resulting structures are distinct for each community. Some people were given the lands of the central casco, named El Moro after the name of the former *hacienda*. These were the so-called *feudatarios*, who had no land but worked as paid labor, and have a relatively poor physical resource, because all their land is in the middle of the cold *pampas*. They do have human resources, however, as this group worked in specialized ways, and within disciplined timetables, as permanent staff on the estate, and they also inherited some infrastructure, such as buildings and machinery, from the estate. Through their organization, they have been able to acquire tractors and other machines, cultivate some land for crops despite the open *pampa* location, and maintain a good number of cattle on their land.

Map 1   SAIS Buenavista: the distribution among the local communities from 1987 (most land is farmed individually)

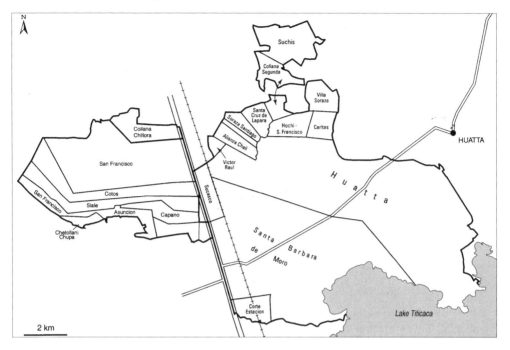

By contrast, the village of Huatta inherited lands of the *pampa*, but also had always conserved their own slope lands around the village. This community contributed laborers to the *hacienda* and then to the SAIS, but on an occasional basis, and never felt part of the great estate. They are weak in specialized skills or work habits. A third kind of case is that of villagers from Capachica, also a peripheral community which was partially involved in providing labor to the SAIS but had other occupations as well. These people were given lands on the *pampa* some 15 miles from their home territory. In the case of this community, very little has been done with their allocation of land, and they have begun with poor physical and human resources.

Huatta

Within the Buenavista ex-SAIS, there are thus varying scenarios. Moving down to a still more detailed level, a study was conducted in Huatta, part of Buenavista including old communally owned land, land allocated from the general breakup of the SAIS, and land separately set aside for ex-workers on the SAIS, some 4,700 hectares. It is this last category of land which has proved the most controversial, perhaps because only a limited number of people were beneficiaries. Two hundred and eight of these beneficiaries were from Huatta; the village population is much larger, but other people had not worked on the SAIS and did not qualify for an allocation. Conversations were held intermittently over two weeks, with the members of the governing body of the community, the *Comité Directivo*.

According to the respondents, the 4,700 hectares had not been well worked in the period from 1987 when they were handed over from the SAIS. The 208 *comuneros* spent most time and effort on their own *chacras* (small farms on the communal land around the towns), and the new communal land was the subject of continued bickering over the relative work contributions from different members. Several members told this writer, in almost identical terms, that communal land had produced only a sack of potatoes for each member, and a little grain, and the sheep and cattle kept were never enough to have marketable surpluses.

Along with the rest of Peru, there was a fairly rapid transition to private working of this extra land from the breakup of the SAIS, a process which was only recognized by the Fujimori government in 1991 when it granted communities permission to sell their land. Official parceling of land began in 1995-1996, and the final inscription of the parcels in the Public Register was due to be completed in 1999, though from what this writer saw, the process will take years to bring to an end because of the costs of inscription, granting of legal title, surveying work, and costs of lawyers and other intermediaries, who have identified a new source of work and income. In addition to the SAIS land, the town of Huatta, as an old community, always had lands of its own—some 1,200 hectares of ancient community lands, worked individually in some 5,500 individual plots, each of them tiny as a result of subdivision over time amongst the over 1,200 people with rights to land.

Most of the results of the process of *parcelación*, are regarded by most of the people directly involved (i.e., the *comuneros* who have acquired the land) as beneficial. This situation could be measured in terms of production levels, but there are no reliable time series, and the process is in any case too young to allow good analyses of this aspect. The adoption of technology or machinery might be another measure, but again the process is probably a long-term one which has not run for long enough to allow for judgement. Most significant for the present discussion is the fact that the flexibility and scope of activities have generally been maintained. Crucially, of the 208 *comuneros*, only about 15 have no other land than the *parcelas* now being formed. The great majority have *chacras* near Huatta, and some have lands elsewhere. Representative of the better endowed farmers is the current President of the *Comunidad*, Timoteo Zapana, who was interviewed in some detail because of his ability to provide details about the evolution of land in the area. He has six plots of land around the village, as well as his *parcela* inherited from the SAIS, and other land rented from the Uros people, near Lake Titicaca. A total of some 50 hectares, in lakeside, *pampa* (plains) and *ladera* (slope land) environments. These different environments are fundamental to our understanding. *Pampa* land is predominantly for grazing, but is also used for the small-scale cultivation of bitter potatoes, *quinua*, and *cañihua*. Ladera land has less frost and better soils, and produces a wide range of arable crops. The lakeside provides good crops when other areas dry out. The central point is that different environments may be combined, by a family instead of a whole community. In this case, flexibility and diversity of resources are maintained within the private holding.

At the other end of the scale, Pedro Pablo Calsin, who accompanied the writer when visiting the area, owns land also as a *comunero*, but has no experience of farming, having worked only in general laboring, and has not been able to work his parcel of land (some ten hectares), which is used now only for his sheep, watched over by himself or a relative, or rented out to other shepherds to use. Most of the time, he is effectively unemployed, and seeks temporary jobs around Huatta, where he lives. Other *comuneros* have varied sizes of plot, from ten to twenty hectares, and a small amount is retained for possible communal use in the future, though no current use is made of it. The size of plot allocated seems to have depended on family size and on the degree of commitment to the former SAIS. None of the *comuneros* consulted, admittedly a small sample of twenty men, admits to having sold their land, but several reported that other *comuneros* had been unable to use their land, and had let it out to bigger farmers, while others were interested in selling their land.

A central point being made in this chapter is the well-established flexibility of farmers' use of land, which has meant that only a small minority have been left with a single, small plot of land. Many *comuneros* have access to other lands through family or *compadrazgo* relations, which allows them to, for example, graze their cattle on slope land when the *pampa* is flooded. This aspect was commented on by most members of the committee. Outside agriculture, there are additional extensions to flexibility for some *comuneros*. Some thirty of the members have lakeside lands, and fish in Lake Titicaca. However, other land resources, such as forestry or mining, have not been developed.

A surprising finding was that no *comunero* combined a significant outside job with his farming. Part-time farming, so typical of small farms in Europe, is not common, and at Huatta all that could be recorded was a hat repairer, three clothes repairers or makers, and two store owners. None of these people spent more than occasional or evening time at their employment. Thus, the existence of outside jobs was not an important incentive for *parcelación* as it might be elsewhere in Latin America (Ruben, Rodríguez and Cortez, this volume). It should be mentioned that some villages in the Lake Titicaca region did have links with outside areas, especially on the eastern slopes of the Andes some 50 to 100 miles away, and substantial numbers of their workers would spend seasons there. This was the case, for example, in villages between Juliaca and Taraco, to the north of the study region.

In clarification, it should be pointed out that other Huatta people—who were not part of the *comunero* group which inherited because they had worked on the SAIS— did have urban jobs combined with their *chacras*, but in these cases, the urban job was commonly the basic employment, and the *chacras* amounted to little more than gardens for domestic consumption of vegetables and a little grain. On the other hand, according to Timoteo Zapana, the majority of *comunero* families (i.e., 120 out of the total of 208) did have wives or children with employment outside agriculture, helping diversification in this way.

Although conservation issues were not studied in the field, in the area around Puno it is not evident that there have been major changes in the natural resource as a result of *parcelación*. Most of this land was formerly under natural grazing, with very little natural tree cover, and little change has occurred, apart from a minor extension of the cultivated area in a few places. Statistically, the census for 1991 does not show an increase in cultivated land, and the *comuneros* interviewed stated that further cropping would be impossible because they lacked the machinery to tackle plowing and working the land. Taking the main cultivated crop (potatoes) as an indicator, there is no real tendency for expansion over the years, as in the 1978-79 campaign 44,383 hectares were planted in Puno province, and in 1997-98, the latest year for which data were collected, there were 43,040 hectares (Puno, 1998). The only major variation over the period occurred in the farm year 1983-84, when only half the usual area was planted, but this was due to massive flooding around the lake which impeded any cultivation.

Technology

In Peru, there is currently great interest in technological change—not in high-technology innovation, but in the resuscitation of traditional technology and its application for sustainable development of rural areas. This "Andean Technology" (Blanco, 1988) includes a variety of water and soil management techniques, including raised fields, ponds, terraces, and a number of traditional crops of very high nutritional value, such as *quinua*, *cañihua*, and amaranth. As such a technological suite was associated traditionally with communal farming, the question arises whether it can also be applied under private holding of land. Some writers have been of the opinion that Andean Technology is only possible under the structure of a highly organized centralized state, in order to administer and build the large structures required especially for the raised fields or *waru waru* (Kolata, 1991; Denevan, 1970; Doolittle, 1990), or for the building of terraces (Sanders *et al.*, 1979; Conrad and Demarest, 1984). However, Erickson (1993) has shown that on the basis of archaeological evidence, and technological logic, it is possible and likely in the Lake Titicaca basin, that small groups or families would have constructed the ancient water management systems. This point is of fundamental importance at the present time, as the reintroduction of ancient technology is being attempted under circumstances of private individual farming, not communal activity.

Apart from the matter of diversity and flexibility, the question arises whether reform affects the ability to adopt new technology, or indeed any technological innovation. It was hoped to be able to adduce some evidence in regard to this question within the current chapter. This is not really possible, but some comments may be made to indicate at least the direction in which technology adoption is going, using the area of the ex-SAIS Buenavista.

Huatta is famous as the area where *waru waru* were first redeployed as an exercise in applied archaeology, starting in 1983. These earthworks, in five separate experimental plots scattered around the town, were abandoned by 1995 and have not been restored (they are "resting", according to most local *campesinos*). In 1999, there were many such abandoned raised field areas all over the lakeside parts of the Puno region; most of these had been operational for just four years as a part of an NGO program. We may now ask about this "failure" and about general attitudes to farming technology.

According to PIWA and CARE, those most keen on adopting the *waru waru* have been the poorest communities, throughout the department of Puno. But everywhere individual plots are being worked, as remarked above, so that tenure differences are not significant. What is different, and possibly of great significance for adoption of technology, is the tenure history, i.e., how current status was achieved and what it resulted in for farmers.

Within the area of the ex-SAIS Buenavista, the period since private working began is too short and too distorted by insecurities over tenure to be able to make a judgement concerning the level of acceptance of innovations. However, from conversations held with some group leaders, it is possible to detect attitudes to innovation and differences between groups. In the three communities where this field study was conducted (Huatta, El Moro, and Capachica), there are three general attitudes. At Huatta, there is evidence of the *comuneros* being more in contact with modernization and the possibilities of help, and these people are anxious to take up machinery and other innovations. El Moro is less so, but may have less need to do so as it is moving toward a specialization in livestock, and the main innovations readily available, already taken up, are moves toward better quality stock, especially Brown Swiss cattle which seem to be the best adapted to this environment. From their location in the middle of the open *pampa*, the people at El Moro can see little benefit in extending crops with the *waru waru* technology, but they have been able to move on to financing plow culture and irrigation with other sponsors, so that dependency on the raised fields is absent. A third case is that of Capachica, where the people are relatively poor, in need of help with crop technology, but unaware or only vaguely aware of the agencies and the possibilities. There have been two long-term experiments with the raised fields at Capachica, and these are seen to have been because of the strong positive influence of the local priest in the village and his encouragement to the farmers.

A new phase in the work of the agencies is beginning, within which both CARE and PIWA are offering only advice and encouragement to adopters, but no monetary gain. There is some evidence (but not from within the field study area of the researcher) that the technology is being adopted by small groups of interested farmers with no difficulty, and that adoption by a whole community is not an essential feature. CARE in particular has proceeded successfully by identifying interested farmer families—not in the three villages mentioned above, but in others around Puno where good contacts have been made—and stimulating them to group together for the specific purpose of working on the raised fields. This is promising for the further diffusion of the technology.

The researcher began with the idea that *waru waru* and other elements of Andean technology would have a special reception, because of their connotations of tradition and sustainable technology. In the event, there is little emotional appeal, and the attitude has been entirely colored by the financial incentives formerly given to communities by agencies keen to have their efforts accepted—money for every hectare planted, food, tools, seed. Under these circumstances, poor people, and those with more education, have been the keenest to adopt. The worst aspect is that once financial help finishes, the technology is left aside.

On the other hand, Andean technology is not compromised by the move away from community ownership and working of land. Where there has been success in adopting the *waru waru* under CARE and PIWA, individuals have been able to adopt just as well as communities.

The other tentative finding, which is unremarkable but confirms an important human dimension described by other writers, is that personal linkages and contacts are fundamental, especially contacts with leaders of the communities which are being targeted. This is the case in a negative sense at Huatta and El Moro, and in a positive sense at the villages attended by CARE and PIWA, and at Capachica. In this latter case, there is a striking evidence of the role of one active promoter—the priest at Capachica—who has organized and encouraged raised fields over a ten-year period.

Some conclusions

The most recent stage of reform, into private farms, is producing a sharply differentiated farming landscape, with winners and losers, as resources become concentrated in fewer hands. The whole process may be criticized as destructive of original communities, and does produce some losers who will leave farming altogether.

The information from this study does, however, suggest that the farming population regards this stage as positive, and that something of the old flexibility and diversity can be retained. In particular, the economies of scope, if not those of scale, that were once widely enjoyed by communities, can be retained by families and small groups. Over the longer term, a sorting process which weeds out inefficient farmers will lead to more productive farming, which is already appearing. Reappearance of the *latifundio* as the logical conclusion to this process will probably be limited, in the same way as it is in developed countries, i.e., by progressive general taxation regimes rather than any special measures for agriculture, and by a more open and competitive market for the land resource. This is certainly preferable to further land reform action, which is always conflictive.

In this less developed region, sustainable development is always an object of concern and research. One very important element of sustainability has been noted, i.e., the *waru waru* raised field system. However, it is still early to judge the potential of this technology for the development process, because of the special help given to it by agencies. One big question is the relation of adoption of the ancient technology to changes in tenure of land. First indications are that the move toward private holdings of land does not deter from technology adoption, and this finding may well be in line with the indications of the archaeologists, that the original adoption of the raised fields was by families and other small groups. This bodes well for the further adoption and spread of the ancient technology.

Notes

[1] Special thanks are due to the British Council in Bolivia and Peru, for support in funding initial visits to the area, and to the Leverhulme Trust for research grants which have supported continuation of the research.

[2] This argument is based upon opinions of Ricardo Vega, Hector Garcia, Raul Paredes and Alipio Canahua; interviewed in Peru.

[3] Dr Sandra Espinoza at the Puno office, Dr Luis Ojeda at the Juliaca office, unpublished file.

[4] J. Paredes, Director of Agrarian Reform, Min. of Agriculture, Puno office; Dr H. Rodriguez, Director of PIWA; Ing. Alipio Canahua, Research Director, CARE International, Puno.

References

Berastain, J.B., "Avances de investigacion sobre la tecnología de waru waru", Vol. 2, producción agrícola. Puno, PIWA, PELT/INADE, 1992.

Blanco Galdos, O., "Tecnologia andina. Un caso: fundamentos cientificos de la tecnologia andina". In: *Comision de coordinacion de tecnologia andina*. CCTA Tecnologia y Desarrollo en el Peru, CCTA, Lima, Peru, 1988.

Caballero, J.M. and E. Alvarez, "Aspectos cuantitativos de la reforma agraria". Inst. de Estudios Peruanos, Lima, 1980.

Dorner, P., "Latin American land reforms in theory and practice". University of Wisconsin, Madison, 1992.

Erickson, C.L., "The social organization of pre-Hispanic raised field agriculture in the Lake Titicaca basin". In: V. Scarborough and B. Isaac (eds.), *Prehispanic water management systems, research in economic anthropology*, supplement 7. JAI Press, Greenwich, CT, 1993.

Fioravanti, E., "Latifundio y sindicalismo agrario en el Peru". Instituto de Estudios Peruanos, Lima, 1976.

Kervyn, B., "L' économie paysanne au Pérou: théories et politiques". In: Morlon (ed.), *Comprendre l'agriculture paysanne dans les Andes Centrales*, INRA, Paris, 1992.

Matos Mar, J., "Hacienda, comunidad y campesinado en el Peru". Instituto de Estudios Peruanos, Lima, 1976.

Mayer, E. and M. de la Cadena, "Cooperación y conflicto en la comunidad Andina". Instituto de Estudios Peruanos, Lima, 1989.

Morlon, P. (ed.), *Comprendre l'agriculture paysanne dans les Andes Centrales*. INRA, Paris, 1992.

Morlon, P., "Parcellaires familiaux et dispersion des risques: l'exemple de l'Altiplano". In: P. Morlon (ed.), *Comprendre l'agriculture paysanne dans les Andes Centrales*, INRA, Paris, 1992.

Morris, A., "The agricultural base of the pre-Incan Andean civilizations". *Geographical Journal*, Vol. 165/3 (1999), pp. 286-95.

Naerssen, T., M. Rutten and A. Zoomers (eds.), *The diversity of development, essays in honour of Jan Kleinpenning*. Assen, Van Gorcum, 1997.

Orlove, B., R. Godoy and P. Morlon, "Les assolements collectifs de haute altitude". In: Morlon (ed.), *Comprendre l'agriculture paysanne dans les Andes Centrales*. INRA, Paris, 1992.

Preston, D., "Re-evaluating sustainability of farming systems in southern Bolivia". In: T. Naerssen, M. Rutten and A. Zoomers (eds.), *The diversity of development, essays in honour of Jan Kleinpenning*. Assen, Van Gorcum, 1997.

Puno, Oficina de informacion agraria, 1998, "Serie historica de la produccion agrícola en el departamento de Puno". Puno, 1998.

Thiesenhusen, W. (ed.), *Searching for agrarian reform in Latin America*. Unwin Hyman, London, 1989.

Zimmerer, K.S., "Soil erosion and social (dis)courses in Cochabamba, Bolivia: perceiving the nature of environmental degradation". *Economic Geography*, Vol. 69/3 (1993), pp. 312-27.

9 Conflict over natural resources and conservation in the indigenous community of Cuzalapa, Western Mexico

Peter R.W. Gerritsen and Nancy R. Forster

Introduction

Mexico's agrarian reform, which began after the Mexican Revolution (1910-1917) and ended in 1992, was one of the most far-reaching in Latin America. Currently, nearly 60% of Mexico's land and 80% of its forests are in the community-based property sector which was established or recognized through agrarian reform (Toledo, 1996). That sector encompasses approximately three million people organized in over 28,000 *ejidos* (agrarian reform communities) and *comunidades indígenas* (indigenous communities) (DeWalt *et al.*, 1994). Yet, despite the scope of Mexico's agrarian reform, access to productive farmland continues to be a problem for a large portion of its rural population (Thiesenhusen, 1995).

There are various reasons for the "land hunger." Community-based property in Mexico is mostly poor quality land situated on steep slopes, and better suited for pasture, woodlands, and forests rather than agriculture. Only 21% of the land controlled by agrarian reform beneficiaries is deemed appropriate for agriculture, and much of that only marginally (DeWalt *et al.*, 1994: 4). In addition, access to community-based land, as well as its management, is largely controlled by local institutions. Mexico's Agrarian Law allows *ejidos* and indigenous communities considerable power to govern their collective landholdings, and to decide how land and resources are allocated and used. Research on common property following publication of Garrett Hardin's *Tragedy of the Commons* (Hardin, 1968) found that such regimes are effective when there is a set of accepted social norms for sustainable, interdependent use of natural resources, limited internal conflict, and the power to exclude people lacking rights (Bromley, 1992). The breakdown or poor definition of social norms and rules, however, can trigger competition for natural resources and their private appropriation.

This chapter examines the institutional context for access to and management of natural resources in the indigenous community of Cuzalapa (referred to as Cuzalapa in the following) in western Mexico. The case of Cuzalapa reveals the increasingly exclusive use of common land by a relatively small group of farmers who have legitimized their claims through their control of community government. This case is also analyzed within the context of biosphere reserve management. The majority of Cuzalapa's land lies within the Sierra de Manantlán Biosphere Reserve (referred to as SMBR or the Reserve in the following), and is thereby subject to its zoning laws, which regulate use and management of land and natural resources.

Tenure institutions in Mexico

Institutions are defined here as the "rules of the game" in society (North, 1990). Tenure institutions govern land and natural resources, while common property regimes regulate individuals' access to natural resources over which they have collective claims (Bromley, 1992). Tenure can be conceptualized as a "bundle of rights and responsibilities" defined through formal and customary social agreements (Dorner and Thiesenhusen, 1992).

The *de jure* tenure regime that governs Mexico's *ejidos* and indigenous communities was constructed in the aftermath of the Revolution, which was fought for "Land and Liberty" *(Tierra y Libertad)* at a point in Mexican history when 95% of rural families were landless (Markiewicz, 1993). The Constitution of 1917 (through Article 27) codified the legal basis for land expropriation and set tenure regulations for the reform sector.

As *haciendas* (the pre-Revolutionary large agricultural estates) were expropriated, the state either restored property to indigenous communities, if they could legally prove their claim, or established *ejidos*, if a group of twenty or more landless farmers petitioned for the land. Rights within *ejidos* was strictly regulated by the legal codes of Article 27 (de Janvry et al., 1997). Land was allocated to the collectivity, and could not be alienated through rental or sale. *Ejidatarios* were allotted an agricultural parcel for individual use, and had to work their land directly without wage labor. Only *ejidatarios* had the right to vote in the community assembly. Access to communal land, beyond the agricultural plots, was secured through the assembly. Strict guidelines governed inheritance of *ejido* rights, and if *ejidatarios* were absent from the community for more than two years, they could lose all rights. Indigenous communities were structured similarly, although with somewhat greater freedom to make internal decisions (ibid.). Article 27 also gave the nation the right of eminent domain over land and water, and the right to restrict property owners in the interest of public good, which, among other effects, set a powerful juridical framework for implementing conservation (Toledo, 1996).

Unprecedented land reform was carried out under the Cárdenas administration (1934-1940), which greatly expanded the number of *ejidos*, regulated their farming practices, and strengthened their ties to the state (Markiewicz, 1993). Following that precedent, the PRI *(Partido Revolucionario Institucional;* Institutional Revolutionary Party), Mexico's governing party since its formation in 1938, used land reform and technical assistance as a form of patronage to control the countryside and maintain farmer support (Markiewicz, 1993; de Janvry et al., 1997). While the state has exerted a great deal of control over agrarian communities in many economic and political dimensions, it has also given their members considerable juridical power to self-govern their collective natural resources and to allot agricultural plots for individual use.

In 1992, Article 27 was significantly modified, one of a number of neo-liberal reforms enacted by the Salinas administration (1988-1994). The reform was a significant moment for Mexico's common property regimes. *Ejidatarios* can now obtain official certification of the boundaries of their agricultural parcels allocated for individual use, after which they can legally sell, rent, and sharecrop that land, and mortgage the parcels as collateral for loans. Sale of *ejido* land to outsiders can be authorized by a two-thirds majority vote of the *ejido*'s general assembly, and that same procedure allows common lands to be privatized and sold (Cornelius and Myhre, 1998). The 1992 reform applied only to *ejidos*, although a similar reform for indigenous communities was enacted in 1999 and is being tested on an experimental basis.

A number of analysts predicted rapid land privatization after the reform, though there is little empirical evidence for that trend (Cornelius and Myhre, 1998; Nuijten, 1998). Yet, the new Agrarian Law may be influencing farmer behavior in more subtle ways, and may be inducing the *de facto* appropriation of common land by individuals.

Tenure reform for conservation

In approximately the same period that Mexico initiated neo-liberal reforms and opened its economy, it also implemented its first legislation to protect the environment. The *Ley General del Equilibrio Ecológico y la Protección al Ambiente* (General Law on Ecological Equilibrium and Environmental Protection) was passed in 1988. Subsequently, an overall strategy for managing Mexico's protected areas, including biosphere reserves, was delineated in the *Programa de Áreas Naturales de México 1995-2000* (Protected Area Program of Mexico, 1995-2000) (SEMARNAP, 1996).

Currently, slightly over 5% of Mexico's land is under some form of protection *(ibid.)*. Biosphere reserves have become a popular form of tenure to conserve biological diversity on land which is already communally or individually owned. The reserves enact land-use regulations without transforming land ownership. They are generally established in fragile areas which have unique biodiversity or endangered plant and/or animal species. While biosphere reserves attempt to involve farmers in conservation activities (Batisse, 1986; IUCN *et al.*, 1991), the zoning regulations imposed on existing properties dramatically alter owners' tenure rights to use land and natural resources (Pimbert and Pretty, 1995).

Biosphere reserves are zoned in more or less concentric circles, resembling a fried egg. The core zone in the center is under strict conservation protection, and all land-use is prohibited. Restricted land-use is allowed in the surrounding buffer zone (Batisse, 1986). Thus, numerous rules and regulations govern land-use in buffer zones. In Mexico, amongst other regulations, landowners must gain permission to change the vegetation cover. Furthermore, forestry requires a detailed management plan, which must be elaborated by professional foresters and approved by the *Secretaría de Medio Ambiente, Recursos Naturales y Pesca* (SEMARNAP: Ministry of Environment, Natural Resources and Fisheries). The latter two regulations also apply to non-protected regions, but enforcement tends to be more stringent in protected areas. In biosphere reserve buffer zones, hunting, gathering, and commercialization of endemic or protected species is strictly prohibited.

It is generally agreed that biosphere reserves are contributing to the preservation of the world's biodiversity (Primack, 1993). Yet, tenure conflicts often arise in biosphere reserves, and can negatively affect biodiversity. Addressing them, therefore, becomes crucial for effectively achieving conservation goals (Wells *et al.*, 1992). Biosphere reserves have also been criticized for failing to establish constructive day-to-day interactions with farmers living within their boundaries, putting at risk both conservation and development initiatives (Wells *et al.*, 1992; Pimbert and Pretty, 1995). In the SMBR, zoning regulations may be creating insecurity over access rights to natural resources, and might be fuelling the appropriation of common land by individuals.

The Sierra de Manantlán Biosphere Reserve and Cuzalapa

The Sierra de Manantlán is a mountain range in western Mexico which extends over approximately 140,000 hectares and rises in altitude from 400 to 2,860 meters above sea level (Jardel, 1992a) (Map 1). It was declared a biosphere reserve in 1987, after the discovery of an endemic species called *Milpilla (Zea diploperennis)*, an ancestor of modern maize. The Reserve is characterized by very high biological diversity. Scientists have identified more than 2,800 vascular plant species and 584 vertebrate species, and expect to register more (Jardel, 1999). It also encompasses 13 vegetation types, including cloud forest (IMECBIO, 1997). Currently, the Mexican government considers the Reserve one of its 25 priority regions for conservation (SEMARNAP, 1996).

The Reserve includes three core zones, which place nearly 42,000 hectares (30% of the total area) under strict conservation protection. The remaining land, nearly 97,700 hectares (70%), is the buffer zone with land-use restrictions. These tenure regulations were imposed on existing properties with their attendant tenure institutions. They include 29 community-based properties (26 *ejidos* and three indigenous communities) with 60% of the land, and 80 private owners with 39% of the area. The scientific field station for the Reserve is state property and encompasses 1% of the area.

Soon after the Reserve was established, its conservation mission was expanded from one-species protection to an integrated conservation project with a regional approach to sustainable development (Jardel *et al.*, 1996). The Reserve currently has great potential for commercial forestry and the harvest of non-timber forest products for medicinal and nutritional purposes (Benz *et al.*, 1994; IMEBIO, 1997). Realizing the dual mission of conservation and development in practice, however, has challenged Reserve managers (Graf *et al.*, 1995; Gerritsen, 1998b).

Cuzalapa is located on the southern slopes of the SMBR and encompasses a total of 23,963 hectares, of which 17,170 hectares (72%) are in the buffer zone and nearly 4,653 hectares (19%) are in one of the core zones (IMECBIO, 1998) (Map 1, see also Map 2). In 1995, the community included approximately 1,330 inhabitants in 302 families in a main village and eleven hamlets (INEGI, 1996). The village has basic services, such as electricity, daily bus service, stores, and running water, but lacks potable water, sewerage, and postal service. Within the past five years, there have been significant improvements in services. Nonetheless, human and material resources are often insufficient, especially in some of the more remote hamlets. Nutritional deficiencies are common among the poor, and deaths are often caused by harsh life circumstances. Most houses are in poor condition and lack maintenance. Those in remote hamlets lack electricity. Illiteracy rates are high among adults, although educational opportunities have improved in recent years for children. While general levels of living are relatively poor compared to the surrounding valleys, there is marked socioeconomic differentiation within Cuzalapa (Gerritsen, 1995).

The historical succession of land tenure regimes in Cuzalapa

Nahua indigenous people inhabited the Cuzalapa valley in the pre-Hispanic period. The Nahua tenure regime provided temporary usufruct rights to families; land for shifting cultivation was redistributed each season. The Spanish conquest brought profound changes to the region. Land rights were drastically altered, and cattle were introduced into the region and allowed to roam freely (Laitner-Benz and Benz, 1994). Prior to the Mexican Revolution, the *hacienda La Loma* operated within part of Cuzalapa's territory (Gerritsen, 1995). A small number of indigenous families worked permanently for the *hacienda*, while a larger number were sharecroppers (Figueroa, 1996).

Further changes took place in Cuzalapa after the Revolution and the *Cristero* War

Map 1   Location of the SMBR and Cuzalapa (SIIR, 1998)

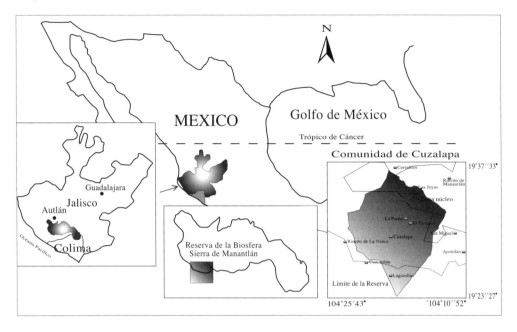

of the 1920s, when *mestizo* settlers came to the community in search of a peaceful place to settle.[1] The indigenous residents did not object since there was enough land. Indigenous and *mestizo* families began to intermarry, and today only a few families can be considered "purely" indigenous. The newcomers quickly allied with the indigenous inhabitants against the *hacienda* owner and, later on, petitioned government agencies in the struggle to recover the community's land. In contrast to the indigenous inhabitants, some of the newcomers could read and write, and they soon moved into important positions in the community (Gerritsen, 1995).

Agrarian reform

The *hacienda* La Loma was taken over by the inhabitants of Cuzalapa sometime between 1929 and 1932. Yet, agrarian reform, which established Cuzalapa as an indigenous community, was delayed until 1950, 16 years after the farmers' formal application and after several years of legal struggle. The presidential resolution which formalized the expropriation of the *hacienda* was executed only in 1964, and even then incompletely, since the state failed to adjudicate over 4,672 hectares of community land, an action still pending (García, 1996). Agrarian reform created significant change in the community by legalizing residents' land rights and, above all, by establishing new tenure institutions.

Cuzalapa's agrarian reform benefited 251 households, and the male heads became official *comuneros* (landholding farmers with voting rights in the general assembly of indigenous communities). Elderly farmers recall that the agrarian reform did not dramatically change land distribution. The *hacienda* had already been taken over some 20 years before, and the reform expropriated land from only some five farmers, either because they were related to the *hacienda* owner or because they did not live in Cuzalapa. Only 15 of the beneficiaries were landless prior to the reform. Existing inequities in land distribution which already existed were not significantly altered by Cuzalapa´s agrarian reform. Inequity was apparently less extreme than today, and was not perceived as a problem by Cuzalapa farmers, since sufficient land was available at that time.

The agrarian reform established new institutions to govern land and natural resources. A directive board *(mesa directiva)* replaced the pre-Revolutionary council of elders *(consejo de ancianos)*, seated in the neighboring indigenous community of Ayotitlán. The directive board includes an executive committee *(comisariado de bienes comunales)* and a vigilance committee *(comité de vigilancia)*. The commissioner of common property *(comisario de bienes comunales*, or more often called *comisariado de bienes comunales)* heads the executive committee, while an overseer *(consejo de vigilancia)* heads the vigilance committee. A secretary, a treasurer, and three assistants *(suplentes)* assist the commissioner of common property, while two secretaries and three assistants assist the overseer. Thus, the directive board includes 12 persons, but in practice the commissioner of common property mainly pulls the strings. Both the executive and vigilance committees are elected to three-year terms by the general assembly, which includes all land holding farmers and, in theory, is the highest authority in *ejidos* and indigenous communities (Rivera, 1994). Currently, the general assembly in Cuzalapa includes some 244 *comuneros*. Internal conflicts, described further below, are so intense that even the number of legitimate voters is in dispute.[2]

Under this tenure regime, farmers (including those who are not voting members of the assembly) gain access to communal land and resources through the general assembly. In practice historically in Cuzalapa, if a farmer needed a specific product, he could simply go to the hills and look for it.[3] Only when he required a large amount of the product was it was necessary to seek approval from the commissioner of common property, as the representative of the general assembly. If a farmer wished to use common land for an extended period, approval from the general assembly was required.

Politics and land access

Agrarian reform in 1950 legalized usufruct rights to community land for the *comunero* households constituted at that time, and established the right to exclude outsiders. Inequities in land distribution that existed before the reform, however, remained and have grown larger since then. Increased inequity is partly due to demographic growth in the face of tenure regulations that generally allow only one heir to inherit the agrarian reform land endowment, and thus become a *comunero*. Yet, the greatest inequities have developed through post-reform allocation of common land by the community government (especially from the 1960s through the 1990s), a process highly mediated by politics. The community institution which was intended to provide equitable access to land and natural resources for those in need has apparently malfunctioned.

From the 1950s onwards, Cuzalapa's directive board has been controlled by a minority of some 30% of the farmers centered on four, originally *mestizo*, families who have dominated decision-making on land allocation and use of natural resources in the commons. This group is known as the *caciques* (local bosses) and is affiliated with the PRI.[4] The remaining farmers are divided almost evenly into the "democratic group", affiliated with the opposition *Partido Revolucionario Democrático* (Democratic Revolutionary Party, PRD), and the *jacqueteros* (the local term for those who change jackets—*cambiar jacquetas*), who function as swing voters. The democratic group has failed to become a countervailing power to the *caciques*, mainly because of internal splits (Figueroa, 1996). The *jacqueteros* are not politically organized and ally with either the *caciques* or the democratic group, depending on benefits to be gained. In most instances they have supported the *caciques*.

Political alliances have conditioned the allocation of Cuzalapa's common land since the agrarian reform. The *caciques* have used their control over the directive board for their own benefit, distributing common land among allies while making it difficult for those in opposition to obtain it. Meetings of the general assembly have been held very irregularly. Many are not convoked officially and are often manipulated. *Comuneros* who oppose the *caciques'* actions have occasionally been excluded from meetings by force, sometimes by local police officers. Names have even been erased from the 1991 "official" list of *comuneros* (the *censo*), thereby depriving the opposition of *voz y voto* (voice and vote), i.e., their right to participate in the general assembly. The *cacique* group's direct linkages with the PRI at the municipal and state levels enabled it to leverage government funds to forge political alliances within the community.

It should also be noted that, beyond political alliances, an additional factor influences land access. Since the 1960s, financial resources have become increasingly important for securing common land. Fences have become necessary to formalize rights to land and to prevent cattle from roaming in the agricultural fields. Since most *comuneros* in Cuzalapa lack the financial resources to fence land, they do not request common land from the directive board (Gerritsen, 1995). Financial resources have also enabled various outsiders to obtain land in Cuzalapa, mainly for grazing purpose (IMECBIO, 1998).

Table 1 illustrates land distribution in Cuzalapa in the late 1990s among *comuneros*. The data represent a sample of 94 *comuneros* (Gerritsen, 1999) and include their agrarian reform parcels as well as the common land subsequently allocated to them by community government. Table 1 shows significant inequities in land distribution among these *comuneros*. Roughly two-thirds have less than 20 hectares, and control approximately one-fifth of the community's land. Approximately one-fourth have between 20-70 hectares, and control nearly one half of the community's land. Finally, 7% of the *comuneros* have more than 70 hectares and control 30% of the community's land. Land distribution in Cuzalapa is clearly less skewed than in many parts of Latin America, but the data demonstrate that significant inequities have developed within this community.

Table 1   Land distribution among *comuneros* in the late 1990s (N=94)

Size of land-holding (ha)	Number of comuneros	% of comuneros	Amount of land (ha)	% of land
<20	63	67%	550	21%
20-70	24	26%	1,251	49%
>70	7	7%	786	30%
Total	94	100%	2,587	100%

Land-use in Cuzalapa

Paralleling the growing problems with land access have been chronic conflicts over natural resource use in Cuzalapa, particularly in the commons. An analysis of the community's land-use history since agrarian reform suggests that the conflicts are linked.

Agriculture has been an important land-use activity in Cuzalapa throughout its history. Today, agricultural practices take place during both the rainy and dry seasons, and vary according to the characteristics of fields. During the rainy season, farmers cultivate rainfed maize on level land using horse-drawn ploughs and tractors, or practice shifting cultivation of maize, mainly on lower hillsides. During the dry season, they cultivate maize and beans in irrigated fields in the lower parts of the valley along the rivers and streams, which provide water for the community's relatively simple, gravity-fed irrigation system. In general, yields are relatively low due to poor soil fertility, disease, and insect pests. Damage from heavy downpours during the rainy season also significantly reduces yields (Gerritsen, 1995).

Forestry and cattle-raising increased in importance during the second half of the 20th century. Both utilize natural resources primarily on common land. The commons are the hilly parts in the community, which are generally covered with forests and secondary vegetation, and are poorly suited for agriculture (IMECBIO, 1998). Local inhabitants have traditionally utilized a wide variety of wood and non-timber forest products from the commons (Benz *et al.*, 1994). Because some community residents have developed commercial uses for common land (forestry and cattle-raising), its relative value for them has increased.

More recently, conservation has become a competing land-use for the commons. With the establishment of the SMBR in 1987, commercial logging, and the hunting and gathering of a great number of plant and animal species have been prohibited. Part of the commons also became part of one of the reserve's core zones (Jardel, 1992a).

Forestry

Commercial forestry in Cuzalapa and the rest of the Sierra de Manantlán took place during two periods: 1940-1970 and 1981-1984. It reached its height in Cuzalapa during the 1960s, when *comuneros* granted a concession to a logging company in return for promised compensation to improve community life and infrastructure.[5] The *caciques* controlling Cuzalapa's directive board, however, managed to pocket a good part of the profits from forestry. Protests from other *comuneros* mounted, but only toward the end of the 1970s was the opposition sufficiently united to terminate the concession. The commercial company was able to maintain its position for such a long period because it was supported by civil servants of some government agencies, like the Secretary of Agrarian Reform and the Mexican army (Jardel, 1992b; Rojas *et al.*, 1997).

A second round of forestry took place in the period 1981-1984, when Cuzalapa established a communal saw mill to harvest dead wood from the community's forests. *Comuneros* who were allied with the directive board made the investment (financed in part with a bank loan) with the professed goal of creating jobs for the other, poorer farmers. Conflicts arose when they failed to share profits from the enterprise, and they began to cut live wood without seeking permission from the general assembly. Strife escalated so dramatically that in 1984 the governor banned forestry in Cuzalapa. *Comuneros* still recall the violence of that period.

Conflict broke out again in 1987 when the *caciques* began negotiations for a new contract with a private logging company. This time, the opposition found an ally in the University of Guadalajara, which proposed to establish a protected area. The creation the Sierra de Manantlán Biosphere Reserve put an end to conflicts over commercial forestry in Cuzalapa (Jardel, 1992b). Yet, new conflicts soon arose.

Cattle-raising

Broadly speaking, Cuzalapa farmers characterize themselves either as *pobres* (i.e., poor farmers), or *ganaderos* (i.e., cattle-raisers, also referred to as *Ricos*: rich farmers). Of all *comuneros*, some 65-70% can be regarded as *pobres* and about 30-35% as *ganaderos* (Gerritsen, 1999). *Pobre* farmers follow a multifaceted livelihood strategy. Farming is diversified and supplemented by a wide array of additional endeavors, including off-farm work. The most common economic activities are maize cultivation, small-scale cattle-raising, wage labor, and collection of non-timber forest products. *Pobres'* land-use is generally subsistence-oriented, particularly in recent years when market prices for maize have been low.

Ganadero farmers employ a more specialized livelihood strategy, with cattle-raising as the dominant activity. Most cultivate maize, but as a secondary endeavor which is mostly carried out by wage laborers and, occasionally, sharecroppers. *Ganaderos'* land-use is more market-oriented than that of the *pobre* farmers, and cattle are commonly sold. Their cattle-raising strategy is extensive in nature, involving few investments. Part of the logic of extensive cattle production involves a continuous effort to secure pasture. Thus, cattle-raisers currently value the commons primarily for the opportunity to obtain pasture (Gerritsen, 1995).

Although cattle have been part of Cuzalapa's landscape since the era of the *hacienda*, it was not until the 1970s that the cattle population began to increase rapidly, in part encouraged by a generous government credit program through Banrural, the government rural development bank (Louette *et al.*, 1997). Migration to the US has also stimulated cattle production, especially since the late 1970s. A 1998 survey indicates that approximately 58% of migrants from Cuzalapa stayed in western Mexico, while some 39% sought their fortune in the US (Gerritsen, 1999). Migrants who head for the US are mainly cattle-raisers' sons who invest their earnings in both land and cattle in Cuzalapa.

In the 1990s, 78% of the *ganaderos* raising cattle in Cuzalapa were *comuneros*, while the remaining 22% were almost all sons of *comuneros* (Gerritsen, 1999). The non-*comuneros* generally graze their cattle on the land of relatives, mostly their parents. Several have purchased land in the community, where they graze their animals and build their houses, a trend which is increasingly common among migrants returning from the US.

During the 1990s, cattle production increased in importance in Cuzalapa, as in other parts of Mexico, stimulated by government incentives and low profits from maize cultivation (Louette *et al.*, 1997; Toledo, 1990). At the end of 1997, the cattle population in Cuzalapa was estimated at 4,500-5,000. Table 2, which is based on a sample of 100 cattle-owning farmers in Cuzalapa (Gerritsen, 1999), shows that the distribution of cattle varies considerably. Approximately one-third of all owners have 20 head or less, and control only 7% of all cattle in the community. These producers can be characterized as *pobre* farmers, while the remainder can be classified as *ganaderos*.

Among the latter, two subgroups can be distinguished. Producers with 20-60 head include 53% of all owners and control 56% of the cattle. Producers with more than 60 head encompass 14% of the cattle-raisers and own 37% of the total herd in Cuzalapa.

Table 2 Cattle distribution among Cuzalapa cattle-raisers (N=100)

Size of herd	Number of cattle-raisers	% of cattle-raisers	Number of cattle	% of cattle
<20	33	33%	301	7%
20-60	53	53%	2,298	56%
>60	14	14%	1,530	37%
Total	100	100%	4,129	100%

As the cattle population has grown, so has demand for pasture. More and more farmers, including those who do not own cattle, have begun to sow exotic pasture species as a cash crop, even on fertile, irrigated fields. In addition, forestland is being converted to pasture at a relatively rapid rate. Louette *et al.* (1998) estimate a 68% increase in the surface under pasture in Cuzalapa from 1971-1993, while Jardel (1998: personal communication) estimates, for more or less the same period, an annual deforestation rate of 0.8 hectare in Cuzalapa.

In summary, cattle production is changing land cover in Cuzalapa. Pasture is displacing agricultural cropland and forests, thereby producing a homogenization of the landscape and an impoverishment of diversity in biological resources. It has also created new economic dependency relationships that only partially follow previous political alliances within the community.

The enclosure of the commons

The full repercussions of extensive cattle production become apparent when we examine its relationship to the process of land appropriation taking place in the commons. Currently, most members of the *cacique* group are cattle producers. For more than four decades, the *caciques* have used political power to pursue commercial interests in the commons, first through forestry and, more recently, through cattle production. With their latest strategy, they have appropriated common land for private use. Farmers recall that the enclosure of the commons started at the end of the 1950s, but it was not until some 10 years ago that almost all was fenced. Only a small area of common land remains freely accessible. It is not clear whether the creation of the SMBR hastened the enclosure of the commons.

Map 2 gives a rough representation of the *de facto* distribution of common land among Cuzalapa farmers, based on information from participatory mapping by key informants. It indicates that cattle-raisers now control most of Cuzalapa's common land encompassing its hillsides and forests. A significant portion belongs to five extended families. As a result, only small parts are now available for collective use. The strategy of the *cacique* group has resulted in a *de facto* loss of access to common land for the majority in the community, and to the *de facto* concentration of that land in the hands of a relatively small group within the community.

While there is still a great deal of conflict in Cuzalapa over the social understandings

Map 2   Relative distribution of common land in Cuzalapa in the 1990s (SIIR, 1998)

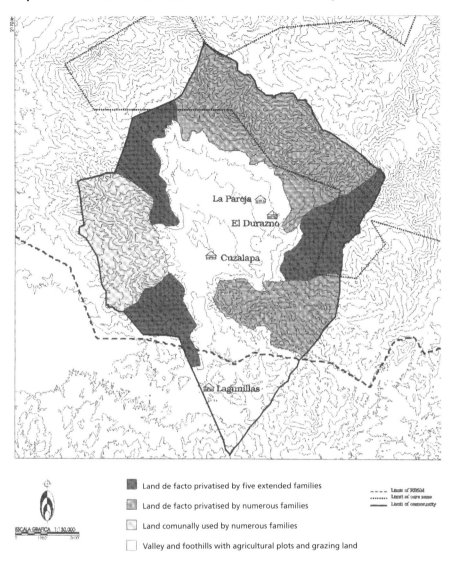

☐ Land de facto privatised by five extended families

☐ Land de facto privatised by numerous families

☐ Land comunally used by numerous families

☐ Valley and foothills with agricultural plots and grazing land

---- Limit of RBSM
.... Limit of core zone
――― Limit of community

ESCALA GRAFICA 1:30,000

implicit in this *de facto* tenure system, it has apparently become the tenure regime that currently governs the commons. *Caciques* who claim property rights to common land increasingly will not let farmers enter their part without permission. They seldom grant permission to graze cattle, although they tend to be more open to requests to harvest firewood or other forest products. Some *caciques* demand that all farmers ask permission, while others still allow some free access. Like any private, individual tenure system, much depends on the persons involved, and on their social and political relationships. Yet, control is difficult because most common land is distant from the village and hamlets, and much happens unseen, at least by outsiders. It has become clear, however, that access has become more limited for farmers, who do not have rights to part of the commons.

The *caciques* with claims to common land have also had the most conflicts with Reserve managers, since zoning regulations of the Reserve restrict their access to land and resources. One of SMBR's core zones, *Las Joyas-Manantlán*, overlaps with land claimed by the cattle-raisers. Technically, all land-use activity is prohibited in the core zone. In practice, however, the Directorship of the SMBR (DRBSM: *Dirección de la Reserva de la Biosfera Sierra de Manantlán*), the government agency responsible for the administration of the Reserve, permits land-use until a solution to the tenure conflict is found.

Discussion

The foregoing sections highlight a number of factors which have influenced changes in land access and natural resource use in Cuzalapa, and which have in turn fuelled conflicts. In the 1970s, government policy provided incentives for cattle production through a generous credit program administered through Banrural. More recently, Mexico's market opening, which started in the mid-1980s and picked up in the 1990s, negatively affected the market price for maize, and may have caused people to turn to cattle production. In 1987, the SMBR enacted land-use restrictions and terminated Cuzalapa's strife-laden forestry enterprise, which may have strengthened interest in cattle. It is unclear how the 1992 reform of Article 27 affected Cuzalapa, since indigenous communities were not subject to the reform, but it might have convinced farmers that new winds were blowing. Further research is required to more precisely determine the relative importance of each of these factors. It is likely that, in combination, they have hastened the *de facto* enclosure of the commons, which was essentially complete by the early 1990s. The fact that the enclosure benefited only a minority raises obvious questions of social justice. Furthermore, cattle production, the land-use strategy associated with the enclosure, most probably has caused loss of biological diversity.

Two major tenure problems currently affect this community. First, Cuzalapa's *de facto* tenure regime is ridden with conflict, and the institutional framework established through agrarian reform is not functioning as intended, although it remains the official system for governing land and resources. Second, SMBR zoning regulations have been laid on top of this poorly-functioning institution for local recourse governance, further complicating matters. The tenure reform enacted through the establishment of the Reserve has greatly reduced the powers of the agrarian reform tenure regime and of local farmers to manage resources, at least in theory. In fact, the zoning regulations are often breached in day-to-day practice. For example, illegal timber cutting and forest clearing still take place. Violators risk being fined by PROFEPA (*Procuraduría Federal para la Protección del Ambiente*, the office of the Federal Attorney for the Protection of the Environment), which is charged with enforcing regulations in the Reserve. Yet, in day-to-day practice, civil servants also negotiate with farmers and make concessions over land-use. It is interesting to note that most Cuzalapa farmers have little or no knowledge about the rules and regulations of the SMBR. Most are unaware of the exact meaning and location of the core and buffer zones, and cannot describe the current restrictions on natural resource use. In contrast, the core members of the *cacique* and democratic group are quite well informed about the Reserve's rules and regulations (Gerritsen, 1998a; IMECBIO, 1997).

It remains an open question whether the government institutions which currently deal with tenure and conservation in rural Mexico have the capacity to solve these tenure problems. As part of the new mission of the Ministry of Agrarian Reform *(Secretaría de la Reforma Agraria)*, the Salinas administration established PROCEDE *(Programa de Certificación de Derechos Ejidales y Titulación de Solares Urbanos:* Program for the Certification of *Ejido* Land Rights and the Titling of Urban House Plots) to implement tenure reform of Article 27. But, PROCEDE was not designed to deal with tenure conflicts, and will not work in communities which have them. Meanwhile, the Ministry of Environment, Natural Resources, and Fisheries (SEMARNAP) administers biosphere reserves, and has a broad mandate to promote conservation and improve levels of living, but has no specific jurisdiction over the tenure institutions created through agrarian reform. Standard strategies used in biosphere reserves to interact with farmers have proven to be insufficient to resolve Cuzalapa's tenure problems.

A common intervention directed at farmers in biosphere reserves seeks to promote ecologically sound technologies for economic activity in buffer zones, and to increase the technical output of farms. Reserve managers generally promote agroforestry, environmental restoration, and soil and water conservation (Wells *et al.*, 1992; IMECBIO, 1997). In Cuzalapa, it has not been possible to implement a coherent intervention program of this type, because of conflicts within the community and between the community and the Reserve's administration. Farmers do not believe such interventions address their most pressing needs, such as resolving conflict over land access. Economic interventions have been dispersed, and reach only a small portion of the farmers (Gerritsen, 1998b).

Another intervention directed at farmers in biosphere reserves is participatory land-use planning. This generally involves "scaling-down" the management program for the whole reserve to individual community-level land-use plans. Generally, rapid and participatory rural appraisals are the methodological tools for involving farmers in land-use planning (Wells *et al.*, 1992; IMECBIO, 1997). In Cuzalapa, a community-level land-use plan was to be formulated in 1998, and initial discussions were started through several unofficial meetings with a small group of farmers. However, planning did not pass beyond the preparatory phase because members of the *cacique* group, including the commissioner of common property, did not want to attend the meetings. *Comuneros* who have traditionally supported the Reserve were unwilling to take a stand against the *cacique* group, and facilitators for land-use planning had to abort their efforts (IMECBIO, 1998).[6]

Internal conflicts of the magnitude of Cuzalapa's are extreme among Reserve communities, but this case illustrates general trends in the SMBR and in other parts of Mexico (see DeWalt *et al.*, 1994). Almost all the agrarian communities in the Reserve have had land disputes, and have experienced administrative irregularities in the implementation of agrarian reform, and many are still unresolved (Jardel, 1999). Furthermore, the appropriation of communal land by individual farmers appears to have become a generalized trend in Reserve communities. Finally, most communities in the SMBR are undergoing land-use change. At varying rates, they are converting forests to cropland and, above all, to pasture (ibid.). Deforestation is advancing most rapidly in the Reserve's north-east and south-west areas; the latter includes Cuzalapa. A number of analysts regard the expansion of cattle production linked to agriculture, the so-called process of *ganaderización*, as one of the major threats to conservation in the near future (Louette *et al.*, 1997; Toledo, 1990).

Conclusions

Cuzalapa is a particularly difficult case in the SMBR, and interventions conventionally used in biosphere reserves to achieve conservation and development goals have proven to be insufficient to resolve its tenure problems. Cuzalapa's *de jure* tenure institution broke down over time as a minority created its own set of rules, with the partial complicity of national institutions which should have protected democratic governance over natural resources. The SMBR's zoning regulations have further complicated Cuzalapa's tenure problems. Currently, two tenure regimes compete in Cuzalapa, fuelling conflicts within the community and with outside agencies, and in particular with the Reserve administration.

To begin resolving Cuzalapa's entangled problems, it is absolutely necessary to better understand the existing tenure systems, in particular how the competing regimes interface, how rules and regulations are applied and bent in practice, and the potential for the current *de facto* tenure regime to become more democratic and equitable. It is likely that a very complex and "messy" picture will emerge. Clarifying it is primarily a task for social scientists, although natural scientists with long-term experience in communities can make important contributions. Establishing protected areas has until now been the task of natural scientists. Conservation in populated reserves, however, is ultimately more about farmers than nature, although one cannot be understood without the other (Gómez-Pompa and Kaus, 1992; Pimbert and Pretty, 1995). Insights into Cuzalapa's existing tenure regimes can provide a basis for conflict management. Yet, mediating conflict and reducing inequities in land distribution will not automatically conserve biodiversity. They are only the first steps to revive or create functional local institutions for governing access to resources and their management.

Notes

[1] The *Cristero* War was a brief religious conflict (1926-1929) which broke out in central and western Mexico when President Calles (1924-1928) attempted to enforce constitutional restrictions on the Catholic Church. The fierce opposition of the conservative *cristeros* slowed progress toward agrarian and other liberal reforms (Thiesenhusen, 1995).

[2] The number of registered *comuneros* in 1991 is reported differently in two official documents archived in the *Registro Nacional Agraria* (National Agrarian Register). The census sent to the Jalisco Agrarian Reform dependency reports 244 *comuneros*, while that sent to the federal dependency reports 216 *comuneros*.

[3] Whenever reference is made to male farmers, it also includes female farmers, unless otherwise indicated.

[4] The term *cacique* is very common in rural Mexico. It is derived from the noun *caciquismo*. The latter "is used to refer to a dominant relation with a local leader, landowner or local politician (the so-called *cacique*). It conveys the idea of a degree of economic or political power, but there is a strong implication of 'influence' and the capacity to manipulate other people's actions" (Torres, 1992, endnote 12).

[5] Apart from the community agreement, a permit granted by the Mexican government is also required.

[6] That same year, preliminary, community-level land-use plans were elaborated successfully in four other agrarian communities, which are less divided than Cuzalapa.

References

Batisse, M., "Developing and focusing the biosphere reserve", *Nature and Resources*, Vol. 22, no. 3 (1986), pp. 1-10.

Benz, B.F., F. Santana M., R. Pineda L., J. Cevallos E., L. Robles H. and D. de Niz L., "Characterization of *mestizo* plant use in the Sierra de Manantlán, Jalisco-Colima, Mexico". *Journal of Ethnobiology*, Vol. 14, no. 1 (1994), pp. 23-41.

Bromley, D.W. (ed.), "Making the commons work: theory, practice, and policy". San Francisco, Institute for Contemporary Studies, 1992.

Cornelius, W.A. and D. Myhre (eds.), "The transformation of rural Mexico: reforming the *ejido* sector". La Jolla, University of California, San Diego, Center for US-Mexican Studies, 1998.

De Janvry, A., G. Gordillo and E. Sadoulet, "Mexico's second agrarian reform: household and community responses, 1990-1994". Ejido Reform Research Project, La Jolla, University of California, San Diego, Center for US-Mexican Studies, 1997.

DeWalt, B.R. and M.W. Rees with A.D. Murphy, "The end of agrarian reform in Mexico; past lessons, future prospects, transformation of Rural Mexico, Number 3". Ejido Reform Research Project, La Jolla, Center for US-Mexican Studies, University of California, San Diego, 1994.

Dorner, P. and W.C. Thiesenhusen, "Land tenure and deforestation: interactions and environmental implications". Discussion paper, no. 34. Geneva, The United Nations Research Institute for Social Development, 1992.

Figueroa B., P., "Lucha campesina, conservación de recursos y ganadería en la comunidad de Cuzalapa, municipio de Cuautitlán, Jalisco". Unpublished M.Sc. thesis. Mexico-City, UAM, Unidad Xochimilco, Division de Ciencias Sociales y Humanidades, 1996.

García L., J.B., "Diagnóstico preliminar de la tenencia de la tierra en la reserva de la biosfera Sierra de Manantlán (I. nucleos agrarios)". Technical Report. Autlán, Mexico, DRBSM, INE, SEMARNAP, 1996.

Gerritsen, P.R.W., "Styles of farming and forestry. The case of the Mexican community of Cuzalapa". Wageningen, Circle for Rural European Studies, Agricultural University Wageningen, Wageningen Studies on Heterogeneity and Relocalization 1, 1995.

Gerritsen, P.R.W., "Percepciones, conocimientos y actitudes acerca de la Reserva: una aproximación, Estudio de caso de Cuzalapa". Technical report. Autlán, Mexico, Universidad de Guadalajara, CUCSUR, IMECBIO, Proyecto de Desarrollo Agroforestal de la Sierra de Manantlán, 1998a.

Gerritsen, P.R.W., "Community development, natural resource management and biodiversity conservation in the Sierra de Manantlán biosphere reserve, Mexico". *Community Development Journal*, Vol. 33, no. 4 (1998b), pp. 314-24.

Gerritsen, P.R.W., "Base de datos socioeconómicos a nivel familiar de la comunidad indígena de Cuzalapa, reserva de la biosfera Sierra de Manantlán". Autlán, Universidad de Guadalajara/CUCSURDERN/IMECBIO, 1999.

Gómez-Pompa, A. and A. Kaus, "Taming the wilderness myth". *BioScience*, Vol. 42 (1992), pp. 271-2.

Graf, S.H., E. Santana, E. Jardel and B.F. Benz, "La reserva de la biosfera Sierra de Manantlán: un balance de ocho años de gestión". Revista Universidad de Guadalajara, Marzo-Abril, 1995.

Hardin, G., "The tragedy of the commons'. *Science*, Vol. 162 (1968), pp. 1243-8.

IMECBIO (Instituto Manantlán de Ecología y Conservación de la Biodiversidad), "Programa de manejo de la reserva de la biósfera Sierra de Manantlán". Documento para consulta. Technical Report. Autlán, CUCSUR/IMECBIO, INE/SEMARNAP, 1997.

IMECBIO, "Diagnóstico integral y plan de manejo de recursos naturales de la comunidad indígena de Cuzalapa, municipio de Cuautitlán, reserva de la biosfera Sierra de Manantlán". Technical Report. Autlán, Universidad de Guadalajara, CUCSUR, IMECBIO, Programa de Desarrollo Regional Sustentable (PRODERS), 1998.

INEGI (Instituto Nacional de Estadísticas, Geografía y Informatica), "Conteo de población y vivienda". Resultados definitivos 1996. Jalisco, Mexico-City, INEGI, 1996.

IUCN (International Union for the Conservation of Nature), UNEP (United Nations Environmental Program) and WWF (World Wildlife Fund), *Caring for the earth: a strategy for sustainable living*. Gland, Switzerland, 1991.

Jardel P., E.J. (coord.), "Estrategia para la conservación de la reserva de la biosfera Sierra de Manantlán". El Grullo, Laboratorio Natural Las Joyas, Universidad de Guadalajara, 1992a.

Jardel P., E.J., "Aprovechamiento y conservación de los recursos naturales en la reserva de la biosfera Sierra de Manantlán, México". Technical Report. Autlán, Universidad de Guadalajara, CUCSUR/DERN/IMECBIO, 1992b.

Jardel P., E.J., "Regímenes de propiedad y manejo forestal: el caso de la Sierra de Manantlán". Paper presented at the Taller de análisis sobre el deterioro de los recursos forestales y el cambio institucional en el campo en México (Febrero 11 y de 12 de 1999). México-City, UNAM/SEMARNAP, 1999.

Jardel P., E.J., E. Santana C. and S.H. Graf M., "The Sierra de Manantlán biosphere reserve: conservation and regional sustainable development". *Parks*, Vol. 6, no. 1 (1996), pp. 14-22.

Laitner-Benz, K. and B.F. Benz, "Las condiciones culturales y ambientales en la reserva de la biosfera Sierra de Manantlán en tiempo de la conquista: una perspectiva de los documentos etnohistóricos secundarios". In: R.A. Palafox (coord.), *Estudios de hombre 1*. Guadalajara, Universidad de Guadalajara, 1994.

Louette, D., P.R.W. Gerritsen and J.J. Rosales A., "La actividad ganadera en la reserva de la biosfera Sierra de Manantlán: un primer diagnóstico". Technical report. Autlán, Mexico: Universidad de Guadalajara, IMECBIO, PDASM, 1997.

Louette, D., L.M. Martínez, R.D. Guevara, J.A. Carranza, R.G. Jímenez, E. Casillas, J.P. Esparza and P. Gerritsen, "Cambio de uso de suelo y actividad ganadera en 4 regiones de la reserva de la biosfera Sierra de Manantlán (1971-1998)". Reporte preliminar. Technical report. Autlán, Universidad de Guadalajara, CUCSUR, DERN, IMECBIO, PDASM, 1998.

Markiewicz, D., *The Mexican revolution and the limits of agrarian reform, 1915-1946*. Boulder, Lynne Rienner Publishers, 1993.

North, D.C., *Institutions, institutional change and economic performance*. Cambridge, Cambridge University Press, 1990.

Nuijten, M., "In the name of the land. Organization, transnationalism, and the culture of the state in a Mexican *ejido*". PhD thesis. Wageningen, Wageningen Agricultural University, 1998.

Pimbert, M.P. and J.N. Pretty, "Parks, people and professionals. Putting 'participation' into protected area management". Discussion Paper 57. Geneva, Switzerland: UNRISD, UNRISD, 1995.

Primack, R.B., *Essentials of biodiversity conservation*. Sunderland, Massachusetts, 1993.

Rivera R., I., *El nuevo derecho agrario mexicano*. Segunda Edición. Serie Jurídica. Mexico-City, McGraw-Hill, 1994.

Rojas, R. (coord.), I. Alcocer, H. Fajardo, G. Martínez, M.A. Márquez, E. Miramontes, D. Ortega, C. Palomar, J.C. Pérez and A. Sandoval, "La comunidad y sus recrusos. Ayotitlán ¿desarrollo sustentable? Caracterización integral del ejido Ayotitlán, municipio de Cuautitlán, Jalisco". Guadalajara, Universidad de Guadalajara/Insituto Nacional Indigenista, 1996.

SEMARNAP (Secretaría de Medio Ambiente, Recursos Naturales y Pesca), "Programa de áreas naturales protegidas de México 1995-2000". Mexico City, SEMARNAP/INE, 1996.

SIIR (Sistema Integrado de Información Regional), "Programa de desarrollo regional sustentable, nivel comunitario. Mapas de la *comunidad* indígena de Cuzalapa". Autlán, IMECBIO, DERN, CUCSUR, Universidad de Guadalajara, 1998.

Thiesenhusen, W.C, *Broken promises. Agrarian reform and the Latin American campesino*. Boulder, Colorado, Westview Press, 1995.

Toledo, V.M., "El proceso de ganaderización y la destrucción biológica y ecológica de México". In: E. Leff, *Ambiente y desarrollo en México*. Volumen primero. Mexico-City, CIIH, Universidad Nacional Autónoma de México, 1990.

Toledo, V.M., "The ecological consequences of the 1992 agrarian law of Mexico". In: L. Randall, *Reforming Mexico's agrarian reform*. Armonk, New York, M.E. Sharpe, 1996.

Torres, G., "Plunging into the garlic. Methodological issues and challenges'". In: N. Long and A. Long, *Battlefields of knowledge. The interlocking of theory and practice in social research and development*. London and New York, Routledge Press, 1992.

Wells, M., K. Brandon with L. Hannah, "People and parks. Linking protected area management with local communities". Washington DC, The World Bank/WWF/USAID, 1992.

10 Land reform, rural organization, and agrarian incomes in Nicaragua[1]

Ruerd Ruben, Luis Rodríguez, and Orlando Cortez

Introduction

Land reform has always been a major issue in the agrarian development debate in Central America. Advocates of land reform programs argued that the subdivision of extensive large holdings was required for political and economic reasons, since small-scale production units could take advantage of expected productivity differences (Dorner, 1992; Thiesenhusen, 1989). In most Central American countries, land reform ended with the establishment of an important sector of cooperative production units. Both the state and major peasant organizations favored the establishment of cooperatives, based on a mixture of technical and political arguments.

Land reform cooperatives initially received many benefits, in terms of access to land, financial services, and technical assistance, especially when they were involved in the production of agroexport crops (i.e., cotton, coffee, and sugarcane). Far less attention has been paid to the formal registration of property rights and the arrangement of internal ownership rights. Moreover, procedures for the management and organization of cooperative enterprises remained rather loose, and frequently failed to meet the required standards. Therefore, free-riding behavior, membership desertion, and ultimately the complete selling of cooperative land occurred.

Land reform in Nicaragua suffered from all these general tendencies. The process of land reform in Nicaragua during the *Sandinista* regime (1979-1990) was originally based on the establishment of large state farms and production cooperatives. Emerging peasant resistance, and subsequent adjustments in the market and institutional environment that surrounded the reform sector, gave rise to parcelation in some cooperatives, and to the transformation of production into service cooperatives in others. When the *Sandinistas* lost the elections in 1990 and the liberal administrations of Chamorro and Alemán took office, state farms were completely dismantled, and further incentives were launched for the registration of individual ownership rights for land reform beneficiaries.

After the start of the land reform process under the *Sandinista* government, subsequent political regimes introduced numerous modifications of land rights, while macroeconomic adjustment programs influenced the access conditions to rural factor and commodity markets. Therefore, the attractiveness of cooperative membership has undergone considerable change over the last ten years. Nicaraguan cooperative performance has scarcely been analyzed from this multi-period perspective, and little comparative evidence is available regarding the relative behavior of cooperative enterprises vis-à-vis individual procedures under similar production conditions.

A rather heterogeneous pattern of rural organization has emerged, and farm households have become engaged in different types of contract choice arrangements. Some land reform enterprises have maintained collective property rights, while other former cooperatives have continued with joint service provision, and some former cooperative members have fully abandoned mutual relationships. Attention should be paid to the individual, household, and group characteristics that influence the selection of these pathways of institutional change, as well as the implications for differences in income level and income composition between cooperative members/former cooperative members and individual farmers. Such an analysis provides insights into the reasons for membership desertion and the selling of land by land reform beneficiaries, and enables the identification of suitable policy instruments that could accompany the process of cooperative reforms in the Nicaraguan countryside.

This chapter focuses on the structure and dynamics of the entrepreneurial cooperative organization established during the first phase of land reform in Nicaragua, with special attention to the process of institutional re-engineering in subsequent phases, and the relative attractiveness of cooperative membership after structural adjustment took place. The second section provides a short overview of the historical background to and the different phases of the Nicaraguan agrarian reform process from 1979 onward. In the third section, major changes in rural organizational forms in the Pacific region are reviewed, comparing the situation during the *Sandinista* period with the adjustments that took place afterward. The fourth section is based on a nationwide survey on income differentiation between farm households related to specific types of social organization. While the relative competitiveness of the cooperative sector is acknowledged, potential reasons for membership desertion and/or the selling of cooperative land are identified. In the discussion, attention is devoted to the available prospects for stabilization of the land reform sector. The chapter is concluded with a number of policy recommendations for reinforcing the land reform sector, and some suggestions regarding technical support for the process of cooperative consolidation.

Land reform in Nicaragua

In 1979, the *Sandinista* government launched a massive program of land reform, based on the expropriation of landed property owned by the former dictator and the confiscation of idle estates. Since the primary objective of land reform was to restructure agricultural production, far less attention was paid to the development of a viable and independent peasantry sector. Instead, state-owned enterprises and landless farmers organized in agrarian production cooperatives (based on collective land ownership) received a major share of all expropriated land (Baumeister, 1998).

Land reform was initially accompanied by subsidized credit programs, technical and managerial support, and tight regulations regarding marketing. Legal aspects were, however, widely ignored and ownership rights were hardly registered. Moreover, former owners did not receive compensation payments. The economic and political limitations of this reform model became apparent from the strong increase in fiscal deficits and the farmers' resistance to the compulsory delivery of their produce for state-determined prices (Spoor, 1994).

In the mid-1980s, the Nicaraguan land reform process changed its orientation, giving more attention in subsequent phases to the redistribution of state farms to the cooperative sector, the titling of individual family farms and their organization in associative enterprises (e.g., service cooperatives, peasant associative shops, etc.). Between 1979 and 1990, the state sector reduced its share of agricultural land from 20 to 9%, while the cooperative sector increased to embrace 29% of all farmland (see also Table 1). Meanwhile, the rural organizational landscape became much more diversified, including both production and service cooperatives, joint titling for indigenous communities, and increasingly also permitting individual titling (de Groot, 1994).

Table 1   Nicaragua: land reform and tenancy structure (1978-1994) (in 000 *manzanas*)

Sector	1978		1990		1994	
	Area	%	Area	%	Area	%
Private property	8,073	100.0	4,398	54.4	5,577	69.8
>500 mzs	2,920	36.2	525	6.5	751	10.5
200-500 mzs	1,311	16.2	925	11.4	1,412	17.4
50 -200 mzs	2,431	30.1	1,702	21.0	2,130	26.0
10-50 mzs	1,241	15.4	1,119	13.8	1,147	14.2
<10 mzs	170	2.1	137	1.7	137	1.7
Reformed sector	-	-	3,675	45.6	2,496	30.7
State	-	-	755	9.3	-	-
Production coops	-	-	895	11.0	663	8.2
Service coops	-	-	1,460	18.0	1,104	13.6
Communities	-	-	171	2.1	171	2.1
Individual	-	-	425	5.2	558	6.8

Source: Stanfield *et al.* (1994).

Note: 1 *manzana* = 0.7 ha.

Major changes were introduced within the Nicaraguan tenancy structure when the *Sandinistas* lost the elections in 1990, and the liberal administration of Chamorro (1990-1995) and then that of Alemán (1995-2000) took office. Emerging conflicts over earlier confiscations and newly granted land titles gave rise to a high degree of instability. New laws permitted the restitution of the expropriated estates that had not been distributed to farmers. Former owners of expropriated land could also make good their claim for compensation to be paid with government bonds (a total amount of US$ 80 million was paid out up until 1994). Some state farms were used to enable the settlement of former guerrilla fighters. Finally, legal procedures were created for the registration of ownership rights for individual land reform beneficiaries.

During the same period, production conditions for the reform sector changed drastically. The liberalization and deregulation of internal commodity markets had taken place in the mid-1980s, in an effort to offer peasant producers more incentive for market production. Major limitations appeared at the output side, when general economic stagnation and urban unemployment brought about purchasing power constraints. For export products, a complex system of dual exchange rates was imposed, allowing the state to acquire a substantial share of the agricultural surplus. High inflation rates and related price distortions on local markets necessitated a series of exchange rate adjustments in the late 1980s and early 1990s. Moreover, restriction of the credit market became effective with the privatization of the banking system and the indexation of interest rates. Consequently, agrarian capital inputs became far more expensive and labor-intensive production systems became more attractive (Spoor, 1994).

Economic reforms and tenancy regulations had important implications for the relative competitiveness of the land reform sector. Agrarian production and service cooperatives have lost some ground in recent years, but still retain control of about 20% of all farmland. Even now that 45% of the farmland has been expropriated, and close to 37% has been redistributed, the debate on land reform in Nicaragua is still largely "unfinished business" (Lipton, 1995), in the sense that ownership rights are not fully guaranteed by the state (and the legitimacy of public laws is not fully recognized by the population) and resource management regimes are subject to continuous modifications. Major questions have emerged with respect to the prospects for the cooperative organization of production and the incentives that are effective in maintaining the cooperative framework. Therefore, attention is devoted to the historical evolution of rural social organizations in the Nicaraguan countryside during the last decade, and to the factors that determine agrarian income differences between different types of rural organization in a more comparative perspective.

Agrarian production and social organization

During the initial stages of land reform in Nicaragua, cooperative organization was generally considered a superior form of production. From the viewpoint of the state, cooperatives provided better opportunities for the effective delivery of inputs, credit, and technical assistance services, as well as for the organization of marketing, while the presence of cooperative units in regions of conflict enabled their integration into military defense activities. Moreover, peasant organizations favored collective production as a way to maintain control over membership and to improve the competitive position of the cooperatives in market exchange.

Decollectivization processes were initiated early in the 1980s, when the *Sandinista* government reviewed the land reform legislation and permitted individual ownership. The spontaneous disintegration of production cooperatives was further reinforced when structural adjustment policies reduced state price controls and necessitated institutional reforms of credit and marketing programs (Catalan, 1994; Clemens, 1994). Finally, devaluation coupled with the sudden collapse of international cotton prices in the late 1980s, implied a dramatic loss of the competitive position of agroexport-oriented cooperatives (Clemens, 1995). When the Alemán government came into office, even more restrictions were imposed on rural finance, and emerging conflicts over land rights made cooperative ownership highly uncertain.

In this section, major changes in rural organizational forms in the Pacific region are discussed, and the situation is compared during the *Sandinista* period with the adjustments that took place afterward. Attention is focused on the Pacific region of Nicaragua, where land reform has been particularly important due to the expropriation of a substantial number of estates belonging to the former dictator. More than half of the land reform cooperatives were located in this region (Baumeister, 1998: 181). Moreover, the Pacific region is very important for national economic development, due to its favorable agroecological potential (i.e., well-drained and fertile volcanic soils that permit the intensive production of annual crops) and the wide availability of road infrastructure, markets, and financial institutions.

Field data were collected from a random sample of 62 production cooperatives/former production cooperatives in 1989, and the same farms and families were visited again in 1997 (Vaessen, 1997). The basic aim was to see how the institutional organization of production had been modified over this eight-year period, and which types of farm households remained within the cooperative framework.

Moreover, major adjustments in the internal organization could be identified. Therefore, attention is focused on changes in membership (size and composition), adjustments in land-use and cropping patterns, and individual member characteristics associated with specific pathways of organizational change.

Descriptive statistics for this cooperative sample are given in Table 2. During the period under review, both available arable land and membership declined substantially, permitting a slight increase in the amount of land per family. Collective ownership of machinery and cattle was drastically reduced. Remaining members are likely to be former founders of the cooperative who maintain strong family ties with other members. When non-founding members leave the cooperative framework, more homogeneous membership reinforces prospects for further cooperation.

Table 2   Resources and membership of cooperatives in the Pacific region (1989-1997)

Characteristics	1989		1997		T-test	
Total area *(manzanas)*	481.7	(537.4)	354.4	(407.8)	2.62	**
Membership (persons)	18.3	(10.4)	12.4	(6.2)	5.45	**
Area per member *(manzanas)*	26.3	(18.0)	28.0	(28.7)	-1.70	*
Family ties (% of members)	58.0	(28.0)	59.0	(33.0)	-0.61	
Male members (% of members)	92.0	(15.0)	90.0	(15.0)	0.97	
Founding members (% of members)	42.0	(25.0)	56.0	(30.0)	-4.31	**
Collective livestock (number)	71.0	(113.6)	10.5	(36.7)	4.29	**
Collective machinery (units)	8.8	(6.6)	3.6	(5.5)	6.48	**
Collective land-use (% of farms)	100		20			

Source: DEA-UNAN/LTC 1989; NIRP/ESECA 1997.

Note: Standard deviations between brackets.

        ** significant at 0.05; * significant at 0.10.

These changes in membership and resource use seem to confirm the general tendency toward decollectivization that could be expected under changing conditions of market liberalization and legal reforms. However, while collective production as a whole declined drastically (in 1997 only 20% of the former cooperatives maintained some collective activities), it did not totally disappear. In fact, three different responses can be identified:

a. *Production collectives:* cooperatives that retain joint production due to their specialization in livestock, commercial cereal production (maize, sorghum, rice) and traditional/non-traditional cash crops (soya, sesame, sugarcane), which require intensive land and labor use.

b. *Service cooperatives:* cooperatives that gave up collective production, but remained engaged in cooperative arrangements for the supply of services, e.g., the channeling of loans to members, the provision of jointly-owned machinery for individual use, and the joint purchase of inputs for individual parcels.

c. *Parcelation:* cooperative members who abandon the cooperative framework and proceed toward individual titling of land ownership, continuing as fully private producers.

Comparing the member and group characteristics of these three segments, some conclusions can be drawn with respect to the reasons for integration/disintegration, and the typical organizational features and production systems associated with partial decollectivization. Table 3 provides a comparison of the underlying factors that motivated institutional change. The upper segment of this table shows a number of structural changes in member and group characteristics between 1989 and 1997. While total membership declined and, consequently, the available land per member increased, differences in land area, group size, and membership composition are not significant between the three categories. Scale economies related to the joint ownership of machinery and/or the maintenance of a common herd, appear to be a major motive behind maintaining the cooperative framework.

The bottom part of Table 3 provides an analysis of the institutional characteristics of the 1997 sample. Smaller (older) families with less land and constrained access to off-farm employment possibilities, tend to remain within the cooperative framework. Surprisingly, their sociocultural background as reflected by previous occupations (e.g., former wage laborers or independent entrepreneurs) had no major influence on institutional choice. Collective ownership leads to fewer land transactions and a lower degree of land allotment. The production systems of disintegrating cooperatives are strongly oriented toward the production of basic grains, whereas service cooperatives are characterized by a more diversified production orientation. Collective indebtedness proved to be a major reason for not being able to proceed with parcelation.

Different pathways for the adjustment of cooperative contracts coexist under broadly similar external conditions. Individual member characteristics have only a marginal influence on contractual choice. Full parcelation is likely to take place within enterprises that have more land available and exhibit less control of their labor force. The transformation of production cooperatives into service cooperatives is generally based on successful past experiences with input supply or machinery services for individual members. Smaller farmers with fewer off-farm employment opportunities stick to the semi-collective framework, due to the burden of their collective debts.

Rural incomes and agrarian stability

Taking into account the coexistence of different strategies for institutional choice, the question of the relative competitiveness of cooperative producers vis-à-vis individual farmers of similar size (farms up to 40 *manzanas* per family) is addressed. Therefore, differences in income levels, income composition, and factor rewards are compared between three types of households:
i)   Members of production and/or service cooperatives who still maintain some degree of cooperation (the remaining cooperative part of the land reform sector).
ii) Former members of cooperatives who fully subdivided their farms (corresponding to the tendency to parcelize).
iii) Private or individual farmers who did not participate in land reform (included as a basis for comparison).

This analysis is based on a nationwide survey on income differentiation between farm households related to specific types of social organization. Data were collected from a stratified sample of 488 households located in three major regions of Nicaragua.

Table 3   Member and group characteristics (1989 and 1997)

Variable	Year	Collective	Services	Parcelation	Sign
Total sample size (N)*		13	16	33	
Total number of members		44	58	114	
Average membership	1989	21.1	19.4	17.7	N.S.
(members per enterprise)	1997	12.5	12.8	12.2	N.S.
Total area	1989	469.1	422.6	532.2	N.S.
(manzanas)	1997	419.2	281.8	364.2	N.S.
Area per member	1989	22.2	21.8	30.1	N.S.
(manzanas)	1997	33.5	22.0	29.8	N.S.
Family ties	1989	57.1	54.8	59.9	N.S.
(% of members)	1997	57.2	57.8	60.6	N.S.
Male members	1989	93.7	87.0	94.1	N.S.
(% of members)	1997	87.7	88.9	92.2	N.S.
Collective livestock	1989	59.5	40.3	90.2	N.S.
(number)	1997	46.1	2.9	0.1	sign
Collective machinery	1989	13.2	8.1	8.0	sign
(units)	1997	12.3	2.8	0.8	sign
Family size (members)	1997	5.2	5.5	6.1	sign
Size private parcel (manzanas)	1997	8.1	15.7	19.1	sign
Land sales (% of farms)	1997	7.7	50.0	63.6	sign
Land allotment (% of farms)	1997	46.2	100.0	93.9	sign
Indebtedness (% of farms)	1997	61.5	18.8	27.5	sign
Off-farm employment (% of farms)	1997	15.4	43.6	60.6	sign
Previous occupation (% wage laborer)	1997	77.2	63.8	68.5	N.S.
Land-use (% subsistence crops)	1997	67.6	69.6	66.3	sign

Note: Significant between-group differences are based on Tamhane and Games-Howell test; significant associations
are based on Goodman and Kruskal-Wallis Tau tests.

* Enterprises interviewed in 1989 en 1997.

Table 4 provides a specification of various income sources. Agricultural income (after payment of variable input costs and hired labor) refers to the net rewards for family labor engaged in arable cropping activities. Livestock income (e.g., change in herds and net sales of milk, eggs, and cheese) is specified separately. Off-farm wage refers to income derived from occasional employment by other farmers, but also includes the rewards for working on collective plots. Non-farm income includes self-employment and salaried labor outside the agricultural sector. Other income includes remittances and other transfers (pensions).

Total household income is somewhat higher in the group of private farmers, but this difference appeared not to be statistically significant. Major differences appear between private farmers and former cooperative members who subdivided their farm with respect to the share of profit and livestock income. Private farmers receive a fairly larger income share from livestock activities, while former cooperative members obtain more than half of their income from arable cropping operations. Similar findings are reported by Davis et al. (this volume). An important difference between currently active cooperatives and private farmers is the higher

Table 4   Income levels and income composition

Income category	Cooperative (N=165)	Parcelation (N=176)	Private (N=147)	Total (N=488)	Anova	Sign (N=488)
Total Income (in Córdovas)	25,982	28,117	34,561	29,525	0.48	N.S.
Agricultural income (%)	41	56*	30*	43	0.00	sign
Off-farm wage (%)	19*	14	9	14	0.02	sign
Non-farm income (%)	15	12	14	14	0.65	N.S.
Livestock income (%)	16	7*	27*	16	0.01	sign
Other income (%)	9	11	20	13	0.12	N.S.

Source: NIRP/ESECA Field Survey, 1998

Note: * Significant differences (based on Scheffe's test)

income share the former receive from engaging in agricultural wage labor. Consequently, household incomes are clearly more diversified in the cooperative context.

In order to gain further insight into the dynamics of the income composition between different categories of farmers, the following income function was estimated:

$$Y_{total} = a_0 + b_1{}^*W_f + b_2{}^*W_a + b_3{}^*W_n + b_4{}^*Y_l + b_5{}^*Y_o$$

where a_0 is the intercept, W represents different labor reward categories derived from farm, off-farm agricultural wage labor, and non-farm non-agricultural activities, and Y represents income from livestock activities and other sources. The coefficients in this function can be understood as income elasticities that indicate the proportional effects of a change in a certain income category on the total household income. Significant differences in the level or slope of this function between the three categories of farm households were verified with the Chow test.

The results are presented in Table 5. The income functions for cooperative members and private farmers give the highest fit, while the model for parceled farmers strongly depends on the farm-level rewards for arable cropping and livestock activities. Farm income is significant in all three specifications: cooperative members are most sensitive to changes in the farm-level wage rate, while parceled farmers are less sensitive, probably due to their lower commercialization rate. Differences between the coefficients for separate income categories proved not to be significant for parceled farmers, while cooperative farmers show more sensitivity to a change in on-farm income (compared to the off-farm agricultural wage rate), and private farmers show more sensitivity to a change in the on-farm wage (compared to the non-agricultural wage rate). Exogenous shocks arising from changes in livestock income or other income sources (e.g., remittances) only lead to proportional income adjustments, and do not exhibit substantial income stabilization effects (coefficients close to 1).

Further analysis of the elasticities for different sources of income, indicates that agricultural production remains by far the most important income component for all types of farmer, although cooperative farmers could also benefit from off-farm employment and, particularly, from engagement in non-farm activities. Non-farm activities seem to be more available to this segment of the rural population, possibly due to their stronger involvement in social networks, resulting in more social capital (Corral and Reardon, 2000; Ruben and van Strien, 1999). It was not possible to explicitly determine the specific individual characteristics associated with different income elasticities. Clemens *et al.* (1999) suggest that rural household incomes in Nicaragua depend on the level of education, the pattern of land-use (perennial crops vs. basic grains), available assets (livestock), and access to credit and social services. Corral and Reardon (2000) point toward high involvement of rural households in the Pacific region in non-agricultural employment, especially amongst higher income quartiles. The focus was on the determinants of income differentiation within a relative homogeneously endowed farm households that only differ with respect to their organizational background.

The results derived from this income analysis can be further used for an appraisal of policy instruments that enable the stabilization of rural farm households. In general terms, income derived from arable cropping activities remains the single most important income source, and all categories of farmers are thus likely to react strongly to improved marketing opportunities or to more efficient input and credit delivery systems. Cooperative members benefit twice as much from an increase in their farm income compared to a similar increase in off-farm wage income. Contributions from non-agricultural income sources remain fairly small and only have a positive effect for cooperative farmers, given their current dependence on seasonal cropping activities.

Economic stability in the Nicaraguan countryside is increasingly challenged by processes of land transfers and membership desertion. While the parcelation of cooperative property enabled some farmers to improve their income position, this was at the expense of a higher concentration of income derived from arable cropping, giving rise to a substantially lower income elasticity for on-farm labor efforts. Otherwise, the incomes of cooperative members have a fairly balanced composition, and are not significantly lower than those of individual farmers with similar resources at their disposal. Parcelation is therefore less perceived as an option for improving economic performance, and has probably far more to do either with declining opportunities on the labor market (related to the low agrarian investment rate) or with the desire to reduce coordination costs. Individual private farmers are distinguished mainly by their higher livestock incomes and less dependency on the labor market. Individual ownership is preferred in this case in order to generate prospects for a genuine peasant strategy of primitive accumulation at farm-household level.

While the relative competitiveness of the cooperative sector is acknowledged, some specific reasons for membership desertion and/or the selling of cooperative land can be identified. Membership desertion is a typical individual strategy for leaving the cooperative framework, usually due to dissatisfaction with internal rules and procedures, unclear definition of membership rights, and incomplete insurance mechanisms (Ruben, 1997). Most former members who leave the cooperative organization, continue as independent farmers within the same region. Otherwise, the decision to sell the cooperative can be considered a collective strategy related to the possibility of gaining access to capital funds accumulation within the cooperative firm. This occurs mostly in the case of more mature cooperatives with older members who are looking forward to their pension (Ruben and Funez, 1993).

Table 5   OLS regression: income elasticities for different farm types

Income category	Cooperative		Parcelation		Private Farmers	
Constant	-2,525		19,500	**	5,284	**
Farm income (Wf)	401.1	**(***)	76.3	**	197.9	**(***)
Agricultural off-farm income (Wa)	202.0	*	-283.1		98.7	
Non-farm income (Wn)	358.0	**	-23.3		31.3	
Livestock income (Yl)	1.07	*	0.92	**	0.99	**
Other income (Yo)	1.05	**	0.54		0.94	**
Adjusted R2	0.93		0.54		0.93	
Chow test (F-stat)	64.40		72.80		14.40	
Income elasticities						
EWf	0.67		0.26		0.49	
EWa	0.05		-0.06		0.01	
EWn	0.13		-0.01		0.01	

Source: NIRP/ESECA Field Survey, 1998 (van Strien, 1998).

Note: ** significant at 0.05; * significant at 0.10; *** coefficients refer to significant between-group differences.

The breakdown of the cooperative framework is thus related to the relative success of earlier operations.

Finally, external market conditions and institutional support regimes tend to be important for cooperative consolidation. Accumulation mostly takes place when access to rural financial markets or off-farm employment is guaranteed. In both cases, funds become available for the purchase of yield-increasing inputs or livestock, giving rise to positive income effects.

Conclusions

Rural organization in Nicaragua has undergone considerable change during the last decades, due to frequent adjustments in the external legal framework and socio-economic production conditions, as well as to growing pressure for the rearrangement of internal rights, duties, and entitlements. Modifications of organizational regimes and contract choice can therefore be considered an endogenous process of institutional re-engineering. From the individual farmer's viewpoint, the attractiveness of cooperative membership is no longer guaranteed by supportive state delivery networks and subsidized financial services, but has to be made effective under competitive market conditions. At enterprise level, access to factor and commodity markets, and the availability of institutional support, as well as of jointly supplied services, are now considered major incentives for maintaining a certain level of cooperation, although the fully collective framework has been almost completely abandoned.

The adjustment of organizational arrangements for resource management takes different directions, depending on the individual and household characteristics of members/former members, the strength of their social networks, and past experiences with entrepreneurial regimes. A distinction can be made between farm households that remain within the cooperative framework due to outstanding debts or the absence of alternative opportunities (e.g., limited access to land or labor markets), and those families that prefer some level of cooperation as a positive strategy for reducing risks and improving competitiveness. The transformation of production cooperatives into service cooperatives mainly took place within enterprises that had already had some experience with joint input purchase or traction services. Full parcelation tends to be the preferred option of farmers with more market-oriented (but extensive) production systems who are better able to complement their income through partial engagement in the labor market.

The process of "purifying" cooperative membership during the last decade, permitted a substantial increase in the amount of available arable land per household. Although no detailed information on land quality is available, this may be one of the reasons why the average family income between existent and dissolved cooperatives is not significantly different. Major variation occurs, however, with respect to the farm household income composition.

Cooperative members derive a major share of their income from individual cropping and livestock activities, supplemented with agricultural wage labor on collective plots. The income from collective activities provides cash resources with which to finance consumptive expenditures as well as investments in their individual parcels. Former cooperative members who opted for parcelation have become far more dependent on their cropping income, and receive a substantially smaller share from livestock and wage labor activities. Compared to individual private farmers, their income composition has become less balanced and more vulnerable to external shocks. Private farmers receive more income from livestock activities, given their higher land/labor ratio. In all cases, improvement of household income strongly depends on agricultural yields and farmgate prices.

Based on this analysis of the influence of farmers' characteristics on the selection of different institutional arrangements for cooperation/non-cooperation and related differences in income composition, it is possible to draw some conclusions regarding (i) the attractiveness of cooperative membership, and (ii) the competitiveness of production and service cooperatives vis-à-vis individual farmers. Membership of production cooperatives remains an important options for less-endowed farm households in more remote regions that are devoted to subsistence crops and have few alternative employment opportunities. Affiliation with service cooperatives takes place when more commercially-oriented crops are cultivated on individual parcels and benefits can be derived from joint input purchase or marketing. Full parcelation mainly occurs when farmers are able to start their individual accumulation process and can cover production and background risks.

Notes

[1] Funds for the fieldwork required for this research were provided by the Netherlands-Israel Development Research Programme (NIRP) Project No. 96-12.1 "Resource Management and Contract Choice in Agricultural Cooperatives". We owe thanks to Michael Carter (University of Wisconsin, Madison, US) for making available the original data from the DEA-UNAN/LTC 1989 cooperative sample. The fieldwork assistance (data collection) provided by Ir. Jos Vaessen in 1997 is gratefully acknowledged. Mrs. Danielle van Strien participated in the processing and analysis of the sampling data set.

References

Baumeister, E., "Estructura agraria en Nicaragua (1979-1989)". PhD dissertation. University of Nijmegen. CDR-ULA Ediciones. San José, 1998.

Catalán, O., "Control de la hiperinflación y ajuste estructural en Nicaragua". In: J.P. de Groot and M. Spoor (eds.), *Ajuste estructural y economía campesina*. Managua, ESECA-UNAN, 1994.

Clemens, H., "La estrategia de desarrollo agropecuario en Nicaragua: oportunidades y limitantes para una reactivación económica democratica". In: J.P. de Groot and M. Spoor (eds.), *Ajuste estructural y economía campesina*. Managua, ESECA-UNAN, 1994.

Clemens, H., R. Cruz and A. Sanders, "Vulnerabilidad y desastres naturales: el caso de los agricultores afectados por el Huracan Mitch en Las Segovias, Nicaragua". Research Paper CDR-ULA. San José, 2000.

Corral, L. and T. Reardon, "Rural non-farm incomes in Nicaragua: patterns, determinants, and implications". World Development (forthcoming).

De Groot, J., "Reforma agraria en Nicaragua: una actualización". In: J.P. de Groot and M. Spoor (eds.), *Ajuste estructural y economía campesina*. Managua, ESECA-UNAN, 1994.

Dorner, P., *Latin American land reforms in theory and practice*. Madison, University of Wisconsin Press, 1992.

Lipton, M., "Land reform as commenced business: the evidence against stopping". In: A. de Janvry, S. Radwan, E. Sadoulet and E. Thorbecke (eds.), *State, market and civil organizations: new theories, new practices and their implications for rural development*. Houndsmills, MacMillan/ILO, 1995.

Ruben, R. and F. Funez, "La compra-venta de tierras de la reforma agraria". Editorial Guaymuras, Tegucigalpa, 1993.

Ruben, R., "Making cooperatives work. Contract choice and resource management within land reform cooperatives in Honduras". Amsterdam, CEDLA/CLAS, 1998.

Ruben, R. and D. van Strien, "Social capital and household incomes in Nicaragua: the economic role of rural organisation and farmers' networks". Report NIRP programme 96-12.1. Paper presented at the XII AASERCCA Conference, Brussels, December 2-3, 1999.

Spoor, M., *The state and domestic agricultural markets. Nicaragua: from interventionism to neo-liberalism*. London, Macmillan. Press, 1994.

Stanfield, J.D., "Un analisis de la situación actual de la tenencia de la tierra en Nicaragua". Wisconsin, Madison, The Land Tenure Center for ASDI, 1994.

Thiesenhusen, W.C. (ed.), *Searching for agrarian reform in Latin America*. Boston, Unwin Hyman Inc., 1989.

Vaessen, J., "The transformation of cooperative organisation in Nicaragua. Contract choice, pathways of change and agricultural performance among agricultural cooperatives". MSc thesis. Wageningen Agricultural University, Wageningen, 1997.

Van Strien, D., "Farm household income analysis in Nicaragua". Field report NIRP 96-12.1. ESECA-UNAN/WAU/HUJI. Managua,

11 Income generation strategies among Nicaraguan agricultural producers

Benjamin Davis, Calogero Carletto, and Norman Piccioni[1]

Introduction

Recent studies show that over 75% of the rural population in Nicaragua lives in poverty, with over a third living in extreme poverty (World Bank, 1995).[2] Nicaragua ranks second only to Haiti as the poorest country in the Western Hemisphere in terms of per capita GDP. The countryside is also torn by conflicts over land ownership that date back to the land reform program of the *Sandinista* revolutionary government (1979-1990). Finally, hurricane Mitch dealt a serious blow to many areas of the countryside, threatening the economic prospects of poor rural households for many years to come. There is concern that unless solutions are found to the low standard of living, land conflicts, and the weakening of medium-term prospects brought on by hurricane Mitch, economic and social instability in the countryside could worsen.

This chapter presents an analysis of poverty and the structure and determinants of income in a population of rural Nicaraguan households. The discussion is based on a 1996 national household survey of agricultural and cattle producers, with extensive detail on income generating assets, agricultural and cattle production, off-farm labor activities, access to institutions and organizations, and individual and household characteristics. The following questions are examined: what the structure and distribution of income and assets in rural Nicaragua are; which household assets and characteristics are associated with poverty; and which assets and institutions hold most promise, from both a household and a policy maker perspective, as part of an income-generation strategy to reduce rural poverty, given the current economic, social, and political context in Nicaragua.

Background

Since late 1987, three consecutive Nicaraguan governments have implemented stabilization and structural adjustment plans with varying degrees of success. The first program, initiated during the Presidency of Daniel Ortega in 1988 with the help of several Nordic governments, failed to stabilize the economy.[3] Following the electoral defeat of the *Sandinista* National Liberation Front in 1990, the government of President Violeta Chamorro (1990-1996), under an agreement with the International Monetary Fund (IMF), implemented a more far-reaching program, which involved the reduction of public spending and the fiscal deficit, restriction of credit, privatization of over 350 state enterprises, liberalization of the financial sector, domestic and foreign trade liberalization, and the drastic downsizing of the role of the state in agriculture (World Bank, 1995).[4] These policies have been continued, in large measure, by the administration of President Arnoldo Alemán, which signed agreements with the IMF in 1997 and 1998.

Although these programs have stabilized the macroeconomy, they have not led to much improvement in the living standards of the majority of Nicaraguans. In fact, the rural poor were the hardest hit by the austerity measures and adjustment policies of the Chamorro Government. Arana and Rocha (1997) show that the distribution of income has worsened since the onset of the stabilization and adjustment programs in 1987. It is increasingly clear that in countries like Nicaragua, macroeconomic success is a necessary, but not sufficient, condition for sustained economic growth. This is particularly true for the agricultural sector, whose recovery the new Nicaraguan government has identified as the key to the economic growth of the country (MAG, 1997, 1998a, 1998b, and 1998c). Further, growth itself is not sufficient to reduce poverty, particularly when this growth leads to increasingly unequal distribution of income.[5] What is required now, as in a number of other developing countries, is more attention to microeconomic problems that inhibit the productivity and response capacity of producers, such as failures in labor, land, and product markets; the absence of agrarian institutions; and the lack of public investment (de Janvry and Sadoulet, 1997).

The reduction of the role of the state in agriculture was a key tenet of the Chamorro Administration's economic policy. The number of *manzanas*[6] of agricultural land supported by government credit dropped drastically, by more than 75% from the 1990/91 planting season to the 1995/96 season. At the same time, the number of *manzanas* of corn and beans supported by credit, the principal crops in Nicaragua, dropped over 90% (BCN, 1997).[7] The prices of inputs were liberalized, and the 1991 devaluation further raised prices of inputs, which were almost all imported. Extension services previously provided by government agencies and the state development bank BANADES were curtailed (Spoor, 1995).[8] By 1996, between only 10 and 15% of producers received any credit or technical assistance. Those few services that existed were provided in large part by non-governmental organizations (NGOs) and projects of international organizations (Davis *et al.*, 1997).[9] Recent government efforts, however, appear to have increased the access of small and medium farmers to extension services, though overall levels of use remain low (Davis and Murgai, 2000).

During the period of *Sandinista* government, the state monopolized the domestic and foreign marketing of agricultural products. In basic grains, traditional intermediaries were displaced, and price policies had a distinctly urban bias (Spoor, 1995). The Chamorro reforms liberalized both foreign and domestic agricultural markets, but without sufficiently promoting institutions that would facilitate competitive markets. While producer and consumer groups quickly stepped in to take over exporting, basic grains markets continue to be underdeveloped, resulting in highly differential participation among households. For both corn and beans, more than half of producing households did not sell their production in 1996. Both the government as well as international organizations have identified commercialization as the key bottleneck for peasant producers (Davis *et al.*, 1997).

The agriculture and cattle sectors accounted for over 29% of GDP in 1999. While growth in the livestock sector has stagnated during the last three years, agriculture has grown at higher rate than the other major sectors of the economy, at approximately 4% per capita annually since 1994 (BCN, 1999). Nevertheless, the recent growth in agriculture is more a result of expansion in planted area, due to the winding down of armed conflict and extension of the agricultural frontier, as well as good prices for export crops such as coffee, than to improvements in productivity (MAG, 1997). For this reason, agriculture remains at a crossroads: with the reduced possibility of growth through expansion of cultivated land, higher levels of productivity are necessary to assure sustained economic growth.

The agricultural sector in Nicaragua, in structural terms, is highly heterogeneous. The response capacity of producers is conditioned by this household level heterogeneity, which is composed of the following elements: control over productive assets, transaction costs, market failures and imperfections, and differential access to agrarian institutions and public goods. Much of this response capacity revolves around the production of corn and beans; almost 80% of agricultural households produce corn, and over half produce beans. Even though households may have diversified into higher value crops or off-farm labor activities, these crops remain an essential element in the economic portfolio of almost all households. This is a response to market failures and economic and social insecurity, in which most households sense the need to assure consumption of these basic grains (Davis *et al.*, 1997). In order to develop successful policy alternatives, it is imperative to understand and take into account household level heterogeneity.

Recent literature on rural poverty in Nicaragua

Few studies exist on poverty in Nicaragua. This is due primarily to the paucity of household level data. Only during the last few years has a concerted effort been begun to catch up in terms of statistical data, beginning with a series of urban expenditure and consumption surveys, as well as the 1993 Living Standards Measurement Survey (LSMS) carried out by the World Bank. The 1993 LSMS had a very limited agricultural module. The LSMS was followed by a population census; a second LSMS was carried out in the spring of 1998, with an expanded agricultural module, using the population census for the sample frame.[10] A number of agricultural household surveys have been carried out in recent years, only one of which has published income figures.[11]

The 1993 LSMS found that over 50% of the Nicaraguan population live below the poverty line, while almost 20% live in extreme poverty. This poverty is overwhelmingly rural. Further, poverty and extreme poverty were somewhat concentrated in Regions I and VI.[12,13] Poor rural households are much more dependent on agriculture, both in terms of own production and wage labor, while food expenditures make up over half their total expenditures. Poor rural households have more family members, while the heads of poor households have significantly less education than non-poor heads of households (World Bank, 1995).

Data sources and the construction of income variables

This study is based on a national household survey of agricultural and cattle producers carried out by the MAG, with the support of the UN Food and Agricultural Organization, during December, 1996. A total of 1,500 households were surveyed, and 1,468 observations from the survey are included in the analysis.[14] For the income analysis, 58 additional observations were excluded, due to lack of information or internal inconsistencies, resulting in 1,410 weighted observations.[15]

In the analysis of the structure of income, a household typology based on farm size is employed. In the land size typology, households are classified into five categories depending on the area they controlled during the survey period.[16] The five categories range from zero to two *manzanas (microfundio)*, two to five mzs. *(minifundio)*, five to 20 mzs. (small landholders), 20 to 50 mzs. (medium landholders), and more than 50 mzs. (large landholders).[17] This division results in the following distribution of households:

Table 1   Household typology based on farm size

	Percentage of households	Percentage of total land
microfundio	20	1
minifundio	24	3
small landholders	29	14
medium landholders	15	22
large landholders	12	60

While the *microfundio* and *minifundio* comprise more than 44% of agricultural households, they hold only 4% of total land area. If one includes the small landholders, then 73% of landholding households control only 18% of the total land area. The overall land Gini coefficient is (.72).

Household income is derived from four economic activities: agricultural production, livestock production, non-agricultural labor activities, and rental land. Non-agricultural and land rental income information come directly from the survey. Net agricultural and livestock income were constructed from the sales and costs of production, including the valuation of output consumed on farm by the household.[18]

Total household income was divided by the number of immediate family members, producing a per capita household income level. This process resulted in an average total yearly household income of C 2,774 (US$329) per capita, in 1996 Córdobas.[19]

A typical problem with using household income data is the high degree of variability inherent in agricultural and livestock production (see Deaton, 1995, for a good discussion). This survey is no exception. A number of producers experienced crop failure, low yields in comparison with their reported technology level, or the death of animals. Because cash flows or monetary savings were not recorded, approximately 16% of households reported net negative agricultural income, and another 16% net negative livestock income. In total, 6% of the households surveyed had an overall negative household income. Many of these households, however, are not poor, at least in terms of assets and income generating potential, and this should be kept in mind when analyzing the characteristics of households located in the lowest income decile.

The structure of income in rural Nicaragua

Although poverty is generalized in rural Nicaragua, the structure and sources of income are very heterogeneous. Income is composed of three principal elements: agriculture (50% of total household income), livestock (25%), and off-farm labor (25%, including migration remittances).[20] Rental income contributes little to total income, and thus is ignored in the rest of this analysis. Beans are the most important crop in terms of income, followed by coffee and corn. For those who grow coffee, it constitutes the most important source of agricultural income. Together, corn and beans comprise 20% of total income, or a little more than 40% of agricultural income. In terms of non-agricultural activities, the largest part comes from salaried labor (12%) and trade (7%). Only 3% of total income (and 12% of non-agricultural income) comes from remittances from permanent migrants.[21]

Control over productive assets strongly conditions the level and structure of income. Table 2 presents an analysis of per capita income by farm size. Sources of income are highly correlated with land size: off-farm income is the principal source of income for smallholders; agricultural income for medium holders; and cattle income for large holders. Total per capita income grows from C 1,026 for *microfundistas*, to C 9,558 for large producers. It can be noted, additionally, in Table 2 as in Figure 1, that the relative share of agricultural income follows an inverted "U". Only 32% of *microfundistas'* income come from agriculture, and this figure jumps to 68% for small producers and then decreases to 39% for large producers. Income from the cultivation of corn and beans follows the same tendency, and accounts for half of agricultural income for *minifundistas* and small producers. In terms of agricultural income, coffee is the most important for medium and large producers.

Table 2   Household income by farm size (1996 Córdobas)

| | | | | | Farm size | |
	Total	micro fundio	mini fundio	small	medium	large
# of weighted obs.	1410	292	335	416	217	150
Household income, per capita	2.774	1.026	1.561	2.091	3.625	9.558
As percentage of total income						
Net agriculture	51	32	57	68	56	39
Net corn	7	4	10	10	6	4
Net beans	15	8	29	25	16	5
Net livestock	24	0	0	10	25	46
Off farm income	25	68	42	22	19	15
Wages	12	50	22	13	6	4
Commerce	7	4	3	3	9	9
Processing	1	2	1	1	1	0
Services	2	5	8	1	1	1
Arts and crafts	0	3	0	0	0	0
Remittances	3	4	9	5	2	1

Source: Authors' calculations.

The relationship between land and income is confirmed in Figure 2, which shows landholdings by income deciles. Total land and grazing land both increase with income. This growth becomes almost exponential for households in the last two deciles. Land used for the cultivation of annuals and perennials (Figure 3) follows the same tendency.

The share of livestock-related and non-agricultural income in total income has a linear correlation with land-size groups. The share of livestock income increases with additional land assets, climbing from zero for *microfundistas* to 46% for large landholders. Meanwhile, the share of off-farm income decreases from 68% for *microfundistas* and 42% for *minifundistas*, to 15% for large landholders.

These shares correspond to the percentage of households that participate in off-farm labor activities (Table 3). Over 70% of the *microfundistas* participate in off-farm activities; the share dips to 36% for large landholders. As for the subcategories of non-agricultural activities, the share of income derived from wages follows the same tendency, from half of the income of *microfundistas* to barely 4% for large producers. On the other hand, the percentage of income from commerce is highest for medium and large landholders.

Table 3   Demographic characteristics and labor activities, by farm size

| | | | | | Farm size | | | | | |
| | | | micro | mini | | | | | | |
	unit	Total	fundio	fundio	small	medium	large	0<20	20>	test
Number of weighted										
observations		1468	297	357	428	225	161	1082	386	
Demographic characteristics										
Age, head of household	years	50,06	47,17	50,06	50,61	49,99	54,00	49,48	51,66	++
Education, head of household	years	2,46	2,61	2,53	2,12	2,24	3,28	2,39	2,67	
Average adult education	years	3,24	3,54	3,16	2,86	3,15	4,05	3,15	3,52	++
Family size	#	6,50	6,15	6,36	6,59	6,67	6,84	6,40	6,79	++
Percentage of households with										
at least 1 member working										
Off farm	%	50	74	50	45	36	36	55	36	--
Wage labor		33	50	34	33	20	21	38	20	--
Own agriculture		95	93	98	97	95	88	96	92	--
Own livestock		30	3	8	31	61	78	16	68	++
Agricultural wage labor		20	32	19	21	9	9	23	9	--
Other wage labor		11	14	16	9	6	7	13	6	--
Own business		22	27	24	17	21	22	22	21	
Professional		5	6	3	5	6	8	5	7	
Student		47	35	54	51	51	44	47	48	
Household		95	92	97	96	96	95	95	96	
Other		11	15	6	10	12	13	10	12	

Source: Authors' calculations.

Means tests in all tables are the following: for 0,1 variables, the null hypotheses is rejected if chi-square >3.84 (2 tails, 10%,*) or 5.02 (2 tails, 5%,**); for continuous variables, the null hypotheses is rejected if t >1.65 (2 tails, 10%) or 1.96 (2 tails, 5%).

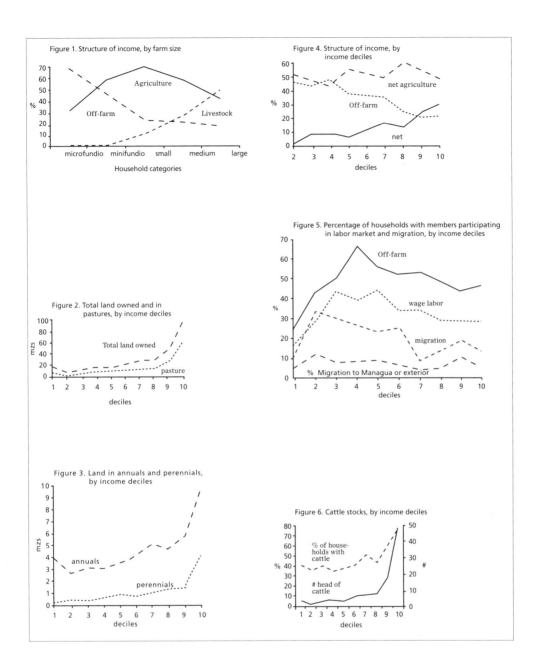

Figure 1. Structure of income, by farm size

Figure 2. Total land owned and in pastures, by income deciles

Figure 3. Land in annuals and perennials, by income deciles

Figure 4. Structure of income, by income deciles

Figure 5. Percentage of households with members participating in labor market and migration, by income deciles

Figure 6. Cattle stocks, by income deciles

Figure 4 shows[22] that agricultural income is the most important source of income across deciles, contributing about 50% of total income. For the wealthiest households as well as for the poorest, agriculture is the main economic activity. Livestock income and off-farm income show opposite tendencies. While livestock income complements agricultural income for wealthier households, Figure 4 confirms that off-farm income is fundamental for the survival of low-income households in rural Nicaragua.[23] It contributes almost half of total income for households in the first four deciles, and then decreases in importance in a linear fashion.

For those households that find themselves in precarious economic straits, non-agricultural income is key to the generation of income for survival. For households in the middle and upper deciles of distribution, where survival is not so precarious, non-agricultural income, which remains substantial, may be used to complement the productive activity of the farm. This phenomenon is apparent in Figure 5, which shows the participation of households in the labor market. The intermediate deciles, from three to seven, have the highest off-farm labor participation. While these households increase their participation in the labor market, the percentage of their non-agricultural or livestock-related income nonetheless decreases, and agricultural income is maintained. This suggests that the non-agricultural income of these households complements the generation of agricultural income.

On the other hand, livestock income is not so important for the rural poor, and is significant only for households in the last third of the distribution. The small contribution of livestock income to total income does not suggest, however, that livestock activity is not important for low-income households, as noted earlier. As can be seen in Figure 6, a high percentage of households in the first deciles have cattle (the story is the same for pigs and horses). Although they earn little income from these animals, these animals serve as instruments for security and savings in the absence of other formal mechanisms, particularly in the case of households with few resources.

Rural poverty in Nicaragua

In order to examine more closely the differences between the wealthier and poorer rural households, a "relative" poverty line (Ravallion, 1992) was adopted; this involves setting the poverty line at a percentage of the national mean of income. For rural Nicaragua, the median income per capita was chosen, which gives a poverty line of C 1,090 (US$130).

In Table 4, the asset position and household characteristics of poor and non-poor households are compared. As expected, poor households have larger families and a higher dependency ratio. Poor households have significantly less of every category of land quality and livestock, as well as lower head of household and family education levels and literacy. Non-poor households also have more equipment and machinery. There is no difference, however, in terms of participation in off-farm labor activities. Further, poor households show a significantly higher incidence of temporary migration, both current and historical. This implies that most migration is low skilled and low paid, and that while migration brings in needed income, it is associated more with surviving poverty than with escaping poverty.[24]

Conversely, while there is no difference in the number of permanent migrants between poor and non-poor households, the latter have a higher share who emigrate to Managua and the exterior (Costa Rica, Honduras, and the US, in equal shares). This suggests the dual nature of migration: temporary, and primarily agricultural and low-skilled migration requiring lower levels of education, is associated with poor households, while permanent migration requiring higher levels of education (as shown before), particularly to Managua and the exterior, is associated with non-poor households.

As expected, poor households received significantly less credit, and had less access to technical assistance, than non-poor households. Nevertheless, there are no

Table 4   Comparison of poor and non-poor households

	Unit	Total	Non-poor	Poor	Test
# of weighted obs.	#	1410	705	706	
Agricultural assets					
Land					
Land in annuals		4,48	5,78	3,18	--
Land in perennials		107	1,70	44	--
Land in pasture		15,13	24,76	5,52	--
Livestock					
Cattle	#	10,49	17,84	3,15	--
Percentage of households with cattle	%	47	55	39	--
Pigs	#	3,33	4,03	2,64	--
Percentage of households with pigs	%	55	62	48	--
Equipment and machinery assets					
Own fumigator		47	56	37	--
Corral		25	37	14	--
Human capital assets					
Family size	#	6,51	5,82	7,19	++
Share of adults in family	%	65	70	60	--
Age, head of household	years	49,90	50,16	49,65	
Average education of adults	years	3,23	3,63	2,82	--
% of households with member working off farm	%	48	49	48	
Migration assets					
Temporary migration					
% of households where member	%				
has migrated to Managua or another country		7	6	8	
migrated during 1996		12	8	16	++
migrated in previous years		17	13	20	++
Permanent migration					
% of households with permanent migration		44	45	44	
have sent remittances		9	10	7	-
live in Managua		15	17	12	--
live in another country		12	15	8	--
Institutional and organizational assets					
% of households that received formal credit		9	12	7	--
% of households that received training		13	12	14	
% of households that received technical assistance		9	9	9	
% of households that participated in an organization		13	13	12	
Agricultural production					
% of households that planted corn	%	78	77	79	
Area planted in corn, primera	mzs	2,22	2,66	1,76	--
% of households that planted beans	%	61	64	58	-
Area planted in beans	mzs	2,14	2,59	1,65	--
% of households that planted coffee	%	17	23	11	--
Technological level					
% of households that used improved seeds	%	10	13	8	--
% of households that used chemicals		44	50	39	--

Source: Authors' calculations

differences in the use of training or technical assistance between poor and non-poor households, which is testimony to the success of alternative institutions such as NGOs and projects in distributing these services more equally (Davis *et al.*, 1997). There is also no difference in the incidence of participation in organizations. In terms of crop choice, a little under 80% of both poor and non-poor households planted corn. Most producers, whether subsistence or commercial-oriented, diversified or not, grow corn in order to assure consumption in the presence of imperfect markets and economic and social insecurity. Non-poor households, however, planted more area in corn, as well as in beans, than poor households. These households also had a larger share planting higher value crops such as coffee, and exhibited a greater level of adoption of agricultural technology.

Examining the determinants of the generation and diversification of income

Many ideas have been advanced regarding the determinants of income generation in less developed countries. Most cite the lack of productive assets, particularly land and skilled labor, coupled with poorly functioning factor markets, as the key determinant of rural poverty. In the most common scenarios, land is either unequally distributed, rendered less efficient by insecure property rights, difficult to accumulate, and/or with access constrained by missing or imperfect credit markets. Land reform, either through government decree or market mechanisms, is still considered an important part of the poverty reduction agenda. Insufficient and/or poorly distributed human capital is also frequently cited, both due to the increased returns in the labor market that accompany higher levels of education, as well as its interactive effects on land-use and family health, etc. These two assets serve as the foundation for the primary axiom of what Lipton and Maxwell (1992) call the "new poverty agenda" of the World Bank and UN development organizations: labor intensive growth.

It is only recently, however, that the World Bank and the other development banks have begun to focus on the poor's lack of access to assets as a fundamental constraint on poverty reduction (Birdsall and Londoño, 1997). Also cited is the inadequate access of the poor to information and appropriate technology, the unequal distribution of public goods/infrastructure, as well as a lack of regional economic development. These three areas are important for their effect on increasing the returns to land and education (see for example, de Janvry and Sadoulet, 1989; Lipton, 1995; Lipton and Maxwell, 1992). The social exclusion school focuses on the presence of social or cultural institutions, such as ethnicity, which affect participation in factor markets and access to market and state institutions (Gore, 1995).[25]

The objective of this study was to determine which household assets and characteristics, market institutions, and infrastructure are associated with income generation and diversification. The specification of the income function, for example, explicitly includes a variety of household assets and characteristics, as well as other factors which form an integral part of development: institutions, infrastructure, and regions. The concept of assets has been broadened to include not only the ownership of different types of land and the accumulation of human capital, but also migration assets. The availability of producer organizations and technical assistance is included as an organizational and institutional asset at the disposal of households. The more typical household demographic characteristics are also considered. Community level variables, such as public goods and infrastructure, are correlated with the regional dummies, and thus excluded from the analysis.

Of previous efforts, Lopez (1995) attempts to test explicitly the different hypotheses of the determinants of income. Lopez shows that human capital (different levels of education) and institutions (in his case, secure land titles), are associated with higher income, and infrastructure/regional development less so, while information/technology (in the form of participation in a government technical assistance program in basic grains) is not. Otherwise most previous efforts to estimate income functions or poverty probits have suffered from methodological problems (see, for example, The World Bank, 1995 and 1996; Reardon *et al.*, 1989; Scott and Litchfield, 1994; Coulombe and McKay, 1996). The typical strategy is similar to the one pursued below, using a tobit or ordinary least squares to model the determinants of household or individual income. Most have used a variety of household characteristics, such as family size, dependency ratio, and gender, as well as the most important assets described above, particularly land and human capital. Some studies have included community variables as well. Problems arise, however, when endogenous and exogenous variables, relative to the decision-making time period of the household, are mixed together as independent variables. This results in problems of simultaneity, which must be taken into account through a system of simultaneous equations, or instrumentalization of the variables.[26]

Here, care has been taken to include only those variables which can be considered exogenous to the household's decision-making process. For the purposes of the study, the decision-making process was considered to be that of the survey period (1996), thus excluding a number of variables which are clearly important to income generation, and have been used in a number of the studies cited above: off-farm labor, livestock holdings, crop choice/diversification, credit usage, and product market participation. Labor market participation is clearly endogenous. Similarly, livestock holdings are too liquid, as cattle and pigs are easily (and likely to be) bought and sold or otherwise disposed of as a consequence of changes in income earnings. Credit is usually approved based on the ability of the applicant to repay the loan; that is, on an appreciation of his or her income-generating potential. The crop portfolio choice (among annuals) is also clearly endogenous. In all cases, the variables needed would have been the choice in the previous period, or a variable expressing past experience (such as employment history) or past ownership of a given good. Level of technology use is also very important, but is again endogenous. Finally, gender is not used as a variable, due to the small percentage of female-headed households and the poor quality of the intra-household data.

Independent variables were prepared in the following fashion. Per capita land assets were classified into four categories: annual,[27] perennial, natural pasture, and forest. The first three land variables are expected to have a positive, though differential, effect on household incomes. Since pastureland is of lower quality, its coefficient is expected to be smaller than that of annual land, and the coefficient of annual land to be smaller than that of perennial land. Squared terms are added for all categories, except for forest land.[28]

Human capital assets are divided into six categories, each in the number of adults with the respective level of education, in per capita units: less than three completed years of education; between three and six years; between nine and 12 years; between 12 and 16 years; and 16 or more years. Again, these variables are expected to have a positive impact on household income. Even the number of adults with little education variable should be positive, due to the increased availability of family labor. It is expected that the older the head of the household, the more income that household will have.

Migration assets are divided into two principal categories: the number of children of the head of the household living nearby, and the number of children living far away (Managua or another country). Based on the descriptive statistics, particularly the comparison of poor and non-poor households, and the individual and household characteristics of migrants, differential returns are expected from these two types of migration, with those who live in Managua or a foreign country having a stronger positive impact on household income.

Organizational assets are characterized in terms of whether organizations were available to households. Regional dummies for geographic location are included, with Region V as the default.

Finally, a variety of interactions between land assets on the one hand, and education and migration assets on the other are tested. The aim is to provide a test of the relationship as to whether human capital and migration assets are complements to or substitutes for land assets. Higher levels of education can either increase or decrease the returns to land. This can take place either through the substitution of family labor on-farm for off-farm labor activities where education receives higher returns, or the complementary effect of increased education on agricultural production. Similarly, migration assets can either reduce the returns to land through the substitution of labor, or increase returns by relaxing liquidity and credit constraints in production.[29] Based on the descriptive statistics presented above regarding higher returns to education in urban areas, as well as the generally underdeveloped state of Nicaraguan agriculture and the intensity of the struggle for economic survival, education and migration assets are expected to serve as substitutes for land. None of these variables proved significant, however, and were dropped from the final specification.

Generation and diversification of income

Total household income was regressed on the set of core variables, using a simultaneous quantile regression in order to correct for heteroskedasticity in the cross sectional data. Three Least Absolute Deviation (LAD) regressions (at the 25th, 50th, and 75th income quantiles) were estimated simultaneously, producing an estimate, by bootstrapping, of the entire variance-covariance estimator.[30] Comparison of the coefficients permits us to see changes in the impact of the explanatory variables at different points in the income distribution.

The results are shown in Table 5. Annual, perennial, and pastureland have a positive and significant impact on household income, with coefficients reflecting differential land quality as postulated. An extra *manzana* of perennial land is worth significantly more than annual land across all three equations, while an extra *manzana* of annual land has greater impact on income than pastureland. Further, for each land type, with the exception of forest, the coefficients are significantly different across equations (as indicated in the last column). The trend indicates that households with higher income experience larger marginal effects. At least part of this effect can be interpreted as the impact of credit and liquidity constraints in an

Table 5   Determinants of income

		25th quantile		50th quantile		75th quantile		Ho=25th=
Regression analysis using simultaneous quantile regression with bootstrapped errors	# obs	1363		1363		1363		
Dependent variable = total household income	Psuedo R2	,13		,21		,31		
								Ho=25th=
		Coef	P>ltl	Coef	P>ltl	Coef	P>ltl	50th=75th=0
Land assets								
annual		257	,00 ***	261	,01 ***	589	,00 ***	*
perennial		1408	,00 ***	2639	,00 ***	4222	,00 ***	***
pasture		95	,00 ***	218	,00 ***	372	,00 ***	***
forest		-11	,73	-89	,14	-51	,80	
Human capital assets								
age, head of household		-8	,60	-13	,51	-22	,53	
less then primary education, adults		254	,04 **	289	,16	495	,15	
primary education, adults		504	,04 **	1411	,00 ***	2138	,01 ***	***
secondary education, adults		834	,24	1983	,00 ***	3348	,23	
preporatory education, adults		2916	,06 *	4685	,02 **	8231	,15	
university education, adults		4306	,05 **	7646	,00 ***	17979	,00 ***	*
Migration assets								
Managua or exterior		225	,24	315	,11	1070	,11	
other		120	,56	-10	,96	-146	,60	
Agrarian institutions								
access to organizations		60	,92	-411	,51	-403	,76	
Regions								
I		-346	,54	-438	,71	1285	,32	
II		-29	,43	-632	,58	1211	,45	
IV		-468	,42	-696	,59	2374	,09	
VI		922	,25	635	,61	2890	,19	
constant		-611	,49	1313	,40	1000	,64	

*** significant at 1%

** significant at 5%

* significant at 10%

environment of severe restriction of financing to agriculture. In 1996, only 11% of agricultural producing households had access to credit, with even lower percentages for poorer households. On the other hand, while the marginal effect is higher for wealthier households, as a percentage of total household income the impact is higher for poorer households, for all land types except forest. This can be seen in Table 6, parts A, B, and C.

Higher levels of education are also associated with increased income, across all equations and levels of education. Again, across all equations, the coefficients reflect quality differences between levels of education, ranging in the 25th quantile

Table 6   Marginal effects of land on income

A. Marginal effect of additional manzana of annual land

	quantile			
	25th	50th	75th	Average effect
Marginal effect	0	0	0	
Total household income at quantile	2.210	6.258	15.244	
Marginal change as percentage of income	0	0	0	

B. Marginal effect of additional manzana of pasture land

	quantile		
	25th	50th	75th
Marginal effect	2.210	0	0
Total household income at quantile	2.210	6.258	15.244
Marginal change as percentage of income	100	0	0

C. Marginal effect of additional manzana of pasture land

	quantile			
	25th	50th	75th	Average effect
Marginal effect	0	0	0	
Total household income at quantile	2.210	6.258	15.244	
Marginal change as percentage of income	0	0	0	

D. Marginal effect of adult obtaining primary education

	quantile			
	25th	50th	75th	Average effect
Marginal effect	0	0	0	
Total household income at quantile	2.210	6.258	15.244	
Marginal change as percentage of income	0	0	0	

E. Marginal effect of adult obtaining secondary education

	quantile		
	25th	50th	75th
Marginal effect	0	0	0
Total household income at quantile	2.210	6.258	15.244
Marginal change as percentage of income	0	0	0

equation from C 254 for less than three years of education to C 4,306 for a university education. There is thus a large payoff to increasing access to education among agricultural households in Nicaragua, across the income spectrum. The marginal effect increases with quantiles, though the differences are significant only for primary and university education. In these cases, even though the marginal effect increases with income, as a share of income the marginal effect of an adult obtaining a primary or secondary education is again more important to poor households, as seen in Table 6, parts D and E.

In terms of migration assets, as expected the Managua/exterior migration assets have a positive impact on income, though the coefficients are not quite significant. Migration assets in general have less of an impact than similar estimations with data from countries like Mexico (Davis, 1997), where rural households have much greater access to non-agricultural labor markets. Finally, neither access to organizations nor regional variables have an impact on income, with the exception of Region IV in the 75th quantile regression.

Conclusion

Across farm households, the structure and sources of income are heterogeneous. Sources of income are highly correlated with land size; off-farm income is the principal source of income for smallholders; agricultural income for medium holders; and cattle income for large holders. The sources of income are also related to the distribution of income; while agricultural income is the most important source for all households across income deciles, off-farm sources complement the income of poorer households, while cattle income does the same for wealthier households.

Poor households are those with low levels of productive assets, and increased access to any productive asset—land, human capital, or migration—is associated with higher household incomes. From the results, policy suggestions for reducing poverty can be drawn. First, increase the access of the poor to land. The size and quality of land holdings are highly significant and associated with the generation of income. While the marginal impact of different types of land increases with income levels, as a share of total income, the marginal impact of an extra *manzana* of any kind of land is more important for poor farmers than for the wealthy. Thus, programs that facilitate land accumulation by poor households (whether owned or rented), or improvements in quality should be part of a poverty alleviation program.[31] While Nicaragua has undergone over the past two decades one of the most widespread agrarian reform programs in Latin America, further land transfers to *microfundistas* and *minifundistas* could lead to a significant increase in income for these households, who are generally among the poorest in the agricultural sector. In terms of poverty alleviation among the smallest landholding households, this suggests that the government should move beyond land titling programs, to either continuing the land reform process or fomenting other mechanisms for land transfers. If more land is not available for these households, either through rent, purchase, or land reform, other viable off-farm employment opportunities must be part of rural development initiatives.

Second, increase the access of poor farmers to agrarian institutions. The lower marginal effect of land with poorer households can be interpreted, in part, as a result of the severe liquidity and credit constraints plaguing producers in Nicaraguan agriculture. Relaxing these restraints could result in increasing the marginal impact of land among poor households. Such a result has been found for Mexico, where part of the income multiplier effect of the PROCAMPO cash transfer stems from relaxing these constraints among producers with low levels of productive assets and seemingly few chances to succeed in an era of reduced government intervention and market liberalization (Sadoulet *et al.*, 1999). This suggests that poor Nicaraguan farmers might also benefit from the income enhancing effects of targeted credit programs, and that given the chance, they can become viable producers.

Third, increase the level of education among poor landed households. Increasing levels of human capital assets also have an important income-enhancing effect, again particularly for poor households. All levels of education, for both poor and wealthy households, are associated with higher incomes, though coefficients reflect quality differences in educational levels. The gains appear to derive primarily from off-farm activities, as there are no complementarities between education and agricultural activities. Similarly, the education results, taken together with the descriptive statistics showing the exodus of higher educated, permanent migrants leaving agriculture, provide evidence that the returns to education are higher off-farm than in agricultural production.

The data suggest two directions for the role of off-farm labor activities in Nicaraguan household income-generation strategies. On one hand are the large number of low-skilled, poorly educated rural agricultural workers, whose participation in labor markets is correlated with poverty; on the other hand, better educated, temporary and permanent migrants who leave agriculture, are associated with increasing incomes. Thus, efforts to increase levels of education in the countryside could have a big poverty alleviation payoff, but only as long as the urban, non-agricultural sector of the Nicaraguan economy can absorb these new entrants.

Notes

[1] We would like to thank Benedicte de la Briere, Annelies Zoomers, Alain de Janvry, Elizabeth Sadoulet, and John Quigley for helpful comments at various stages of writing this paper, and Jaya Sil for early work with this data. Any errors are ours.

[2] Arana and Rocha, 1997, using the same data but a different poverty line, conclude that 88% of the rural population lives in poverty; see also MAS, 1996.

[3] See Spoor, 1995, Uttling, 1991, and Martínez Cuenca, 1992, for a discussion of the failure of the *Sandinista* stabilization program.

[4] See Arana and Rocha, 1997, for a discussion of the economic and social impact of these policies.

[5] Arana and Rocha, 1997.

[6] 1 *manzana* = 1.75 acres = 0.7 hectares.

[7] While the total amount of credit to agriculture has increased since 1997, most of this increase came from private banks and was directed toward agroexport crops such as coffee (MAG, 1998d).

[8] Recently BANADES itself was closed.

[9] Recent efforts by the MAG may have increased access to technical assistance on the part of small and medium producers, though survey data is not available to test the impact of these programs (see MAG, 1998b).

[10] Data should become publicly available during 2000.

[11] Nitlapán-UCA (1995) carried out an agricultural household survey of Regions I, V, and VI, which collected income information. Net income variables were not constructed, however. In 1995, FIDEG carried out a nationwide, 6,000-observation household survey focusing on gender issues (Renzi and Agurto, 1996), but again income information is not available. Finally, Ruben, Rodriquez, and Cortez (1999) refer to a 1998 nationwide, 500-observation survey focusing on farm incomes, with which we are not familiar.

[12] Preliminary results from the 1998 LSMS show that rural poverty decreased slightly, though significantly, between 1993 and 1998. See references in Davis and Murgai (2000).

[13] The regions comprise the following departments: I-Nueva Segovia, Esteli, Madriz; II- Leon, Chinandega; III-Managua; IV-Matagalpa, Jinotega; V-Masaya, Granada, Carazo, Rivas; VI-Boaco, Chontales, Rio San Juan.

[14] The data is representative of all regions of the country with the exception of the two departments of the Atlantic Coast.

[15] See Davis *et al.* (1997) for more detail on the creation of this sample, and Steiner (1995) for a description of the basic grains survey sampling methodology. This sample was drawn from a larger, 5,600-observation national basic grains survey. The universe from which the sample was drawn is all households using land for agricultural or livestock purposes, greater then one tenth of a *manzana*, and less then 500 *manzanas*. The survey is thus not strictly representative of agriculture at the national level, since cooperatives and the *latifundio* were excluded, although it is designed to be representative of the vast majority of agricultural and cattle producing households in Nicaragua. Producers with more than 500 *mzs.* of land comprise less then 1% of all producers.

[16] This includes land which is owned by the household, plus land rented in during the whole agricultural cycle, and excluding land rented out.

[17] An adjustment was made to take into account differences in land quality between cultivable land, pastures, and *tacotal*/forest. Cultivable land is given a weight of one; pasture, 0.75; and *tacotales*/forest, 0.5. The land variables used in the econometric analysis do not include this quality adjustment, since we include each type individually.

[18] The value of corn produced by the household, but consumed by animals, was counted as an input into livestock production. See Davis (1997) and Davis *et al.* (1997) for more detail on the construction of the income variable and how home consumption was valued.

[19] Using an exchange rate of 8.4 C/US$.

[20] The result that 25% of income comes from nonagricultural activities is similar to results shown by household surveys in other Latin American countries with the same level of development. For example, nonagricultural income represented 22% of total income in Honduras, and 18% in Paraguay (Lopez and Romano, 1995; Lopez and Thomas, 1995). Two countries with more developed industrial and service sectors, Mexico (Davis, 1997, and Sadoulet *et al.*, 1999) and Chile (Lopez, 1995), reported percentages more in the 50% range.

[21] Permanent migrants are those who were not living in the household during 1996, the year the survey was conducted.

[22] In this figure, we excluded decile one, due to the larger number of households with negative incomes.

[23] In some countries, diversification into off-farm activities is also associated with increased incomes (Reardon *et al.*, 1992, for Burkina Faso), while in others (such as India) diversification and income have a negatively sloped relationship (Walker and Ryan, 1990).

[24] It must be remembered, however, that with only cross sectional data we cannot assume causality.

[25] Recent World Bank studies have also played special attention to ethnic and gender issues in rural poverty.

[26] One study estimated the equations separately by occupation of the head of the household (non-working, agriculture, wage, self-employed), and specifically took into account this endogeneity by using a two-stage Heckman procedure. The OLS portion of the procedure, however, was marred once again by the inclusion of endogenous variables (Coulombe and McKay, 1996). Glewwe (1991), in his study of the determinants of household welfare in Cote d'Ivoire, explicitly discusses the endogeneity problem, and even uses simultaneous equations for a few community-level variables, but still includes some questionable variables, such as the household net debt position, savings, transfers, and current livestock holdings.

[27] Almost no irrigated land was recorded in the survey.

[28] We are unable to model the impact of land title security on income due to limitations in the survey data. Though land title conflicts are thought to have an important negative impact on agricultural productivity, and are thus a main focus of government and World Bank programs, Nitlapán-UCA (1995) and Davis *et al.* (1997) found that land title insecurity was not the main concern of agricultural

producers. Hopefully, analysis of the 1998 LSMS and a new panel of the 1996 FAO survey will be able to determine the effect of land title insecurity.

[29] From another perspective, migration and education assets, by increasing the potential for income diversification, thus spreading income risk and allowing for more risk-taking in agriculture, serve as complements to agricultural production.

[30] See Deaton, 1997, for an introduction to the benefits, in the presence of heteroscedasticity, of the LAD estimator, and StataCorp, 1999 for a description of the simultaneous quantile estimator.

[31] Davis *et al.* (1997) also found that the rental market had lead to a more progressive distribution of land.

References

Arana, M. and J. Rocha, "Efecto de las políticas macroeconómicas y sociales sobre la pobreza en el caso de Nicaragua". Mimeo, May 1997.

Birdsall, N. and J. Londoño, "Asset inequality matters: an assessment of the World Bank's approach to poverty reduction". *American Economic Review*, Vol. 87, no. 2 (1997), pp. 32-7.

Central Bank of Nicaragua, "Indicadores económico". Gerencia de Estudios Económicos, Managua, February 1997.

Central Bank of Nicaragua, "Indicadores económico". Gerencia de Estudios Económicos, Managua, December 1999.

Coulombe, H. and A. McKay, "Modeling determinants of poverty in Mauritania". *World Development*, Vol. 24, no. 6 (1996), pp. 1015-31.

Davis, B., "Economic reform and the determinants of income among agricultural households in Mexico and Nicaragua". Doctoral dissertation. University of California, Berkeley, 1997.

Davis, B., C. Carletto and J. Sil, "Los hogares agropecuarios en Nicaragua: un análisis de tipologia". Food and Agriculture Organization of the United Nations and the University of California, Berkeley, November 1997.

Davis, B. and R. Murgai, "Between prosperity and poverty: rural households in Nicaragua". IFPRI and The World Bank, April 2000.

Deaton, A., "Data and econometric tools for development analysis". In: J. Behrman and T.N. Srinivasan (eds.), *Handbook of development economics*, Volume III. Amsterdam, Elsevier, 1995.

Deaton, A., *The analysis of household surveys. A microeconomic approach to development policy.* Baltimore, The John Hopkins University Press, 1997.

De Janvry, A. and E. Sadoulet, "Investment strategies to combat rural poverty in Latin America". Giannini Foundation Working Waper no. 459, University of California, Berkeley, 1989.

De Janvry, A. and E. Sadoulet, "Agrarian heterogeneity and precision policies". Paper presented at the Latin American Seminar on Agrarian heterogeneity and differentiated policies, Mexico, November 27-29, 1997.

Glewwe, P., "Investigating the determinants of household welfare in Cote d'Ivoire". *Journal of Development Economics*, Vol. 35 (1991), pp. 307-37.

Gore, C., "Introduction: markets, citizenship and social exclusion". In: G. Rodgers, C. Gore and J. Figueiredo (eds.), *Social exclusion: rhetoric, reality, responses.* Geneva, International Labor Organization, 1995.

Lipton, M., "Growing points in poverty research: labour issues". In: G. Rodgers (ed.), *New approaches to Poverty analysis and policy*, Vol. 1: The poverty agenda and the ILO. Geneva, International Labor Organization, 1995.

Lipton, M. and S. Maxwell, "The new poverty agenda: an overview". Mimeo. Institute of Development Studies, UK, 1992.

López, R., "Determinants of rural poverty: a quantitative analysis for Chile". Mimeo. The World Bank, 1995.

López, R. and T. Thomas, "Rural poverty in Paraguay: the determinants of farm-household income". Mimeo. Department of Agricultural and Resource Economics, University of Maryland, College Park, 1995.

López, R. and C. Romano, "Rural poverty in Honduras: asset distribution and liquidity constraints". Mimeo. Department of Agricultural and Resource Economics, University of Maryland, College Park, 1995.

Lopez, R. and A. Valdés, "Rural poverty in Latin America: analytics, new empirical evidence, and policy". Technical Department, Latin America and the Caribbean Region, The World Bank, 1997.

Martinez Cuenca, A., *Sandinista economics in practice*. Boston, South End Press, 1992.

Ministry of Agriculture and Cattle (MAG), "Marco de políticas y acciones para el ciclo agrícola 1997-1998". Managua, 1997.

MAG, "Marco de políticas y acciones para el ciclo agrícola 1998-1999". Managua, 1998a.

MAG, "Elementos para una política de desarrollo rural". Transferencias para la modernización del campo. Programa agrícola, CONAGRO/BID/PNUD, Managua, 1998b.

MAG, "Una ruta para modernizar la Nicaragua rural", Mimeo. Managua, 1998c.

MAG, "Boletin Trimestral". Managua, 1998d.

Ministry of Social Action (MAS), "La Pobreza en Nicaragua". Managua, 1996.

Nitapán-UCA., "Diagnóstico de la producción agropecuario". Análisis de encuesta rural 1995. Report prepared for the Proyecto de Tecnología Agraria y Ordenamiento de la Propiedad Agraria, Managua, 1995.

Ravallion, M., "Poverty comparisons: a guide to Cconcepts and methods". LSMS Working Paper, no. 88, The World Bank, 1992.

Reardon, T., C. Delgado and P. Matlon, "Determinants and effects of income diversification amongst farm households in Burkina Faso". *Journal of Development Studies*, Vol. 28, no. 2 (1992), pp. 264-96.

Renzi, M. and S. Agurto, "La mujer y los hogares rurales Nicaraguences". Managua, FIDEG, 1996).

Sadoulet, E., A. de Janvry and B. Davis, "Income transfer programs: PROCAMPO in Mexico". Mimeo. University of California, Berkeley, and IFPRI, August 1999.

Scott, C. and J. Litchfield, "Inequality, mobility, and the determination of income among the rural poor in Chile, 1968-1986". Working paper: DEP53. London School of Economics Suntory-Toyota International Centre for Economics and Related Disciplines, March 1994.

Spoor, M., *The state and domestic agricultural markets in Nicaragua. From interventionism to neo-liberalism*. New York, St. Martin's Press, 1995.

Steiner, M,. "Area frame sampling methodology for the 1994/95 Nicaraguan agricultural survey". Mimeo. US Department of Agriculture, August 1995.

Uttling, P., "Economic adjustment under the *Sandinistas*: policy reform, food security, and livelihood in Nicaragua". Geneva, UNRISD, 1991.

Walker, T. and J. Ryan, *Village and household economies in India's semi-arid tropics*. Baltimore, The Johns Hopkins University Press, 1990.

World Bank, "Ecuador poverty report, parts I and II". Report No. 14533-EC, 1995.

World Bank, "Republic of Nicaragua poverty assessment". Volumes I-II. Latin American and Caribbean Regional Office, 1995.

Part 3

Livelihood and land-use

in a global competitive sphere

12 Globalization and survival of the smallholder producer: a case study of land-use change in Tingambato, Mexico[1]

Laura Paulson

Introduction

Over the last quarter century, Mexico's development has been characterized by shifting state policies and globally driven agricultural transformations, leading to both environmental change and economic marginalization of millions of rural producers. Mexico is modernizing its agriculture sector in order to make it more globally competitive, a process which translates into disinvestment in small-scale production, increasing the emphasis on new technologies, and a conversion of land-use to promote higher-value export-oriented crops (Barkin, 1990; Barry, 1995; Sanderson, 1986). This shift in policy toward a more globalized food sector has resulted in profound transformation of local and regional agricultural economies.

In this context, small-scale producers are being pressured to participate in broader, more competitive economic spheres. Changing patterns of trade, distribution, land ownership, and labor migration have led to a more homogenous marketplace and political reality, presenting new challenges to the adaptability, resiliency, and competitiveness of the small-scale producer. How these changes will affect smallholders and their relationship with their environment and resources is a topic that is now receiving substantial academic attention (Bebbington, 1997; Stonich *et al.*, 1994; Zimmerer, 1997). Some studies have shown that small-scale producers of non-traditional exports are particularly vulnerable to the changing market and production conditions of a more global economy (Marsden, 1997; Stanford, 1991), in part, because the adoption of non-traditional, higher-risk crops undermines household food security and requires increased responsiveness of small-scale farmers to market fluctuations (Marsden, 1997). The Mexican avocado sector provides an example of how farmers in the non-traditional sector are adapting. However, with scholars just beginning to turn their attention to the Mexican avocado sector (see, for example, Stanford, 1998, and forthcoming), relatively little information currently exists with respect to how small-scale farmers will become articulated within the larger industry, and what transformations in agricultural strategies and land-use will take place at the local level as a result of regional and global restructuring (Stanford, 1998).[2]

Land-use is most appropriately evaluated within the context of numerous political, social, and economic factors which influence the individual actions of producers. In this paper, use is made of a case study of the adoption of avocado production by farmers in Tingambato, Michoacán, Mexico in order to explore how some of these factors (e.g., agricultural policy, land reform, institutional restructuring) are shaping agricultural land-use. The response of small-scale farmers to opportunities in the avocado sector, illustrates how some producers are responding to the loss of national agricultural support and increasing pressure of economic integration. The pattern and process of agricultural adaptation has been complex. While producers have shown remarkable resiliency and adaptability to wider industry forces and policy shifts, overall, small-scale producers in Tingambato are experiencing globalization in two ways: they are exiting agriculture altogether, or they are being marginalized to a separate market system within the avocado sector. These trajectories can be traced to an array of complementary policies (e.g., credit, land reform, phytosanitary requirements) designed to increase the competitiveness of the Mexican agriculture sector.

This chapter is divided into three sections. First, an overview of the avocado industry in Michoacán and the special characteristics of Tingambato is given. This is followed by an examination of the industry trends, their relationship to national agricultural policy and local level changes in land-use since the 1970s. Finally, by placing the case study within the context of recent industry trends and current policy shifts, local constraints and opportunities for adoption of avocado production are examined, and the extent to which producers participate in and respond to agricultural change at the local level is explored. This study draws on local ethnography, Mexican Agricultural Census data, and results from a land cover change analysis carried out by the Institute of Ecology of the National Autonomous University of Mexico (UNAM) for the avocado-producing zone of Tingambato.

Overview of the avocado industry

The state of Michoacán leads the world in avocado production. While most Mexican avocado is earmarked for the domestic market, approximately 2-3% is exported, primarily to the European market. Combined, Mexico produces approximately 45% of the global supply (Gledhill, 1995; INEGI, 1997; USDA, 1997). Michoacán produces 85% of Mexico's total avocado output, the majority originating from the Uruapan region, to which Tingambato belongs. Over the last 30 years, the Uruapan district has undergone profound land-use change, characterized by a significant shift in production from maize and a diversity of native tree crops toward cultivation of the export-quality Hass avocado, now the state's most important commercial crop. Between 1970 and 1991, the area planted with Hass increased from 5,114 to 63,581 hectares (DGE, 1975; INEGI, 1997), with estimates at 100,000 for 1998 (Stanford, 1998: 5). Similarly, avocado contributes enormously to the economy, generating one and a half billion *pesos* (about US$ 200 million) in 1996 (INEGI, 1997). Furthermore, Mexico is the sole provider of processed avocado (e.g., frozen avocado, guacamole, oil, and paste) to the US. Exports to the US have increased dramatically from US$ 3.9 million in 1989/90 to US$ 13.2 million in 1992/93 (Sanchez Colin y Rubi Arriaga, 1994), representing a 338% increase. Even so, processed exports represent only about 3% of total production (USDA, 1997). While Mexico continues to export processed avocado to the US, the fresh export market is receiving increased attention due to the recent opening of the US market to Mexican fresh avocado to 19 northeastern states during the winter months of November to February.

Avocado is well-suited to the climatic and ecological characteristics of Michoacán. In fact, local sources indicate that native *(criollo)* varieties have been grown in the region for hundreds of years and were introduced to other regions of the world as cash crops following Spanish colonization. Although *criollo* varieties have been traded on local and regional markets for decades, many *criollo* orchards were grafted over with Hass in the 1960s as producers looked for ways to increase the quality of the avocado. Plentiful rainfall, low frost risk, and rich soils provide optimal conditions for Hass production. There are four blooming seasons during the year, depending on where an orchard is located. In areas above 2,000 meters, growers can leave the fruit on the trees for up to six months without damage to yields, because it does not ripen until picked. This has provided Michoacán a unique opportunity to market its avocados year-round, both domestically and globally (Smith, 1992), enabling farmers to take advantage of seasonal constraints on production in other avocado-producing regions.

Production is highly varied and defined by a distinct class structure reflecting, in part, the broader structure of Mexico's agricultural sector, which has a long history of communal, private, and mixed land tenure arrangements. In 1970, 81% of orchards were held by private producers (DGE, 1975). More recent studies (Stanford, 1998) indicate that this figure has declined to 75%. Privately-owned orchards average about 40 hectares in size, but range from five to 400 hectares. Those belonging to *ejido* and indigenous producers tend to average about two hectares per orchard (Alvarez-Icaza *et al.*, 1993).[3] Avocado production is capital-intensive, and typically the wealthiest and largest producers own the best land in the region, and have personal financial capital to invest in production. Thus, at a regional level, the most productive lands, highest yields, and best-quality fruit are produced and controlled by an elite group of producers.

Small-scale producers, on the other hand, typically have minimal or no support structure, limited financial resources, and more marginal land. Frequently, these farmers invest little in pre-harvest production practices and, as a result, produce low yields of low-quality fruit. It is these latter producers which characterize Tingambato. These farmers are being forced to quickly adjust to new competitive production conditions without the financial and technical resources of their large-scale competitors, and without the political clout to leverage the support they require. Faced with a limited resource base, smallholders in Tingambato are particularly vulnerable to changing and evolving economic and political conditions within the local and regional economy.

At an altitude of 1,980 meters and encompassing an area of 24,577 hectares, Tingambato possesses both rich forest reserves and an ecological environment well-suited to the cultivation of a variety of high-value crops. Eighty-four percent of the land is held by producers organized into two *ejidos* and three indigenous communities, and unlike the tenure patterns in the wider region, the *ejidos* and communities of Tingambato hold some of the best land in the municipality. Agricultural systems among indigenous communities and *ejidos* reflect a diversity of strategies combining rainfed maize cultivation, commercial avocado production and forest extraction, although the intensity of these strategies has varied over time. Approximately 60% of indigenous land is now dedicated to avocado cultivation, indicating the increasing importance of this crop to the economies of the indigenous groups in Tingambato. The most recent statistics available indicate that private landholdings comprise 15.8% of the total land area and vary in size from five to 30 hectares (Paulson, 1999: 92). Although communal farmers hold the greatest percentage of land in Tingambato, private producers are entirely dedicated to avocado production and have greater access to capital, technologies, and producer networks.

Agricultural policy and commodity restructuring

Over the last century, agricultural production in Tingambato has been characterized by a gradual shift from semi-subsistence food crop production to an engagement with commercial cash crops and integration into markets. In the early part of the century, large swaths of forested area in the Tingambato valley were cleared for the cultivation of maize, beans, and wheat in order to meet local agricultural development needs associated with population increases. During the 1960s, green revolution technologies provided the primary incentive for a dramatic increase in area cultivated in wheat in northern Tingambato. In southern Tingambato, farmers supplemented basic grain cultivation with income from a diversity of tree crops, including peach, *criollo* avocado, and *chirimoya (cherimoya)*, where climatic and ecological conditions enabled their cultivation.[4] In fact, from 1950 to 1960, *chirimoya* was the most important cash crop for Tingambato's economy. By the late 1960s, however, *chirimoya* was rapidly being replaced with the export-quality Hass avocado. The region's focus on avocado has resulted in a 36% reduction in overall forest cover (Rosete *et al.*, 1997: 12), and a change in agricultural crop mix from basic grain and semi-commercial diversified tree crop production *(criollo* avocado, peach, *chirimoya)* to Hass avocado (Alvarez-Icaza *et al.*, 1993; DGE, 1975; INEGI, 1997; Rosete *et al.*, 1997; SAGAR, 1997).

Interviews with farmers, and data from a recent study on land cover change in Tingambato, indicate that the major expansion of avocado began in the late 1960s. This coincides with the introduction of Hass avocado to Tingambato about 30 years ago by a small group of wealthy, private producers. Although avocado has always been grown on a small-scale in Tingambato, usually in home gardens and around fields, it was not until the 1970s that production became more commercially oriented. By the early 1980s, production was increasingly directed toward export markets, such as France and Japan, as wealthy, innovative producers from the wider region began to look for new market opportunities and send consignment shipments abroad (Smith, 1992; Stanford, 1998). In 1997, the US lifted its 83-year phytosanitary ban against Mexican avocado, thus fostering a shift toward increased standardization of avocado quality and further opening up trade possibilities.

Private producers and *ejido*/indigenous producers responded differently to agricultural policy shifts from the 1970s to the mid-1990s. While private producers generally shaped and strengthened the industry through their own initiatives (Stanford, 1998), participation by small-scale, limited-resource producers depended heavily on the availability of production incentives and disincentives created through national agricultural policy change. For the most part, production incentives, such as price supports and subsidized inputs, encouraged small-scale farmers to continue with maize production at a somewhat consistent level during the 1970s and 1980s, while avocado production was dominated by entrepreneurial producers with sufficient capital and know-how. Policy instruments, intended to provide incentives to small-scale, primarily *ejidal* producers during the earlier decades of production, rarely reached their goals. One such incentive was a program of commercial fruit production implemented by the National Commission for Fruit Production (CONAFRUT), and the Michoacán State Forestry Commission. This program provided rural producers with free avocado trees during the 1960s. While these programs were critical to providing small-scale producers with the initial capital to establish an orchard, small producers lacked the technical and financial capability to maintain their orchards, and many of them failed (Stanford, 1998).

In 1981, a number of factors triggered a major economic crisis in Mexico that affected small-scale, semi-subsistence grain producers and avocado producers differently. Facing a downturn in the oil market, the fiscal deficit arising from failures of the SAM program and a significant drop in the value of the *peso*, the national economy entered a deep recession.[5] Between 1982 and 1988, public investment in agriculture fell by 68.2%, the guaranteed price of maize fell 43.7%, input subsidies were reduced for fertilizer and access to irrigation, and interest rates offered by *Banco Nacional de Crédito Rural* (National Rural Credit Bank, or BANRURAL), the state agricultural lending institution, rose to 32.4% for basic grain producers and 35.9% for producers of other crops (Gledhill, 1995). In Michoacán, BANRURAL temporarily suspended operations altogether in the early 1980s (Calva, 1991). While these austerity measures negatively affected producers of basic grains in Tingambato as well as in the wider region, avocado growers responded by becoming more responsive to market signals, expanding commercial contacts and searching out new market opportunities. But avocado production also became more expensive as costs increased and market prices declined, adversely impacting some producers (Smith, 1992). Only the wealthiest producers were resilient and capable of surviving this period of economic stagnation. Both low-income producers of basic grains and unsuccessful avocado producers were forced to abandon their fields and seek wage work outside the region.

By the late 1980s and early 1990s, a combination of factors led to increased adoption of avocado production by *ejidos* and indigenous communities in Tingambato. A gradual withdrawal of state-subsidized credit, inputs and services exacerbated production and purchasing constraints for producers of basic grains. Looking for more profitable opportunities during this period, several areas of Tingambato were illegally cleared of forest to establish orchards (Paulson, 1999). The first to take advantage were small-scale private investors. Local ethnographic data reveals that a significant portion of indigenous land was illegally sold to private producers, who subsequently established orchards in these areas (Paulson, 1999). In one case, *comuneros* (members of an indigenous community) claimed that the forest was diseased, leaving them no alternative but to burn it down and turn the area into avocado orchards (Paulson, 1999). By the mid-1990s, small-scale maize producers were pressured further into exiting from maize production. The 1994 devaluation of the Mexican *peso* essentially lowered the guaranteed price of maize, and the government's refusal to raise prices to the now higher international level placed extraordinary constraints upon small-scale maize producers (Appendini, 1998). After seeing the success of orchards established by private producers, members of *ejidos* and communities with the resources to do so began to plant avocado in their fields as a diversification strategy. Success of these orchards motivated other *ejido*/indigenous farmers to shift to avocado, even if only one tree at a time. Over 64% of cultivable area in Tingambato is now planted with avocado, and about 98% of all avocado grown is Hass, while 2% is *criollo* grown in home gardens (Paulson, 1999).

While the overall trend since the early 1980s has been a gradual withdrawal of the state from agricultural decision-making, since the mid-1990s the state has reconfigured its relationship with the agriculture sector, with greater emphasis on high-value export-oriented commodities. While initially there was minimal state support for the avocado industry, creating an environment in which wealthy, elite producers could shape the industry, the government is increasingly influencing production and market conditions through a series of liberalization measures, and by forming state-producer alliances designed to increase the competitiveness of the industry. Although the late 1980s and early 1990s saw increasing diversity among adopters of avocado production, policy shifts are now exacerbating inequities in participation in the industry.

Local opportunities and constraints affecting adoption of avocado production

In the 1990s, smallholder *ejido* and indigenous farmers demonstrated an increased interest in avocado production throughout the Tingambato area. Several factors have played a key role in either encouraging or discouraging smallholders from cultivating avocado. The elimination of state support for grain production coupled with new incentives for higher-value fruit and vegetable production have translated into greater willingness to adopt new agricultural land-use strategies. Yet the conversion to avocado demonstrates more than an economic response to market opportunities. It also can be interpreted as a response to market uncertainties and a change in land tenure protection. In this section, the various factors which have inhibited or facilitated a shift to avocado production are examined.

Land reform

As Mexico moves toward full integration into a free-market economy, the government has determined that the traditional land management structure—the *ejido*—has been a key element in the lack of competitiveness of the agriculture sector. The *ejido* has traditionally been viewed as a structure which discourages investment in land improvements because individual parcels are not legally owned. Thus, increasing the opportunity for *ejidos* to improve their productivity includes giving smallholder farmers adequate title to their land. But, unless accompanied by a set of appropriate complementary policy reforms, it also increases smallholders' vulnerability to more powerful market forces and the opportunity for large-scale commercial interests to push them out of agriculture altogether.

In 1992, Mexico reversed its law, allowing *ejidos* to sell, transfer, or rent out their land. This is being accomplished through the *Programa de Certificación de Derechos Ejidales y Titulación de Solares Urbanos* (Certification Program for *Ejidal* Rights and Titling of Urban House Lots, or PROCEDE), a government-sponsored land titling and regularization program. As yet, however, it is unclear to what extent the reform of Article 27 and its program, PROCEDE, have influenced recent developments in land-use change. By altering the legal basis of tenure in order to make land available for large-scale production, the reform was expected to drastically increase large-scale commercial farming throughout Mexico. In Tingambato, however, this structural policy change has only served to legalize practices which have taken place for decades, and legitimate speculation in avocado production, undermining the *ejidos*' fragile hold on some of the most agriculturally-productive land in the municipality.

A change in land tenure has been a primary factor in the introduction and establishment of avocado in Tingambato. All of the *ejidos* and indigenous communities have engaged in illegal sales, rentals, and transfers of land for decades, usually at their own discretion, and promoted by the most powerful groups within each. However, the reform has enabled the consolidation of land within *ejidos* which have not voted to disband. More powerful producers within the *ejidos* are buying up land from those with less resources, usually at bargain prices, for their own personal benefit, while leaders in the indigenous communities have frequently sold portions of forest and communal land to outsiders for their own financial gain, in many cases weakening the internal organization of the communities. Some indigenous communities and *ejidos* have seen large portions of their land sold off to private producers. For example, there is speculation among several *comuneros* that *aguacateros* (larger-scale private avocado producers) offered one community a large sum of money and assistance with building needed infrastructure in exchange for the land (Paulson, 1999). In another community, individual members sold their parcels to a private contractor who is constructing a new state highway through the area (Paulson, 1999).

How has PROCEDE affected avocado production in Tingambato? Overall, it has created a sense of uncertainty and fear. PROCEDE promised new benefits, such as tenure security and increased access to credit, by providing the title needed to meet collateral requirements of lending institutions. But *ejidos* cannot obtain full titles, which are required by banks, unless they vote to disband. Even if the *ejidos* had proper title to their parcels, there is a general fear that the bank would take their land away if they were unable to pay their debts. To some degree, fear and uncertainties about the program have encouraged the *ejidos* to maintain the status quo. It is this very insecurity in tenure which has actually motivated *ejido*, and to some extent indigenous, producers to make improvements to their land. Producers willingly plant trees as a way to reinforce tenure and demonstrate a commitment to their land.

Access to credit and subsidies

Since the early 1990s, the Mexican rural agricultural finance system has been undergoing structural and organizational changes consistent with agrarian reform policies designed to modernize the agriculture sector. Several factors have figured prominently in the restructuring of finance in the countryside: privatization of state-owned banks, the massive unpaid debt *(cartera vencida)* accumulated by the *ejido* sector as a result of decades of uncontrolled lending to *ejidos* by the government-run agricultural lending institution, *Banco Nacional de Crédito Rural* (National Rural Credit Bank, or BANRURAL), and the need for reduction of the state's fiscal burden (Gledhill, 1995, Myhre, 1998). Creditworthiness is determined by a combination of factors including borrowers' repayment history, current earnings, scale of production, and the ability to provide collateral (usually land). Historically, credit has been channeled to large-scale, export-oriented private producers and *ejidatarios*, leaving more marginal *ejidos* and indigenous communities without any means of increasing their productivity through technological advances, improved inputs or land improvements because of lack of access to financial capital. Following implementation of the land reform program in 1992, many *ejidatarios* were under the impression they would gain access to credit if they completed the land titling process. Instead, many *ejido* members are finding that the benefits promised by the land reform program are out of their reach.

In Tingambato, the absence of widely available and easily accessible credit has been one of the major constraints for producers. Currently, there are limited options for financing rural production in Tingambato, and access to these depends heavily on producer category (e.g., commercial versus subsistence, large-scale versus small-scale), land tenure arrangements, and crop choice. There are three types of financing: commercial bank credit backed by FIRA (the Agricultural Trust Fund of the Bank of the Mexico), BANRURAL funding for private commercial producers and credit associations, and PROCAMPO subsidies for those producers not eligible for alternative sources of financing.[6] Although BANRURAL continues to operate in strategic areas of the state, the availability and accessibility of BANRURAL credit remains scarce in the municipality. First and foremost, BANRURAL has been restructured to operate more like a private, commercial bank, determining that small-scale producers such as those in Tingambato are too risky to invest in.[7] Second, as a result of corrupt municipal practices which have misallocated good-faith debt repayment efforts by conscientious *ejidatarios*, the *ejido* debt in Tingambato has yet to be reconciled.[8] Together, these have placed extraordinary financial constraints upon local small-scale producers belonging to *ejidos*, while at the same time discouraging producers from resolving their debts and fostering a sense of mistrust of local government. In summary, no forms of traditional credit are available in Tingambato, and small-scale producers with limited resources must rely on PROCAMPO as their main source of support (for another example, see Schüren, this volume).

Until 1998, the state offered no direct subsidies or fiscal incentives for avocado production. Recent changes within the PROCAMPO program, however, have provided new incentives and mechanisms for producers to shift from basic grain production to higher-value crop production, such as Hass avocado. During the first five years of operation (1993-1997), only basic crops were eligible for subsidization under PROCAMPO. In Michoacán, these included soya, beans, wheat, maize, rice, barley, sorghum, and oats. In 1998, PROCAMPO coverage was extended to all crops, including fruits and vegetables. Eligibility for payment for perennial fruit crops depends on the number of trees per hectare or the percentage of land used for tree cultivation. In the case of avocado, the government requires ten trees per hectare. Producers are also allowed to mix avocado with maize or another crop, but at least 10% per hectare must be planted with avocado for the land to be eligible for PROCAMPO subsidies. This also ensures that those maize producers who attempt to switch to avocado do not jeopardize their PROCAMPO eligibility: they can still receive subsidies while their *milpas* (agricultural field dominated by subsistence maize production, but may include several different crops) are in transition.[9] In 1998, 67% of PROCAMPO payments went toward maize cultivation and 4% toward avocado, with an average payment of $NP 625.50 per hectare (approximately US$ 65) (Paulson, 1999). Avocado, a capital-intensive crop, is much more expensive to produce than maize, but can be highly remunerative. While the PROCAMPO subsidy will never meet the cost of orchard establishment or maintenance, trees will render some yield, however minimal in volume and quality, providing small-scale producers with a source of financial security.

The government asserts that PROCAMPO was set up as a supplement to other already functioning programs, some of which are intended to stimulate producers to invest resources from PROCAMPO in capital and/or to form associations with other producers in order to become more productive (Alcala *et al.*, 1996). But most farmers interviewed indicated that the subsidies do not cover all of the costs of production, leaving no resources to reinvest. Rising input costs, coupled with the declining guaranteed price for maize, has meant that it has become cheaper for many farmers to purchase maize than to continue cultivating it. New incentives, such as the inclusion of avocado within the PROCAMPO crop structure, may further encourage small-scale producers to shift to avocado production through a slow transitional process. The consequence of such a shift, however, could be a future loss of land tenure protection, as farmers who find it difficult to adequately maintain their orchards or who face market instability, risk losing their land to wealthy, more entrepreneurial producers.

New employment opportunities

Both neoclassical and Marxist economics predict the transformation of small-scale peasant farmers to either capitalist producers or wage earners under advanced capitalist agriculture (Ellis, 1988). Avocado has brought new wealth to Tingambato for some, but above all, new sources of employment for many. The introduction of avocado into the region has drastically changed migration and employment patterns at both the local and regional levels. Similar to other Michoacanos, many Tingambateños spent time in the US or in other regions of Mexico working as agricultural wage laborers in the 1960s, 1970s or 1980s. Many believe there is no longer a need to migrate since the local economy has improved. In fact, in-migration is increasing due to Tingambato's importance in the avocado industry. While several of the wealthier private landowners in the municipality have chosen to reside in Mexico City, Morelia, Uruapan, or even Texas, some families move to Tingambato in order to establish medium-scale fruit growing operations. Others come to the area to obtain seasonal jobs working in the orchards, packing houses, and tree nurseries.

Since the 1990s, employment patterns have drastically changed with an emphasis on flexible, temporary, and seasonal labor. In some cases, these same flexible wage positions have created new opportunities for upward mobility. High complementarity in labor demand between the avocado industry and rainfed maize production provides new and accessible possibilities for small-scale producers to enter avocado production. Because the main harvesting season for avocado is from November through February, many farmers are able to complement their subsistence maize production with seasonal jobs when the need for household farm labor is at its least intense (see Bee, this volume, for another example). While rainfed maize farming is labor intensive, avocado production, with the exception of the harvesting and distribution processes, is primarily capital-intensive. Through seasonal orchard jobs, some Tingambateños have accumulated finance capital and technological capability, allowing them to establish their own small orchards (for another example, see Wells, 1990, 1997).

Phytosanitary policy and harmonization of quality

A series of new measures and regulations has been established by the state government since 1995 in an effort to harmonize standards and facilitate the export of Michoacán's avocado to the US. While the overall trend since the early 1980s has been a gradual withdrawal of the state from agricultural decision-making, since the mid-1990s, several actions have signaled the reconfiguration of state policy toward agriculture. This shift is characterized by increasing emphasis on building alliances and linkages with producer networks within export commodity sectors, and an increasing government role in defining avocado quality.

In 1994, the state began to establish local organizations and committees as one mechanism for implementing phytosanitary campaigns which would facilitate the export of avocado to the US by increasing the quality of avocado. While initially compliance was voluntary, in 1996 participation became mandatory. In that year, the federal government passed legislation establishing phytosanitary requirements and specifications for the transport and movement of avocado and other fresh fruits and vegetables. Furthermore, state-producer alliances determined that the phytosanitary requirements and quality standards should apply to domestic as well as export fresh avocado. Highway inspection stations as well as certification requirements have been established to protect the principal production zones from pest infestations (Paulson, 1999).

One result of this new legislation is to restrict access to the export avocado market to only the most resourceful, wealthy and politically well-connected producers in the region. By possessing a certificate indicating that an orchard is free from quarantined plant diseases and pests, a producer has access to both domestic and global fresh avocado markets. Producers who are not able to obtain a certificate must sell their avocado to the processing market. Financial assistance was initially provided by the government to the 1,500 producers who voluntarily entered the program, as well as for establishing local plant health committees to set up campaigns within each avocado-producing municipality in the region. These committees are headed by some of the most elite producers in Michoacán. Most producers initiated into the program were wealthy, private commercial producers, with personal financial capital, close ties with political organizations (Stanford, 1998), and proximity to information sources about the certification and inspection program.

Orchard certification is not only mandatory, but also very costly and thereby discriminates against small-scale producers with limited resources. In 1994, costs incurred for the region-wide program reached approximately US$ 14,285, increasing to US$ 160,000 by 1998 (Paulson, 1999: 72). While 1,500 producers were registered with the program, the USDA only approved 65 for export certification, and then financed the strict and capital-intensive phytosanitary regime through loans to the Mexican government. The state government is no longer providing financial or technical assistance to new producers entering the program, making it difficult for resource-poor smallholders to access the technologies disseminated through the campaigns. With an estimated 6,000 producers in the industry (Stanford, forthcoming), this leaves a massive quantity of producers without recourse.

Since October 1997, the local Committee for Plant Health (*Sanidad Vegetal*) in Tingambato has been operating out of the offices of a local *ejido*. Although the statewide program has been operating since 1996, it did not initiate a campaign in Tingambato until late 1997. While the goal of the program is to eradicate pests and diseases of avocado in order to comply with USDA import requirements, it is essentially creating marketing channels which favor some producers over others. "Freeing" an orchard of plant pests and diseases is believed to ensure yields of high-quality fruit. This is accomplished primarily through a strict regime of orchard inspection and maintenance, and through tighter regulation and control of all avocado entering and leaving quarantined areas.

The requirement that every avocado producer in Tingambato be registered with the *Sanidad Vegetal* committee in order to transport their fruit, provides both opportunities and constraints for commercialization, depending on the class of producer. All producers are required to pay a registration fee of one *peso* per tree or 100 *pesos* per hectare. Once registered, producers may seek technical assistance with eradication, but the cost of any extra inputs, such as pesticide chemicals, is borne by the producer. Those producers with minimal economic resources face either indebtedness or marginalization in marketing. By not subscribing to the program and completing the certification process, their fruit is branded as low-quality and therefore marketable only for the food processing industry (e.g., frozen avocado, guacamole, avocado oil and paste). In the alternative, *Sanidad Vegetal* will allow the producer to subscribe to the program on credit. While this certainly provides some benefit to the small-scale producer, just as it would to the large-scale producer, the former is more likely to become further indebted and many resent their forced participation in the program. At the time this study was carried out, 1,300 hectares of avocado were registered with the program in Tingambato.

Even if a low-income producer manages to subscribe to the program, the costs of obtaining phytosanitary certification are exorbitant, and thus virtually exclude poorer smallholder producers from the program. Table 1 shows the average cost of production for the export market, which has steadily increased since 1995. The information in Table 1 generally refers to production costs for yields averaging 15 metric tons per hectare. In reality, yields vary anywhere between three and 15 metric tons per hectare, depending on orchard size and degree of inputs utilized. Small-scale producers tend to have the lowest yields, largely because low-resource producers frequently invest the absolute minimum required for production, skimping on pre-harvest care. The regional avocado producers' union in Uruapan estimates a production cost of NP$ 3.10 per kilo for an eight t/h yield. Most of this cost is represented by the high cost of agrochemicals.

Table 1   Average cost of avocado production *(pesos* per hectare)

Category	1995	1996	1997	1998
Cultural practices*	2,140	2,140	2,924	3,663
Fertilization**	4,931	5,620	6,165	4,699
Phytosanitary control	2,546	3,088	3,327	5,875
Other***	1,428	1,095	1,195	1,700
Harvest	1,932	966	1,272	1,272
Total	12,977	12,909	14,883	17,209

Source: USDA Foreign Agricultural Service, 1997; AAL Uruapan, 1998 (see Paulson, 1999).

*   "Cultural practices" refer to labor costs for cleaning and maintaining orchards.

**   The USDA and AAL have different categories for fertilization and phytosanitary control.

***   "Other" includes property and social security taxes, union dues, and subscription fees for Sanidad Vegetal program.

Therefore, reducing the extent to which agrochemicals are used reduces overall production costs. The average farmgate price offered for domestic fresh avocado in November 1998 was NP$ 3.60 per kilo, although prices vary depending on which market produce is directed to and the season in which it is sold. The processed food market offers the lowest price, about NP$ 2 per kilo. Small-scale producers in Tingambato who are not able to take advantage of fresh avocado export opportunities because of lack of capital to ensure high-quality produce, and/or lack of access to export markets, produce for the processed avocado market.

Producer organization

With an adequate supply of high-quality fruit ready to be exported to the US, producers and the state have realized that they need to be better organized in order to survive in a more competitive market. Although the government and private sector made some attempt to cooperate in the industrialization and commercialization of fresh produce, primarily through CONAFRUT and other parastatal agencies, in the 1970s and 1980s (Sanderson, 1986: 76) there were few powerful or effective unions or other producer organizations in the avocado industry. Those organizations that did exist tended to exhibit dynamic qualities and typically established horizontal linkages, with no connection between production and marketing (Stanford n.d.). The benefits of membership were obscure and membership roles increased and decreased depending on whether it was harvesting season (Stanford, forthcoming).

Since 1996, more concerted efforts at organization have been made, both within already established organizations and between organizations and state agencies. Several producer organizations are shifting their priorities from production-related problems to a focus on marketing and distribution related issues (Stanford, 1998). One of the largest and most active local unions is the *Asociación Agrícola Local* (AAL) *de Productores de Aguacate de Uruapan Michoacán*, founded in 1968, with 130 members as of 1998 (Paulson, 1999). Prior to 1997, this union focused on offering member discounts for pesticides and holding seminars on new grafting techniques and orchard maintenance, for example. As of November 1997, the month the first US export season opened for Mexican fresh avocado, the union began to focus on marketing, supply, and distribution problems. New efforts are being made in the areas of consumer marketing, technical assistance, phytosanitary campaigns and price recommendations to producer members, dissemination of information through newsletters, and weekly price quotes.

In November 1998, Michoacán's state governor inaugurated a new 110-member, producer-owned integrated exporting company. AMIMEX, S.A. de C.V. *(Aguacateros de Michoacán Mexico)* was originally founded by 50 producers of which 42 (or 85%) are authorized to export avocado to the US. At the time of its inauguration, membership had expanded to 110 members with control of 40% of the total certified avocado area in Michoacán, or 4,300 hectares (La Voz, 1998). In addition to the exporting company, which was primarily set up to facilitate commercialization of its product abroad, AMIMEX is also expanding into packing and processing operations.

The inauguration came on the heels of a drastic setback for the Michoacán avocado industry. Just a few weeks earlier, oversupply to the international market caused the price to plummet, creating concern and panic within the industry. Nevertheless, the industry has recognized that the saturation of the market with Mexican avocado is a result of its own disorganization (La Voz, 1998). As a result of the fiasco, the state government called for all producers to stop harvesting their fruit, and by late November/early December 1998 only 14 of approximately 70 packinghouses in the region remained open. The governor is also strengthening efforts to create an organization capable of monitoring the three most important elements for successful exportation, i.e., market price, supply, and quality of product (La Voz, 1998). Market elements are the key to survival of the industry as a whole, but *ejido* and indigenous small-scale avocado producers are the most vulnerable to problems of oversupply. They have typically been the last class of producer to switch to Hass avocado, and many of their orchards have not yet been brought into production due to the lag time between initial planting and maturity (approximately 3-5 years). As the area cultivated with avocado increases, both in Tingambato and in the region, it is imperative that producers organize in order to avoid future supply problems. Future disorganization and loss of control over market supply could spell disaster for the newer entrants to the industry.

Producers in Tingambato indicate that their means of marketing their avocado depend greatly on distributors who come around to orchards to negotiate with producers. The lack of a vehicle to transport their own fruit to packinghouses increases the chance that they will be forced to act as a "price-taker" in the marketing process, with minimal leverage to negotiate. Frequently, entire harvests are purchased, but it is also fairly common for distributors to choose only the highest quality fruit from particular trees within an orchard. Once the sale has been negotiated, distributors send trucks and pickers (or contract out a picking company) to collect the produce.

Few small-scale *ejido* and indigenous producers from Tingambato are active in associations outside Tingambato. A local producers' union (AAL) was established about 20 years ago, but it has never been well-organized. It does not have an office or regular meeting place, but occasionally gathers at the offices of Tingambato's largest *ejido* for meetings. The union is dominated by many of the same producers who head the local Plant Health committee. Those who are "active" recognize the few benefits they received in the past and the need to better organize. Because many of the small-scale *ejido*/indigenous producers are new participants in avocado production, they do not share a cohesive history with the more well-established producers in the municipality, nor do they possess the political experience to negotiate within the more globalized context of the avocado industry. Furthermore, deep divisions within *ejidos* and indigenous communities discourage some producers from willingly interacting with other, more powerful, producers within their same communities.

Conclusions

This chapter illustrates the relationship between agricultural restructuring, land-use change, and smallholder participation in the Mexican avocado sector. While environmental features have been critical to defining land-use capability in Tingambato, policy reforms modifying the broad array of producer incentives and government support structures for Mexico's farmers have provided a new context in which land-use decisions are made. Over the past 30 years, land-use in Tingambato has undergone a profound transformation as a result of regional and global social, political, and economic factors driving the expansion of the export avocado industry in Michoacán. As policies become increasingly focused on assimilating and adapting to global economic forces, the state has refocused its efforts on ensuring the avocado industry remains competitive, by strengthening alliances with wealthy, powerful producers and promoting a policy environment in which only the most resilient survive. In this context, it is clear that the survival of small-scale producers in the Michoacán avocado industry is, at best, fragile.

Land reform, implemented in 1992, was thought to be the key to ensuring the competitiveness of the agriculture sector. It has become clear, however, that land reform alone will not determine the competitiveness of smallholder farmers, unless it is accompanied by appropriate policies that enable the reform to benefit those for whom it was intended. In Tingambato, the reform of Article 27 and its program, PROCEDE, have enabled the consolidation of land within *ejidos*, exacerbating already existing deep divisions among *ejidos* (and indigenous communities). While illegal sales, rentals, and transfers of land have existed for decades, enabling the expansion of avocado production in the municipality early on, the context in which this change in property relations is taking place has shifted from one of outsiders penetrating the property structures of *ejidos* and indigenous communities, to increased fragmentation of lands within and greater consolidation of holdings among the most powerful groups within these entities.

With the integration of the avocado sector into the global marketplace, high-quality, high-yield production has become increasingly critical for survival of the industry as a whole. The reduction of state-supported credit and price subsidies has placed significant constraints upon the smallholder producer's ability to access the expensive technologies (equipment and agrochemical inputs) required for a competitive product. PROCAMPO, the state's poverty alleviation program, is the only means of support available to most small-scale farmers in Mexico. Although initially intended to encourage farmers to reinvest resources in land improvements, smallholders have found it difficult to manage even the basic costs of grain production due to the structural limitations discussed previously. In this sense, production is being channeled away from small-scale producers, toward more efficient, larger-scale producers. Alternatively, the inclusion of avocado in the PROCAMPO crop structure over the past year has provided an incentive to smallholders in Tingambato to diversify their crop portfolios. The low subsidy and the high cost of orchard establishment and maintenance preclude any drastic transition to avocado production; however, many smallholders are overcoming this obstacle by planting just a few trees at a time. Once the trees mature and begin to produce, the income earned from the sale of the fruit provides capital for additional expansion of orchards. The downside to this is that farmers, because of capital constraints, ultimately become more vulnerable and at greater risk of losing their land resources should the market fail.

Opportunities for commercialization are critical to the small-scale producer's ability to survive in the avocado industry. These opportunities are defined by access to markets, the extent to which producers are capable of organizing marketing practices, and participation in the government-sponsored phytosanitary certification program. Access to these opportunities is highly dependent upon class and scale of producer, financial capital, and political connections with powerful regional unions. Furthermore, the ability to compete effectively depends on accurate, timely, and available market information and a reciprocity in producers' interaction with marketing agents and organizations. Participation in the orchard certification program, above all, determines for which market a farmer will produce. By requiring producers to participate in order to have their fruit transported to a packing house or processing facility, but at the same time requiring a fee for participation, the program thereby limits who can participate. Those farmers with limited economic resources, while able to participate on credit, face either marginalization or further indebtedness. The requirement that all neighboring orchards must be certified in order to certify a particular orchard could result in increased maneuvering by wealthier orchard owners to rent or buy neighboring orchards.

Several points lead to the conclusion that the increasing globalization of the avocado sector is creating inequities among different sets of producers. First, the establishment of avocado production in Tingambato, as well as its expansion, at least through the 1980s, is attributed to wealthy, private entrepreneurs who began cultivating the improved variety in the *municipio* in the late 1960s. These producers financed production with their own capital and developed close alliances with state agencies and party leaders in Michoacán, the same phenomenon which was occurring industry-wide (see for example, Stanford, 1998). Many of these same producers head the local avocado producer's union and the local Plant Health committee, and at the same time are connected to some of the most powerful and exclusive producer organizations in the region. This elitist domination of the sector has impeded access to information and resulted in technological weaknesses in smallholder production processes. Semi-reliance on brokers and intermediaries for technological information and for marketing and distribution services, has eliminated the smallholder's autonomy in post-production decision-making.

Second, migration and labor patterns have dramatically changed within Tingambato as well as within the industry. The proliferation of packing houses, tree nurseries, and larger-scale orchards has developed a significant market for wage labor, practically eliminating the need for Tingambateños to join labor migration networks and increasing the incidence of in-migration of outsiders looking for seasonal wage work. While some Tingambateños have inevitably joined the rural proletariat, para-doxically, many have used the availability of seasonal work to provide the finance capital and technological capability necessary for small-scale orchard establishment.

Despite the challenging constraints small-scale producers in Tingambato face as a result of recent commodity restructuring and policy reform, they have nevertheless shown adaptive capacity and a willingness to participate in avocado production. Although demonstrating some degree of adaptability, complex new production and market conditions have arisen which increase the vulnerability of the small-scale producer in the avocado sector. While many smallholders remain committed to their land and their farm livelihoods, even if it means a change in crop structure, their ability to survive will depend greatly on the extent to which they are capable of renegotiating their role within the industry and are provided appropriate policy options to carry this out.

Notes

[1] This chapter is based on research carried out with financial support from the Latin American Area Center and a grant provided by the National Aeronautics and Space Administration (NASA) to conduct a comprehensive study of the economic and demographic causes of land-use change in Mexico under the direction of Dr. Diana Liverman. Funding to participate in this workshop was provided by the Graduate and Professional Student Council of the University of Arizona and the Latin American Area Center. Special thanks go to Hallie Eakin, Martjan Lammertink, and Dereka Rushbrook for their careful editing of and helpful comments on an earlier draft.

[2] For the purposes of this study, small-scale is defined as less than 10 hectares and generally refers to indigenous and *ejido* producers.

[3] An *ejido* is a communal land management structure created as a result of the Mexican Revolution, in which members hold land in usufruct. Until 1992, *ejido* members were not legally permitted to rent, sell, or transfer their land.

[4] *Chirimoya* is a fruit belonging to a family of fruits consisting of guanabana, nona, and *chirimoya*. Tingambato had a reputation for producing the sweetest and best-tasting *chirimoya* in the region. *Chirimoya* is still sold in local and regional markets, but is produced on a very small scale in home gardens.

[5] SAM (Sistema Alimentaria Mexicana) was a food self-sufficiency program implemented by President Lopez Portillo in 1980. SAM attempted to use price incentives to promote increased productivity in the agricultural sector, particularly among small-scale producers of basic grains. The program provided services such as food distribution, subsidized electricity and irrigation, and lower interest rates. It was dismantled due to fiscal problems related to the oil crisis after only two years of operation (Sanderson, 1986).

[6] PROCAMPO (Program of Direct Support Payments to the Countryside) was initiated in 1993 as a financial assistance program to soften the impact of market liberalization policies on small-scale farmers, and to ease the transition from a system of price supports and state-supported credit to a system without such support. PROCAMPO initially provided direct case subsidies to farmers who agreed to cultivate one of several selected basic food crops. Farmers are paid on a per hectare basis, rather than a yield basis, with subsidies varying annually.

[7] This restructuring entails several new lending policies: BANRURAL has purged its client base of thousands of inefficient, indebted, small-scale producers, it has overhauled its administrative units to function more efficiently, it requires land titles as a requisite for extension of credit, and largely lends to credit associations in order to better manage its risk.

[8] BANRURAL, in an effort to collect its debts from the *ejidos*, delegated the responsibility for collecting payments to the municipal government, with the requisite that until those individuals within *ejidos* who owe money repay their debts, the bank will not extend credit to anyone. Claims of corruption by the municipal government are rampant; instead of handing over the collected payments to the bank, the municipal government is using the money for its own expenses.

[9] There is no information available, however, as to the class of producer currently receiving PROCAMPO for avocado cultivation. Because a producer must have signed up for the program in 1992, 1995, or 1996 and avocado was not a subsidized crop at that time, it is inferred that the avocado currently being subsidized is for new plantings on parcels previously dedicated to other crops. (See Paulson, 1999, for more detail).

References

Alcala, Elio, L.M., M. Del Carmen Brunt Rivera, de la Luz Parcero Lopez y Teofilo Reyes Couturier, *Campesinos: Articulo 27 y Estado Mexicano*. Mexico, DF (INAH), Plaza y Valdes Editores, 1996.

Alvarez-Icaza, P., G. Cervera, C. Garibay, P. Gutierrez and F. Rosete, "Los umbrales del deterioro: la dimension ambiental de un desarrollo desigual en la region Purepecha". PAIR-UNAM, Michoacán. Mexico, DF, Fundacion Friedrich Ebert, 1993.

Appendini, K., "Changing agrarian institutions: interpreting the contradictions'. In: W.A. Cornelius and D. Myhre (eds.), *The transformation of rural Mexico: reforming the ejido sector*. Center for US-Mexican Studies, University of California, San Diego, 1998.

Barkin, D., *Distorted development: Mexico in the world economy*. Boulder, Westview Press, 1990.

Barry, T., *Zapata's revenge: free trade and the farm crisis in Mexico*. Boston, South End Press, 1995.

Bebbington, A., "Social capital and rural intensification: local organizations and islands of sustainability in the rural Andes". *The Geographical Journal*, Vol. 163, no. 2 (1997), 189-97.

Calva, L., "Probables efectos de un tratado de libre comercio en el campo Mexicano". Distribuciones Mexico, DF, Fontamara, S.A., 1991.

Direccion General de Estadística, "V censos agrícola-ganadero y ejidal 1970". Estado de Michoacán, Mexico, DF, Direccion General de Estadistica, 1975.

Ellis, F., *Peasant economics: farm households and agrarian development*. Great Britain, Cambridge University Press, 1988.

Gledhill, J., *Neoliberalism, transnationalization and rural poverty: a case study of Michoacán, Mexico*. Boulder, Westview Press, 1995.

Instituto Nacional de Estadistica, Geografia e Informatica, "El sector alimentario en Mexico, edicion 1997". Aguascalientes, Mexico: INEGI, 1997.

La Voz de Michoacán, "Revatinga entre aguacateros propicio la caida del precio". November 26, 1998.

Marsden, T., "Creating space for food: the distinctiveness of recent agrarian development". In: D. Goodman and M.J. Watts (eds.), *Globalising food: agrarian questions and global restructuring*. London, Routledge, 1997.

Paulson, L.J., "Globalization and survival of the smallholder: the role of agricultural restructuring in land-use change in Michoacán, Mexico". Unpublished M.A. thesis. Latin American Area Center, University of Arizona, Tucson, 1999.

Rosete, F., J.A. Ordoñcz y O. Masera, "Dinamica de cambio de uso del suelo y emisiones de carbono en la meseta purepecha: el caso de la comunidad indígena de Santiago Tingambato". Unpublished manuscript. UNAM-Instituto de Ecologia, Morelia, Michoacán, 1997.

Sanchez C., S. and M. Rubi Arriaga, "Situacion actual del cultivo del aguacate en Mexico". 1994 Yearbook, California Avocado Society, Inc., 78, 1994, pp. 61-74.

Sanderson, S.E., *The transformation of rural Mexico: international structure and the politics of rural change*. New Jersey, Princeton University Press, 1986.

Secretaría de Agricultura, Ganaderia y Desarrollo Rural, "Libreta agrícola 1997, Distrito de desarrollo rural". Unpublished document. Uruapan, 1997.

Smith, A.P., "The battle for green gold: the North American free trade agreement—the implications for the avocado market". Unpublished M.A. thesis. Cornell University, 1992.

Stanford, L., "Peasant resistance in the international market: theory and practice in Michoacán, Mexico". *Research in Economic Anthropology*, Vol. 13 (1991), pp. 67-91.

Stanford, L., "Mexico's empresario in export agriculture: examining the avocado industry of Michoacán". Paper presented at the 1998 meeting of the Latin American Studies Association, Chicago, Illinois, September 24-26, 1998.

Stanford, L., "Examining the social dimensions of agricultural 'organization': the case of the avocado industry of Michoacán". In: G. Rodriguez and R. Snyder (eds.), *Strategies for resource Management, production and marketing in rural Mexico*. University of California, San Diego, Center for US-Mexican Studies, forthcoming.

Stonich, S., D.L. Murray and P.R. Rosset, "Enduring crises: the human and environmental consequences of nontraditional export growth in Central America". *Research in Economic Anthropology*, Vol. 15 (1994), pp. 239-74.

USDA, "Attache report on the Mexican avocado sector". Foreign Agricultural Service, 1997.

Watts, M. and D. Goodman, "Agrarian questions: global appetite, local metabolism: nature, culture and industry in fin-de-siecle agro-food systems". In: D. Goodman and M.J. Watts (eds.), *Globalising food: agrarian questions and global restructuring*. London, Routledge, 1997.

Wells, M.J., "Mexican farm workers become strawberry farmers". *Human Organization*, Vol. 49, no. 2 (1990), 149-56.

Wells, M.J., "Legal discourse and the restructuring of Californian agriculture: class relations at the local level". In: D. Goodman and M.J. Watts (eds.), *Globalising food: agrarian questions and global restructuring*. London, Routledge, 1997.

Zimmerer, K.S., "Discourses on soil loss in Bolivia: sustainability and the search for socioenvironmental 'middle ground'". In: R. Peet and M. Watts (eds.), *Liberation ecologies: environment, development and social movements*. London, Routledge, 1997.

13 Economic strategies of rural producers: a comparison of *ejido* and Mennonite agriculture

Ute Schüren

Introduction

Especially since the establishment of agriculturally very productive Mennonite colonies in their neighborhood, *ejidatarios* in the Chenes region of the Mexican state of Campeche have been increasingly confronted with the criticism that their failure to obtain sufficient yields from their fields is due to their laziness and ignorance. These allegedly characteristic features are explained either as an outcome of governmental paternalism or as cultural traits of the Maya-speaking rural population in general. As one civil servant put it: "How come that Mennonites immigrating from other regions, who are not accustomed to the local environment and often work without irrigation systems, obtain such high yields while our *ejidatarios* do not get along with all our help and governmental programs?" (interview, Hopelchen, Aug. 12, 1994).

In the following, a comparison is made of the agriculture methods of Mennonite and of *ejido* producers. It will be shown that fundamental differences in the importance attributed to land and farming as a basis for livelihood exist which reflect different economic strategies. Low yields are not typical of Mayan culture, but simply a result of the increasing economic and environmental strains households have to cope with. The discussion will concentrate on the production of corn, the major crop cultivated by both groups as well as in the Chenes region in general.

The Chenes region: a brief economic history

The municipality of Hopelchen (also known as Chenes region) is situated on the tropical frontier of the northeastern part of the Mexican state of Campeche (see Map 1).[1] The region is characterized by more or less extended plains or small valleys, and broad, conical hills and ridges of relatively high relief (the *montaña*) which rise toward the south. In the northern part, between fields, pasturelands, plantations and settlements, the landscape is covered with dense scrub and deciduous seasonal forest. In the southern area, some parts of high tropical forest remain. Soil fertility and depth vary considerably. Soils are often thin and the ground surface is littered with chunks of limestone rock. Mechanized land is restricted to areas of deeper soils and poorly drained bottomlands (*ak'alché*). Especially in the extreme northern and southern part, soils are very stony and only few areas are suitable for working with a tractor (Wilhelmy 1981: 133; Wilson 1980: 33; Berzunza Herrera, 1989: 14, 68; Ayuntamiento de Hopelchen, 1992: 10; Gates, 1993: 110; Sales Gutierrez, 1996: 42-56).

In the rural area of Hopelchen, the infrastructure is still very deficient and several settlements can only be reached by dirt road. The main problem for development is the supply of water. As a karst region, the Chenes has almost no surface water and rainfall percolates very rapidly through the porous limestone. Access to groundwater from deep wells, which may dry up during the dry season

(November to April), is limited. Generally, the groundwater level drops from north to south. But there is a high variability even within small areas. Around Ich Ek, for example, groundwater is found at 25 meters. Only a few kilometers to the north, in San Juan Bautista Sahcabchen, it lies at 140 meters (Berzunza Pinto, 1991: 116; Wilhelmy, 1981: 74-87).

A large part of the municipality's rural population is bilingual (Yucatec Maya and Spanish). Most of the Maya speakers live in villages with *ejido* organization[2], while in the regional center Hopelchen and three other larger settlements (Bolonchen, Dzibalchen, Iturbide) a Spanish-speaking *ladino* population controls most commercial activities and conducts some farming.[3] Also, Low German-speaking Mennonite colonists, who began to immigrate into the region in the 1980s, make up an increasing part of the population.

Although Hopelchen remained relatively isolated until 1943, when a paved road to the urban centers Campeche and Merida was constructed (Aranda González, 1985: 184), the economy had been incorporated into the international market as early as the 18th century. Workers from all over the Yucatán peninsula and other parts of Mexico came to the region to extract tropical forest products, mainly chicle (the resin of the *chicozapote* tree, *achras zapota)* for US chewing gum production. In the late 1940s, US manufacturers introduced artificial substitutes for the resin and reduced their imports drastically, and the chicle boom came to an end (Ponce Jiménez, 1990; Peña, 1942: 47; Konrad, 1987, 1995; Ramayo Lanz, 1997). Agrarian reform in the Chenes region was pushed forward during the presidency of Lázaro Cardenas (1934-1940). But it was only after the breakdown of chicle production that agriculture based on the *milpa* (the traditional swidden system)[4] became the primary economic strategy for the major part of the population living in *ejidos* in the center and the south of the Chenes (Schüren, n.d.a and n.d.b). However, the lack of local wage-labor opportunities forced many inhabitants of Hopelchen to emigrate temporarily or permanently to the urban centers of the Yucatán peninsula, namely Campeche, Merida and, since the 1970s, to the tourist enclave of Cancun.

Government development programs started in the second half of the 1960s in a few *ejidos* with the installation of small irrigation projects for collectively organized *ejidatarios*. But due to malfunctioning equipment—and a therefore risky production under high credit costs with low value crops—poor access to market, and strained relations between members of the collectives, these projects were not successful (Messmacher, 1967: 147; Gates, 1993: 143-151). In 1995, groups in two *ejidos* (Ich Ek and Suctuc) were working with an outdated irrigation system, operating just some of their wells. In the 1970s, within the framework of President Echeverría's large-scale investment program for rural development (PIDER), more governmental measures were introduced, including the distribution of credit and equipment for commercial bee-keeping and the mechanization of *ejido* lands. Also, infrastructure in the villages (e.g., the construction or extension of systems of potable water and electricity) was improved and some roads were built. Some ambitious projects were pushed forward. In the 1980s, more than 10,000 hectares of bottomlands (of which only about 5,000 were actually used for production) were cleared in Chunchintoc and 500 hectares in Xmaben to produce dry rice. But these projects soon proved to be disastrous, not only for the natural environment but also economically for most of the *ejidatarios* (interviews with *comisarios ejidales*, Xmaben March 2, 1996, Chunchintoc March 9, 1996; Gates, 1993: 169).

Map 1   The municipality of Hopelchen Campeche

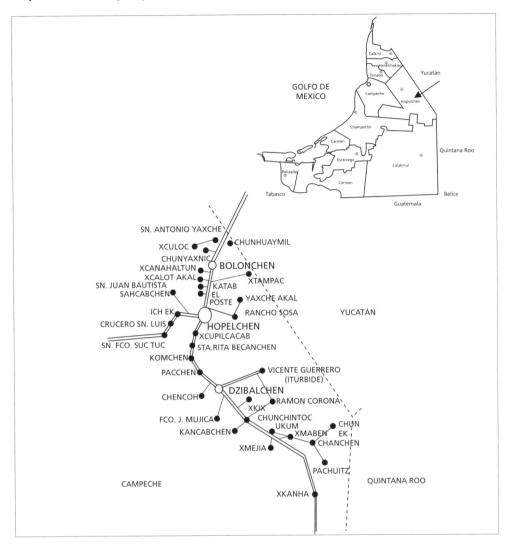

Generally, the mechanization of agriculture did not improve living conditions in many *ejidos*, but fostered the producers' dependence on the government and on expensive means of production (pesticides, hybrid seeds, fertilizers, gasoline, tractors, etc.). From the very beginning, the amount of mechanized land per producer, and especially the technology offered to the *ejidos*, was insufficient for them to make a profit. *Ejidatarios* were subjected to the control of government agencies including the Rural Credit Bank. Their agricultural knowledge was rejected. Crop failures were frequent and the producers, increasingly confronted with fraud and politics, lost much of their motivation. Credits could not be repaid and the majority of *ejidatarios* of the municipality fell into loan default.[5] However, at the time of the introduction of "modern agriculture," the traditional *milpa* system was already under much stress in many parts of the Chenes region. In the northern part, almost no areas of high forest were left. Because of population pressure and extensive commercial clearings, the *milpa* fallow cycle was already very reduced. Consequently, yields had decreased notably (interviews with *ejidatarios* in Bolonchen, March 6, 1996; Hopelchen, Feb. 13, 1996; Campeche, March 28, 1998; Xcupilcacab, Sept. 19, 1994; interview with civil servants, Hopelchen, Feb. 23, 1996).

Today, there are striking differences concerning land-use, supply with machinery, access to markets, etc. among the agricultural producers of the Chenes region. The spectrum of production techniques ranges from traditional forms of swidden agriculture, to the use of modern irrigation systems. In addition to corn *squash*, beans, cotton, tomatoes, and watermelons are cultivated. Cattle, poultry and pig raising, citriculture, horticulture, the production of honey, and embroidery are also important for the rural economy. In the southern part, lumber, chicle, and other forest products are still extracted on a small scale.

There are currently 36 *ejidos* in the Chenes zone. They differ considerably in the size of their land grants and in the number of their members.[6] Forms of production within the *ejidos* are far from homogeneous. This is partly a consequence of government modernization programs directed at selected groups of *ejido* members, which had to be formed in order to obtain credit. An increasing number of especially younger men (*avecindados* or residents, sons of *ejidatarios*, colonists, etc.) are without official *ejidal* land rights, although many of them are unofficially allowed to till fields in the territory of the *ejido*.

In general, rainfed agriculture practiced by the majority of producers is a risky undertaking. Production is constantly threatened by erratic rainfall patterns. Decreasing yields during the last decades can be attributed, at least in part, to climatic changes resulting from the still ongoing ecological devastation of the adjacent tropical forest and the lack of an adequate resource management by the forest industry. What is more, tropical storms and hurricanes may pass between August and October. They often ravage the countryside and destroy fields entirely, leaving the agricultural producer with total crop failure. In 1995, for example, hurricanes Opal and Roxana devastated large areas of Campeche, and flooded settlements and cultivated lands. Nevertheless, agriculture in the Chenes region can still be profitable. Especially private agricultural entrepreneurs with large farms till their fields quite successfully, as do most Mennonites. In the following section, their farming methods are examined and compared with agricultural production in Xcupilcacab, a village with *ejido* organization.

Mennonite production[7]

As mentioned, Mennonite colonists first arrived in Campeche and the Chenes in the early 1980s, after land had become scarce in their former settlements in northern Mexico. They were well received and their presence became an important economic stimulus, especially for regional commerce. After their arrival in Hopelchen, land increased in value and became an important commodity.

At first, the Mennonites bought large tracts of private land (up to 10,000 hectares) belonging to former ranches. Many of them included territory appropriated by *acaparadores* who had obtained titles for national lands from the government in order to resell them. Since the New Agrarian Legislation offers the possibility for the long-term renting of *ejido* lands, since 1993 groups of colonists have begun to rent *ejido* territories of various qualities (ranging from long-term fallow areas to mechanized land). In 1996, an illegal sale of 15,000 hectares of communal land in one *ejido* took place. Often Mennonite colonists had invested a considerable amount of labor in order to make the land arable. With their heavy machinery, they were totally independent of governmental aid, and even constructed their own wells. Due to this investment, their land increased considerably in both quality and value (interview, Nuevo Progreso, March 18, 1998).

Most of the Mennonites wear a typical costume. Men are often dressed in checkered shirts, "cowboy" or baseball hats, and trousers with fly. Women's and girls' dress consists of wide, dark skirts, stockings, high-necked shirts or dresses, scarves with fringes, and broad-brimmed hats with colored ribbons. Mennonites live endogamously in isolated villages and neighborhoods known as *campos*, or on private farms.[8] Groups differ in their attitude towards modernization. Some are more conservative and have strict behavioral norms and a strong religious orientation; among other things, electricity and radios are forbidden. Conservative Mennonites own horse-drawn carts and are not allowed to drive cars. They hire trucks and drivers, who charge high amounts for transporting persons and goods. Mennonites in other settlements are more open and have begun to drive their own vehicles. Typical of Mennonite culture in general, is a protestant work ethic. Hard work is considered an important virtue. To sweat is seen as a sign of diligence. Other principles of life are humility, modesty, and piety. Especially women and girls seldom speak Spanish fluently. They are kept in relative seclusion, and are expected to behave in a reserved manner. Although there is a strong communal unity and the practice of mutual aid, in the colonies there are considerable differences with regard to access to land, capital, and machinery.

While Mennonites in many ways reject the "modern ways" of the surrounding culture, in terms of agriculture they are quite up to date. Almost the whole process of production is mechanized. Most farmers have their own tractors and other agricultural machinery. They all use hybrid seeds and chemical inputs (fertilizers, herbicides, pesticides). Some producers have installed modern sprinkler irrigation systems.[9]

Mennonite agriculturalists own their land individually.[10] Land tenure and production area vary considerably in size. In Nuevo Progreso, which is situated about 20 kilometers from the town of Hopelchen, individual farmers own, on an average, 100 hectares of land. Generally, 15 to 20 hectares are cultivated. But there are also some colonists who own and till much larger areas (interview with a Mennonite agriculturalist, Hopelchen, Nov. 11, 1994). Two Mennonite producers near Xcanahaltun, for example, till, all in all, up to 360 hectares.[11]

The division of labor is determined by sex and age. Mennonite farming relies a lot on family labor. To have many children is strongly desired, and households are quite large. Several couples have more than ten children. Nevertheless, at harvest time, farmhands from all over the municipality, including *ejidatarios*, are increasingly occupied. Work in the colonies is attractive, because Mennonites usually pay higher wages than local *ladino* farmers. In 1998, for example, wages were N$ 60 a day, more than double the official minimal wage (N$ 27) (interview with a Mennonite producer, Nuevo Progreso, March 18, 1998).

Most Mennonites practice intensive, rainfed agriculture. The major cash crop is corn. In contrast to *ejido* producers, corn is not important for household consumption,

ECONOMIC STRATEGIES OF RURAL PRODUCERS

and almost all is sold at official prices to National Warehouse Depositories (ANDSA or CONASUPO in Hopelchen, Dzibalchen, and Bolonchen). Yields of up to five tons per hectare are frequent. According to official data, between 1994 and 1997 they averaged more than three tons per hectare, with the exception of 1995 when hurricanes Roxana and Opal devastated the fields (see Table 1).

Table 1   Mennonite corn production with rainfed agriculture 1994-1997

Operation/Year	1994	1995	1996	1997
Area sown (ha)	3,179	3,735	3,909	3,879
Area of total failure (ha)	0 (0%)	3,100 83%)	55 (1%)	177 (5%)
Area harvested (ha)	3,179	635	3,677	3,702
Production (ton)	9,537	635	13,606	12,306
Producers (abs)	193	178	N/A	N/A
Average area sown per producer (ha)	16	21	N/A	N/A
Average harvest per producer (ton)	49	4	N/A	N/A
Average production on area sown (ton/ha)	3	0	3	3
Average production on area harvested (ton/ha)	3	1	4	3

Source: Own calculation based on data from SARH/SAGAR Campeche and Hopelchen (N/A = not available).

Note: Agricultural cycle spring/summer: Yalnon,[12] Xcanahaltun, Nuevo Progreso.

Table 2   Mennonite watermelon production on irrigated fields 1994-1997

Year	1994	1995	1996	1997
Area sown (ha)	33	64	200	100
Production (ton)	525	N/A	4,000	2,000
Production area sown (ton/ha)	16	N/A	20	20
Producers (abs)	4	N/A	7	N/A

Source: Own calculation based on data from SARH/SAGAR Campeche and Hopelchen (N/A = not available).

Note: Agricultural cycle autumn/winter: Nuevo Progreso.

The area of total crop failure ranged from zero to less than 5% of the total area sown, except in 1995. The yields obtained equal those of other private farmers in the Chenes area, but differ considerably from those of the majority of *ejido* producers (see below) and of peasants on small private plots.

Mennonites who also practice agriculture with irrigation obtained the highest and most secure yields. Main products were watermelons (Table 2) followed by tomatoes. Sorghum and corn were cultivated as forage crops.

As can be seen, the irrigated area sown with watermelons increased between 1994 and 1996 by six times, and was reduced by half due to credit problems between 1996 and 1997. Today, Mennonite producers are quite successful with their watermelon production. According to official data, yields of, on average, 20 tons per hectare are obtained. Individual producers may harvest up to 33 tons per hectare (interview with a Mennonite producer, Hopelchen, April 7, 1995).

Mennonite farmers generally work with credit (from BANRUAL and private banks). They also receive PROCAMPO.[13] Farmers with irrigation systems selling watermelons and tomatoes may also obtain credits from their buyers: at the beginning of the production cycle, contracts with commercialization agents guarantee the purchase of their product. In recent years, exports to Central America or the US, with payment in US dollars, have been arranged. This well-planned commercialization excludes middlemen, and provides relatively high, and safe, cash incomes.

Although Mennonites are not a homogenous group and farming differs in terms of means of production, a few generalizations can be made. Most producers practice a highly mechanized and commercially oriented agriculture. Their main products, corn and watermelons, almost exclusively serve as cash crops. Mennonites use sufficient inputs, permitting high yields. Also, a large part of the articles of consumption (meat, cheese, bread, eggs, vegetables, milk, clothing, etc.) are produced by the households themselves, thus reducing expenses to a minimum. Being incompatible with their creed, Mennonites reject many consumer goods (TV, radio, etc.). Parents educate their children to become farmers as well. Schooling is local, limited to a few years, and children are taught basic reading, writing, and arithmetic skills. Thus, spending on education is low. The major part of the income can be reinvested in production, while crop insurance (which may help to recover capital of production in case of crop failure) and savings secure its continuity even in times of crisis.

Often, Mennonites purchase implements for agriculture in groups, buying at factory prime cost. Thus, costs of production can be considerably reduced. Commercialization is well-organized and capital is often saved in US dollars, thus avoiding the devaluation risk of the Mexican *peso*. Since Mennonite farmers own machinery, they are able to use their tractors adequately and on time according to agricultural needs. Often, they have their own workshops and are able to repair damaged parts and even make spare parts. Increasingly, they offer their services and machines to other agriculturalists in the Chenes region. This includes the drilling of wells, the repair of agricultural machinery, and the tillage of private and *ejido* lands.

Xcupilcacab: an example of *ejido* production

Xcupilcacab, a village with approximately 800 inhabitants (1995), is situated just to the south of the town of Hopelchen (see Map 1). The settlement is quite old and dates back at least to Colonial times. *Ejido* organization was introduced in 1927 when Xcupilcacab received its first land grant. In 1989, its forest extension of 62,780 hectares was incorporated into the Calakmul Biosphere Reserve. The *ejidatarios* have still not received any compensation for this, which is one of the reasons they refuse to participate in PROCEDE, the official program aimed at the privatization of *ejido* lands. Although much pressure was put on the *ejido* by the staff of the *Procuraduría Agraria*, the governmental institution responsible for the execution of this program (Schüren, 1995, 1997a, and n.d.a.), until 1998 *ejidatarios* applied for neither titles for house plots nor for certificates for their individual parcels and the common lands of the *ejido*. The *ejido* has at its disposal 3,446 hectares of land. Only a small part of the whole area is used for mechanized agriculture, which was introduced by the late 1970s. All people, *ejidatarios* and residents, who participated in its preparation have access to the *mecanizado* (interview, Xcupilcacab, March 23, 1995).

According to census data recorded in 1995[14], mechanized land was unevenly distributed among *ejido* members and residents of Xcupilcacab. Of the sample, 84 households (70%) were involved in agricultural corn production, and 72 (60%) had access to mechanized land. Nevertheless, plots differed considerably in size. The majority of producers had smallholdings of less than four hectares. Only five households (about 6%) possessed more than five hectares of mechanized land (see Table 3l), usually between seven and 12 hectares. However, even their plots were smaller than the average production area (more than 16 hectares) Mennonites were tilling in the same period.

Table 3   Access to mechanized land in Xcupilcacab

Land (ha)	Number of households	
N/A	1	(1%)
0	11	(13%)
<1	36	(43%)
1-2	20	(24%)
3-4	11	(13%)
>5	5	(6%)
Total	84	(100%)

Source: Household census, spring 1995 (N/A = not available).

Note: Total hectares were 157.74[15]. N=84 households.

Many household heads interviewed (including small and middle producers) stated that they used to work larger plots. The reason for the decrease in mechanized agriculture was the cut back of credit and the reduction of the state controlled price of corn. Due to loan default with the government program PRONASOL and with BANRURAL, none of the producers had access to official credit programs. Although many of them received PROCAMPO (at that time, at N$ 350 per agricultural cycle and hectare), the amount was not sufficient to cover production costs and urgent cash needs. Besides that, the payments usually arrived too late for the current agricultural season.[16] Others stated they did not have enough time to till a larger area, because they were engaged in wage-labor.

Producers work individually on the mechanized land. In general, only varieties of hybrid corn are planted. Often *squash* for the production of seeds is cultivated, too. Beans are rarely sown. Many peasants cannot afford to buy seeds. Although quality decreases from one production cycle to the next, they select seeds of hybrid corn from last year's harvest. To prepare the fields, a tractor has to be rented either from the *ejido* or from a private owner living in the village. There are only two tractors available in Xcupilcacab. What is more, frequently one or the other of the machines breaks down. Expensive spare parts then have to be purchased and brought in from Campeche City. This may threaten the whole process of production. To get one's fields prepared on time (that is, in accordance with climatic conditions) is of utmost importance if one wants to obtain good yields. Nevertheless, under present conditions this is rarely achieved. The preparation of the fields frequently has to be carried out long before the rains set in. At the time of planting, weeds have already taken over and seeds cannot develop adequately.

Capital is also needed to buy fertilizers and herbicides. Only very few producers apply the optimal amount, and some do not use chemical inputs at all. Exact data on the application of chemical inputs on mechanized land are only available for a reduced number of households. About 62% did not use herbicides at all. Only about 14% of the 64 households investigated applied the optimal amount of herbicides.[17] With relation to fertilizers, clear data are only available for 54 households practicing mechanized agriculture. Only five producers (9%) applied the optimal amount. Twenty-one households (about 39%) used only half or less. Fourteen (about 26%) producers applied no fertilizer at all.[18]

Table 4   Corn yields per hectare on mechanized land in Xcupilcacab

Number of households		Yields (kg)
5	(7%)	0-100
17	(24%)	101-500
29	(40%)	501-1,000
8	(11%)	1,001-1,500
13	(18%)	>1,501
Total 72	(100%)	

Source: Household census, spring 1995.

Note: Agricultural cycle spring/summer 1994. N=72 households.

In sum, rainfed mechanized agriculture as practiced in Xcupilcacab depends on a certain amount of capital investment for the renting of machinery as well as for the purchase of chemical inputs and high quality seeds. Costs of production per hectare vary considerably between producers. Only a small group is able to employ all inputs needed for a successful production. Thus, the majority prepare their fields insufficiently. Due to the restricted access to tractors, producers have to perform most agricultural operations without the help of machinery. Supported by other household members, they spend much time and labor clearing their fields, sowing, fertilizing, weeding, and harvesting by hand. Frequently, they carry their crops home on their shoulders. Only a few producers can afford to employ farmhands. Yields per hectare obtained in the *mecanizado* differ considerably. In the agricultural cycle spring/summer 1994, corn yields ranged from around zero (in five cases) to more than 2,500 kg per hectare (in two cases). The majority of households (46, i.e., 64%) had yields of between 101 and 1,000 kg, while 19 producers (26%) obtained yields of up to 2,000 kg per hectare (Table 4).

Milpa agriculture

In contrast to the Mennonites, almost 40% of the households in Xcupilcacab practicing agriculture cultivated *milpas* (either exclusively or in addition to mechanized fields, Table 5).

Table 5   *Milpa* and mechanized agriculture in Xcupilcacab

Households (practising agriculture)	Milpa alone	Mecanizado alone	Milpa and mecanizado combined	Not available
84 (100%)	11 (13%)	50 (60%)	22 (26%)	1 (1%)

Source: Household census, spring 1995.

Note: According to sown area agricultural cycle spring/summer 1994. N=84 households.

Table 6   *Milpa* area planted in Xcupilcacab *(roza* and *cañada)*

Number of households		Land per household (ha)	Milpa roza (total area in ha)	Milpa cañada (total area in ha)	Total milpa area (ha)
1	(1%)	N/A	N/A	N/A	N/A
50	(60%)	0	0	0	0
4	(5%)	<0.5	0.5	1.5	2
16	(19%)	0.5-1	2.5	13.5	16
1	(1%)	1-1.5	0	1.5	1.5
11	(13%)	1.5-2	8	14	22
1	(1%)	2-8	0	8	8
Total 84	(100%)	###	11	38.5	49.5

Source: Household census, spring 1995 (N/A = not available).

Note: Agricultural cycle spring/summer 1994. Total hectares were 49.5.[19] N=84 households.

In comparison to mechanized agriculture, the *milpa* system has several important advantages. Seeds sown in *milpas* are local varieties, which are much more resistant to drought, flood, and pests than hybrid corn. What is more, they can be stored much longer and are, according to informants, more tasty. These traditional *(criollo)* varieties are still carefully selected by each producer. Also, beans, *squash* (for seeds) as well as some other crops (yam, chile, camote, jicama, etc.) may be planted together, while in the mechanized fields mainly corn and *squash* thrive. *Milpas* can be prepared without machinery and need less inputs than mechanized fields. Therefore, even after the introduction of "modern agriculture" the swidden system has not been given up, although development agencies still polemicize against it. *Milpas* have always served as insurance against the risks of mechanized production, and were intended to fulfill the households' consumption needs. Due to the lack of capital for production, *milpa* agriculture is again gaining importance. If registered, also *milpa* producers have access to PROCAMPO. According to census data, in 1994 households planted up to eight hectares of *milpa*. A *milpa* of the first year (i.e., after the initial clearing of the bush) is called *milpa roza*, while a *milpa* during the consecutive years is named *cañada* (Table 6).

Although the swidden system is generally considered a traditional form of agriculture in the Chenes region and other parts of the Yucatán peninsula, it has been considerably modified in recent years. Most *milpas* of today have considerably fewer crop varieties than in former times (Warman, 1985: 29). Since yields especially depend on the amount of the available vegetation to be cleared, the reduction of high and medium forest inevitably leads to a decline in fertility and an increase in the growth of weeds.

Table 7   Corn yields per hectare on *milpa* plots in Xcupilcacab

Yields (kg)	Number of households	
0-250	12	(36%)
251-500	16	(49%)
501-750	3	(9%)
751-1,000	1	(3%)
1,001-1,250	0	(0%)
1,251-1,500	1	(3%)
Total	33	(100%)

Source: Household census, spring 1995.

Note: Agricultural cycle spring/summer 1994. N=33 households.

In former times, no chemical inputs were applied, and after two or three years *milpa* plots had to be abandoned while new *milpas* were cleared. Yields were much higher than today, and could reach up to four tons per hectare in areas of virgin forest (Ewill and Merrill-Sands, 1985: 95, 107; Steggerda, 1941: 177-186). *Ejidatarios* worked up to six hectares (150 *mecates*) of *milpa roza* and *cañada*. Corn was grown not only for household consumption but also as a cash crop. The surplus was sold to local tradesmen. The decline of high forest in the area of Xcupilcacab was noted already in the late 1930s. Since then, peasants have had to walk many hours to find plots of forest suitable to turn into fields (interview with two former *ejidatarios*, Campeche, March 28, 1998, and Xcupilcacab, Sept. 19, 1994). Today, some households in Xcupilcacab apply fertilizers. These producers do not have to move their *milpas* as often and can reduce walking distances to a minimum. According to census data obtained in Xcupilcacab in 1995, the time needed to get to the *milpas* was estimated by informants to range from ten minutes to two hours by foot or 45 minutes by bicycle. Some producers work the same plots for many years without any fallow period, while those who cannot afford to buy fertilizers still change their *milpas* in the traditional way. Fallow periods vary between one and 15 years (in most cases, however, they last only five to six years). Current yields are much lower than in former times. In 1995, 85% of the households practicing *milpa* agriculture obtained yields of only 500 kg per hectare. However, one producer who applied fertilizer was able to obtain three times as much corn (Table 7).

In sum, the *milpa* system practiced by about 40% of the agricultural producers in Xcupilcacab serves to secure, at least in part, the subsistence base of rural households without needing capital investments. Nevertheless, if possible, fertilizers are bought in order to obtain higher yields.

Commercialization and consumption

The data presented so far show that only a few households in Xcupilcacab were able to sell some of their produce. The amount sold ranges from 300 kg to more than ten tons. Only the two largest producers could sell their corn at official prices (N$ 650 per ton) to ANDSA or CONASUPO. The majority sold the corn to local merchant middlemen, who paid only N$ 500 to 550 per ton, or even less. People accept these lower prices for several reasons. They avoid the considerable costs of transportation to ANDSA or CONASUPO, and do not have to wait there for hours or days before their produce is accepted. Often the purchasing centers refuse part of the corn, or reduce the price due to its (alleged or real) poor quality. What is more, the purchasing centers do not pay in cash, but by check, which has to be cashed at a bank. Since banks often run out of money, producers have to return repeatedly, each time spending money on fares. What is more, contracts with money-lending merchants have to be fulfilled in order to repay debts.

The average amount of corn sold by the producers of Xcupilcacab is about 1,223 kg per year (Table 8). After production costs, this comes to an average yearly income of between N$ 642 and N$ 795.[20] In comparison, to obtain a sufficient corn production on mechanized land, expenses of N$ 710 per hectare,[21] as a minimum, are necessary. Considering the poor income from corn cultivation, and even including PROCAMPO payments, it is obvious that most producers from Xcupilcacab are not able to invest more capital in their agriculture.

Data on household corn consumption also vary strongly. Today, not only *milpa* crops but also those produced on mechanized land are often used for household consumption. On the other hand, some *milpa* cultivators have to sell so much of their corn in times of cash shortage, that later they are obliged to repurchase this important means of subsistence at elevated prices in order to feed their families. Generally, the amount of corn available for household needs averages around 1,100 kg, but ranges between zero and 4,000 kg depending on household size, consumption patterns, and yields obtained. Taking into account household composition and minimal per capita requirements, the amount of corn available for consumption can be calculated (Table 9).

The surplus recorded in Table 9 served as seeds, reserve food, or animal feed. Depending on the amount available, corn consumption may vary strongly.

In sum, with the exception of a few middle-size producers, most households of Xcupilcacab cultivate only small plots and obtain low yields. Of the 84 households practicing agriculture, 68 (80.95%) sell less than the average amount of corn (about 1,223 kg; Table 8), while 23 households (27.38%) do not even produce enough to fulfill their minimal requirements of food (Table 9). However, the amount needed for animal consumption, seeds for the next production cycle, and as an economic reserve for years of total crop failure, has not been taken into account.

The renting and selling of ejido land

In 1995 and 1996, the *ejidatarios* of Xcupilcacab rented their entire mechanized area to foreign investors, who wanted to plant cotton. To most observers, this strategy confirmed the negative image of the "lazy" *ejidatarios* of the Chenes cited above. Would agricultural producers rent their most important means of production if they were hardworking? Nevertheless, a closer look at the local *ejido* economy makes it clear that the renting of mechanized land can be easily explained in terms of economic rationality. As one *ejidatario* puts it: "Even if you sowed six or seven hectares of corn on mechanized land, it wouldn't be profitable at all. Therefore, it is preferable to prepare only one or two hectares in the *milpas* to feed the family, and to look for wage-labor while renting the *mecanizado* to others" (Interview, Xcupilcacab March 30, 1995).

Table 8   Commercialization of corn in Xcupilcacab

Number of households		Corn sold to O ANDSA or CONASUP	Corn sold to local merchant middleman (kg)	Total corn sold (kg)
1	(1%)	N/A	N/A	N/A
56	(68%)	0	0	0
4	(5%)	0	1-500	1,500
8	(10%)	0	501-1,000	7,500
2	(2%)	0	1,001-1,500	3,000
3	(4%)	0	1,501-2,000	6,000
1	(1%)	0	2,001-2,500	2,500
1	(1%)	0	2,501-3,000	3,000
2	(2%)	0	3,001-4,000	8,000
1	(1%)	0	4,001-5,000	5,000
2	(2%)	0	5,001-8,000	16,000
1	(1%)	0	8,001-12,000	12,000
1	(1%)	14,000	0	14,000
1	(1%)	23,000	0	23,000
Total 84	(100%)	Total	###	101,500

Source: Household census, spring 1995.

Note: Agricultural cycle spring/summer 1994. N=84 households.

Table 9   Corn available per capita for household consumption in Xcupilcacab[22]

Balance (kg) minimal requirement	Number of households	
N/A	1	(1%)
No corn for household consumption	3	(4%)
Less than minimal amount of corn required for consumption	20	(24%)
Minimal amount of corn required and slightly more (up to 100 kg)	20	(24%)
Surplus of 101-200 kg	17	(20%)
Surplus of 201-300 kg	8	(9%)
Surplus of 301-400 kg	4	(5%)
Surplus of more than 400 kg	11	(13%)
Total households	84	(100%)

Source: Based on data of the household census, spring 1995 (N/A = not available).

Note: Agricultural cycle spring/summer 1994. N=84 households.

The rent obtained was very low (N$ 300 per hectare per year, plus PROCAMPO). However, the *ejidatarios* avoided the high costs of production on mechanized land, and were able to produce some corn for household consumption on their *milpas*. Also, the village inhabitants were employed as cotton pickers and could obtain safe wages without having to migrate to other places. Thus, total income was much higher than it would have been had they cultivate corn on the mechanized land themselves. Since the retreat of the cotton farmers, in 1997, *ejidatarios* in Xcupilcacab have offered their land to Mennonite producers.

Conclusion

The 1992 agrarian legislation has opened up the possibility to transform *ejidal* (and communal) lands in Mexico into private property. By joining the PROCEDE program, *ejidatarios* (and members of the Mexican indigenous communities) can now get certificates and titles for the parcels they are working, certificates for the communal land of the *ejido (tierra de uso comun)*, and titles for their house lots *(solares)*. Legally, they can form agrarian associations—with the state or with private entrepreneurs—within their *ejidos* and communities. Above all, the selling or long-term renting of *ejido* land is now permitted, and there are fewer prerequisites for making private investments in the *ejido* sector. Government officials argue that especially the "indefinition of *ejidal* rights" causes *ejidatarios* not to invest in their land, and thus not to prepare it adequately (e.g., Téllez, 1993: 7).

The case of Xcupilcacab, however, shows that the mere distribution of land titles will not necessarily lead to a solution of the actual problems. The majority of *ejidatarios* do not restrain from investments in their production because they have no title for their *ejido* parcel, as Tellez suggests, but because they lack the money to maintain their production. When asked about their main problems, *ejidatarios* never mentioned the question of land tenure. They referred instead to their lack of capital and to the deficient infrastructure. *Ejidatarios* especially stressed the need for irrigation systems to make corn production more secure and to allow the cultivation of more profitable products.

Thus, most *ejidatarios* in the Chenes region did not care much about PROCEDE. As in other parts of Mexico, land ownership follows customary regulations. Distrust of the program was widespread. Especially, in the first years of PROCEDE, most *ejidatarios* refused to participate. Among other things, they feared taxes would be collected in the future. What is more, they wanted to avoid the time-consuming work of preparing measurements. Thus, the *Procuraduría Agraria* supervising PROCEDE is currently increasing its pressure on the *ejidos*. Titles and certificates, for example, are now becoming a requirement for credit and PROCAMPO payments (Schüren, 1995 and n.d.a).

The situation of Xcupilcacab's corn producers is fairly typical of many other *ejidos* in the Chenes region. It reflects the gradual process of displacement of the rural poor. Associations with "more effective" private investors are promoted by the government. Since a "new" land market has developed, especially due to Mennonite immigration, this process has much intensified in recent years. Being without capital, *ejidatarios* are in a weak position. Investors can bring down the prices for land easily due to the urgent cash needs in and the competition between *ejidos*. *Ejidatarios* rent and sell their land as a response to economic constraints on their agricultural production. As the case of Xcupilcacab shows, in contrast to the Mennonites, most *ejido* producers lack the minimal requirements—mainly in terms of sufficient capital and infrastructure—to make production profitable. To obtain good yields from mechanized agriculture, considerable capital investments are necessary. Even in *milpa* production, the decrease in fertility makes the use of chemical inputs more and more necessary. Unless savings are available, crop failure inevitably leads to decapitalization and to a vicious circle of loan default *(cartera vencida)* and further economic decline. Most *ejido* producers in Xcupilcacab are indebted to BANRURAL or to credit programs. It is almost impossible for them to obtain new credit. Instead of spending the financial aid from PROCAMPO on means of production, it is often used to repay debts or to obtain necessary consumer goods. Frequently, no capital is available for the next production cycle.

Especially since the liberalization of the prices of the main agricultural products and the increase in the costs of production after the national financial crisis of December 1994, many *ejidatarios* have stopped tilling their fields themselves. Economic differentiation and land concentration have become more pronounced. While the majority of poor peasants have partly or completely reduced planting in the *mecanizado*, a few well-to-do *ejidatarios* have managed to accumulate large tracts of land. They often have better access to infrastructure and can afford to occupy farmhands as well. It is only these people who manage to produce a surplus[23]—which, however, is moderate compared to the income Mennonite farmers obtain. The majority of poor peasants in Xcupilcacab are unable to reproduce their households with their agricultural production alone.

Different strategies have to be combined.[24] In the *ejidos* of the Chenes, especially honey production is important and does not interfere with *milpa* or mechanized agriculture (see e.g., Ewill and Merrill-Sands, 1987). Women's contributions to the rural households' income is essential. In addition to their housework, they are occupied as farmhands and in the urban services, and sell animals, fruits and vegetables grown in their gardens, or home-made crafts. Generally, in the municipality only few wage-labor opportunities exist, mainly on large private agricultural or poultry farms and in the service sector. In villages and towns that have access to main roads, there is a pattern of daily migration to Campeche, Merida, and local towns. Nevertheless, seasonal wage-labor (predominantly in the construction industry of Campeche) is more frequent.

The data presented demonstrate that the deficient production of corn in *ejidos* cannot be attributed to the alleged laziness of the Maya-speaking peasants. On the contrary, deficient production results from environmental and economic constraints that force households to combine several strategies in order to survive under conditions of poverty. Often, the necessities of wage-labor come into conflict with those of agriculture. Many men in Xcupilcacab who work on poultry farms, for example, have to do so seven days a week, and often for more than eight hours a day, just to receive a fairly low income (interview, Xcupilcacab, Aug. 29, 1994). Thus, there is not enough time left to take care of their fields.[25]

However, there are also important cultural differences between Mennonites and *ejido* producers in the Chenes region, and these influence their choice of economic activities. Mennonites have been farmers for many generations. For them, farming is not simply one of several important economic strategies, but a whole way of life. To give up agri-culture would mean giving up membership of the Mennonite community with all its social and economic advantages. What is more, farming helps them to preserve an important degree of autonomy and avoid intensive contacts with the Mexican state and society.

The situation in the *ejidos* is completely different: social mobility and integration into the larger society and status system are desired as the only way to escape poverty and the stigma of being rustic. Therefore, many rural producers in *ejidos* prefer to invest what little money they have in the education of at least one of their children, rather than in their delicate agriculture.[26] Education is a prerequisite for social advancement and may open possibilities for better paid jobs, mainly in the state bureaucracy.

Especially younger men and women look for employment in the urban sector, migrate temporarily or permanently to the cities of Campeche, Cancun, or Merida, while money returns help to subsidize the households of their parents.[27] Under present conditions, agriculture is hardly able to secure the subsistence of producers in *ejidos*. What is more, it offers no attractive prospects for their children's future.

Notes

[1] On December 31, 1996 the southern part of Hopelchen (which comprised 34% of its former territory) was ceded to the newly created municipality of Calakmul, which includes the Calakmul Biosphere Reserve (founded in 1989) (Diary de Yucatán Jan. 2, 1997). New population data for the actual territory of Hopelchen are still not available. Before the division of its territory, the municipality was about 11,302 square kilometers in size and made up about 19.9% of the state territory of Campeche. In 1995, Hopelchen had almost 42,000 inhabitants and the population density was 3.7 persons per square kilometer (own calculation based on official census data cited in Sales Gutierrez, 1996: 41, 57-68).

[2] The *ejido* was introduced by the government after the Mexican Revolution as a system of collective land tenure offered to landless petitioners in rural areas. While the land was kept under the domain of the nation, membership was limited to a group of (mostly male) officially recognized usufructuaries. These *ejidatarios* had the permanent right to work the land and participate in the decisions of the *ejidal* assembly *(asamblea ejidal)*. Ejido land grants were first given to inhabitants of villages, later to workers on former *haciendas* and to colonists of the so-called New Centers of *Ejidal* Population (NCPE). Generally, the *ejido* territory consists of an urban zone *(zona urbana)* where the houses are built, an area for collective use *(área de uso común)*, and often individual plots worked by *ejidatarios* and their families. The usufruct right to land could only be ceded or inherited to one selected person. Until the 1992 changes of the agrarian legislation, *ejido* members were obliged to work the land personally. They could lose their *derecho agrario* in case of longer absence. *Ejido* land could not be legally sold, mortgaged, leased, or otherwise alienated; however, these practices have been widespread. Today, under the 1992 agrarian legislation, the renting of land is permitted and, provided that the *ejido* goes through the official land titling program PROCEDE, the selling of individual plots is possible (see Schüren, 1997a, for a more detailed discussion of the *ejido* system and the new agrarian legislation).

[3] In the countryside, Maya-speakers average 70% of the population. In the town of Hopelchen, the capital of the municipality, they make up between 30 and 40% (interview with the director of the National Bureau of Indian Affairs, INI, Hopelchen 5/3/93). For a profound discussion of the actual ethnic and linguistic composition of the municipality, see Gabbert n.d.: Part IV, Chapter V.

[4] A vast corpus of literature exists on the traditional *milpa* system of the Yucatán peninsula. See especially Terán and Rasmussen, 1994; Steggerda, 1941: 89-152; Redfield and Villa Rojas, 1936: 42-86; Villa Rojas, 1945: 56; Ewell and Merrill-Sands, 1987; Warman, 1985; Hostettler, 1997: 269-291. For *milpa* agriculture in Campeche and the Chenes region, see Peña, 1942, I: 97; Quintal Aviles, 1976: 11-22; Faust, 1993: 276-333; Gates, 1993: 109-120; Schüren, 1997b.

[5] See Gates (1993) for a profound and critical discussion of the effects of modernization policies in Campeche.

[6] Land grants range from 960 to more than 90,000 hectares, including so-called forest extensions *(ampliaciones forestales;* see Schüren n.d.a and n.d.b). The number of *ejido* members (1993) varies between 17 and over 400 ("Relación de autoridades municipales y número de *ejidatarios* de los *ejidos* del área de influencia...", n.d. [1993] Archive, Secretaría de la Reforma Agraria, Promotoría de Desarrollo Agrario, Núm.3, Hopelchen, Campeche).

[7] The Mennonites are descendants of an Anabaptist movement which emerged during the Protestant reformation in sixteenth-century Europe. The name is derived from their leader, Menno Simons, who

guided the group as from 1536. Already in former times, this religious community was characterized by an agrarian way of life. Most Mennonites live in separate colonies, do not participate in politics, and insist on their self-sufficiency. They reject the interference of the state in their internal affairs (e.g., education, military service). Mennonites have a long history of repeated migration. From the Netherlands, they moved through Poland (East Prussia), Russia, Canada, and the US. The first Mennonite families (most of them arriving from Canada) came to Mexico in the 1920s, where at first they settled in the states of Chihuahua and Durango, and later in Zacatecas and Tamaulipas. From there, Mennonite groups spread to Campeche, Belize, Costa Rica, Paraguay, and Bolivia. See Sawatzky (1986) for a history of Mennonite colonization in Mexico.

[8] For the Mennonite colonies in and near the Chenes region, there are no actual population data available. According to 1994 census data of the Centro de Salud, Hopelchen (SAA), the largest settlement—Nuevo Progreso—had more than 1,000 inhabitants (originating from Zacatecas) living in 12 *campos*. Two independent Mennonite families live near Xcanahaltun. In 1998, other settlements were established near Iturbide (50 families from Tamaulipas) and Komchen (about 50 families from Chihuahua). Therefore, their actual number is estimated at around 2,000. Immigration of Mennonites still continues.

[9] In the Chenes region, irrigation systems are crucial for success in agricultural production. At least two agricultural cycles are practiced, and independence from the erratic rains is possible. In their general survey of *ejido* households in Mexico, Davis *et al.* (1999) found out that access to irrigation was the most important factor for differential levels of agricultural incomes among rural producers.

[10] Although the Mennonite elders conducted land negotiations, and obtained only one title for the whole colony, the community keeps its internal land register in which individual property is documented (Sawatzky, 1986: 153, 206; Nuhn, 1976: 44).

[11] Data obtained from SARH/SAGAR (Ministry of Agriculture; until 1994 briefly called SARH: *Secretaría de Agricultura y Recursos Hidraúlicos*; after 1994, renamed SAGDR or SAGAR: *Secretaría de Agricultura, Ganadería y Desarollo Rural)* Campeche and Hopelchen, 1994-1998; interview, Huechil 6/3/96.

[12] Yalnon is situated in the municipality of Hecelchakan close to the border of Hopelchen.

[13] The government program PROCAMPO (since October 1993) is a financial aid program directed at agricultural producers of corn, rice, cotton, beans, and other crops. It is intended to compensate for the fall in prices (due to their liberalization after Mexico joined NAFTA) for 15 years. In 1998, for example, Mennonite farmers were registered as a group with 2,500 hectares in Nuevo Progreso alone (interview with a representative of SAGAR, Campeche 31/3/98). However, Mennonite producers often receive their PROCAMPO very late, because they are known for evading political conflict (interviews with a shopkeeper and a Mennonite producer, Hopelchen Sept. 20, 1994; April 7, 1995). Some Mennonites also participated in the program Allianza Para el Campo in order to obtain government support and credit for the installation of irrigation systems (interview with a Mennonite producer, Nuevo Progreso March 18, 1998).

[14] Socioeconomic census data were collected in 120 households (89% of the total number of 135) with between them 635 members. Also, formal and informal interviews were held with *ejidal* and village authorities as well as with other people between 1994 and 1998. Without the friendly help of the inhabitants of Xcupil, this investigation would not have been possible. I am very grateful for their cooperation. Especially, I would like to thank *Indalecio Lara Pech* for his collaboration. He and his family not only supported the project indiscriminately, but also became true friends.

[15] In the census data of 1995, only a slight difference between access to land and sown area was recognized. Sown area was 147.74 hectares (agricultural cycle spring/summer 1994).

[16] Compare Paulson (1999) for similar problems among smallholder producers of avocado in the Mexican state of Michoacán. See Davis *et al.* (1999) for a general discussion of the impact of PROCAMPO in the Mexican *ejido* sector.

[17] The optimal amount on mechanized land was considered to be two liters per hectare at a price of

N$ 50 (interview with a representative of SARH/SAGAR, Hopelchen March 24, 1995). 15.63% used on their fields half of the amount, or less, of *líquido* required, and 7.81% applied more than half (household census, spring 1995; N=64).

[18] The optimal amount of fertilizer per hectare was estimated by producers to be four sacks of 50 kg at a price of between N$ 200 and N$ 220 (interview with a representative of SARH/SAGAR, Hopelchen March 24, 1995). Fourteen producers (25.93%) applied more than half of the amount of fertilizer needed (household census, spring 1995; N=54).

[19] In the census data of 1995, there was only a slight difference between sown area and total *milpa* plots (50.8 hectares).

[20] The former amount is based on the average unofficial price of corn (N$ 525), while the latter is based on the official corn price in 1995 (N$ 650).

[21] This is the amount counting only the costs of seeds, chemical inputs, and tractor use for the preparation of one hectare of land. Costs of harvest, transportation, shelling of corn, and other operations that may be carried out by household members without the use of machinery are excluded (interview with a representative of SARH/SAGAR, Hopelchen March 24, 1995).

[22] The amount of corn available for consumption is related to household composition and minimal requirements of corn. Household composition was coded (in conformity with number, age, and sex of members) according to the system employed by Wilk (1997: 243; see also Hostettler, 1997: 242-245, 266) to obtain per capita consumption data. These data were related to the amount of corn minimally required to feed one consumer, as established by Stuart (1990: 138, quoted in Hostettler, 1997: 332). Stuart suggests a minimal daily per capita requirement of shelled corn of 450 grams (or a yearly amount of 164.25 kg). This represents an intake of 1,625 calories, or 73% of the recommended caloric intake of 2,216 calories per person per day.

[23] Similar processes of differentiation in peasant communities are described by Bee (1999) for grape producers in Chile.

[24] This trend has also been recognized for households in Mexican *ejidos* in general. Davis *et al.* (1999) showed that between 1994 and 1997, off-farm activities were the main source of income recorded in their survey.

[25] For a general discussion of similar strategies of livelihood diversification, see e.g., Ellis, 1998.

[26] According to census data obtained from 120 households in 1995, the amount of money spent per year for the education of children in Xcupilcacab ranged from N$ 60 to N$ 3,000, and often was above spending on agricultural production.

[27] See also Davis *et al.*, 1999, for a general discussion of the role education has for members of *ejido* households.

References

Aranda González, P., *Apuntaciones históricas y literarias del municipio de Hopelchén, Campeche.* Mérida, Maldonado Editores, 1985.

Ayuntamiento de Hopelchén, "Estudio socio-económico municipal, Hopelchén: ayuntamiento de Hopelchén". Comité de planeación para el desarrollo municipal, 1992.

Berzunza Herrera, R., "Geografía del estado de Campeche". Campeche, Gobierno del Estado, 1989.

Berzunza Pinto, R., *Estado de Campeche.* Monografía. Campeche, Talleres Gráficos del Gobierno, Instituto de Proposiciones Estratégicas, 1991.

De la Peña, M.T, "Campeche económico (2 volumes)". México, DF, Gobierno Constitucional del Estado de Campeche, 1942.

Ellis, F., "Household strategies and rural livelihood diversification". *The Journal of Development Studies*, Vol. 35, no. 1 (1998), pp. 1-38.

Ewell, P. T. and D. Merrill-Sands, "*Milpa* in Yucatán, a long-fallow maize system and its alternatives in the Maya peasant economy". In: B.L. Turner II and S.B. Brush (eds.), *Comparative farming systems.* New York/London,The Cuilford Press, 1987.

Faust, B.B., *Cosmology and changing technologies of the Campeche Maya.* Ann Arbor, Michigan, UMI, 1988.

Gabbert, W., "Ethnizität und soziale Ungleichheit auf der Halbinsel Yucatán, Mexiko, 1500-1998". Unpublished thesis. Freie Universität Berlin, Berlin, n.d.

Gates, M., *In default, peasants, the debt crisis, and the agricultural challenge in Mexico.* Boulder, Westview Press, 1993.

Gubler, R. and U. Hostettler (eds.), *The fragmented present, mesoamercian societies facing modernization.* Möckmühl, Anton Saurwein, 1995.

Hostettler, U., *Milpa agriculture and economic diversification in a Maya peasant society of Central Quintana Roo, 1900-1990s.* Ann Arbor, Michigan, UMI, 1996.

Konrad, H., "Capitalismo y trabajo en los bosques de las tierras bajas tropicales mexicanas, el caso de la industria chiclera". *Historia Mexicana*, Vol. 36, no. 3 (1987), pp. 465-505.

Konrad, H., "Maya *chicleros* and the international chewing gum market". In: R. Gubler and U. Hostettler (eds.), *The fragmented present, mesoamercian societies facing modernization.* Möckmühl, Anton Saurwein, 1995.

Messmacher, M., "Campeche, análisis económico-social". México DF, 1967.

Nuhn, H., "Landerschließung und Kulturlandschaftswandel an den Siedlungsgrenzen im Waldland, gelenkte Agrarkolonisation an der Siedlungsgrenze im tropischen Regenwald Zentralamerikas". *Göttinger Geographische Abhandlungen*, No. 66 (1976), pp. 25-61.

Ponce Jiménez, M.P., "La montaña chiclera Campeche, vida cotidiana y trabajo (1900-1950)". México, DF, CIESAS, 1990.

Quintal Avilés, E.F., "Informe, investigación realizada en el municipio Hopelchén, Campeche,durante la primavera y verano de 1976". Unpublished report, 1977.

Ramayo Lanz, T., "Repartir lo indivisible, los mayas de la montaña, Campeche y la tierra, la guerra de castas". In: G.M. Negroe Sierra (coord.), *Guerra de castas, actores postergados.* México, DF, Unicorno, 1997.

Redfield, R. and A. *Villa Rojas, Chan Kom, a Maya village.* Chicago, University of Chicago Press, 1934.

Sales Gutierrez, C., "Campeche, apuntes económicos y sociales". México, DF, 1996.

Sawatzky, H.L., *Sie suchten eine Heimat, deutsch-mennonitische Kolonisierung in Mexiko, 1922-1984.* Marburg, N.G. Elwert Verlag, 1986.

Schüren, U., "Neoliberal policy and the peasantry in rural Campeche, current trends". In: R. Gubler and U. Hostettler (eds.), *The fragmented present, mesoamercian societies facing modernization.* Möckmühl, Anton Saurwein, 1995.

Schüren, U., "'Land ohne Freiheit', Mexikos langer Abschied von der Agrarreform". In: K. Gabbert *et al.* (eds.), *Land und Freiheit* (Lateinamerika, Analysen und Berichte 21). Bad Honnef, Horlemann, 1997a.

Schüren, U., "Zwischen Pflanzstock und Traktor, die Landwirtschaft yukatekischer Klcinbauern im Wandel". In: E. Schriek and H.-W. Schmuhl (eds.), *Das andere Mexiko, indigene Völker von Chiapas bis Chihuahua.* Gießen, Focus Verlag, 1997b.

Schüren, U., "Política neoliberal y economía de los campesinos en el municipio de Hopelchén, estado de Campeche". In: H. Carton de Grammont and M. Basaldúa Hernández (coord.), *El ajuste estructural en el campo mexicano, efectos y respuestas*, Vol. III (O. Baños Ramírez and G. Torres (eds.), Nueva ruralidad, migración, empleo y organización campesina, cambios y perspectivas). Forthcoming.

Schüren, U., "La revolución tardía, reforma agraria y cambio político en Campeche 1910-1940". In: R. Gubler and P. Martel (eds.), *Yucatán a través de los siglos.* Forthcoming.

Steggerda, M., "Maya Indians of Yucatán". Washington, DC, Carnegie Institution, 1941.

Téllez, L. (coord.), "Nueva legislación de tierras, bosques, y aguas". México, DF, Fondo de Cultura Económica, 1993.

Terán, S. and Ch. Rasmussen, *La milpa de los mayas, la agricultura de los maya prehispánicos y actuales en el noreste de Yucatán*. Mérida, Talleres Gráficos del Sudeste, 1994.

Villa Rojas, A., "The Maya of East Central Quintana Roo". Washington, DC, Carnegie Institution, 1945.

Warman, A., "Estrategías de sobrevivencia de los campesinos mayas". México, D.F, Universidad Autónoma de México, Instituto de Investigaciones Sociales, 1985.

Wilhelmy, H., *Welt und Umwelt der Maya, Aufstieg und Untergang einer Hochkultur*. München, Piper, 1981.

Wilk, R.R., *Household ecology, economic change and domestic life among the Kekchi Maya in Belize*. DeKalb, University of Illinois Press, 1997.

Wilson, E.M., "Physical geography of the Yucatán Peninsula". In: E.H. Moseley and E.D. Terry (eds.), *Yucatán, a world apart*. Alabama, University of Alabama Press, 1980.

14 Agro-export production and agricultural communities: land tenure and social change in the Guatulame Valley, Chile

Anna Bee

Introduction

There have been dramatic changes in the agrarian landscapes of Chile since the mid-1970s that have had important implications for land tenure patterns and for labor market structures in the national economy. Chile has promoted non-traditional exports as part of a general outward looking economic strategy to the extent that between the mid and the late 1980s, non-traditional export grew at a rate of 222% (Barham *et al.*, 1992). Several export sectors have been particularly successful, including forestry products, fish and fish products and fruit and horticultural produce. For example, Chile is now a major southern hemisphere exporter of fresh fruits, providing consumers in the northern markets with a variety of low cost fruits out of season. The expansion of agribusiness in areas of Chile supplying the world market with these types of exports has led to a radical transformation of the rural sector (Gwynne, 1999).

Large-scale commercial farmers have generally enjoyed the benefits of the export growth more than the small-scale farmers have (Gwynne and Kay, 1997). It has been argued that Chile's impressive agro-export growth has concentrated land ownership, thus reducing peasant access to land and stable employment (Carter and Mesbah, 1993). Agricultural production systems have become increasingly capitalized, active land markets have developed, and there has been a dramatic increase in levels of female and seasonal employment (Barrientos, 1997). As Chile has become further integrated into the world market, peasant farmers have found it increasingly difficult to remain competitive. There is an increasingly large economic disparity between capitalist and peasant farming, and even under the recent "reconversion" in Chilean agriculture, the peasant economy remains precarious (Kay, 1997). However, these changes are locally specific. A heterogeneous rural population experiences the expansion of non-traditional exports in different ways (de Janvry *et al.*, 1997; Paulson, this volume). The expansion of export production does not necessarily herald the destruction or marginalization of more "traditional" forms of agricultural production. In some cases, the local systems of land tenure and community political and social organization have allowed the small-scale farmers to negotiate the form of their relationship with the export sector.

This chapter explores the expansion of the fresh fruit sector and its impacts on one valley system in Chile's Fourth Region[1]. It focuses on the land tenure system in the valley (including communal land holdings) and the development of a land market resulting from the development of the export economy. It is argued that there is a vital link between the locally specific land tenure system in the valley and the shape and form of export agriculture. In the case under consideration, there has been an incomplete transformation of agricultural production systems. While export production has expanded dramatically in this area and some local small-scale farmers have been marginalized, the pattern is complex. Small-scale farmers in some cases remain an important part of the productive landscape, producing crops for the domestic market alongside the large, highly capitalized firms producing for export. A section of the chapter explores some of the issues surrounding changing land tenure patterns and the concomitant changes in community relations.

Export agriculture and land tenure in the Guatulame Valley

The Guatulame Valley is located in the Fourth Region in Chile's semi-arid Norte Chico. This part of Chile had traditionally been characterized as a relatively poor and underdeveloped region. However, this situation changed dramatically in certain areas of the region where the production of export crops has come to dominate. The most important export crop in this region, and indeed in the Guatulame Valley, is the table grape, which represents one of Chile's most successful fruit exports. Between 1977 and 1986, the international prices of table grapes increased by 50% (Korovkin, 1992). As producers began to recognize the profitability of this particular crop, land under table grape production increased tenfold between 1974 and 1987 with 70% of the total production from this land used for export (Gwynne, 1991).

The Guatulame Valley bears testament to the effects of the push toward export production, prompted by a shift to neo-liberal economic principles and the acceptance of the theory of comparative advantage with table grapes coming to dominate the region. In the basin of Chañaral Alto (in the Guatulame Valley), there were no table grapes planted in 1980; in 1994, however, there were 1,800 hectares under export table grapes (Gwynne and Ortiz, 1997). The majority of the grapes are grown on large-scale estates (known as *parronales)* owned by commercial farmers who have received financial support from international marketing companies. Producers need to have significant capital to start a grape farm, as the total cost of buying land, obtaining water rights, and caring for vines until production starts has been estimated at approximately US$ 35,000 per hectare (Gwynne and Ortiz, 1997). In the majority of cases, it is the large-scale farmers who have been able to capitalize on the fruit export boom, although some small-scale farmers have become involved in fruit production, and many have become involved in waged work on the grape farms. The next section explores the form of land tenure in the Guatulame Valley, and how this relates to the expansion of the agro-export sector.

The patterns of land ownership in the Guatulame Valley are the products of centuries of change accelerated in the last few decades through agrarian reform and the growth of export agriculture. Some of the forms of land ownership are specific to the region, while others are representative of other areas in Chile. The pattern of land ownership in the Guatulame is complex and difficult to unravel, and becoming more so with the increased rates of land exchange in some areas. Using a combination of studies (Bee, 1996; Gwynne and Meneses, 1994; Meneses, 1989) it is, however, possible to identify three "typical" forms of land ownership in the Guatulame:
1. Small-sized farms derived from agrarian reform.
2. Private property that survived the agrarian reform.
3. Agricultural communities.

This chapter is concerned mainly with the interaction of categories 2 and 3[2]. Two types of private property can be described. The first type comprises the large estates that were subjected to agrarian reform. These were not the dominant types of land ownership in the Guatulame, but they did exist. One local land-holding family had their landholdings significantly reduced during the reforms, and were left with two properties with a combined total of 148 hectares. There were other landowners with significant properties, but although their properties were large they were not equivalent to 80 basic irrigated hectares (BIH) and they were not reformed (Gwynne and Meneses, 1994). While this was the pattern following the agrarian reforms, it has undergone considerable alteration with the development of a land market as a result of the local table grape economy. Many properties have been consolidated into larger farms that have been inserted into the export economy. There are several local or regional farming families, who stand out as having capitalized on the drive to export and are now very significant in large-scale grape production in the valley. They have been active in purchasing land, and each family has several large farms employing significant numbers of both local and migrant workers. These families dominate grape production in the Guatulame Valley.

The second type of private property comprises those that were less than 80 hectares and therefore not subjected to agrarian reform. This type of land was generally significantly smaller than 80 hectares. Most of this land had been farmed for long periods by families possessing no legal title to their plots. When the agrarian reforms began, land ownership was regularized and title to the land assigned to the families who could prove they had traditionally been farming a specific location. These plots have therefore generally been passed down through generations, the agrarian reform process altering only the legal situation of land tenure. As agro-export production expanded in the region, some of these smaller scale farmers became involved in table grape production for export. These farmers generally have much less autonomy than the large-scale commercial producers, and are frequently tied into contractual arrangements with the packing and exporting companies that allow them little leeway for expansion and require them to roll over their debt for consecutive years. A similar pattern has occurred amongst the farmers in the reformed sector who adopted export production but have found themselves unable to meet their contractual arrangements with the export firms. As a result, many small-scale farmers have fallen into irretrievable debt and have decided to sell their properties. They either remain in agriculture (working as employees on the large-scale grape farms) or leave agriculture entirely (Murray, 1997).

The third characteristic form of land tenure in the Guatulame is found in the agricultural communities. These communities, with their complex systems of land holding, were not directly altered by the agrarian reforms, although the agrarian reform legislation did subsequently affect them. Since the mid-1980s, they have played a crucial role in the development of the grape economy, as sources of land (and labor) for grape production. They are also the sites where, to a certain extent, the traditional system of agricultural production has been maintained with the attendant social and political organizations of the communities (JUNDEP, 1991; McBride, 1936). Each community is composed of a fixed number of members (comuneros) who hold "rights" (derechos) to use the communal land and form the community committee. In the Fourth Region in 1993, there were 166 communities with 12,731 community members undertaking some form of agricultural production. With a total population of 76,386 and a total landholding of 946,932 hectares, they constituted 58% of the rural population of the Fourth Region and occupied 25% of the land.

Table 1   Agricultural communities of the IV Region

Province	Number of communities	Families	Rural population	Percentage of comuneros
Elqui	20	1,488	8,928	39.8
Limari	116	7,959	47,754	80.0
Choapa	30	3,284	19,704	61.0

Source: CODEFF, 1994.

Within the communities, land ownership is based on three types of exploitation, one of which is individual while two are communal. The individual form of ownership is in the form of *goce singular*. This is land usually located in the fertile valley bottoms and is the site of the *comunero*'s house and small plot of agricultural land. The first form of communal land is known as *las lluvias* or "rainfed land". Here the land is moderately used for cultivation of crops such as cereals. The *lluvias* are situated on the hill slopes and are sometimes irrigated, but more commonly rely on the scarce rainfall. The community grants the use of these lands to a *comunero* for a certain number of years, then on death or migration, another *comunero* may receive the right to use the land. The third type of land within a community is the common land *(campo comun)*. This forms the major part of the community's land and is located on the arid hillsides above the *lluvias*. The *campo comun* is used for the pasturing of animals, particularly goats, and also for the collection of fuel.

Having briefly described the land tenure patterns in the Guatulame, this chapter now moves on to explore the changes that have occurred in these patterns as a result of the expansion of the export economy. The focus here is the interrelationships between land tenure and social change in the agricultural communities and export production. The following section traces the legal changes that have affected the status of land tenure in the communities, and how these in turn have led to the development of a land market in some communities.

Land markets in the communities: increased pressure on limited resources

It has been argued that since the early 1980s, the communities have been strongly challenged by both external and internal forces (Scott and Litchfield, 1993: 9), and that the development of a land market within the communities and for community land is one of the main challenges: "The communities have been seriously weakened as producers of local property rights in recent years as a result of three factors: (a) the degeneration of common grazing land into limited open access; (b) legislation allowing the individual ownership of land by *comuneros* within the community and (c) the alienation of community land to non-members." The alienation of community land to non-members is perhaps the most important factor in the weakening of the communities' traditional economic, political, and social organization. This has been evident in the Guatulame Valley where some communities have developed an active land market, with many of the purchasers not being members of the community, while other settlements are not legally able to dispose of communal rights to non-members.

The origin of this division between communities lies in Decree Law 5 of 1967, which allowed for the Regularization *(Sanemiento)* of individual and collective ownership within the community. The process of regularizing the land tenure has three components. Firstly, the area occupied by the community has to be mapped and defined. Secondly, a list of *comuneros* is drawn up. The final component of the process is to determine which individuals and families have a historical connection to the community. In the majority of cases, there was no legal title to the land, but a person who could prove a tradition of residence on and use of a plot of land could apply to have it legally recognized[3]. An important caveat to this legislation was the fact that all the *comuneros* had to be in agreement before the decision to regularize land tenure could go ahead. In many communities, the *comuneros* did not all agree to take up the opportunity and, as a result, the majority of the communities still had not regularized their land ownership by 1995. Of the nine communities in the Guatulame, only two had delimited their boundaries and regularized their land ownership in the early 1990s.

The distinction between the communities, with regards to land tenure, really came into focus after Decree Law 108 in 1978 allowed for the sale of communal land to people who were not members of the community (Gwynne and Meneses, 1994). It is presently only legally possible to sell to individuals who are not *comuneros* in communities with regularized land ownership. As the growth of the grape economy in the valley has led to the development of an active land market as producers have sought suitable land for table grape cultivation, the community lands have come under increasing pressure.

The communities' leaderships and the government ministry for land *(Bienes Nacionales)* deemed certain controls necessary to inhibit the diminution of communal autonomy and the complete transfer of communal land to non-members. A limit of 10% of communal land was set as the maximum any individual could own in any one community (companies are not allowed purchase community land). This limit was reduced to 3% in 1990, but there are of course methods for bypassing the legislation. The most common is for various members of a family to purchase *derechos* in their name. Thus, if we examine the list of recent transactions for the community of Chacarillas it becomes evident that for the two dominant landholding families, female members have bought several *derechos*. Since 1988, two of the women from the major export producing families have bought 14 rights between them. The women are ostensibly buying the land to circumvent the legal limit on private ownership; they will not actually become involved in the exploitation of the land.

In the Guatulame Valley, the difference in the legal status of individual and collective ownership within the various communities has produced dramatically different patterns of agricultural production. These patterns have become more obvious with the expansion of the table grape economy in the region. Although the community legislation of recent years has sought to define and limit the exchange of land within the communities, especially its removal from communal use and transfer to the private sector, a land market has always been present and since the early 1980s has become much more influential.

Regularized exchange of land in Tome Alto and Chañaral Alto

To explore the changing nature of land tenure patterns in the Guatulame Valley and the alterations to the agricultural production systems, this chapter now focuses on two contrasting settlements. Chañaral Alto is located in the community of

Chacarillas where the land tenure has been regularized. The community is composed of 216 *derechos*. The village of Tome Alto is located in the community of El Tome where land tenure has not yet been regularized and there are 106 *derechos*.

Chañaral Alto, the larger of the two villages (population 2,232 in 1992), is located higher up the river valley than Tome Alto (see Map 1). Traditionally, the economy of the village was based on small-scale farmers (with plots of less than five hectares) producing tomatoes, beans, peppers, garlic, and melons for urban centers in Chile. However, the community has experienced the effects of the dynamic land market in the valley, as a significant number of *comuneros* have sold their land to large-scale producers. The village has developed into an important local center for the grape economy, attracting significant investment directly into export agriculture, and also into other areas such as local services. This has led to an increase in agricultural and non-agricultural waged employment amongst the population of the village. It has also been experiencing an increase in population, as people are attracted to the economic opportunities presented by the export sector. The dynamic land market and the expansion of the grape economy into the village have altered certain systems of production; the traditional small-scale producers have to a large extent been marginalized.

Tome Alto is a much smaller village with a population of approximately 500. It has a much more stable population base and, if anything, the population has decreased slightly over the last two decades. The small-scale farmers have a reputation for producing high quality tomatoes, which are cultivated intensively on small, plastic-covered plots known as *casetas*, irrigated with water from the Guatulame River. Other crops grown include beans, peppers, and avocados. In Tome Alto, community land has not been sold to large-scale producers, and so the community lands remain intact and export production is excluded from the village. Therefore, in this village the majority of the population are directly involved in cultivating crops for the domestic market.

Explanations for these differences between the villages need to take into account the wider economic conditions that have led to the expansion of export production in the valley. The changing forms of agricultural production have prompted the development of a land market within the communities; a land market that is especially marked within communities where land can be sold to the commercial farmers. There was, however, an incipient market for land in the communities, prior to the various decree laws affecting land tenure. Exchanges occurred without legal designation, and it might be that these exchanges continue alongside the regulated exchange of land registered with *Bienes Nacionales*. To reiterate, the situation is complex with markets for agricultural and non-agricultural land and exchanges between small-scale and large-scale producers, and between *comuneros* and non-members.

There appears to be three distinct types of land exchange within the communities. The first is the exchange of land within a community for small-scale agricultural production. In these instances, plots of between 0.5 and 2 hectares are exchanged, usually between residents of the community. For example, in Tome Alto one family had purchased land for the production of tomatoes. In total, they had purchased seven plots *(casetas)*. The second type of exchange is the purchase of land for the purpose of house building. The plots of land in this example are small, approximately a quarter of a hectare, and will not be used for agricultural production. Moreover, they are generally purchased from the state, rather than from a local landowner. In

Map 1   The Guatulame Valley

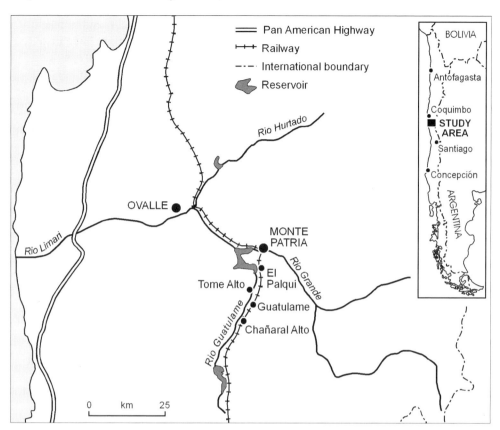

Chañaral Alto, two women who participated in the research stated that they had purchased small plots of land on which to construct their houses. For each of these women, the purchase of land represents a stake in the future life of the village through house ownership. Yet, in neither case was the land to be used for agricultural production beyond the family garden plot. The third type of land exchange involves the sale of land for commercial exploitation, usually for the installation of vineyards.

Sale of land for "commercial" exploitation[4]

It is this third type of regularized land exchange that has had the biggest impact on access to land for the small-scale producers and the changing agricultural production systems. For example, in the village of Chañaral Alto, which lies at the heart of the community of Chacarillas, the regularization of the land tenure system and the subsequent shift to private ownership has transformed the local land market. The small-scale producers within the community have been able to sell their land to third parties, generally large-scale producers. The small-scale farmers could not compete with the sweeping changes in the local agricultural economy, as the majority lacked the capital to start producing export table grapes. This situation was at various times compounded by low prices for domestically oriented crops, and so many families sold a proportion, or all, of their lands. By 1990, 126 of the 216 community "rights" had changed hands, with the majority of them going to the commercial farmers who were not previously community members. These commercial farmers have installed vineyards, transforming the village into an important center for table grape production. At the same time, the small-scale producers generally remained in the community, to work either permanently or seasonally in the vineyards and associated packing plants. Interview data suggest that the pattern of crop dominance in Chañaral Alto has changed significantly, and several individuals referred to the period when Pinochet overthrew Allende and then stopped supporting the poor farmers. When a land market developed, local *campesinos* sold up:

"...Men arrived and offered us a good price for the land. Times had changed and so people were fed up. They said 'everything is so expensive' and they sold up everything, their little plots of land. So now there's nowhere to plant tomatoes" (Alicia, Chañaral Alto).

Another interviewee from the village suggested that:

"If it weren't for the grapes, the people would work on the tomatoes, as they did in the past. Nearly everyone worked on the tomatoes..... I think it is better for people to have their own land and the means to work it. It's better for people to work like that and not have to work for someone else" (Sara, Chañaral Alto).

In contrast, in the communities without regularized land ownership, such an active land market has not developed, and commercial grape farming has not substantially taken off. For example, in Tome Alto there are no large-scale grape farms and the landscape is dominated instead by small plots of land under the plastic protection used for the tomato crops. As land tenure is not regularized (thereby preventing *comuneros* from selling to a third party), vineyards have failed to encroach on the settlement, and the list of community rights showed very few of them changing hands (in 1994, no rights had been sold to large-scale producers). However, the production of tomatoes does not necessarily provide the farmers with a reliable income. Low prices or frost-damage are just two of the factors that can reduce the profitability of the tomato crop. One of the interviewees in Tome Alto eloquently explained the importance of tomato cultivation in the village, but also emphasized the inherent risks:

"Well, with the tomatoes when things are good, then it's okay. We buy things. For example, we have a small van that we bought because of the tomatoes, but life is very sacrificial, very hard. The life of the farmers is very hard and sometimes it's not for profit. For example, this year was very hard for us. We lost absolutely everything. We are just waiting and hoping to get work on the grapes, to go and work in the grape packing plants. There we will earn a bit of money" (Maria, Tome Alto).

Even though large-scale grape production has not physically arrived in the village, the villages have not been excluded from involvement in the grape economy (Bee, 1996; Barrientos *et al.*, 1999). Many are actively involved as employees in the fields and packing plants of the grape economy, exploiting the new seasonal employment opportunities. This is a result of the synchronization of the grape and tomato cultivation calendars. When work on the tomatoes ends in November, the harvesting of the grapes begins. An intriguing situation has therefore developed in Tome Alto with respect to the articulation of traditional farming systems and the expansion of modern large-scale commercial agricultural production: the population is able to combine work on their own land with work in the grape economy (especially during the harvest).

"We arrived here (Tome Alto) in 1979 and no women [or men] went out to work in the packing plants...One year, we heard that Don Jaime [commercial farmer] was looking for workers, and so we went with our husband's permission. We were the only ones from Tome Alto to look for work....then one year they were short of workers and they asked us if we knew anyone. We took some women who wanted to work and now everyone works.....The village is deserted during the summer" (Rachel, Tome Alto).

In general, though, it must be emphasized that the village remains dominated by small-scale production, and that the villagers very much identify themselves as *campesinos* rather than waged workers. As one interviewee concluded: "The things from the house we buy from the tomatoes, because the work from the vineyards is no big deal."

The social and political implications of markets for community land

The changes occurring in communities throughout Latin America as a result of the increasing globalization of agriculture have diverse impacts; both positive and negative (see Morris, this volume). This is the case in the Guatulame, where the weak development of a land market has been significant for many aspects of community life, including the social and political dimensions. Property in rural areas is but part of the wider system that exists in any political community. Yet in communities that have their bases in communal control over land resources, land will play a pivotal role in the overall cohesion of political, economic, and social structures. At the community level, the importance of the development of a land market should not be underestimated as a point of reference for not only the dramatic economic and agricultural transformation, but also some of the recent social and political changes that have taken place within the communities.

One of the most striking changes brought about by the expansion agro-export production in Chile as a whole, and a change that is certainly evident in the Guatulame, is the increase in the level of female employment (Barrientos, 1997; Dias, 1991; Lago, 1992; Valdés, 1988). In the Guatulame, women are employed throughout the year, but their employment is especially concentrated during the grape harvest when they work in both the fields and the packing plants (Bee and Vogel, 1997). For these temporary waged workers (*temporeras*), work in the grape economy provides increased independence and family income.

"Well, the women here aren't as feminist as in other countries....but the women here are not totally confined to the house. In spite of everything, the woman can have her own money and buy her own things. She can decide what to buy rather than relying on the men to give her money and tell her what to buy" (Patricia, Chañaral Alto).

The majority of the women from both villages now work in the grape economy, although the women from Tome Alto are more likely to work for shorter periods than the women from Chañaral Alto. Whilst the work on the grape farms and in the packing plants is extremely hard, the women value the opportunity to earn their own wage, and hence have greater input into household expenditure:

> "I bought my washing machine with the money from the grapes. Before I had to get up at 6 am and do the washing before going out to work. So I decided to save my money and buy a washing machine" (Ximena, Tome Alto).

The sweeping changes in the agricultural sector, in which women had previously been marginalized as "unpaid family labor", have created opportunities for them to rework household relations (Bee and Vogel, 1997). In Tome Alto, the majority of the women combine work in both the "traditional" sector and the export agricultural sector, negotiating both waged and unwaged work. Work in the grape economy brings some material benefits, but is seen as a supplement to work on the family land. In Chañaral Alto, the women have a much greater variety of employment outside the grape economy than the women in Tome Alto do, and as women (and men) become increasingly excluded from land ownership, waged employment will become even more vital.

Another issue associated with the expansion of export agriculture in some villages, is the increased level of migration to these villages during the summer harvest. Every year, between November and January, a large number of migrants arrive in Chañaral Alto looking for work on the vineyards and in the packing plants. These migrants, in the eyes of the local population, bring with them many social problems, including violence, drug abuse, and increasing promiscuity. The expansion of export agriculture is therefore seen to have contrasting impacts on the community:

> "The parronales have brought good things and bad things to the village. They give you the opportunity to earn money, sometimes lots of money, to be able to study or to be involved in a business. But they also bring problems, especially from the outsiders. There is always an increase in parties and drugs and robberies during the harvest" (Sergio, Chañaral Alto).

In some instances, the interviewees commented on the positive changes brought about in the village by the growth of agribusiness. For example:

> "I think that if they [the grape farms] had not come, well just imagine how this town would be. Because people have been able to buy things, people who previously lived miserably now have TVs, refrigerators, good beds, things like that. People have done well by these jobs on the parronales" (Patricia, Chañaral Alto).

However, even taking into account some of the benefits of the wage earning potential opportunities of the export economy, the alienation of community land in Chañaral Alto and the addition of large-scale producers to the list of comuneros will have had an effect on the cohesion of the community organization. Traditionally, the community organization—which is composed of the comuneros—has had significant political control within the rural areas of the Fourth Region. The leader of the community has frequently had ties to the national political powers (and been able to use their influence in local politics and community organizations). Thus, as community membership is effectively opened to incorporate large-scale farmers and members of their families, the community organization will discover a new set of priorities. No longer oriented toward small-scale producers and their concerns, it will be diluted with members indirectly connected with the village and community. The production of crops such as tomatoes and melons for the domestic market will become increasingly marginalized within the community.

The national government has also been faced with this problem of farmers producing for the domestic market, especially the *minifundistas*. Since the onset of the democratization process, the state has been faced with a number of dilemmas. For example, it has proven exceptionally difficult to have total control over the land regularization and land transfer processes. While the government abdicated complete control over the land exchange process during the height of the push toward export agricultural production, the livelihoods of the small-scale producers have been significantly threatened by the development of an active land market, as has been the case in many parts of the Guatulame Valley. Some of the recent reconversion projects have been aimed at strengthening the productive capacity of the small-scale producers. In some instances, this has involved encouraging and supporting the cultivation of non-traditional exports, such as flowers and bulbs (Kay, 1997). In others, it has involved supporting more traditional forms of agricultural production. A prime example of this is the proposal to build a tomato packing plant in Tome Alto. The community has obtained financial support from INDAP (Institute for Agrarian Development) and technical advice from JUNDEP (a local NGO). The plant will serve the local farmers by acting as a center for packing and selling their tomatoes. It represents a significant support mechanism for the small-scale farmers, within a village still oriented toward the domestic market.

Traditional producers and products have also been supported through the provision of credit from INDAP, and while many small-scale farmers have large debts that they cannot pay, the credit available to them is vital. The communities act as a way of channeling the credit and technical advice. One local NGO has run several technology transfer groups aimed at both men and women, and covering many aspects of productive capacity from tomato irrigation to market gardening. Project coordinators generally approach the community leaders in an attempt to find suitable people for incorporation into the projects. The community leaders are therefore able to introduce certain members of the community to technical assistance. Overall, many of the irrigation and technical support projects are channeled through an agreement between the community organizations and the various government agencies involved. While there are projects in both Tome Alto and Chañaral Alto, it is felt by all the members of the NGO involved that in the former village they are much more successful. This might be because the village is smaller, making initial contact and continued interaction with the villagers easier, but it might also be because the villagers in Tome Alto are more supportive of projects aimed at helping small-scale production.

Concluding remarks

The capitalization of land brought about by the development of a mild marketization process has had wide ranging implications for the agricultural communities of the

Guatulame Valley, many of which were not anticipated by the national government. As the production of table grapes for export has expanded, new land markets and systems of labor organization have developed. Some communities have maintained their control over and access to communal land, as without legally defined ownership of land within the communities, the land remains largely outside the realm of large-scale export production. In other communities, with regularized land tenure, community members have been selling land for large-scale export production. Changing land tenure patterns in the various communities have had repercussions on labor and community organizations. In the village of Tome Alto, small-scale agricultural production has continued with only superficial changes, although the population is involved in seasonal work in the grape economy. Access to communal land and maintenance of "traditional" community structures remain of fundamental importance in this village. On the other hand, Chañaral Alto has experienced the development of an active land market and greater social change as a result of its role as a local center for export production. This role grew out of a number of factors, including the fact that community land could be sold for export production. The alterations in land tenure and labor organization have had ramifications that cut deep into the social fabric of the traditional agricultural communities. The expansion of agro-export has provided the populations of the agricultural communities with new employment possibilities, but has also brought the traditional communities' social and political structures under increasing pressure.

As Chile continues to promote the expansion of non-traditional agricultural exports, the exporting areas will continue to experience changes in land tenure and social and political organization. In this particular instance, some of the "traditional" agricultural producers have been able to maintain their small-scale production for the domestic market. This does not mean, though, that they are not involved in the export economy; it is just that they are able to work in the grape economy at certain times of the year to earn extra income. The expansion of the grape economy in the Guatulame has led to the development of a complex set of interactions between various sectors of the rural economy. The pattern is by no means a simple one, and there is a need to develop a nuanced understanding of the impacts of export expansion on a heterogeneous rural population, if responsible and reactive polices for the support of small-scale producers are to be developed. The fact that small-scale agriculture remains viable in some areas of the Guatulame Valley is not the direct result of government policies. It is instead the result of a combination of factors, including the non-regularization of land tenure in the communities and the production calendars of the domestic and export crops. This case study illustrates that, even as they face the risk of being further marginalized, the rural population negotiates the locally specific and contradictory impacts of the globalization of agriculture.

Notes

[1] The research for this chapter was undertaken between 1993 and 1994. The primary research method was structured interviews based on a standard questionnaire. Through a combination of quota sampling and snowball sampling, the questionnaires were administered to a total of 135 individuals (women and men). Extended in-depth interviews were also carried out with selected female respondents and key informants. The research was made possible by an ESRC studentship. For further details, see Bee, 1996.

[2] In the Guatulame, most of the small-sized farms resulted from the expropriation of six estates in the El Palqui area, three of which belonged to members of the Prohens family. *Asentamientos*, formed from the expropriated land, were set up under the transitional control of CORA, and the land was eventually transferred to the beneficiaries in plots averaging between 5.2 and 12.0 hectares. The larger plots were compensation for poorer quality land. The actual subdivision of the land took place between 1973 and 1977, that is, during the years of the military dictatorship (Gwynne and Meneses, 1994). Most of the beneficiaries were former tenants (inquilinos) of the estates. Thus, during the mid-1970s, a significant number of small sized farms were created in the El Palqui area, representing an expansion of the small-scale production sector at a time when wider economic changes were having a dramatic effect on the agricultural sector.

[3] An officer of the land registry *(Bienes Nacionales)* described this process. He also emphasized the point that while the agricultural communities have existed for a long time, their legal history is relatively recent. This has meant that for the majority of communities, regularizing land tenure would be an extremely complicated process (Personal Interview, November, 1993).

[4] In this case, "commercial" refers to the larger scale enterprises rather than the small plots used for tomatoes, etc.

References

Barham, B., M. Clark, E. Katz and R. Schurman, "Nontraditional agricultural exports in Latin America". *Latin American Research Review*, No. 27 (1992), pp. 43-82.

Barrientos, S., "The hidden ingredient: the role of female labour in Chilean fruit exports". *Bulletin of Latin American Research*, Vol. 16, no. 1 (1997), pp. 71-81.

Barrientos, S., A. Bee, A. Matear and I. Vogel, *Women and agribusiness: working miracles in the Chilean fruit export sector*. London, Macmillan, 1999.

Bee, A., "Regional change and non-traditional agricultural exports: land, labour and gender in the Norte Chico, Chile". Unpublished PhD thesis. Department of Geography, University of Birmingham, 1996.

Bee, A. and I. Vogel, "Temporeras and household relations: seasonal employment in Chile's agro-export sector". *Bulletin of Latin American Research*, Vol. 16, no. 1 (1997), pp. 83-95.

Carter, M.R. and D. Mesbah, "Can land reform mitigate the exclusionary aspects of rapid agro-export growth?" *World Development*, Vol. 21, no. 7 (1993), pp. 1085-100.

CODEFF, Proyecto "Perfil ambiental de la zona semidesertica de la IV Region". Comité Nacional Pro Defensa de la Fauna y Flora, Santiago, Chile, 1993.

De Janvry, A., N. Key and E. Sadoulet, "Agricultural and rural development in Latin America: new direction and new challenges". Working paper No. 815. Department of Agricultural and Resource Economics, University of California, Berkeley, 1997.

Diaz, E,. "Investigacion participativa acerca de las trabajadoras temporeras de la fruta (estudio de casos)". Centro El Canelo de Nos, Santiago, 1991.

Gwynne, R.N,. "Chile to 1994? More growth under democracy?" Economist Intelligence Unit, Special Report number 2065, 1991.

Gwynne, R. "Globalisation, commodity chains and fruit exporting regions in Chile". *Tijdschrift voor Economische en Sociale Geografie*, Vol. 90, no. 2 (1999), pp. 211-25.

Gwynne, R.N. and C. Kay, "Agrarian change and the democratic transition in Chile: an introduction". *Bulletin of Latin American Research*, Vol. 16, no. 1 (1997), pp. 3-10.

Gwynne, R.N. and C. Meneses, "Climate change and sustainable development in the Norte Chico: land, water and the commercialisation of agriculture". Occasional Publication. School of Geography, University of Birmingham, No. 34, 1994.

Gwynne, R.N. and J. Ortiz, "Export growth and development in poor rural regions: a meso scale analysis of the upper Limari". *Bulletin of Latin American Research*, Vol. 16, no. 1 (1997), pp. 25-41.

JUNDEP, "Diagnosico de la situacion de las mujeres de las comunidades agrícolas de las poivincias de Choapa y Limari". Unpublished report. Ovalle, 1991.

Kay, C., "Globalisation, peasant agriculture and reconversion". *Bulletin of Latin American Research*, Vol. 16, no. 1 (1997), pp. 11-24.

Korovkin, T., "Peasants, grapes and corporations: the growth of contract farming in a Chilean community". *Journal of Peasant Studies*, No. 19, no. 2 (1992), pp. 228-54.

Lago, M.S., "Rural women and neo-liberal model". In: C. Kay and P. Silva, *Development and social change in the Chilean countryside*. Amsterdam, CEDLA, 1992.

McBride, G.M., *Chile: land and society*. New York, Octagon Books, 1936.

Meneses, C., "Efectos geosociales de la modernizacion agrícola observados en la propiedad de la tierra y en el desplazamiento de cultivos tradicionales en los valles del semiarido". Paper presented at the XII Congress of geography, University of La Serena, Chile, 1989.

Murray, W., "Competitive global fruit export market: marketing intermediaries and impacts on small-scale growers in Chile". *Bulletin of Latin American Research*, Vol. 16, no. 1 (1997), pp. 43-55.

Scott, C.D. and P. Litchfield, "Common property and economic development: an analysis of Latin American experience in the light of contemporary theory". Unpublished monograph. London School of Economics and Political Science, University of London, 1993.

Valdés, X, "Feminizacion del mercado del trabajo agrícola: las temporeras". In: Mundo de mujer-continuidad y cambio. Santiago, Centro de Estudios de Mujer, 1988.

Final reflections

15 Land and sustainable livelihood: issues for debate

Annelies Zoomers

Understanding livelihood

The authors of this book explore the changing role of land in the livelihood strategies of rural dwellers, and sketch a picture of current transformations of the countryside in various countries in Latin America. More specifically, attention is focused on the changes of livelihood and land-use as the consequence of temporary migration (especially in traditional communities with communal land management systems in Bolivia, Mexico and Peru); land privatization in Peru, Mexico, and Nicaragua; and the influence of the global competitive sphere on farmers in Mexico and Chile. The various chapters analyze in detail the implications of changing land tenure regimes for the land-use (agricultural production and environmental sustainability), the income generating capacity of farmers (is greater access to land still a way out of poverty?), and the sociocultural aspects of life, including social prestige and power relations. To what extent do security of tenure and access to land affect development opportunities?

Recently, much has been written on the subject of livelihood and livelihood strategies (e.g., Bebbington, 1999; Carney, 1998; Ellis, 1997; 2000; Zoomers, 1999) and—in spite of the difficulty involved with translating these into unidimensional policy goals—more efforts are being made to take the farmers' preferences and priorities as a starting point for policy-making (see Appendini, this volume). Rather than looking at the rural poor as passive victims, policy makers now acknowledge that farmers play an active role. Families constantly weigh different objectives, opportunities, and limitations as a consequence of external and internal circumstances that change over time. Rural livelihood depends on the way families respond to change, resulting in the reallocation of land, labor, and capital resources, and it is increasingly recognized that to be successful in reducing rural poverty, we must focus on the whole rural society and economy, not just the agricultural sector. "Accordingly, reducing rural poverty will depend on achieving three crucial objectives: increasing agricultural productivity, creating rural non-farm employment, and protecting natural resources and the environment" (*Land Policy Newsletter* 9, May 2000). The sustainable livelihood approach is increasingly accepted as a new approach to alleviating poverty.

The various chapters in this book show that the rural population cannot be depicted as a homogeneous group with common characteristics and interests. In the general description of rural life, a common characteristic is the spatial variety of various farming systems, production relations, and types of organization. In addition to this kind of heterogeneity, there is an important degree of diversity at the household level: rather than specializing in one activity, most farmers have a broad portfolio of different activities (multi-tasking), ranging from agriculture to a range of non-farm activities and various types of temporary migration. Within these portfolios, it is often possible to identify some degree of interdependence between the activities, meaning that activities are mutually linked and have some kind of internal logic (see Zoomers, 1999: 31-32). In developing their livelihood strategies, farmers have to deal with risk and insecurity (e.g., due to seasonal influences and the vulnerability of the natural conditions). Their opportunities will highly depend on the availability of assets (land, capital, labor, etc.), institutional support (credit, technical assistance), and infrastructure.

The rural population, including the poorest groups, is clearly far more heterogeneous than commonly assumed. Making generalizations about livelihood strategies—or presenting fixed categories—is impossible for several reasons:

- Livelihood strategies arise in different geographic settings (mountain areas and tropical rain forests, in close proximity to urban areas or in isolated areas, etc.). Livelihood strategies form part of a specific context and are difficult to compare.
- Each family has its own starting point: some are in infra-subsistence situations, others are at subsistence level or have surplus production. Processes of upward and downward social mobility are not so unilinear as many assume: it is assumed that the poor sell their land and become the victims of further deterioration, and that the rich buy land and are in a favorable position to achieve improvement. Various examples show that this is not true in many cases. There are substantial groups of "poor rich" (people who used to be poor) and "rich poor" (people who used to be rich but are now poor), showing that the path of development can be rather erratic and unpredictable.
- The driving forces behind livelihood strategies vary considerably and are expressed by various goals. Some families focus on income improvement, while many seek to minimize risks or enhance their prestige within the community. In addition to studying the portfolio of activities (what farmers do), we need to distinguish between strategies engendered by pull factors (i.e., taking advantage of opportunities) and those engendered by push factors (coping with crisis); strategies in response to periodic change (seasonal factors) or structural changes (land scarcity, erosion, etc.); strategies designed to consolidate the existing situation or to generate dynamic processes of change; and strategies with curative elements (to solve existing problems) or preventive ones (designed to avoid problems).
- Livelihood strategies differ depending on the distribution of work among and within families. No two strategies are identical, not even among households that appear to have exactly the same features. The roles of the actors (the women, men, children, adults, etc.) figure within a varied strategy, resulting in differences in the allocation of work. Whereas in some households the activities are spread among the different members of the household (everybody does everything), other cases reflect a high degree of specialization. The interests of a household's individual members will not always be consistent with the family goal, and vice versa. Variations in personal abilities and motivation affect the interrelations between the various activities and the degree of internal cohesion. Conflict and competition may arise between the activities and the household's members: what benefits the individual need not necessarily benefit the family, and vice versa.
- Livelihood strategies or strategic behavior will not necessarily bring about the desired results. The success of farmers in improving their position (social mobility) is related less to strategic actions (what they do) than to location-related factors (where they operate), and to access to networks of information and people, coincidence and timing, and the presence of buffer mechanisms.
- The results of livelihood strategies are multidimensional: no single strategy serves all objectives simultaneously. Socioeconomic success (generation of income) may

have a negative impact on food security, the environment, or other aspects related to overall wellbeing. In addition to considering economic results, sufficient attention must be paid to the implications for food security and social, cultural, and agroecological aspects.

The above shows why it is difficult to compile a fixed typology of livelihood strategies (see also Zoomers, 1999: 46-47). Generalizing about livelihood strategies is a dangerous thing to do. Livelihood is like a Pandora's box: there are many concealed aspects inside it. Another complication is that livelihood strategies are a moving target. They should be conceived of as a stage, not as a structural category.

Livelihood strategies and land

Instead of classifying farmers on the basis of what they own (how much land they have, etc.), we need to distinguish them on the basis of what they do (their portfolio of activities) according to their objectives and priorities. Given certain circumstances (i.e., quality and location of the land being the same), land-use and the implications for rural livelihood are mainly determined by a combination of characteristics at the household level (i.e., objectives and priorities, the family cycle, etc.), and factors at the village level (e.g., multifunctionality of land, institutional arrangements, etc.). The link between livelihood and land is determined by the following factors.

Objectives and priorities

Both livelihood and the use of land depend largely on the objectives and priorities of the farmer's household. Some farmers are dedicated to optimizing their economic results (e.g., the producers of non-traditional crops for export; see Paulson, Bee, and Schüren, this volume), in other words, to attaining the maximum possible production while minimizing the costs. Others will be much more interested in using their land for food production, or as a place of residence.

The objectives and priorities of households are difficult to reduce to fixed entities. Rather than focusing exclusively on income maximization, most pursue several objectives simultaneously, with priorities that vary depending on the circumstances. In Latin America, most households aim at a combination of the following goals (see also Brunschwig, 1996: 383, 397):
- To secure the long-term productive capacity of resources (such as land, livestock, pastures, water, and tools), including the minimum labor force necessary for social reproduction. This is a first priority objective; risks are unacceptable.
- To maximize net income generated by the available resources. This is a second priority objective; risks are somewhat acceptable.
- To improve the quality and quantity of the productive resources. This is a third priority objective; risks are acceptable.

In other words, farmers try to grow some of the food they need, to earn monetary income through non-agricultural activities, and to manage capital in the form of livestock. "(...) The crops are intended to feed the family, and financial income is guaranteed through raising livestock and selling labor" (Brunschwig, 1996: 383, 397). A complex of different and changing priorities influences farmers' lives.

Even though generalizations are always dangerous, an important determinant of livelihood and the use of resources, including land, is the family development cycle (also known as the family lifecycle).[1] Dependent on the cycle a household is in (i.e., the labor supply), the goals and priorities of farmers vary, particularly when it comes to access to and use of resources. Especially in the case of the rural poor, the development potential of the family is strongly affected by demographic variables, particularly fertility, mortality, and migration rates. As households expand and children grow up, labor capabilities and consumption needs change and contribute to improvements in affluence and development options; this has direct implications for access to and the use of land and other resources.

Usually the development cycle begins with the marriage of a couple with limited production potential (the couple receives a share of household capital) and low consumption requirements. Few newlyweds have their own land at the beginning. Instead, they work the land of their fathers. During this period—in which they await their share of the inheritance—migration is a rather common way of earning money.

With the birth of the first child, however, the external orientation often makes way for a more introverted perspective. In many cases, and if possible, both husband and wife stop migrating—or migrate only when such is absolutely necessary—and try to subsist from agriculture in their own village. Some try to obtain sufficient land through a variety of means (leasing, sharecropping, trading, etc.), while others prefer to remain in the migration area and/or move to the city.

As the number of children increases, consumption needs rise, first without adding to the household's income situation. As the children grow up, and thus the household's labor supply expands, households improve their circumstances and level of affluence, and do their best to consolidate the situation. While the parents and youngest children work the land, the older children earn additional income through migration (working as casual laborers) or attend school (investment in education). Rather than saving for the future, as was done in the previous situation, the families aim to reap the fruits of their labor and to improve their situation. At this stage, the children's contribution of capital increases, thus diversifying income and giving rise to favorable opportunities for upward mobility and improvement. Farmers who invest in their agricultural livelihood at this point, clearly differ from households that choose a new course (migration to a city or settlement area).

When the children get married, they often claim their share of the inheritance, even though in many areas they should officially wait for their parents to pass away. For the parents, the amount of available land effectively diminishes. Moreover, as families grow older, the labor contribution by family members ceases, and the income level tends to diminish. Finally, with the segmentation into new household units, resources dwindle through inheritance. The parental household is reduced to two persons with close ties to the new households of their married children. Sometimes the parents are absorbed into the household of one of their children.

Basically, households shift along a scale of relative wealth. As they acquire more labor power, their means of existence (which includes access to land) changes accordingly. Farmers are not a static group; they experience different levels of affluence during their lives. In certain periods, they are interested mainly in accumulation or consolidation; at other times, they focus on compensation and survival, or on increased security or risk reduction. This makes a flexible typology preferable to fixed categories. Four types of strategies can be distinguished.

Accumulation strategies

Accumulation strategies involve establishing a minimum resource base and preparing for future expansion. They are applied in particular by newlyweds and families with young children, as these groups tend to be relatively poor and seek to amass resources for future improvement. The dominant goal is to obtain the minimum maneuvering space necessary for upward social mobility. Accumulation strategies are usually guided by a long-term strategic view of future income sources.

An important example of a accumulation strategy is *land acquisition* (frequently preceded by a period of temporary migration), which often begins the moment the first child is born. Access to land is initially obtained through inheritance and marriage. Expansion of the land base often takes place through the establishment of a wide variety of sharecropping arrangements: farmers get access to the land temporarily by returning capital, inputs, or labor. Only later do they have enough capital to purchase or lease land on a more permanent basis. Along with the rising level of affluence and expansion of their land, however, farmers become inclined to accumulate through labor recruitment; after a period of working the land exclusively with family labor, reciprocal labor exchange may be intensified, followed by the recruitment of paid laborers.

Consolidation strategies

As things get better, attention gradually shifts to consolidation, i.e., investments are made to stabilize the family's wellbeing and short-term quality improvements. They are applied mainly by fairly wealthy households that have achieved a level of affluence after a period of upward mobility. These households have surplus assets to invest. In most cases, family members are older (children have grown up and contribute labor and capital).

Consolidation will often go hand in hand with land improvement and agricultural intensification. As soon as farmers have sufficient land, they shift their priority from acquiring more land to achieving qualitative improvement. They do so by purchasing better land from neighbors or in the colonization area, or investing in the productivity of the existing land, e.g., erosion control, increased use of agrochemicals, etc. Such efforts may coincide with agricultural intensification, e.g., introduction and expansion of irrigation, introduction of new varieties, etc. In some cases, the expansion of land and agricultural intensification means that the children need no longer resort to migration.

Other examples of consolidation strategies are investing in children's education, the purchase of a second home or improving the living environment; or the purchase of luxury goods and other consumer items.

Compensatory and survival strategies

These strategies prevail among two categories of farmers: households that are dealing with a *temporary crisis* (e.g., occasional crop failures, loss of labor power and capital, etc.), and poor farmers with a structural shortage of land (due to sale, erosion, soil degradation, etc.) or labor power (especially incomplete families, including widows and widowers, the elderly, and abandoned women). Victims of downward social mobility, these households use often try to break out of the situation by selling land, livestock, and/or other goods as a response to a crisis; the moment they do so depends largely on the level of affluence and the available amount and value of buffers. The capital obtained through selling is used to buy food and other essentials.

Other strategies intended to compensate for losses or promote survival include permanent or temporary migration; saving and economizing, i.e., restricting consumption and expenses in periods of scarcity (families switch to less expensive food, skip festivals, and remove children from school etc.; exchange, borrowing, and barter (e.g., working land that belongs to others, exchanging goods, working for payment in the form of food in times of food shortage, etc.).

Finally, many of these families rely on external support provided by the children or family members. This strategy is most common among older families, including widowers and widows, who used to have sufficient land or labor power, but have distributed their possessions among their children.

Security and risk-reduction strategies

Many farming families try to reduce insecurity. This does not mean, however, that risk minimization is a goal in itself: families will in general be inclined to reduce insecurity to an acceptable minimum, especially in circumstances with a hostile environment, e.g., in the higher areas of the Andes.

An important example of a security and risk-reducing strategy is diversification. This involves both crop diversity (the association of crops) and income diversity (multi-tasking). Planting two or more varieties simultaneously (intercropping) diminishes the risk of plagues and disease, and protects crops from inclement weather. Other risk-reducing strategies include the spreading of agricultural production over various agroecological zones in mountain areas, installing irrigation channels, and introducing drought-resistant crops. Multi-tasking provides farmers with the possibility to shift income sources in cases of crisis.

In addition, an efficient mechanism for farmers to cope with risk situations is sharecropping. Others give priority to stockpiling, i.e., creating buffers by purchasing livestock, textiles, etc. A special type of stockpiling strategy is to invest in social relations (networking); households use this practice as a "savings account" for their security (this is the opposite of the selling strategy).

In conclusion, depending on the family development cycle and the level of prosperity (and given a particular set of objectives and priorities), households opt for a particular combination of strategies and sub-strategies (see Table 1).

A family—depending on the situation it is in—can adopt a different relation with the land. In the context of a farmer's livelihood strategy, priority (often after the fact) is given to land acquisition (accumulation) or improvement (consolidation); when land is exchanged, sold, or rented out, this is often a compensatory and survival strategy applied in the event of a crisis; when an attempt is made to achieve security or

Table 1 Livelihood strategies in response to increasing levels of prosperity and family development cycle

Type of farmer/ stage in family development cycle	Dominant strategy and goal	Sub-strategies
A. *Newlyweds and young families* with small children, who are relatively poor but seek to accumulate resources for future improvement	*Accumulation* To establish a minimum resource base and prepare for future expansion	*Temporary migration* *Land acquisition* *Labor recruitment*
B. *Consolidating households* (children have grown up) that have achieved a period of upward mobility (fairly wealthy)	*Consolidation/income* maximization Consolidation and quality improvements; achieving qualitative improvement of production means	*Land improvement/ agricultural intensification* *Education* *Consumption* *Housing/residence*
C. *Disintegrating households* experiencing downward social mobility and/or households experiencing a temporary crisis	*Compensation and survival* To break out of the slump or at least to remain afloat in their current situation (survival)	*Migration* *Saving and economizing* *Selling* *Exchange, borrowing and barter* *External support*
D. All types, but especially poorer households	*Security and risk-reduction* (often combined with A, B or C)	*Diversification* *Sharecropping* *Stockpiling*

Source: Based on Zoomers, 1999.

reduce risks, this often takes the form of a change in the use of land (multicropping, etc.). Depending on their wealth, farmers may adopt sharecropping and stockpiling strategies. It is difficult to describe the importance of land in general terms, because its importance in the livelihood strategies of farmers is a moving target.

Coincidence and timing

Important factors that influence the link between land and livelihood—and, more specifically, the extent to which this link will contribute to social mobility—are coincidence and timing, i.e., the sequence of events. The importance of this dimension is often overlooked, and no attention is paid to these factors in the literature on rural development. Similar livelihood strategies will not necessarily generate similar results, even other circumstances and the access to resources (i.e., land) are the same.

Examining situations where farmers have taken similar actions but accomplished dissimilar results, reveals the importance of coincidence and timing. Two farmers with the same amount of land, labor, and capital may achieve entirely different results by using these means in different ways at different times. Their ultimate success is largely determined by the sequence in which they develop activities and the order in which they implement changes. Farmers who invest wisely at the right moment and right place are especially likely to improve their situation. Purchasing a piece of land and investing in cultivating non-traditional crops for agro-export may be a ticket to success for some farmers; others, who experience crop failure during the first year, may find the same strategy to be the beginning of continuing misfortune. They are forced to sell their land and livestock to pay their debts, and will never recover. Illness, arguments with family members, and a temporary lack of money are crucial factors in determining whether farmers improve or deteriorate. Crop failure is not necessarily a disaster, but it can become an insuperable tragedy if it recurs year after year or coincides with illness; in these cases, people cannot migrate and will sell their production means (land, livestock) to pay for their medicine. Many changes for the worse are brought about by a combination of loss of labor power (migration, illness, death of family members or draught animals) and crop failure (often inherent to certain climate zones). Only after a few consecutive crop failures does the situation become desperate and improvement impossible, especially for farmers who have taken out credit (usually the wealthier ones). Indebtedness due to crop failures can propel relatively wealthy farmers into a downward spiral.

It is therefore difficult to generalize about the best way to achieve improvement. No set course of development exists; much depends on the conjunction of circumstances.

Multifunctionality of land

In economics, land is conventionally classified as a separate factor of production, alongside labor and capital; entrepreneurship is sometimes included on this list. In the current policy debate on land privatization, there is much emphasis on the need to develop a free land market (and to abolish existing obstacles to land transfers, such as land ownership ceilings, restrictions on transferability, and land-use conditions), but there are several reasons why it is difficult to treat land as a normal and freely tradable capital good.

Land does not behave in the same way as capital or labor, because it is tied to a specific location. Although one may refer to a "free" land market, this does not usually mean that the new owner can freely dispose of his land, breaking the historical and/or cultural ties between the land and the original population, and/or putting an abrupt end to the old usufruct. Even though the new owner might in principle be free to use the land, his neighbors might restrict his degree of liberty.

Markets in land are in reality markets in land rights, i.e., during a transaction, what is transferred is a property document rather than the property itself. Thus, land transfer is not directly visible and does not necessarily have a noticeable influence on the local situation. In many countries, there is no direct link between ownership registration and the land register (el catastro), and thus there is often no relationship between documents and reality. The official title does not always correspond with the local perception: landownership relations are often a layered reality in which earlier rights are still operative. Moreover, the use rights to land will not always coincide with the use rights to other resources (water, trees, etc.). Nor is the land market comparable with labor and capital as far as the operation of the price mechanism is concerned. The total supply of land is fixed, whereas labor and capital supply is not so bound to such a maximum. The price of land is largely based on sitespecific characteristics (location, soil quality), and cannot be perceived as a neutral indicator for land scarcity; no two parcels are identical, because they are never situated on the same spot.

Another problem arises from the fact that land prices are often based on the economic function of the land. In practice, however, land often performs different functions at the same time. The chapters of this book show that land is a multi-functional asset. For some groups, the ownership of land is mainly a status symbol; for others it is a production factor or a source of capital; for yet others, land serves mainly as a place to live or to relax. It also performs a role as territory, especially for indigenous groups (cultural patrimony), but also for nature conservation.

Current policy discussions about land markets and efficient use (see also Volume 1, this series) ignore the multifunctionality of land. Because of this multifunctionality, the value of land cannot be expressed in a single price ticket. While it can generally be posited that labor and capital are of little value without land, land performs a vital function even without other production factors. Land resources play multiple roles, which vary according to the circumstances:

- Land—being an engendered space—plays a different role for men than it does for women; access to land (and perception) is highly dependent on generation (the majority of landless *comuneros* are relatively young, e.g., they are the sons of *comuneros*); still, land plays an important role in connecting generations.
- Access to land and secure tenure are necessary conditions for increasing agricultural production. There is a variable link between access to land and agricultural income; circumstances (access to capital, availability of labor, knowledge, etc.) determine the way land is used and what form of income can be derived from it.
- As things get better for a household, the chances increase that the land will be used for cattle-raising (especially by the wealthier households) and/or capital-intensive crops; there is also an increasing tendency toward specialization (non-traditional agro-export), and people are more likely to acquire land to, for example, extend their agricultural activities, or build a residence and/or use it for recreational purposes.
- As things get worse for a household, the chances increase that the land will be used for consumption crops (multicropping); insufficient farm income is compensated for by off-farm income, including migration. In the event of an emergency, the land will be sold or rented out.
- The buying and selling of land (including exchange and sharecropping relations) constitutes an important way of adapting to change and/or overcoming crisis. Farmers are very aware of the value of their land; many see it as a savings account to which they can occasionally turn.

In the literature, the sale of land is usually depicted as the beginning of an irreversible processes of land concentration, which ultimately leads to *descampesinación* (distress sales). This is true in certain situations (examples are given for Chile and Mexico, this volume), but in other situations, opposite tendencies can occur. Land transfer is often a cyclical, and reversible, process that forms part of a farmer's livelihood strategy: the sale of land enables him to survive a temporary crisis and/or to switch to new nonagricultural activities (income diversification). The purchase of land enables farmers to create a buffer, i.e., a reserve of money, derived for example from migration. Households with more land have more flexibility, also because they can spread their land-use.

Over the course of time, some households succeed in buying additional land, while others decide to dispose of it (*decampesinación*). It is important here that selling and/or purchase patterns should not be viewed as mutually exclusive processes which necessarily result in a oneway evolutionary trend. Changes in landownership must sometimes be seen as an irreversible process, but in other cases, it is reversible: vendors become purchasers, and vice versa; buying and selling can also go together. There have certainly been considerable oscillations at the household level over the generations: farmers who are currently recorded as vendors of land were buyers in a earlier period. The difference between a buyer and a seller is often not structural, but a distinction governed by the phase of the family development cycle and by income variation (Zoomers, forthcoming; see also Foster, 1993).

Policy implications

Although the title of this book is *Land and Sustainable Livelihood in Latin America*, it is difficult to generalize about the degree to which there is a mutual relation between land tenure and livelihood, and the consequences of this for rural development. In many cases, the Latin American countryside has become far more complex and diverse than before. "A large proportion of former *haciendas* or *latifundios* have been successfully converted into medium-sized modern capitalist enterprises, relying mainly on wage labor, using advanced technology, and integrated into the domestic and international markets" (Kay, 1996: 33). The *minifundistas* (small landholders) have changed as well: some have benefited from new market opportunities, new products, subcontracting links with agro-industries, support from NGOs, and other opportunities (see also Zoomers and van der Haar, 2000).

The majority of the *minifundistas*, however, have diversified their livelihood and become dependent on off-farm income sources. The traditional category of *minifundistas* has increasingly become a heterogeneous group, each *minifundista* combining agricultural and non-agricultural activities with temporary migration; only some of the rural labor force is tied to the land, and—also as the result of globalization and the introduction of modern communication technology—farmers have become more mobile than in former times. Particularly in the Andes region and the Mexican highlands, large numbers of farmers are no longer permanently based in their area of origin. They alternate between their own land and "outside" land (owned by migrated family members or agro-industrial firms). The land issue, and the use of land, is no longer determined by the local situation, but needs to be analyzed in the context of transnational communities. Many farmers have become "split-location *campesinos*" (Thiesenhusen, 1995), using their land increasingly as a safety net and not so much as a production factor.

Many *campesinos* who have been forced off the good farm land they formerly worked, now cultivate steep slopes and other land that is marginal for farming and often divided up into tiny plots, on which they destroy ground cover and forest and promote soil runoff. Areas of formerly agricultural land have lost their fertility and become desert areas (e.g., in the Andes region) or are now used as pasture (e.g., in the Amazon basin). Much of the land is no longer, or has never been, suitable for farming.

Greater access to land, and the improvement of land tenure relations, has been a traditional recipe for reducing rural poverty levels across Latin America. In the 1990s, land redistribution was still regarded as an appropriate instrument for alleviating rural poverty. "An effective land policy can gradually remove the constraints on the access to land, improve productivity, increase incomes and improve living conditions, especially for the rural poor" (World Bank, 1996: 27). However, this formula needs to be reconsidered in the light of the diversity of livelihood strategies, and in view of the heterogeneity of production environments at the local level. In many areas, rather than being a way out of poverty, land policy (i.e., improving the land tenure situation) may have contributed to the stabilization of man-land relations, but has not helped improve the income situation. In many cases, land is no longer seen as a source of income, but is used increasingly as a safety valve (land serving as insurance against unemployment, and as a pension fund for household members). Given this situation, the question is: to what extent is greater access to land a way out of poverty?

Where land policy does affect the livelihood of farmers, the focus is generally on the implications of getting access to land, or to extra land, and the consequences for their investment behavior, i.e., their willingness to invest in increasing production or sustainable land-use (conservation). Very little has been said about the extent to which access to land also affects the non-agricultural side of earning a living, or the extent to which landownership has an impact on and is intertwined with other rights (e.g., voting rights, participation in communal activities). Changes in land tenure affect land-based agricultural activities (investments in increasing production and sustainable land-use), non-agrarian pursuits (including migration), and the social and cultural aspects of life, including social prestige and political power. It even has implications for the extent to which households are able to benefit from development projects, because target groups are often defined on the basis of access to land and tenure relations.

Little research has been done on the implications of the loss of land or of land acquisition for the livelihood strategies of farmers. In some instances, loss of land will be compensated for by income diversification or intensification; in other instances, the size of the land holding may be expanded at the expense of non-agricultural activities. Much remains to be learned about the interaction between land tenure and livelihood, and the consequences of this for the various members of the household. Decisions on selling or buying land and the moment such decisions are made must be related to the household's other objectives or activities. An analysis of investment strategies by settlers in the Amazon Basin showed that before farmers give priority to the purchase of land, they give priority to other matters: "Initially, they invest in education for their children and expand their farming systems to include both cash crops (including labor-intensive higher value and higher risk crops) and livestock. Subsequently, additional farm land is reclaimed, sharecropped, leased or purchased; and the settler branches out into non-farm activities. As incomes rise, many settlers prefer to hire labor for the more arduous tasks and to use family labor for social or more lucrative activities" (Scudder, 1991: 148-184).

Those searching for a new policy must try to connect with current reality. Land is more than an economic asset: it covers a range of entitlements, and must be interpreted as a part of broader livelihood strategies. "People manage an array of resources or assets (natural capital, social capital, human capital, physical capital) within a dynamic context in which assets and decisions-making interact" (Hoon, Singh and Warmali, 1997). The livelihood approach is broad and multidisciplinary, and is not easily linked to sectoral policy approaches. Whereas in the current debate land titles and registration are seen as ways of resolving land problems, policy should aim at strengthening the adaptive and coping strategies of the poor, and incorporate an empowering, participatory focus.

The present time is characterized by constantly increasing mobility and the virtualization of life: "We live in a network society in which people are globally connected and locally disconnected" (Castells, 1996). Rural life is rapidly changing, with increasing levels of international migration and the functioning of farmers in a global competitive sphere. It is questionable whether present policy, which emphasizes the free transfer of private land, is still sufficiently in tune with the modern age. Future land policy should concentrate less on perpetuating oldfashioned man/land relations (granting individual property titles) and begin searching for more flexible solutions. The chapters of this book show that access to land and security of tenure play an important role in rural life, but that their importance cannot be described in neutral terms. Sustainable development is not so much a function of access to land: security of life and potential welfare highly depend on having access to *place* (the characteristics of the locality) and to territorial and institutional space.

Note

[1] Chayanov stressed [at the beginning of the 20th century] that "farmers' households do not seek to maximize profits or income. They aim to satisfy certain essential needs related to family composition. Their members cease working once such needs have been met, which means that the farmers modulate their sales according to their monetary needs (i.e., they produce and sell proportionately less when prices are higher)" (Kervyn 1996: 427).

References

Bebbington, A., "Capitals and capabilities: a framework for analyzing peasant viability. Rural livelihoods and poverty". *World Development*, Vol. 27, no. 12 (1999), pp. 2012-44.

Brunschwig, G., "El Alto Valle de Canete: el matorral y la puna". In: P. Morlon (ed.), *Comprender la agricultura campesina en los Andes Centrales de Peru—Bolivia*. Institut Francais d'études Andines and Centro de Estudios Regionales Andinos "Bartolome de las Casas" Cusco, Peru, 1996.

Carney, D., "Sustainable rural development. What contribution can we make?" Paper presented at the Department for International Development's Natural Resources Advisers' Conference, July 1998.

Foster N., "Land for the peasantry: looking for the market". In: W. Glade and C.A. Reilly (eds.), *Inquiry at grassroots*. Inter-American Foundation, Virginia, 1993.

Hoon, P., N. Singh and S.S. Wanmali, "Sustainable livelihoods: concepts, principles and approaches to indicator development". A draft discussion paper. Paper presented at the workshop Sustainable livelihoods indicators. Social Development and Poverty Eradication Division, UNDP, New York, August 1997.

Castells, M., "The rise of the network society". In: *The information age: economy, society and culture*, Volume I. Cornwell, UK, 1996.

Ellis, F., "Household strategies and rural livelihood diversification". Unpublished paper. Norwich, United Kingdom, 1997.

Ellis, F., *Rural livelihoods and diversity in developing countries*. Oxford University Press, Oxford, 2000.

Kay, C., "Latin America's unequal and exclusionary rural development in the neo-liberal era". Unpublished paper. Institute of Social Studies (The Hague) and Grupo de Investigaciones Agrarias (Chile), 1996.

Scudder, T,. "A sociological framework for the analysis of new land settlement". In: M.M. Cernea (ed.), *Putting people first. Sociological variables in rural development*. Second edition. Oxford University Press, 1991.

Thiesenhusen, W.C., *Broken promises: agrarian reform and the Latin American campesino*. Boulder, Westview Press, 1995.

World Bank, "Bolivia: poverty, equity and income: expanding earning opportunities for the poor". Unpublished paper. Country Operations Division I, Country Department II, Latin America and the Caribbean Region, Washington, 1996.

Zoomers, A., *Linking livelihood strategies to development. Experiences from the Bolivian Andes*. Amsterdam, Royal Tropical institute/CEDLA, 1999.

Zoomers, A. and G. van der Haar (eds.), *Current land policy in Latin America: regulating land tenure under neo-liberalism*. KIT/Vervuert, Amsterdam, 2000.

Zoomers, A., "Se vende propiedad: el mercado rural de la tierra en Santa Cruz (Bolivia)". In: D. Pacheco and M. Urioste, *Las tierras bajas de Bolivia a fines del siglo XX*. Consorcio Fundación Tierra, ACLO/CEDLA/CIPCA/QHANA, La Paz, forthcoming.

Map Chile

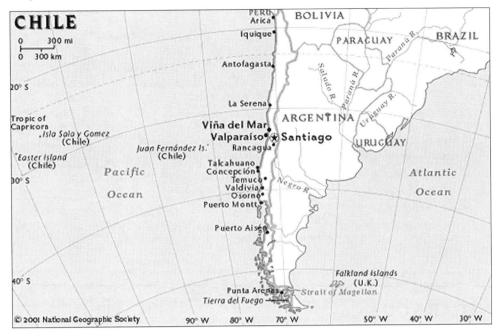

Map Mexico

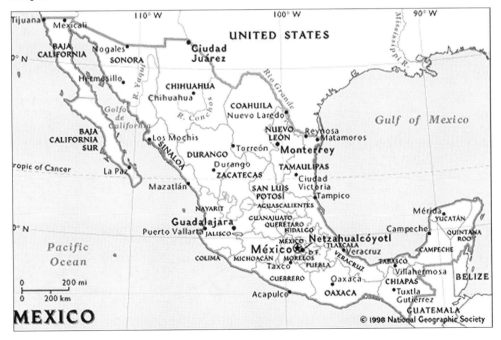

Map Nicaragua

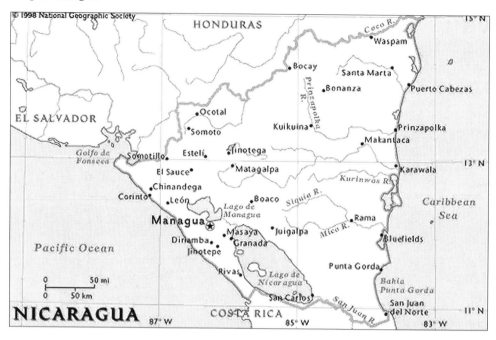

Map Peru

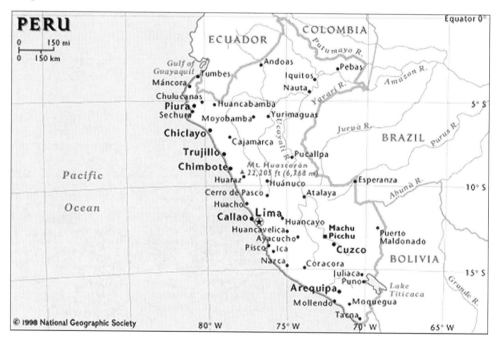

Map Bolivia

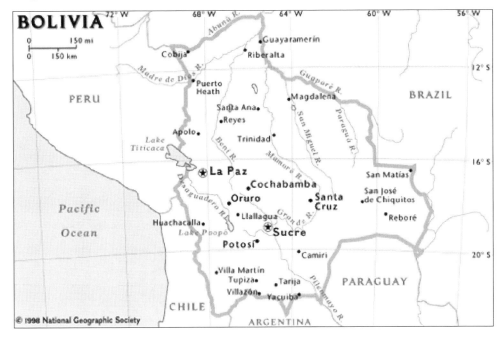